THE MENTAL HEALTH OF CHILDREN:

SERVICES, RESEARCH, AND MANPOWER

The Mental Health of Children: Services, Research, and Manpower

REPORTS OF TASK FORCES IV AND V AND THE
REPORT OF THE COMMITTEE ON CLINICAL
ISSUES BY THE JOINT COMMISSION ON
MENTAL HEALTH OF CHILDREN

HARPER & ROW, PUBLISHERS

NEW YORK, EVANSTON, SAN FRANCISCO, LONDON

1817

Official distribution of this book has been made possible through a grant from the Foundation for Child Mental Welfare, Inc.

FIRST EDITION

STANDARD BOOK NUMBER: 06-012227-7

LIBRARY OF CONGRESS CATALOG CARD NUMBER: 72-123940

Designed by Sidney Feinberg

Contents

Prenatal Period • Infancy • Preschool • Grade School • Junior High and High School • Appendix A: Psychosocial Disorders in Childhood and Adolescence • Appendix B: Recommendations by the Clinical Committee of the Joint Commission on Mental Health of Children on Research • Appendix C: Utilization of Paraprofessionals in Clinical Settings • Appendix D: Psychopharmacologic Agents • Appendix E: Statement on Racism by the Committee on Clinical Issues • Appendix F: A Clinician's Overview • Appendix G: Recommendations by the Clinical Committee of the Joint Commission on Mental Health of Children • References

Figures and Tables

I

PROGRAMS OF PREVENTION AND REHABILITATION RESEARCH AND ITS USES, AND MANPOWER

REPORT OF TASK FORCE IV

Edited by Seymour L. Lustman, M.D., Ph.D.

The Commission reports in this volume focus on a number of crucial issues related to the mental health of children. Each of the three studies points to deficiencies in our services to children, the shortages in manpower, and the gaps in our knowledge of normal and abnormal child development. However, the analyses of these common problems, and the solutions proposed, often vary according to the task assigned to the Commission study groups. The discussions of services to children, for example, range in topic from administrative and organizational problems to clinical issues centered on the individual child. The analysis begins with the Report of Task Force IV on Issues in Research, Manpower, Rehabilitation and Treatment, and Prevention.

—EDITOR

Task Force IV

Introduction

Task Force IV was charged with the responsibility of studying and formulating recommendations on issues in research, manpower, rehabilitation, and treatment, as well as prevention. We met this challenge by discussing issues among ourselves, by assigning Task Force members to special subcommittees, and by contracting for special studies.

Based on the assumption that mental health was the concern of many different disciplines, an interdisciplinary committee was appointed and given the task of exploration and recommendation in the area of research, prevention, rehabilitation, and manpower. The Committee very quickly realized that the fundamental thread running through all of these very broad areas was one of both basic and applied (such as assessment) research. Accordingly, our first unifying concerns had to do with maintaining and promoting a research atmosphere and broadening our information base in all of the areas described in this report.

Given the time, and the massive task, we attempted to look at the problems from the vantage point of the traditional disciplinary conceptualizations. We made an effort to look at psychiatric aspects of the problem, psychological, social work, education and special education, pediatrics, law, dynamic demography, architecture, sociology, anthropology, economy, among other trains of thought. We quickly realized, as Donald R. Young has put it, that: "Every profession necessarily has a technical language of its own, a system of values, and its preferred ways of working. These professional subcultures facilitate the accomplishment of professional tasks, but they are handicapped to inter-professional communication. Words change in their meaning from one profession to another, and, of course, each has terms that are exclusively its own."

The task of accommodating special interests and uniquely different focuses and conceptualizations into the Task Force proved too much for this effort. It was not possible to develop a unique, commonly understood language, or a commonly understood conceptual framework. Accordingly, the reader should understand quite clearly that all of the reports published in this volume do not represent a complete consensus of the interdisciplinary Task Force, and it is expected that some members of diverse professions or scientific disciplines will not readily understand what is being said by others. This is particularly true in terms of the therapeutic framework, wherein there were people who, by virtue of their profession, had been deeply immersed in clinical responsibility, and others who, by virtue of their profession or scientific discipline, had never experienced clinical responsibility.

In spite of this, there was a considerable, and impressive, agreement about many things. Perhaps the most important of these was the feeling of the Task Force that its effort cannot be considered a static, one-shot examination of these massive, ever changing problems, but that it had to be thought of as a dynamic process of constant surveillance, data gathering, and assessment—with perhaps the most important aspect of this being the interdisciplinary communication of the people involved. We very frequently used and recommended the idea of a "consortium" in which relatively involved disciplines could communicate and affect one another.

My personal response to the experience leads me to stress these two factors: the first is the necessity to view all problems within a research framework, and the second is the necessity for an ongoing interdisciplinary consortium which would both educate its members and develop a commonality of language and conceptualization, which would prove most helpful for further study of this complex field.

In the pages which follow, we will summarize some of the major thought, discussion, and study engaged in by all the members and contractors. The papers and studies done for and by the Task Force are listed in Appendix B at the end of this report.

Seymour L. Lustman, M.D., Ph.D. (editor)
Chairman, Task Force IV

Research

When the initial discussions of this Task Force were held, a major difficulty emerged, namely, the apparent and actual discontinuities among the four areas of Research, Manpower, Treatment and Rehabilitation, and Prevention which were given to the group as its concerns. In order to fulfill the task of identifying major relevant dimensions and deriving short-run and long-run strategies in these complex areas it was necessary to develop an emphasis which would be purposeful and, at the same time, be sufficiently broad and comprehensive in order to include the diverse issues which emerged from our early discussions. This represents a dynamic view of both the scientific and the clinical dimensions of mental health, rather than a static problem-solving focus.

While many approaches were possible, and since the rationale for grouping the four substantive areas of the Task Force was not explicit, the members of the group agreed to a perspective in which research issues and researchable questions would provide criteria for the selecting and formulation of items of high priority. This decision has probably led the Task Force into some difficult intellectual and possibly impractical positions, but it has enabled the group to avoid a spurious appearance of omniscience. Rather, it allowed the Task Force to explore in a number of directions and permitted an open-ended state of affairs rather than closed dogmatic conclusions, nor was any attempt made to insist on consensus.

Using research considerations as criteria of judgment, the Task Force was able to formulate its recommendations, not in an absolute prescriptive fashion, but with the understanding that most current knowledge is in the process of becoming obsolete. One result of this guiding assumption is that all recommendations are tentative and lead to the formulation of issues rather than ready-made substantive solutions. This does not mean that all action is halted or that innovation is squelched. Rather the Task Force members could press beyond the problems posed by meeting immediate needs and could formulate some areas for further inquiry. Such an approach creates some problems, but these are more likely to provide opportunities for clarification of thinking and the promotion of inquiry rather than premature generalization and poorly planned action.

With respect to research as a primary area of concern for the Task Force, Dr. Lustman explicates the issues which emerged from the Task Force deliberations. His paper is presented below, followed by a summary statement of research recommendations.

Mental Health Research and the University

In view of the fact that the existence of the Joint Commission on Mental Health of Children (called the Oswald Bill) owes so much to the late President John F. Kennedy, it is singularly appropriate to start this report with two of his favorite quotations. I will state these since they delineate so precisely a crucial dimension of the research problems to which the Commission must address itself.

Kennedy said: " . . . I am reminded of the story of the great French Marshal Lyautey, who once asked his gardener to plant a tree. The gardener objected that the tree was slow growing and would not reach maturity for a hundred years. The Marshal replied, 'In that case, there is no time to lose. Plant it this afternoon' " (O'Hara, 1966).

The second reflected his increasing maturity in terms of the limitations of power when he stated, "Every President must endure a gap between what he would like and what is possible" (Sorensen, 1965).

If we consider the limitations of our current substantive research knowledge and power, it is abundantly clear that we will have to endure a considerable gap between what we would like and what is possible, and, more than that, we must preserve the soil and plant the trees today which may not flourish for a very long time.

Another way of stating this is the need to consider the area of research from a short-range and a long-range view. Of greater import is the interrelationship between these views; the degree to which they can complement each other and the degree to which they may come into destructive contention. From such an appraisal it may be possible to more clearly approach priorities in terms of recommendations.

One could start such a discussion from the base of a conciliatory compromised conclusion, by stating that the country, the professions, science,

9

and the university face a momentous challenge; that by acting as a unified consortium, that challenge can be met; and that in so doing the separate components will only stimulate and strengthen one another. To a certain extent, this may be true—however, by starting from such a noncontroversial conclusion we may avoid contention, but we preclude the benefit of debate.

That there are hazards is abundantly clear. In a series of frank editorials, Grinker (Feb. 1967, Mar. 1967) has clearly delineated some of them. Nevertheless, few of these issues are being debated. Accordingly, I will make no attempt at reconciliation and instead will attempt to delineate further some of the problems to be faced.

BASIC CONCEPTS

A pressing conceptual need, stressed by all men of science, is to remain aware of the difference between research and research utilization. It seems necessary to continually restate the difference between basic research, which is process-oriented and directed toward new knowledge, and research utilization, or technological development, which is practical, task-oriented, or product-oriented.

The Joint Commission on Mental Health of Children represents a confluence of humanist-activist pressure and professional and scientific response. Under the humanitarian and compassionate pressure of "meeting the needs" of an applied field such as mental health, it is unfortunately easy to forget that the general direction as well as the speed of all technological development depends on the reciprocal appropriate current from basic to applied science. The short-range and the long-range views—like science and technology—are symbiotic. However, as Oppenheimer (1959) succinctly put it, "Our concern . . . is that this symbiosis be benign for both."

In a simplified schematic sense, we can conceptualize research utilization as an interaction of four complementary sectors. One is a body of substantive research data usually thought of as basic research; the second is the assessment of need; the third is the development of applicable techniques, which includes appropriately rigorous assessment; and the fourth is the development of a delivery system by which they can be made available to society.

Viewed from this perspective, the short-range view is under the sway of strong humanistic appeals in which deficits are vigorously stressed and in which the quality of preventive and rehabilitative efforts are to be equally available for all. Such considerations tend to converge with ever increasing concentration on needs and delivery systems. This can be thought of as one aspect of the work of the Commission that is long overdue. The difficulty lies in the morass of conflicting basic research, and the paucity of scientifically based preventive and interventive techniques. Considering the substantive basic research available, it is evident that some decisions will be premature in the sense that conclusions will be reached before research has been done and will be based on professional consensus. Such planning has a different probability of success than the planning which is based on research. One should remain mindful that planning based on consensus produced the Edsel.

Perhaps this can be made clearer by a brief reference to the history of polio control. The need was clear, many delivery systems were available, but the production and trial of a vaccine did not stem from this. It had to await the germinal research of Enders and the many basic scientists who made tissue culture work possible. Prior to this, the preventive and rehabilitative work in the area was disorderly, if not chaotic, characterized by claims and counterclaims. With the development of a vaccine the delivery systems problem almost solved itself. Although many of our medical schools have become preoccupied with it, "delivery system research" can hardly be considered the protogenic inquiry in our field. To the extent that it preempts the attention of rare scientific talent, and to the extent that it alters the scientific training environment, it must be seriously questioned.

If I may be permitted a caricature, the commitment of the major resources of our greatest universities to the "delivery system research area" is like asking our most significant theoretical physicists to preoccupy themselves with automotive engine systems. Not that such questions aren't important, but are they of such import as to override long-range, basic research needs?

RESEARCH PLANNING: AN OVERVIEW

In an oversimplified way, we have available to us two strategies for the planning of research. The first of these is in terms of need; and the second is planning, based upon historical knowledge of the way science proceeds.

Having once stated "the need is great," we have in fact made such a global description of the research deficits of the area of mental health that it becomes extremely difficult to explicate any further direction or plan. One possible approach might be a statistical conceptualization in which planners, for better or worse, would make decisions based on frequency counts of need. Anything other than a statistical approach—but equally valid—presents one with the problem of individual value judgments. Accordingly, some people make judgments about need in terms of their own concept of "sickest." This term usually refers to those children least accessible to the known and available techniques of intervention or rehabilitation.

I do not favor such approaches. There is great doubt that the cost, suffering, and loss to society are any greater in an autistic child than in an extremely bright, creative youngster who is so neurotic that he cannot function in school or society. Neither a statistical nor a value judgment approach to research planning is judicious, because it does not take into account the independence of investigators, and would preclude the heuristic impact and possible breakthrough from relatively insignificant diseases (in terms of incidence). One such example would be the heuristic impact on biochemical research of research on phenylketonuria in spite of the extreme rarity of this condition. Planning based on need and value judgment is no more meaningful than alphabetical listing, starting with A—abuse, adoption, and autism—all the way to Z—zoophobia.

It is also essential to remain aware that all current research planning in terms of need is predicated on a humanistic, egalitarian philosophy of life and an equally strong conviction that money and directed effort can produce scientific results. It is as if our political beliefs, our humanism, and our affluence lead us to believe that we can legislate away the troubles of mankind by appropriating large enough sums of money to appropriately designated research areas. In this endeavor, we are propelled by a veritable epidemic of sloganism and advertising techniques.

I think this error stems from a stubborn confusion of basic science with development or technology. While, as stated above, there is admittedly an overlap, it exists primarily in those areas of "ripeness," a matter to which I will refer in a moment. Technology can be heroically mobilized and directed by legislation; science much less so, if at all.

The second strategy stresses the dynamic relationship between available knowledge and technology. To adequately plan for short-range research gains, one must explore the basic research data with a view toward what areas for development have been made "ripe" by work such as tissue culture, rather than listing priorities of statistical needs. Painful though it may be, we must bear in mind that the preventative or therapeutic tools for such a condition or conditions as schizophrenia are not at hand because our researchers have not as yet unlocked the nature of the disease or diseases. Were we able to increase, by some magic, the number of mental health workers and facilities by tenfold or a hundredfold, and deliver them singly or in groups to all, we would be no closer to an understanding of, or a treatment or treatments for, schizophrenia. This is not to confuse making available the best we have even if it is ameliorative; I have no intent to disparage that high purpose. However, we must do this knowing that the definitive intervention can come only from fundamental research. There is a crucial difference between the two, and there is no utility in confusing one with the other.

SHORT-RANGE RESEARCH PLANNING

I would like to suggest that two strategic approaches to short-term research are possible. The first, as indicated above, is that the probabilities of pay-off will be enhanced by programing research in those areas in which the state of the field (in a research sense) seems "ripe," rather than in those areas in which the need seems greatest. This is based on the historical survey of how research usually blends into development or intervention. The success of a crash program such as radar, the bomb, or a vaccine is not predicated on the need, but rather on the ripeness of the area, how close to a developmental phase the preceding basic research has come. However, given a critical level of maturity in the underlying research, technological development can then be directed and facilitated.

I do not intend in this report to cover all such areas of maturity but would like to give an example of what I have in mind. I think it has been substantially documented that the development of the human child depends on the availability of a consistent, nourishing, stable, caretaking person. In the usual family, this is the mother. We have abundant and consistent clinical and developmental empiric evidence of the devastating impact of a lack of mothering from more than fifty years of research, particularly in certain kinds of institutions. It is clinically documented that certain variations in early mothering will lead to "failure to thrive," and to a host of developmental arrests and deviations. I do think that this area of the impact of mothering on development is ripe for concerted and planned research. I would like to contrast this with a condition such as autism or schizophrenia in which the research goals must be long-range, since not enough is known of the nature of the disease for short-range planning.

The second short-range goal would be *assessment research,* aimed at a closer understanding of existing programs and as an integral part of new programing. In terms of assessment research, we are currently struggling with the results of decades of following a humanist-activist model rather than a research model. Without appropriate assessment or evaluative research, "demonstration project" planning can lead to a Tower of Babel, and many of our most cherished professional beliefs will remain more closely linked to prejudice than to wisdom.

Although such research is demeaned and considered unglamorous by many, it is crucial and difficult work. One cannot overestimate the complexity of evaluation research or the necessity for great sophistication. While this is undoubtedly true of all intervention or preventive programs, I would like to focus on treatment intervention as one example. The methodological complexities have made it extremely difficult to do convincing research in this area, and an obstinate lack of humility has prevented us from viewing the problem in terms of indications and contraindications for one or another of a host of therapeutic interventions. Instead, we continue to ask simplistic, inappropriate questions such as: "Does psychotherapy work?" or "Does psychoanalysis work?" or "Does drug A, B, or C work?" Moreover, as the question is asked today, it no longer has the scientific tone it formerly had. It has a ring of panic in it as a pragmatic, expedient response to the host of responsibilities to which mental health has been "volunteered," i.e., the war on poverty, the war on crime, the war on war, the war on drug abuse, urban redevelopment, riots, education, etc.— let alone the traditional problems of neuroses and psychoses.

Given the complexity of a paradigm which would run Patient A (with hundreds of variables) in Life Situation B (with hundreds of variables) getting Treatment C (with many variables) from Dr. D (with innumerable variables) at Time and Place X (with its host of variables), one readily sees the methodological problems involved and one can appreciate the desperate need for manageable simplification. Nevertheless, it is noteworthy that attempts still go on to reduce such complex interactions to a two- or three-variable model of research.

It is abundantly clear that good assessment programs for existing therapeutic modes are imperative, and that if they are sophisticatedly conceived they can yield a great deal of information about underlying processes as well as indications and contraindications. It is thoughtless to expect psychotherapy, as we currently know it, to have a dramatic impact on infantile autism, but it is inordinately hazardous to assume that it has no impact on hysteria or phobia or other neurotic states.

Perhaps an example will clarify the meaning of the need for sophisticated assessment research. If one looks at the admission statistics from the state of Connecticut, one finds that new admissions to the state hospital system have increased 55 percent since 1955. Readmissions during the 1960 to 1967 period increased 253 percent and have accounted for more than half of the total admissions ("Department of Mental Health Reports," 1967). This is reflective of a massive humane endeavor which takes an empiric, researchable question as its basic postulate: i.e., sick people are better off *out* of hospitals than inside them. In spite of the iatrogenic impact of hospitalization on some patients, the generalization of this proposition to all patients in hospitals, as a debilitating factor, has never been demonstrated.

Evaluation, such as it is, has focused on the patient population and has *not* been extended to the impact of such serial hospitalization on family, children, and communities. The values of such a therapeutic endeavor as revealed in such statistics are laudable humanistic efforts, but can hardly lend support to the idea that this is a scientifically based therapeutic endeavor. It is sadly reminiscent of the story of the man whose progressive deafness was not helped by existing hearing aids. He set about to build a huge hearing aid of his own. A friend viewed his efforts and the resulting contraption and asked, "Does it work?" "No," said the man, "but it sure makes people talk louder."

Nor have we attended sufficiently to such factors as the 366 percent rise in the birth rate of hospitalized women reported from Michigan

(Shearer *et al.*, 1968), or the fact that this is a small percentage of a presumably even greater rise in the overall birth rate related to the "open door" hospitalization policy. This exists, in spite of our scientific suspicion of a genic factor in psychotic conditions or our scientific suspicion of familial, interactional etiologic effects.

Nor have we attended to the suspicion, expressed by some sociologists, that the "open door policy" (as practiced in the American state hospital system) may be related to an increase in bizarre crime.

Although many people are aware of the distressing impact on dependent children of such serial, home-to-hospital-to-home psychotic environments, the definitive research has not yet been done.[1] At the same time, there is every reason to suspect that this program brings about grievous disturbances in the development of children. If we were to rephrase this mental health program arbitrarily in terms of foster parent care, I have no doubt that every professional and nonprofessional involved would disqualify an ambulatory psychotic mother and/or father who is hospitalized two to six times per year, and with varying degrees of drug control when out of the hospital, as a good candidate for being a foster parent. Yet, we are in effect condoning this with biological parents in our current hospital policies. The assessment of such programs must become more sophisticated and must include the impact on children, families, and the community as well as the status of the patient himself.

Another case in point is the "child guidance clinic" movement in America. Started as a "demonstration project," it has never been adequately assessed. Some professionals think it is poor, others marvelous. The question of poor or marvelous *for what* has never been meaningfully approached. Assessment is almost invariably reported as effort—how many children and families seen, number of interviews, etc., rather than effect or process by which effect is produced. This seems to be the forthcoming fate of the "community mental health center" movement. Nevertheless, it is possible to rectify both. This becomes an urgent thought when one realizes the utility of such neglected assessment in terms of self-corrective feedback to planners and therapists.

LONG-RANGE RESEARCH PLANNING

A historic view of the progress of science reveals the reasonable thought that one requires a very large scientific establishment consisting of many individuals or small groups of individuals working on their own or related projects. From this broad base, the probability is enhanced that a single

1. However, the early research finds of Anthony (1968 and two studies to be published) have begun to document quite impressively the disadvantageous impact on developing children in "psychotic" homes.

individual or small group of individuals, with sufficient creative genius, will either conceptualize something completely new or resynthesize a field anew. It is these "breakthroughs" which represent the best of basic science and are paradigmatic for the subsequent technological developments which come in their wake.

Again, it would seem reasonable to study *where* such science occurs and in *what* atmosphere it occurs. If one does this, one is led to the central, if not exclusive, position of the university. Every aspect of science either happens within a university or is closely related to the university—certainly in the sense of people trained in the university. If the United States did not have a large, and probably the world's finest, university system, it would be appropriate to request funds to set up such a system. It was this university complex which made American science preeminent.

The original intent of federal funding was to enhance it. There are many who feel that this intent was like trying to push a huge boulder "just a little way down the mountain." Universities are now in the position of increasingly enhancing national health planning.

The broader aspects of this situation have been described by Barzun (1968). His recent, pithy commentary stresses that the American university " . . . is getting to resemble the Red Cross more than a university, with direct help to whomever is suffering now"; and further, the possibility exists that it may have destroyed itself by turning into "a public utility."

Since I am speaking of preserving the atmosphere of the university, of extending it and safeguarding the kinds of innovative people it attracts— as a calculated risk for science—it is worth paying some attention to the university itself.

The basic, or perhaps I should more appropriately say the *ideal,* university consists of a community of free and independent scholars, each engaged in the acquisition and transmission of knowledge. The great vitality of the American university system has come from its heterogeneity in the sense that it consists of a large number of very different kinds of institutions, each with its own specific charge. This ranges from the extremely practical mission of certain agricultural colleges to the freest kind of scholarly tradition as represented by schools such as Yale, Harvard, the University of Chicago, and others. That these universities are in a process of great change is self-evident. It is imperative that the appropriate bodies of educators, citizens, scientists, and politicians arrive at some basic conception of the primary mission of universities within the United States.

If I may quote Yale president Kingman Brewster (1967), "The survival, as well as the quality, of civilization depends greatly upon the effectiveness of continuous discovery and learning in our universities. The effectiveness of American universities depends greatly upon free competition for students, faculty, and new ideas among hundreds of ambitious institutions. The effectiveness of this academic competition depends greatly upon the ability of some of the strongest institutions to direct their own destiny, free of political interference, free of dependence upon outside dictate."

Speaking at Boston College on April 20, 1963, the late President Kennedy stated the problem as follows: "I want to impress on you as urgently as I can, the growing and insistent importance of universities in our national life . . . our national tradition is *variety* . . . it remains the task of each of our institutions to shape its own role among its differing sisters" (O'Hara, 1966).

I would hold that it is this quality of the self-directed, free academic enterprise—different, diversified, heterogeneous, and dedicated to discovery and learning—which is crucial to the well-being and future of science in the United States. This is certainly true of all fields, but particularly of the chaotic state of scientific endeavor in the mental health sciences.

The major part of research relevant to mental health continues to be forthcoming, primarily from medical schools, and secondarily from certain graduate departments in those aspects of the social and biological sciences which are called behavioral sciences. The medical school has a tradition of its own, which cannot avoid carrying a considerable responsibility of providing facilities for patient care, since this care is an essential part of the experience of medical education and research. This is not usually a matter of service exclusively for service's sake.

It is quite clear that the modern university can no longer exist without adequate federal aid for its operations. Since, in recent years, this has become increasingly tied to part of a service demand for the citizenry, one must seriously question the relationship between quantities of service, education, and research. In addition, it would appear that there is some danger of foreclosure in the interests of maximizing equal care—by that I mean foreclosure in direction and area of research growth. There is usually a difference between "expedient" and "basic." This is, however, not the only conflict which is potentially harmful for scientific growth. Another is that of the position of the investigator caught between short-range and long-range goals, particularly as they relate to current funding practices.

FINANCING

There are essentially three sources of research funds and salaries for research people. These are the university facilities themselves, private foundations, and the federal government. Of these, the increasing expense involved in operating an appropriate institution and doing research has made it mandatory that federal aid be perhaps the most crucial aspect (Swain, 1962; Abelson, Jan. 1963, Feb. 1963).

By current practice, the largest proportion of research funds is granted to investigators who apply via appropriate study section review for projects.

Although such projects are renewable, they tend to average about three years per request and tend to support the salary of the principal investigator and his staff, as well as the expenses of conducting the research. This has developed a number of problems.

The first of these is the difficulty of establishing appropriate criteria of scientific merit which can be used with fairness across a tremendous range of studies which have addressed themselves to essentially different phenomenology. In recent years, this has put an unnecessary hardship on those investigators who do clinical research. The multivariant phenomena which they investigate—if they are to retain their relevance—do not readily lend themselves to the better-explicated criteria of scientific rigor which are more appropriate to sharply circumscribed studies, usually having little or no clinical relevance. As a result of this, clinical research is in a decline, and every effort must be made not only to preserve it but to invigorate it and revitalize it. It seems imperative to introduce such concepts as "appropriate rigor" and "relevance" to the funding concepts used. All of our clinical research is complex and will continue to suffer unless cognizance is taken of that complexity. The area should be supported financially if it is "appropriately" rigorous and systematic. Methodological complexity is a lesser error and is certain to be more productive ultimately than irrelevance.

The second hardship such project research brings about is the fact that principal investigators are forced to delineate small, doable projects, rather than to concentrate on a career in a programmatic sense. The only exception to this has been the small, rather successful Career Awards program operated by NIMH.

Another debilitating factor in this model is the uncertainty and instability of the academic or the research setting for the investigator. He must conceive of a project in order to get his salary and the salary of his staff. If he wants to continue, he must prematurely (while the project is in midstream) initiate an additional request for a supplementary grant or else conceive a new project, etc. What this has resulted in is a loss of the time and energy of the principal investigator, who functions under the duress and anxiety of this instability. I think it is fair to assume that these people represent the best-trained scientific talent available and must now give a great deal of their time to fund raising and administration.

To summarize, such short-range, project, or product research tends to place investigators under an unnecessary and self-defeating burden of insecurity—necessity to "go where the money is"—which tends to vitiate faculty self-determination. This programing plus a service orientation will diminish faculty self-selection and self-direction, which in turn cannot help but alter the atmosphere in which scientists work and in which new scientists are trained.

In addition to this, one must consider the fact that since universities can no longer function without federal aid, they are obliged to go in the direction where federal funding dictates. In the current and foreseeable future it will be easier to get service funding than research funding. This will be particularly true of universities which ally themselves with mental health centers or heart, stroke, and cancer centers. This, then, brings about a subtle change in the direction and in the function of the university which tends to produce a homogeneity within the American university system, with each medical school being responsible for an appropriately sized catchment area, which strains its service responsibilities. Some future historian may chronicle that: "Before they were forced to become commissioners of health, deans of medical schools were considered to be educators, and their institutions, subsequently called catchments, were highly esteemed as centers of learning." Indeed, one day, the same might be said of the corporate executive functions of university presidents, in contrast to their traditional role as great educational leaders.

I do not for a moment mean that such concerns aren't crucial concerns of citizenry, government, and perhaps some universities. I merely question the priority and the devastating impact of preempting the traditional university function of all schools for this purpose. Viewed from this perspective, i.e., changing university function, I can see no compelling reason why such necessary facilities and institutions cannot be constructed *outside* of university control—particularly if other means of academic financial support can be devised.

The dangers of such a continued direction are already apparent, particularly in the rather ominous professionalization of the graduate school. The Ph.D. degree, once granted for original contribution to research, is now granted to engineers. The prerequisite of a scholarly contribution to one's field has been grievously eroded. If this continues to be the case in *all* universities, one cannot help but wonder where the future cadre of scientific talent will develop.

The physical sciences already demonstrate the impact of such planning and funding. At the same time, they are not as paradigmatic for the general university as are the health sciences—in particular, medical schools. The medical school is prototypical of emerging university–federal government homogeneity—and psychiatry is prototypical of that evolving relationship.

What has occurred to university departments of psychiatry because of mental health planning and mental health centers will happen soon to departments of medicine and surgery with the appearance of heart, stroke, and cancer institutes in a similar pattern. Since medical schools cannot survive without federal aid, the question remains, "In what form can they exist?"

Within psychiatry, as a result of meeting the demands of federal planning and funding, there has developed an ominous possibility of a leveling —a pedestrian, monotonous uniformity of departments throughout the country. This will be primarly in the service of the aforementioned larger, humanistic movement of helping all people and equalizing all care. While much can be said for this, and I am myself sympathetic to it, science has and will continue to suffer, particularly in terms of the coming generations of scholarly innovators.

If we preoccupy ourselves with delivery systems, we will continue to lose sight of the more crucial and difficult problem of what is to be delivered. There are some areas, such as polio vaccine, in which the disparity is not so great and the priorities may be different. However, these areas are few, and somewhere within the national planning, the first priority must be to innovators.

The federal government must address itself to maintaining an optimal climate in which the Einsteins and the Enders can emerge without a loss of developers. Again, by this, I do not intend to demean the contribution of technology; it is more a matter of priorities and a wish to ensure a benevolent atmosphere in which the symbiont can survive.

In the past, both aspects have been encouraged within the United States by the great diversity throughout our educational system. The value to the country of the ferment that comes from such heterogeneity, in terms of different kinds of universities, should never be underestimated.

Given the harsh realities of funding practices, the only antidote must be to deliberately plan for self-determination on the part of institutions. This variety has served the country incredibly well in the past, and is the only way to guarantee the effervescence and excitement so crucial to the educational and scientific enterprise.

This does not mean a "parochial elite," but is an antidote to the possibility that each of the medical schools, via controlled planning, will tend to become responsible for the short-range health needs of the country. Some universities must be preserved for the *long-range* health needs.

What I see as perhaps the only hopeful alternative is large block grants to institutions which will permit them the necessary freedom of self-determination in their faculty, teaching, research, and missions. If we add "the evolution of health research" to the following, Haskins (1968) has succinctly stated the issue:

Like successful biological evolution, successful social evolution must constantly guard against discarding the essential with the trivial. . . . It would be difficult to find a more appropriate general caveat for our time than this of exercising due care that, in embracing new and experimental courses on myriad fronts of movement with the ardor that we must, we do not at the same time discard long-tested values and long-tried adaptive courses which, if they are lost, will only have, one day, to be re-won—and probably at enormous cost.

The university, as an educational and scientific institution, may be in just such jeopardy. It may become very costly to re-create a scholarly atmosphere if we continue to alter it.

On a broader level, it is incredible to me that the educational enterprise—which has served the country so well—should have to justify its existence on any other level than the increased benefits to the country of an educated citizenry. The health and welfare of its citizens is a matter of prime priority to government and has had abundant university consultation. However, it would be a tragic and short-range decision to completely pre-empt the values of the university from its long-range obligations by making this its major function.

SUMMARY

In summary, the long-range research needs of the country can be approached as one small segment of the larger issue of the function and status of the university in modern life. It calls for a sober reappraisal of the mutual obligations and mutual impact of the university and the "outside world" (government, industry, and the community) upon each other. To date, this is a matter which has concerned educators far more than scientists. The issues are best described in the following incisive and lucid comments of Robert Maynard Hutchins (1969):

> Every institution in society must serve society. Otherwise it will not last very long. But the question is what is the special, peculiar, unique service a university can render? How many different kinds of service can a university render without ceasing to be one, or without becoming incapable of rendering the special, peculiar, unique service it could offer? If a university is expected to meet every need, respond to every demand, and yield to every pressure, how does it avoid becoming totally other-directed? What then is its claim to that freedom traditionally called academic? If it may properly respond to some demands and reject others, what is the standard of acceptance or rejection it should apply? Obviously the ordinary test of action, the test of purpose, is meaningless if the university's purpose is to do whatever the society wants. Yet we all have a vague feeling, even yet, that there are some things a university ought not to do and some things it cannot do without ceasing to be a university.
>
> There can be no objection to a community's setting up institutions to reflect what it thinks it wants at any given time. What it wants it should—or at any rate it will—try to get. The university, I suggest, is the institution that performs its highest, its unique, service to society by declining to do what the society thinks it wants, by refusing to be useful, in the common acceptation of that word, and by insisting instead that its task is understanding and criticism. It is a center of independent thought.

There can be no doubt that the gradual emergence of the university from its classical monastic seclusion has had an enormously beneficial effect on all concerned. One major function of the university must remain that of a reservoir of highly skilled, specialized talent for the practical problems of government, industry, and the community. It is by now obligated to so remain a vital force in civilization.

And yet, one must even question the developing concept of the itinerant consultant—which is the lot of many professors of science. I do not know if it is possible to have it both ways—perhaps it is a matter of degree—but it must be possible to function as such a reservoir without completely relinquishing the concept of university as a community of highly individual, independent, free scholars.

If we focus on psychiatry, besieged by service needs, community needs, national mental health, etc., the problem of basic research can seem a luxury rather than a crucial urgency. This is further complicated by the multidisciplinary nature of the enterprise as well as by the multitheoretical characteristics of the field. It can be a bewildering morass which should concern all psychiatrists and health workers.

From the viewpoint of the incomplete nature of the research results of *all* theoretical systems, methods, and disciplines, great humility on the part of all thoughtful scientists seems appropriate. Practically, it may call for eclectic departments of psychiatry. This does not mean departments composed of eclectics. At this stage of scientific progress, most scientists would agree that this blunts the probe and blurs the exploration.

I refer, rather, to an overall eclecticism arising from a community of experts representing their own disciplines with integrity, dedication, and security. In such a department, psychiatry, pediatrics, education, and psychoanalysis can stand, contribute, and grow alongside neurophysiology, biochemistry, neuropharmacology, and the social sciences. In the unconditional freedom of the university tradition, each specialist must be free to immerse himself in the complexities of his own research area. He must also be free to collaborate—not by assignment but by inner direction. If there is to be fruitful, multidisciplinary collaboration, it will best arise spontaneously from such an intellectual climate, rather than from a calculated financial need. It cannot be programed, for it depends too much on the ripeness of the moment, the people, the methods, and the communication.

I remain convinced that when the time is at hand for basic research collaboration between disciplines, the best of it will come as highly individual, inspired spurts, rather than from premeditated calculation. Perhaps the best one can do to enhance this probability is the preservation of the most fertile soil, i.e., the provocative skepticism of university heterogeneity. In such a structure, whether through intrigued interest or irritated awareness, multidisciplinary communication and teaching occur.

The nation, science, *and* the university will each lose something very important if the community of free scholars, and the communication so made possible within the university, is altered. The future interdependent development of all begs for a tolerant reevaluation by men of vision.

RECOMMENDATIONS ON RESEARCH

1. The Task Force considers as a matter of highest priority the concept of establishing and preserving a national research climate which will optimize the productivity and opportunities of creative individual researchers. It is assumed that a very broad concept of child development encompasses the basic disciplines of biology, the social sciences, the behavioral sciences, education, and the medical sciences. This means that encouragement and fostering of scarce research talent be undertaken in these disciplines as well as in combinations of specialties, e.g., city planning, architecture, and dynamic demography; special education, etc. Thus, research can contribute to the promotion of normal child development and suggest the problems and the directions of answer searching that must continue if the various practice fields are to improve their techniques and revise and expand their knowledge base.

2. Owing to the possibility of steering by the very nature of funding practices, we would consider it crucial to preserve a national eclecticism in research which would prevent premature foreclosure in research direction. Although we are not at the moment concerned with issues of territoriality among the basic disciplines, we think there is much to be gained by mutual exchange of experts in their own areas.

3. The Task Force is concerned about the protection of basic scientists and scholars whose work does not clearly fall as yet into readily applied techniques. We think a distinction should continue to be made between research and development, and that support for development must not be given at the expense of basic research. Short-range project research should be planned on the basis of "ripeness" of moment, i.e., what aspects of basic research knowledge are close to a developmental phase, rather than some vague concept of "meeting the need."

4. Existing patterns of support seem more designed to fit the needs of the established researcher. We are concerned with the need for overall support mechanisms other than short-range project support. Support for training of researchers should be increased, and those showing talent should be encouraged to stay in research. We are convinced that this desirable goal would be enhanced if support were shifted to programmatic career planning rather than project support. We would be interested in exploring the area of identification of, and encouragement to, innovative people.

5. We are concerned with methods of supporting development. This is thought of as delivery techniques and systems having to do with the im-

plementation and delivery of mental health services to children. We also recognize that such problems must be related to children's services delivery generally, and to the entire system of services in health, education, and welfare.

6. We consider it crucial to redefine demonstration projects as innovative efforts which *include* evaluation and assessment as a central orientation. To prevent the spawning of a massive proliferation of "demonstration projects" which present us with the dangers of a Tower of Babel, it is necessary to stress that no demonstration project should be funded without appropriate rigor and relevant assessment techniques, appropriate and relevant to the phenomena being studied. Evaluation should be *necessary* where funds are used for demonstration, rather than *desirable*. Of greater import, the utility of such self-correcting feedback information is enormously important to the *process* of developing new programs and techniques.

7. In view of the multidisciplinary nature of research in this field, and with a view toward preserving a national eclecticism, criteria for scientific merit, when funding is involved, should explore such concepts as "appropriate rigor" and "appropriate relevance" to the phenomena being studied.

Manpower

One of the recurrent themes that emerged in Task Force discussions of manpower and other topics was the problem of defining child mental health goals. All members contributed ideas and views without arriving at any consensus. Since this kind of problem is not resolved through discussion, and is one which results in intellectual discomfort if left as a permanent unresolved issue, it was agreed that Dr. Otto Pollak delineate the problem of goal definition in child mental health, especially with reference to manpower. Dr. Pollak's paper treats the issue in depth, both sociologically and psychologically, and it is included in the report as one of the major contributions that emerged from the discussions and deliberations of the Task Force. It is listed below, together with papers and studies on various aspects of manpower contributed by a Subcommittee on Manpower, chaired by Dr. Raymond Feldman. The titles are as follows: "Mental Health Goals in Child Rearing and Child Care," by Otto Pollak, Ph.D.; "Needed: A Scientific Basis for Manpower Utilization in Mental Health Services," by Joseph Whiting, Ph.D., James Carper, Ph.D., and Raymond Feldman, M.D.; "Considerations Regarding Manpower Study," by Otto von Mering, Ph.D.; "Toward an Understanding of Manpower Pools, Their Training and Development in Relation to Populations with Different Mental Health Risks," by Otto von Mering, Ph.D.; "Needed: Mental Health Manpower Development and Training Patterns," by Otto von Mering, Ph.D.; "Suggestions for Alleviating Manpower Shortages in the Child Health Services," by Otto Pollak, Ph.D.; "Present Status of the Clinical Field," Raymond Feldman, M.D.; "Mental Health Services for the Community: Process, Requirements and Solutions," by James W. Carper, Ph.D., Joseph F. Whiting, Ph.D., and Raymond Feldman, M.D.; "Implications for Mental Health of U.S. Department of Labor and U.S. Office of Economic Opportunity Programs for Children," by James Carper, Ph.D.; "Community Functioning, Manpower Utilization, and Impact Evaluation," by Joseph F. Whiting, Ph.D.

Along with Pollak's "Goals" paper, the subcommittee's contributions point up the dilemmas and the possible solutions for resolving the manpower difficulties in the child mental health field. As Feldman, Carper, and Whiting indicate, conventional ideas about using present manpower resources in the traditional mental health professions in order to meet present or future needs have many aspects which appear to be unrealistic and unrealizable. The papers of Von Mering and Whiting converge upon similar issues.

One problem becomes apparent if one looks at population trends. In 1965, the nation's total population for all ages totaled 194,600,000; the projected growth by 1980 is 235,291,000. This is a percentage increase of plus 80 percent. The increase in child population under the age of fifteen for the same period is from 59,900,000 in 1965 to an estimated 72,800,000 or a percentage increase of plus 82 percent. During the same fifteen-year period, 2,000,000 more babies are expected to be born. These population increases, according to the Bureau of Health Manpower of the U.S. Public Health Service, will bring substantial increases in need. Indeed, Fein, in *The Doctor Shortage* (1967), points out that during the next decade the total increase in demand for medical services may be about plus 25 percent. The estimated increase in physicians is about plus 19 percent, or possibly plus 13 percent, if new foreign-trained physicians are not available. The supply of physicians would not meet the total increase in demand, and certainly would not take into account the impact of new medical discoveries, changes in service settings, and increased availability of services.

When one looks at the total health manpower picture, the supply has increased greatly and will continue to increase. It will, however, never meet the increased demand for services, even if the highest estimate of increased health manpower is realized. In general, more than 3,700,000 health workers in all categories are needed by 1975. This would require a rate of increase in production of health workers 50 percent higher than between 1955 and 1965. Of course, the most difficult increase to achieve will be among the more highly trained professions and among teachers, researchers, and skilled technicians. That this is not likely to occur is shown by the rather static production of physicians. In 1965–66, the population of twenty-year-olds from which medical students are drawn totaled 2,791,000. Medical school admissions were 8,206, or 3.3 per 1,000 twenty-year-olds. Estimates for 1975–76 indicate there will be 3,993,000 twenty-year-olds, and that 14,500 to 15,000 medical school admissions will be made from this group; thus, the rate per 1,000 twenty-year-olds will be 3.6 to 3.8. This means that the opportunity to enter medicine in 1975 will be about the same as in 1960, when 8,794 out of 2,281,000—or 3.9 per 1,000 twenty-year-olds—entered medical school.

When one realizes that the demand for medical services is expanding much faster than either the increased capacity of schools to train or the available number who will enter the medical profession, then the inability of medical and health services to meet the demands of children's needs and those of their families is underscored. Under present conditions, neither the health professions nor the training resources can meet the requirements placed upon them either now or in the foreseeable future. Nevertheless, the professions and their knowledge and skills, their control and access to the service settings and resources, and their roles as trainers and educators cannot be discounted. Indeed, they are indispensable if one is even to begin to solve the shortage problem. The crucial area of training needs continual examination and research, in and of itself. Given the state of flux in the area of treatment goals, training for "what" becomes an important issue to be researched.

Our various papers and discussions, as well as the ongoing research by Dr. Joseph Whiting and the American Psychiatric Association's Division on Manpower Studies, led the Task Force to choose as one of its core themes the utilization of manpower. If a major focus is on how manpower is to be used, in what settings, and for which populations, then one can examine the available manpower pools and assess the likelihood of obtaining candidates for those jobs which need to be performed and, equally important, the possibilities of training resources expanding and/or revising their present operations in order to equip new manpower pools with required knowledge and skills.

By focusing on the problems of manpower utilization, these other areas of recruitment, training, and placement are amenable to national planning and can also be formulated as research issues. The Task Force has identified at least three different issues related to utilization, namely:

the community health requirements as defined by the community as well as by the professionals;

the operations of education and training establishments; and

the existing service structures that deliver health and related services.

The utilization of personnel has to be formulated in its relationship to the above-mentioned areas. This leads to an estimation of the state of the national mental health and related professions, as well as the roles of the community, educational resources, and the service structure arrangements. In this exploration the following questions are raised: How do people choose their health services and get them? Which professionals give services? How do they receive their training, and how does their knowledge about services affect recipients of services? The Task Force recommends that such queries be made the basis of future inquiry into manpower needs and deployment policies.

Under this concept of utilization the Task Force recommends an intensive study of structures in the present arrangements, e.g., hospitals, clinics, residential treatment centers, schools; it also recommends examining new and emerging structures, such as the community mental health centers, comprehensive neighborhood health centers, regional medical plans, etc.

Under this rubric, there is an implication for manpower development which ranges from the addition of more of the traditional professionals to the total manpower pool in order to supply an increasing demand, to a new definition of traditional occupational functions; e.g., consultation collaboration, supervision, and most recently, "new careers." The concept of manpower should not only be one of available jobs and available people to fill them, but rather how these are balanced with respect to the functions of meeting community health needs, educational resources, service structures and the existing manpower, and occupational and professional practices. The Task Force recommends that studies of occupational functions, manpower resources, and their relationships be explored and studied in order to make intelligent decisions.

The Task Force recommendations are future-oriented. They demand a reconceptualization of current thinking about manpower recruitment, development, and utilization, not in an ex-cathedra manner, but rather with the principle of development of an ongoing informational base which would take into account the community attitudes and the three basic requirements as noted above.

The Task Force also recommends that serious rethinking and analysis be applied to the utilization of both professionals and trained nonprofessionals and their relationships to the new service structures, with an emphasis on the new ways of delivering skills. This means that trials of these new manpower resources be made in both traditional settings and new community-based service organizations. We urge that research in these areas guide the development of new careers and new service settings.

The awareness of the importance of community definition of health care must be understood as being a basis of public education, one which could lead to community understanding of how manpower should be used. Otherwise, community support will be more rhetorical than real, and the development of new manpower will be made more difficult.

Attention must be paid to educational and training resources and the modes of organization which will be necessary for the training and development of manpower for new service structures. Since the expansion of already overloaded training resources, as well as the initiation of new training resources will take considerable time, planning should begin immediately.

Although the Task Force was not able to fully explore the issues in mental health training, we recognized that these are interconnected with the development of manpower. In general, the Task Force inclined toward a more efficient training in mental health, not only for those centrally concerned with mental health, but also for those whose professional work has mental health implications of which they are only dimly aware. Such training is especially important for teachers, pediatricians, parents, recreation group leaders, police, and others whose activities and interactions with children can potentially enhance mental health goals; however, the means for incorporating mental health into specific training and educational activities for such professionals is beyond our present scope and would require long-term study. We simply point to the importance of including mental health as an integral part of the training of all those who work with children.

One set of issues that emerged through the manpower discussions of Task Force IV was the need for clarification of the goals that child mental health manpower would be fulfilling. Dr. Pollak's paper is reproduced here in full, as expressing the best formulation that the Task Force was able to obtain.

Mental Health Goals in Child-Rearing
and Child Care

INTRODUCTION

Any exploration of manpower utilization requires the identification of
the purposes toward which such manpower is directed. Evaluative research,
similarly, presupposes a determination of the purpose of the activity to be
evaluated. In the mental health field, however, we find relatively little
attention given to a formulation of goals. The literature seems to be preoccupied with the descriptions of various forms of pathology, with genetic
explanations of syndromes, and with the description of processes and techniques. The use of the professional helper and its risks, such as counter-
transference, etc., seems to have attracted considerably more interest than
the goal of such use.

In historical perspective this situation becomes more meaningful
than it appears to be at first. The purpose of the psychoanalytic effort was
primarily understanding and only secondarily therapeutic. Freud's first
Introductory Lectures pointed out the distinction between the organically
oriented physician, who encourages the patient to expect improvement in
the near future, and the psychoanalyst, who describes the treatment as
painful, time-consuming, and uncertain in outcome (Freud, 1966). When
pressed for a definition of the goals of psychoanalysis, the older Freud
could still promise nothing except the transformation of neurotic fears
into everyday misery (Waelder, 1960)—a considerable improvement in
Freud's terms. Of course, the suffering of humanity could never accept the
Freudian position of reality and its problems, and in the optimistic atmosphere of the New World the psychoanalytic pessimism was transformed
into a therapeutic optimism, which insisted on the use of psychiatric
knowledge for the improvement of the human condition, as an ally to
child-rearing, as a guide to married life, and ultimately even as a guide

30

to successful aging (Erikson, 1950). Philip Rieff (1966) has pointed out the insistence of modern times to receive help, rather than clarification, from psychiatry, and Paul Halmos (1966) has recently identified many statements of optimism on the part of professions practicing social case-work and psychotherapy which seem to respond to this claim of suffering and bewildered yet optimistic humanity.

This transformation of a pessimistic view of reality in science into an optimistic practice on the way from Europe to America is not unprece-dented. It has happened in criminology with the shift from Lombroso's pessimism to the optimism of American prison reformers and psychiatrists studying juvenile delinquency (Grünhut, 1948).

There is no question that the American attitude of belief in the useful-ness of dynamic psychiatry for the improvement of child-rearing and human interaction in general is the only rational alternative to man when faced with this body of knowledge. Pessimism with regard to the success of inter-vention is a self-fulfilling hypothesis. As long as we believe that human behavior is wish-relevant, it seems unacceptable in the American world view to think of professional intervention as not following the goals of improvement.

It is therefore remarkable that so little attention has been given, even in this country, to the specification of these goals. Here we come up against a cultural lag between scientific tradition and the results of social change. At the period in which psychoanalytic findings were made, adult people frequently suffered from the pathological consequences of generally re-stricted and specifically sex-repressive child-rearing. At the same time, the world was not yet shaken by two world wars and the specter of a third one which threatens universal annihilation. People needed a remission from restraints, and psychiatrists and patients and—in the progressive educa-tion movement—teachers and students entered into alliances of liberation. Liberation, however, needs no specific goal. Its direction goes "from" rather than "toward." As a matter of fact, specific goals must express them-selves as constraint and, as such, appear to contradict the purpose of liberation. In modern times, however, the impending stress of atomic war-fare, of riots in metropolitan areas, the threat to parents of children's turning to the damaging use of drugs, seem to present restraints as goals of therapy. These restraints are seen as mental-health-serving intervention, rather than remissions.

Actually, two factors seem to work against the specification of such goals: (1) the identification of the mental-health-serving professions with the psychoanalytic model, that is, with a model of liberation; and (2) the unconscious identification of many therapists and teachers with their pa-tients and students. It is the tragedy of intervention with character disorders that it creates a danger of seduction to the therapist, a seduction of joining the patient in the enjoyment of impulse release and in the defiance of the

reality principle, which is the eternal challenge to developmental experience. To have specific goals for child-rearing and intervention means,
therefore, a betrayal of the psychoanalytic tradition and a renunciation of
the principle of *not* using therapeutic intervention for the vicarious enjoyment of pathology.

PROBLEMS OF ADAPTATION

It is the historical contribution of Erikson (1950) and Hartmann
(1958) to have expanded the psychoanalytic perspective to the relationship of the individual to his environment and to the total life-span. Problems of adaptation are, by definition, goal-connected. Manpower utilization
in the professions serving the mental health of children must concern itself,
in part, with problems of adaptation. This is not to say that the problem
of solving intrapsychic conflict will not remain one of the major areas of
human existence, requiring the intervention of psychiatrists and social
workers. It is to say, however, that mental health care which takes its model
only from modes of intervention directed at the solution of intrapsychic
conflict will leave part of the task undone (Rapoport, 1960), and probably
that part of its task which has become more crucial to human survival
than it ever was. Even help with adaptation is not enough. A goal of
positive enabling has been suggested in the recent literature (Gladwin,
1967). This may be interpreted as a mental health goal, directed at helping
children to develop creativity in bringing about benevolent social change.
The cynic may say that adolescents seem to develop this ability simply out
of intergenerational conflict, but the cynics will be wrong if they equate
adolescent rebellion with benevolence.

INTRAPSYCHIC CONFLICT AND SOCIAL CHANGE

It is traditionally stated that intrapsychic conflict is based on the incompatibility of the pleasure principle and the reality principle, on the
incompatibility between attitudes formed in childhood and the opportunities and requirements of adult life. Recent developments on this
national scene, however, suggest that the conflict between libido and destructiveness in all three areas of psychic life seems to be of equal, if not
greater, importance. An economy of abundance gives a degree of leeway
to the pleasure principle which periods of scarcity have never known. A
culture of child-rearing which has been based on an ideology of permissive-
ness has similarly expanded the range of permissible impulse gratification
and restricted the demands of the reality principle. The sexual revolution
has made the postponement of libidinal gratification a much more ques-
tionable requirement than it formerly was ("The Sexual Future of Man,"
1967). A world in which the whole experience of earning a living is

related to employment in large-scale organizations has made independence a lesser requirement of adulthood than could have been fathomed in the nineteenth century. What has not yet become permissible, however, is the replacement of love by hate as the dominant principle in superego structure. This is perhaps the outstanding plight of the Negro in the United States. His closeness to political power, his sudden sensitivity to history, and his awareness of being watched by the newly independent nations have brought about a situation in which hatred of white people becomes something approaching an ethical demand (Fanon, 1963). It has been noted that Negro children show a formerly unknown degree of anger. It is within the awareness of every school administrator that the destructiveness of young Negroes presents itself not as deviance—felt or pretended—but as a justified expression of the Negro existence under modern conditions in the United States. When superego exhorts hatred and condemns love, the intrapsychic conflict of a large number of children and adolescents certainly represents a challenge of the first magnitude to the mental-health-serving professions. It must not be forgotten that the anger of the Negro child and his hatred for the white may release also the anger and hatred of the white children, and that a white "backlash" may have to be considered as a threat to the mental health development of white children.

Another intrapsychic problem that is likely to make its appearance will be the recurrence of hatred in people who thought that their feelings for Negroes were positive. The white liberal rejected by Black Power will find it difficult to maintain the stance of love conquering hate and may be forced into feelings toward Negroes paralleling the feelings of Negroes toward the whites. In areas where violence is encouraged and destructiveness redefined as a means of obtaining justice, the problem of maintaining the supremacy of love over hate, of libido over thanatos, becomes a problem of Negro and white in unexpected quarters. In the light of these developments, the maintenance or the establishment of such libidinal supremacy over the destructive forces which now are assuming the mantle of legitimacy appears to be a mental health goal of the first order (O. Pollak, 1966). In discussing all this, one is reminded of Freud's prophetic statement that, given our drive disposition and our environment, "love for fellow man must be considered just as indispensable for the survival of mankind as is technology" (Freud, 1948, as quoted by Cohen, 1966).

DESTRUCTIVENESS IN THE SERVICE OF DEVELOPMENT

The establishment of libidinal supremacy, however, does not hold much promise of being a tenable achievement without some clarification of the goals of destructiveness which do not interfere with adaptation. In this connection it should be pointed out that the process of development, in itself, furnishes a vast area of targets for the innate destructiveness of man. Every phase of development which chronological experience has left behind presents a risk of remaining cathected to such a degree that it interferes with age-appropriate thinking, feeling, and acting. The child leaves permanent "footprints" for the adult. Health development can provide targets for aggression. He who can direct his aggression into a vigorous destruction of his arrest in childhood experiences has probably a better chance for mental health than he who must direct it against the family member, a neighbor, or a person whom he does not want to have for his neighbor.

Another object for destructiveness is man's fantasies of perfection— in self and in others. One of the most pernicious aspects of perfection fantasy is the idea that development is an experience of increments. When we call somebody infantile, we really accuse him not only of arrest; we accuse him of wanting to be adult and child alike. The accusation could well be extended against the person who in the later decades of life fights the decline in physical power and the mental capacities of retention and coordination, who fights the loss of physical attractiveness and the loss of interpersonal powers. In a period in which the advances of medicine produce longer and longer life-spans, the ability to live with the experience of loss as a continuous theme of the melody of life seems to be an essential mental health goal.

In this light it would seem to be desirable to reorient child-rearing and child care from a time perspective which reaches its end with the attainment of young adulthood, to preparation for adequacy in coping with the total life-span. This reorientation has been started by Erikson (1950) in the conceptualization of the developmental goals of generativity and integrity. It deserves further elaboration and incorporation into the goals of child-rearing and child care. To foster personal success experiences is not only the goal of psychiatric therapies (Masserman, 1962), but also a mental health principle which should guide preventive and maintenance efforts by the child-rearing profession. Since many of our children will attain an age in which the experiences of retirement and of chronic disease are the main theme of living, personal success experiences will have to be formulated in the dimensions of maintenance and conservation as well as in terms of growth and acquisition. As the adult has to overcome his romance with his own childhood, so has an aging person to overcome his romance with adulthood. Problem solving is, therefore, a process which lasts as long as life and can never be approached with the idea of one-time efforts leading to permanent solutions. Again, a psychiatric concept must be extended to child-rearing. Gerald Caplan (1964) has formulated the essence of treatment goals as the attainment of new ways of problem solving. In the perspective of adaptation to the problem of development over the total life-span, the readiness to look for new ways of problem solving becomes a mental health principle also of child-rearing. This becomes particularly important in our time of rapid technological and social change, in which no way of problem solving remains appropriate for any length of time, in which education and reorientation become permanent propositions, and in which the learning dilemma becomes a greater threat to competence, adequacy feelings, and a positive self-image than ever before. It becomes a mental health principle to use "self" not as something to be produced and then put to use without further effort but as something to be repetitively adapted and reformulated to physical and social change (Perlman, 1957).

MASCULINITY AND FEMININITY

Another area of adaptation is represented by the changing roles of men and women in our society. The concept of penis envy has blurred our conception of the adaptive problems faced by women and men alike which have come about through the entrance of women into social roles formerly reserved for men. The unease of women over their increasing difficulty in attaining or retaining their "femininity" has entered the national awareness. The accusation of the maternal performance of domineering women by Strecker (1948) and his followers has set off a line of psychiatric condemnations of women as "Moms" (Erikson, 1950) which has now become almost part of public opinion and of the self-image of women, at least in our middle-class population. Completely overlooked is the fact that the "masculine" behavior of many women is required by the functions which they have been forced to assume in modern society. Their earning power is needed for the maintenance of the standard of living in many families. Their decision making and authoritative stance at home are enforced by the absence of the father from the family during working hours. Our educational system and political values extol and demand the equality of men and women. Our tradition of sexual morality puts the responsibility for enforcement on the female partner in every premarital encounter between men and women. This puts every girl on a date into a maternal stance vis-à-vis her escort. The dominance in women is further stimulated by the dependency into which modern organizational life forces their husbands in the matter of daily experience. Depleted by the demands on his adulthood during working hours, the husband returns to the home in a mood of regression with a pronounced need for nurture which his wife is supposed to meet. That under such conditions women can be accused, and can accuse themselves, of a lack of femininity seems to be a misunderstanding of necessary adaptations which requires of the mental health-serving professions remedial help rather than indictment by reference to antiquated models of sex-appropriate behavior. It would seem to be imperative that the mental health-serving professions set for women the mental health goal of self-acceptance with respect to the elements of masculinity which modern conditions demand (Cohen, 1966).

GROUP IDENTITY AND ITS COST

In recent days the public school system has been challenged over and over again to provide more instruction in Negro history. In this context the mental health aspects of ethnic identity must be explored. Perhaps the most outstanding example of a fight for ethnic identity against the odds of history is presented by Judaism. Over 2,000 years of dispersion, many Jewish people have resisted the attempt to submerge themselves in the ocean of Gentile populations, to accept their religion, their ways of life, and to attain the comforts of security at the price of losing their identity. It does seem likely that many Negroes are about to make the same historical choice. Interestingly enough, they do that at the time at which the white majority is showing signs of accepting integration as a goal of societal development.

No mental health movement can present a value system which would oppose identity formation and identity maintenance. What it must do, however, is enable people to know, and pay the price of, identity formation. Every identity formation in a way represents segregation and, as such, the loss of a wide range of potential partners for interpersonal exchanges, for capitalizing on man's nature as an open system, and for the extension of his libidinal propensities. Identity, although affirmative to self in one way or another, must say no to alternatives. Where this becomes group policy, the price is heavy in terms of the reactions on the part of those groups which are rejected by this identity formation. In simple terms, it is impossible to have identity without having enemies, to have group identity without being a minority, to be a minority without being potential targets for the hostility of the majority. To decide for the identity of Black Power at the historic moment at which the "white" majority is adapting itself to integration is a momentous decision which should not be made without awareness of the probable consequences. In this sense, Negro children may have to learn more from the history of the Jews than from their own. What mental health principles would have to show as impossible in this context is the improbability of having identity and integration together.

ATTAINMENT OF INTERPERSONAL COMPETENCE

Since human beings are open systems, the ability of relating to others in terms of strengthening exchanges is a condition of growth, development, maintenance, and delaying deterioration. In this process the individual must make a number of significant shifts which depend for their success on his ability to cope with the experience of rejection, active as well as passive. We know from psychoanalytic discoveries how difficult and threatening it is to reject as well as to be rejected. Still, in the process of growing up, an individual must learn to proceed from dyadic relationships to triadic relationships, from living with the mother to living with the mother and father, from living with one's parents to living with one's siblings, from living with one's siblings to living with one's schoolmates, with colleagues, with marriage partners, with one's own children, etc. We must shift from the small organization of the family to the large organization of the school, from the student-serving organization of the school to the production-serving organization of employment, from small organizations in which one is important to large-scale organizations in which one is employed and declared to be unimportant in the end through retirement.

It is the basic experience of human encounter beyond the dyadic relationship that one must make choices and becomes a dependent variable of the choices made by others. In every small group the leader must decide at whom to look and whom to engage in interaction, to whom to shift his attention; in other words, whom to single out, whom to reject, and in each case, for how long. Similarly, the followers must learn to make decisions about whether to follow the leader or to oppose him, to strive for the attainment of leadership positions themselves, to accept being a follower; and every such decision implies that somebody is being rejected and will react to rejection. It is a mental health demand of the first order, therefore, to learn to distinguish between rejection and destruction, to become aware of one's own rejecting and to be able to find the strength to cope with the phenomena actively and passively. A child would have to learn that, within every instance of being rejected, there exists a potential freedom to be chosen by another, and on the other hand, every act of rejecting potentially liberates him from immobilization in human interaction.

Interpersonal competence means, then, not only the ability to give and to receive constructively from another, but also the ability to refuse interaction and to withstand the refusal by the use of alternatives. Implied in these developmental tasks is the ability of coping by seeing alternatives, of using them in reality and not becoming victim of them in fantasy. To keep one's options open increases one's power of meeting rejection, of combating the feeling of being destroyed when an open system closes itself in interaction with you, and it ultimately protects the individual in meeting the difficulties of existence in large-scale organizations, be it in education or employment.

To be prepared against the feeling of vulnerability by rejection is becoming the most important personality equipment in our time. Our thinking on mental health has been captivated by life experiences which relate to personality development from infancy to adolescence. Within this framework of chronological time, emphasis has been put on experiences within the sphere of family life and on encounters with the peer group in school and gangs.

I should like to propose that this framework of theoretical orientation needs an extension relative to the impact of bureaucratic arrangements upon development of the self-concept and the mental coping tasks which functioning in a corporate society requires. From the moment the child enters school, he encounters the experience of being relatively insignificant in relation to large numbers of peers and of being exposed to forces which are sometimes only dimly perceived. Of necessity, there will be many experiences of rejection because the large numbers of pupils make it impossible for the teacher to respond to every child at the moment at which he needs it. This experience is repeated in employment during adult life. Most Americans are wage earners or salaried in a large-scale organization, be it in government, industry, hospital care, or education. Again the individual experiences rejection and failure of response as a repetitive occurrence during working hours. Again he is exposed to the impact of decisions which he cannot foresee, which are made by people of whose existence he may not even be aware, and, in general, to a feeling of being dependent on forces which are overwhelming and practically impervious to the impact of his own actions. Figuratively speaking, most of us in our working life have about the power of a passenger in a jet. In school, as well as in employment, we experience that peers are advanced ahead of us, sometimes also that younger people become our supervisors or attain other positions in the hierarchy to which we feel entitled. In dynamic terms we are stimulated into transference of feelings of sibling rivalry and of the resentment of the aging father toward his sons.

Alternatives, however, must be geared to the present and to the future. Only for these two dimensions of time is it possible to make choices; "about the past, as past it is impossible" (Aubert, 1965). To dwell on alternatives not chosen in the past is not only unproductive; it is also misleading. The alternatives that one has not chosen are never exposed to reality testing, whether they be represented by human beings, material things, or mental experiences. They can be adorned in fantasy with all the characteristics of perfection. No falling short of expectation will ever be expressed in relation to them. But, on the other hand, dwelling on them may use up time which would otherwise be available for new adventures in testing available alternatives. It is therefore a principle of mental health to equip personality with alternate opportunities for response in the present and the future and to liberate it from the prison of dwelling on alternatives not used in the past. The job which one could have taken but did not take, the profession which one could have chosen but did not choose, the specialization which one should have developed in one's occupation but did not develop, the friends whom one should have made but did not make, are meaningless for coping with the challenges of life. The job which one can still take, the friendship which one can still seek, the specialization in one's occupation which one can still develop, these are the coping alternatives which can enhance, or at least support, the positive self-image on which all strengthening interaction ultimately depends.

The ability to maintain various options of response in relation to the experience of rejection, or at least incomplete acceptance, in a civilization of large-scale organizations must be supplemented by the ability to cope efficiently with complexity. It is important not to be left stranded with only one way of responding to the challenges of modern life. It is equally important not to be immobilized by the apparent availability of too many alternatives. One of the greatest difficulties of adolescents in modern education is that they are not helped to cope adequately with mass communication and competitive claims of the available funds of knowledge. In the effort to increase standards, to carve out academic careers for themselves, and ultimately to maintain a positive self-image, all college and university teachers are steadily increasing the burden of the undergraduate and graduate students. At the same time a claim is made on the time of the student for nonscholastic activities in the service of "the well-rounded personality." While considerable attention is being given to the alienation of our adolescents from the establishment and explanations are offered in terms of family dynamics which would suggest that adolescents act out the hostility of their parents against authority, it is frequently overlooked that the educational system, functioning with professional self-respect, continuously increases the feeling of inadequacy in the students which it is supposed to serve. An educational system which does not bend its efforts to making the educational task manageable for the students presents a mental health hazard that should not remain outside the concern of the mental health-serving professions or be overshadowed by the traditional concern with the damaging aspects of family dynamics.

Mental health under such conditions would require a positive self-image which cannot be destroyed by failure to reach the pinnacle of the educational or bureaucratic hierarchy, which cannot be damaged by the daily encounter with rejection and nonresponse, and which can find fulfillment in the small-scale organization of the family, either of childhood or of adulthood. In a sense, this requires a reorientation of mental health personnel from looking upon the family as a major source of emotional damage to one of emotional recuperation.

It is by now widely recognized that the family is a social system in which the improvement of one family member may result in the deterioration of another or, at least, cannot be maintained without having the other family members share in the gains of therapy (Burgum, 1942; O. Pollak 1956). However, professional and paraprofessional manpower, no matter how well utilized, will never suffice for mental health care if the family is not enlisted as a therapeutic agent. This would imply a new mental health goal, namely, to help parents and siblings to function as therapeutic agents. This will become doubly necessary under the new trends of home care and community mental health. Obviously, it is not enough to take safeguards against sending patients from mental hospitals to family settings in which their pathology originated and is likely to be stimulated again. The finding of another "nonhospital" setting and the provision of extramural professional help will prove to be insufficient if we cannot help families to become adept both in the prevention of mental disorders and in the assistance to intervention by professional helpers where mental disorders have occurred. The greatest contribution of dynamic psychiatry to modern civilization may well turn out to be the enrichment of the repertoire of family function by the addition of mental health care. Parents in the psychologically altered strata of the population have assumed—at least by intent—responsibility for the prevention of mental health hazards in child-rearing (G. Pollak, 1963, 1964). The whole field of family life education bears witness to this phenomenon of benevolent social change. Mental health goals in this respect, however, should not be confined to parents. They should extend to brothers and sisters, and they should include the development of skills in interpersonal relations which would lend effectiveness to the intent.

THE COMMUNITY

Finally, the family has to serve yet another function in reaction to the complexity of our mass civilization. The incredible advance of the physical and life sciences and the unalterable process of change in scientific opinion put the individual under a permanent onslaught of scientific guidelines which claim his time beyond the range of the feasible, and put him under the almost continuous pressure of anxiety over the outcome of tests, the cancer-conducive impact of his nutrition, the heart disease-conducive quality of his way of life, and, in the political sphere, scare him with the permanent threat of atomic annihilation. With this onslaught of threats the family must assume the function of claiming its independence from the experts, of assigning its own priorities within the range of possible avenues of health care, and must refuse the avalanche of advice about the appropriate conduct of life or child-rearing which, within a period of ten years, is likely to be changed in the manner of normal scientific development. This is not to say that scientific advance does not have guidance to offer the individual. It is to say, however, that the family must provide the coordinating and value-directed selecting function with which alone the individual can continue to live in our time without having to feel the helplessness of a dependent variable (O. Pollak, 1967).

Rehabilitation and Treatment

The Task Force Subcommittee on Rehabilitation and Treatment, recognizing the extensiveness and complexity of these fields, limited its work to identifying the rehabilitative-restorative requirements of mentally ill children as functions to be repaired or restored in different settings, ranging from hospitals and clinics to schools and families. Dr. Carl Fenichel, who chaired the subgroup, contributed his thoughts on the use of educational settings as resources for rehabilitative work, and these are included in his paper. Central to Dr. Fenichel's position is that of those in need of rehabilitative services one should distinguish between (1) those children who are unable to function and develop normally because of neurological, mental, emotional, and/or behavioral disorders and (2) those children who are socially disadvantaged because of poverty and minority-group status and therefore unable to function and develop normally. Fenichel focuses upon the first category, from which he also separates out the child with presenting neurotic symptoms, who can be helped by the services of the child guidance clinic. Fenichel develops the argument for more extensive use of educational settings with special groups to rehabilitate the seriously disturbed child and then proposes a series of programs, namely: screening, consultation, and referral centers; preschool home training; special day school programs; adolescent and young adult rehabilitation centers. These are discussed below as excerpted from Fenichel's paper "Rehabilitation of the Seriously Disturbed Child."

SCREENING, CONSULTATION, AND REFERRAL CENTERS

Rehabilitation through special education cannot begin without a thorough interdisciplinary examination and evaluation of the deviant child. A comprehensive developmental and psychoeducational assessment with recommendations of each child's special treatment and educational needs should be made as early as possible by a team that may include a pediatrician, psychiatrist, neurologist, psychologist, speech and language pathologist, ophthalmologist, audiologist, educational specialist, and/or any other professional disciplines available and considered essential for the proper educational placement of the disturbed child.

Without adequate knowledge of the physical, mental, social, and emotional status of the child, no educator can plan and program for that child's specific needs. Without special planning and programing based on interdisciplinary findings, special education has neither meaning nor purpose and ceases to be *special.*

Every community should establish screening centers located in community mental health centers, hospitals, public health centers, local schools, clinics, voluntary agencies, and/or mobile units where, on the recommendation of a physician, clinic, school official, or public health official, any child suspected of a physical, mental, or emotional disorder will be given a complete physical, neurological, and psychological examination.

These centers could become the focal point for the coordination of all the services involved in the total program. Each center will assume responsibility for following up its own recommendations and referrals and for ongoing, periodic reevaluations to make certain that appropriate and adequate community treatment, training, and educational facilities are made available to meet its recommendations.

Each screening center will establish an ongoing relationship with the client and with the agencies recommended to work with the client to ensure that the changing needs of each disturbed child are adequately and appropriately met through childhood and adulthood.

A PRESCHOOL HOME TRAINING PROGRAM

Following the comprehensive examination and evaluation, a home training program should be immediately provided by appropriate public or voluntary agencies for the special training and education of disturbed children and for the training and guidance and counseling of their parents.

A team of educational and other specialists will work with the child and with the parents to help reduce and alleviate the child's specific disabilities and problems in language, learning, behavior, coordination, and self-management. Group guidance sessions for parents will help them learn educational and training techniques to program for their child's growth and development at home until he is ready for eventual admission into an organized school program.

It is hoped that early identification and intervention through special training and education can reduce and sometimes eliminate the severity of a child's mental and emotional disorders. An early program of special education may help correct much of a child's maladaptive behavior and inappropriate learning patterns before they become too ingrained. Without early preventative measures through educational intervention, what would have been a manageable problem can frequently become unmanageable and create serious behavior, learning, and personality problems. Early training, special education, and rehabilitation of disturbed children can often prevent the development of secondary and more serious handicaps.

In Regular Classes

Despite the growing network of special educational facilities and services for the disturbed child, wherever feasible and desirable such children should be placed in regular public school classes. Many of the techniques of special education can be applied successfully in the regular classroom. However, this will involve individuation of instruction, flexibility of programming, and the acceptance and understanding of the child's educational and behavioral problems and needs. Much will depend on the ability of the school and teacher to provide a meaningful program to meet the disturbed child's specific problems and needs. The presence of handicapped children in a regular classroom will require extra planning and efforts by the teacher, creative and supportive supervision, the services for part of the day of resource or itinerant teachers for individual instruction, as well as the services of other available disciplines where necessary: pediatrics, psychiatry, speech pathology, psychology, and counseling.

In some settings the special or resource teacher sees the disturbed child in her "resource room" and works with him in those areas in which he needs help most. The resource teacher not only acts as counselor to the children she sees, but as consultant to the regular teacher who has the child in her class. She helps the regular teachers understand the child's problems and sees that they have any special instructional guidance, techniques, and material needed.

The itinerant teacher is used when there are too few handicapped children in any one school to justify having a full-time resource teacher. The itinerant teacher serves a number of functions and helps the regular teacher in ways similar to those of the resource teacher, working with individual children and teachers on a consultant and tutorial basis.

In Special Classes

The trend today is toward separate, self-contained classes within regular schools for many of the more disturbed children. The environment of the special class is more normal than that of the completely segregated special school. It is usually closer to the child's home, thus minimizing the transportation problem. It can be partially integrated with regular classrooms in the same building. However, the special class does have partial physical and social isolation. It results in greater cost of special equipment and in the inconvenience of supervising and administering separate classrooms.

Many modfications are being introduced to reduce the disadvantages of the separate class and to utilize the special teacher more effectively. There are the partially integrated classes where children stay with the special educational teacher for part of the day and in regular classes the remainder of the day. A child may participate in regular classes in art, physical education, music, shop, domestic science, and any academic areas in which he can hold his own and benefit therefrom.

Special Schools

For children who, because of the severity of their disturbances, cannot be accommodated in special classes within a regular school, special schools should be established under public school auspices or by voluntary agencies with governmental and public support.

The special school has several advantages over the special class. It is easier to administer a single school than a number of special classes in different schools. It simplifies control and supervision, and facilitates the use of skills of specialized teachers and other personnel, as well as specialized equipment.

Often when a single school district cannot adequately meet the needs of its disturbed children, two or more adjoining school districts can, by formal action of their boards, create a joint district to provide special schools. Together, the joint school districts share expenditures, space, coordinated leadership, and trained personnel.

State departments of education should also encourage and support the establishment by voluntary agencies of specialized day treatment and educational centers to meet the specific needs of the most severely disturbed children who cannot benefit from any of the existing facilities within the public school setting. Such demonstration schools usually provide a more highly individualized and innovative program, a smaller teacher-child ratio, more flexibility and experimentation in curriculum and programing, and a wider use of other clinical, interdisciplinary services.

Home Instruction

Many school systems provide home instruction for children who are unable to leave their homes and attend public school classes. Among the children requiring such services are the physically weak, orthopedically disabled children; children whose physical or emotional health would be endangered by the excitement, infections, or injuries involved in mingling with normal active children; children with frequent and severe uncontrollable seizures.

The "home teachers" in such a program must be able to work and plan independently, teach many subjects and a wide range of grades, as well as work with the specific needs and problems of many different types of handicapped children.

In some communities where school systems operate educational TV stations, or where educational closed-circuit TV is available, television instruction can supplement the work of the home or hospital teacher. Homebound students may also participate in the regular classroom program of instruction via telephone hookups. The homebound child hears the teacher and the children in the classroom and, by turning a switch, can be heard in the classroom.

While for some handicapped children there may be no other alternative to home instruction, it certainly is not to be recommended as a long-term program for most disturbed children. With few exceptions, most disturbed children can benefit more from a group than from an individual setting. For many isolated and withdrawn children a one-to-one relationship would only feed their very pathology and need to cling to a dependency figure that each child wants all to himself.

Many disturbed children's major problems are in the areas of interpersonal relationships and group living. Through properly planned group activities and interactions in a classroom, disturbed children can and do help each other develop the capacity to work and play and live together—something they must achieve if they are to remain and function within the community.

Day Hospitals

Up to now the day hospital program has been used chiefly for mentally ill adults. However, a few communities have organized day programs for severely disturbed children and adolescents.

The day hospital program enables the patient to spend the night with his own family. It is not only less costly than residential facilities, but it keeps the child more related to home and community and reduces the likelihood of his becoming overdependent on institutional living.

A program of special education, occupational therapy, and recreational and vocational training should be an integral part of the day hospital facility for severely disturbed children and adolescents. Arrangements may be made by the hospital to have children transported to appropriate programs in special schools and centers.

THE ADOLESCENT AND YOUNG ADULT REHABILITATION CENTER

Coordinated efforts should be made by every state's educational and rehabilitational agencies to encourage and support facilities organized by public and voluntary agencies to meet the educational, social, recreational, and vocational needs of severely disturbed adolescents and young adults who cannot benefit from existing special educational programs beyond the elementary school level. Such rehabilitational services are also needed to help adolescents and young adults in mental institutions make their way back to community life. Mental health officials recognize that many of the young people in mental hospitals and residential centers could return to their homes if transitional rehabilitation resources were available within their communities.

The programs in such rehabilitational facilities should include special education, organized recreational and socializing experiences, guidance and counseling, sheltered workshops, and prevocational and vocational training for productive work experiences and skills.

Through continued observations, aptitude tests, and exposure to real work tasks, these rehabilitation centers should assess and determine the handicapped person's abilities and potential for various kinds of occupations ranging from professional and skilled vocations to business, domestic, clerical, and unskilled work in various types of settings: competitive, semi-competitive, and sheltered workshops.

These centers should be responsible for training in specific work skills and in the use of equipment essential for selected occupational goals. The rehabilitation program should also include training and guidance in work tolerance, in appropriate work habits, and in social skills needed to get along with others in job situations.

The rehabilitation center should also have an evening program of academic remediation, socializing and recreational experiences, and individual and group guidance for adolescents and young adults who are holding down jobs in the community but who need supportive services to maintain themselves on the job and in the family and community.

The aim of these centers should be to help make as many of these young people as possible into productive wage earners leading meaningful lives and contributing to their own and to society's well-being.

Dr. Dorothy Miller focused on the identified mentally ill children, especially the institutionalized population, normally under treatment in the state hospitals. Finding the hospitalization experience inadequate and especially dismal for rehabilitation outcome after a five-year follow-up of releases from California child populations in hospitals, she suggests a set of recommendations and supporting argument as follow in this excerpt from her "Rehabilitation of Mentally Ill Children: A Position Paper."

In this paper I have suggested that if the children in our state and local mental hospitals and correctional facilities are ever to rejoin society and to attain any measure of life outside of a custodial situation, great effort must be directed to their rehabilitation. Such children desperately require our best professional attention, concern and study; they comprise a large segment of all of the most seriously mentally ill children in the United States, and yet, at present, they are receiving the least amount of professional care and concern, and have available to them the poorest and fewest of the resources necessary for their adequate care, treatment and rehabilitation. I have suggested that most traditional techniques of child psychiatry have failed to appreciably help such children and that public institutions have become "psychiatric graveyards" or warehouses for many of these children. I have conducted two preliminary studies regarding the type of population served in a state hospital, the rehabilitation services given after their release, and a follow-up study of the outcome of such care. Both studies show how difficult the entire problem is, and how dismally we have failed with our present rehabilitation services.

Without all of these components however, no such reconstruction of the self can occur. A foster home placement is not enough, financial aid is not enough, professional counseling is not enough. Rather all of these—and more—must be made available to each child in a concerted, adequate, and planned manner before we could hope to achieve the solution to such a difficult problem.

But we are discussing children—not yet so totally damaged by fate and experience as to be beyond all hope of repair. We must take up the task.

Therefore, I recommend:

1. A continued and enlarged study of the nature of the problems and the types of rehabilitation programs available to institutionalized children.

2. The widest use of special education techniques in the teaching and training of these poorly socialized children.

3. The support and development—perhaps from the ranks of the poor—of a new career program for parent-surrogates—not mere foster parents, but rather a special reference group, trained to develop self-esteem and social competency in these bereft children. These persons will be a new "sociological professional," trained as a special stable reference group for special types of mentally ill children. Such reference groups must become the child's significant others, his source of identity and security. Such pseudo-professionals must have special status and support, both financial and psychological, in recognition of their special and heroic task. Such persons may be the child's actual parents.

Present Federal, state and local funds and programs designed to serve mentally ill children must be coordinated to develop a new social strategy for the mentally ill child. Stigma, shame, neglect, and ignorance must be attacked on a broad front, and a new, now hopeful, total social system must develop to support the reference group and socialization groups' efforts with individual children.

In my view, this is what is necessary if we are to seriously affect the fates of our mentally ill children.

The area of treatment is highly complicated by the different conceptual frameworks that constitute the therapeutic assumptions of physicians and others engaged in treatment processes. Usually one tends to regard treatment as the appropriate intervention in order to remediate a *diagnosed* condition. Often, however, in the child mental health field, diagnoses are labels which do not necessarily have easily corresponding treatment techniques. Dr. Victor Gioscia and his colleagues have contributed a study of "Dimensions and Innovations in the Therapy of Children" (1968).

A literature survey was made by a multidisciplinary research team organized to examine the interrelation of the "dimensions" of therapy and selected aspects of "innovations" in the therapy of children. Five dimensions, conceptualized as independent, were cross-related to one another. These five dimensions are: (1) functions (behavior, feeling, or diagnosis of the patient); (2) social organizations (those social organizations in which functions occur); (3) modes (the facilities, techniques, and modalities of therapy); (4) staff (those who do therapy); (5) evaluation (criteria and scientific methods used in the evaluation of therapy).

Five innovative aspects of each dimension were used for categorizing "innovations." These were conceptualization, range, time, status, and demand. Thus, the project selectively reviewed the highlights of the published literature since 1962 pertaining to the therapy of children to "code" the information retrieved according to criteria schematically presented in a sixfold table.

The constellation of vocabularies used by clinical writers, schools or theories of therapy, and models of clinical philosophies is described and discussed. Innovative models are highlighted.

The group reviewed a large amount of clinical literature; however, when viewed as a percentage of the entire output of clinical writers who in the last few years concerned themselves with aspects of the profession which converge on the mental health of children, these reviews can be regarded as only a small fraction of the whole. Our prior knowledge and experience provided us with some selective criteria, and our twin focus on dimensions and innovations further limited the scope of our work.

Clinical literature is usually more concerned with the qualities than with the quantities of human experience. For that reason, and for others, recommendations presented in this chapter should be understood to represent reflections and not quantifiable conclusions, clinical generalizations, or trends. They are presented as hypotheses which are regarded as highly plausible. While they may not be universally regarded as the best possible methods of fostering the mental health of children, they represent an effort to seek parsimonious generalizations, to hew to a line of thinking which seems realistically feasible, not merely an assemblage of "good ideas, but unworkable."

The following is a summary of the project and incorporates some of the major recommendations presented to the Task Force.

It was recommended that the NIMH sponsor, in connection with its clearinghouse activities, studies which would develop techniques for evaluating material which should be quickly retrieved and more rapidly disseminated to the relevant professional practitioners.

Official taxonomies are numerous, but even more numerous are the numbers of "schools of thought" and "models of madness." In recent years, the number of models has increased, while at the same time moving beyond exclusively medical and/or psychological models of madness. Especially evident is a trend toward a focus on disturbed patterns of interactions rather than a predominantly intrapsychic model.

The Task Force endorsed the research recommendation that a policy of national eclecticism be adopted to *encourage* research conducted under differing theoretical orientations, and that this policy foster an increase in interdisciplinary work rather than a mandate to do so.

Promising trends toward this goal were noted in the development of behavioral science versus a cross-disciplinary approach and in the "system theory" approach as an aid to adequate conceptualization.

One of the clearest trends in the literature we reviewed was the increasing inclusion in clinical writing of the social aspects of the life situations of children requiring clinical attention. The increasing attention to the possibility of causal roles of ethnicity and social class in the precipitation of mental illness was followed by increasing attention given to urban epidemiological pressures.

We therefore recommend the continued effort of agencies at federal, state, and local levels who have various political, social, and clinical roles to explore further channels of liaison to avoid conflicts between their respective roles. For example, at the federal level, HUD and HEW might well continue ways of mutually devising strategies in which the housing and mental health needs of children are jointly planned and funded.

Furthermore, we strongly urge that cross-cultural studies and comparisons of mental health trends be largely expanded, and that liaison between federal and international clinical organization be similarly formally instituted. This recommendation is particularly crucial for those children who increasingly experience more and more of the worldwide forces which generate or facilitate circumstances of illness. Both long-range and short-range planning for such forms of liaison seem necessary.

Distinguishing techniques as novelties consonant with a basic clinical philosophy from modes as the constellation of all such techniques, we found that new clinical philosophies are in evidence and that new modes of treating children are being devised. Except for drugs and electrical therapies, we have *not* found that traditional modes are being replaced by these innovations, but, in general, are thriving as well-established sets of techniques. *We have found a trend to include in treatment the social relations which are diagnosed as causal and determinative of mental illness in*

*children, along with a related trend to include increasingly large social or-
ganization in diagnostic assessments.* However, as noted in our previous
recommendation, there is a large gap between diagnosis and technique, so
that "social treatment" is a term to which it is hard to attach a specific
meaning.

1. Children should not be forced to experience hospitalization until
every available alternative has been investigated, it being our conviction
that the analysis of state hospitals, for example, reveals them to be mas-
sively alienating institutions in need of drastic social reorganization. *Children's needs and adult needs should not be in the same service. Children's
services should be separate and should not be regarded as a therapeutic
agent for the adult.*

2. The wide gamut of therapeutic intervention would best be approached from studies stressing indications and contraindications.

3. Crisis therapy teams, related to such issues as suicide, drug-induced
psychosis, death of a parent, etc., should be established under the aegis
of the community mental health facilities now in process of construction.

4. Since we are not education specialists, but are clinical specialists,
we strongly urge that steps be taken by the Office of Education to re-
examine the entire philosophy of education in the United States, with a
view toward rectifying what we regard as a major deficit, i.e., that, by and
large, most institutions of education ignore the matter of "emotional learning" by focusing almost exclusively on cognitive learning, with little or no
thought given to attempt to synchronize stages of emotional and cognitive
mastery. In view of the increasingly heavy burdens of socialization being
placed on the school by reason of changes in family responsibility, we see
attention to this matter at the highest levels of government to be the first
order of priority. Since even a massive reorganization of the schools would
take almost a generation, we recommend, as a short-range strategy, that
every encouragement be offered to clinicians to participate in the gradual
introduction into schools of the professional knowledge which is their professional competence.

The traditional triumvirate of clinical professionals, i.e., psychiatrists,
psychologists, and social workers, seems now to be experiencing, in addition to changes within its own ranks, changes in the number and kinds of
professionals and "paraprofessionals" who are joining it in the tasks of
treating the nation's children. For this reason (and for others) the trend
we observe is that clinical and paraclinical roles are increasing by being
redefined, partly reflective of and partly causing a redefinition of the nature
of therapy. As new responsibilities emerge, new staff roles are called for,
which, in turn, alter the responsibilities clinicians and their newfound
partners share. The trend toward the inclusion of social relations in therapy brings with it a set of new tasks, which do not always harmonize with

the traditional ones. The best strategy is not always increasing specialization, since cooperation, coordination, consultation, and integration are not thereby facilitated.

We therefore recommend:

1. That primary priorities be allotted after a census of mental health needs has been taken, after which allocation of functional responsibilities may be made in proportion to manpower availabilities, and that remuneration for service be given second priority, it being our view that this cart is far too often found in front of the horse.

2. That deficits in manpower discovered in the above procedure should be translated into training mandates, deliberately encouraging enrollment in understaffed professions by offering subsidized educational grants and/or draft deferment, as third order of priorities.

3. That education and training of paraprofessionals *not* be undertaken on an *ad hoc* "crash" basis, but instead be translated into an appropriate number of paraprofessional civil service ranks for which standardized educational procedures ought to be devised (e.g., assistant nurse, assistant doctor, assistant psychologist, assistant teacher, assistant social worker, etc.).

4. That work study programs for graduate students be devised using the NIMH fellowship programs as a model for the development of assistant professionals.

5. That a design and staffing breakthrough be deliberately sought to replace as quickly as possible the present asylums called mental hospitals, which should be charged with the responsibility to approximate the therapeutic situations in which therapy is known to work best, i.e., small patient-to-staff ratios.

6. That deliberate efforts be made to reconstitute the specialists of community organization workers in social work and counseling psychologists in psychology, these having apparently suffered a dilution over the years until their present condition was reached.

7. We anticipate that conflicts will arise between clinical and civic roles among so-called indigenous workers. Thoughts should be given to modes of mediation by clinicians and such workers in equal representation, on the premise that freedom in one role is contagious for the other.

EVALUATION

We find the official philosophy of scientific studies, i.e., one or another variant of positivism, to be relatively inapplicable to most clinical situations, it being nearly impossible to meaningfully measure changes in well-being or well-feeling. If patients had to prove, with the rigor required of most evaluation studies, that they required help, almost no one would be treated, since almost no one has demonstrated that his patients got better because, and only because, of his treatment strategies. In addition, "comparable" human beings tend to exhibit annoying idiosyncrasies which confuse careful research strategies. Clinical samples derived from investigators using comparable techniques tend to be too small for high-powered statistics. We hold strongly the conviction that the naturalistic methods of therapy ought to be required to meet naturalistic criteria of evaluation. The Task Force recommendation of concern for "appropriate rigor" to an area much in need of less rigor and more flexible evaluation was endorsed.

The study group supports the Task Force research recommendations:

1. That the concept of appropriate rigor be adopted as the philosophy of clinical research programs, making it possible to assemble data pools (similar to the one in Maryland) which compare "comparably" diagnosed patients treated in "comparable" ways.

2. That, as in systems engineering, wherein the abbreviation "R and D" (research and development) describes two-faceted programs, the abbreviation "D and E" be officially promulgated to announce the adoption of the policy that demonstration *and evaluation* are similarly inseparable aspects of projects which seek to test a new clinical stratagem.

3. That periodic census be taken by investigators trained in assembling clinical data which is comparable in as many significant variables as possible not only as a way of "measuring" the effectiveness of tax-supported programs, but also as a way of assessing when and where outmoded techniques might require continuing education, since techniques once taught but presently outmoded have a way of enduring nonetheless.

Three studies were undertaken for the Task Force which focused on the mental health needs of children of three minority-status groups. These are: "Position Paper on the Mental Health Needs of the Negro Child," by James Comer, M.D.; "An Overview of Mental Health Problems of American Indian Children," by Dorothy Miller, D.S.W., and Joan Ablon; "Mental Health Needs of Spanish-Speaking Children in the New York City Area," by Joseph P. Fitzpatrick, S.J., Ph.D., and Robert E. Gould, M.D.

These represent somewhat different approaches, but they are appropriate for the different problems that are investigated. The American Indian child growing up in as colonial a situation as any found under nineteenth-century imperialism manifests unique problems of captive people kept apart and subjected to the demands and standards of their subjugation. This is reinforced by historical development of a military and political nature and maintained by a pseudo-apartheid practice on the part of present-day authorities.

The Negro child, coming from an equally disastrous historical tradition of slavery, followed by more than a century of second-class citizenship, and beset at present by the vicissitudes of urban ghetto life and declines in the quality of urban life style, requires a different set of interventions if the Negro child is to gain competence or mastery of his environment as well as a sense of self-esteem.

The Spanish-speaking minority, namely, the Puerto Rican émigrés to New York City in recent decades, represent another group whose life style in their culture of origin is inconsistent with the harsher demands of an industrialized urban culture. The linguistic barrier can create additional problems of adjustment and create further risks for young children growing up in the cross fire of these divergent cultural expectations.

The recommendations and supporting discussion of these studies are excerpted and follow below:

AN OVERVIEW OF THE MENTAL HEALTH PROBLEMS OF INDIAN CHILDREN

1. *There should be more systematic research focused on the mental health problems of Indian children to provide adequate data for policy and program development.*

We would recommend that basic studies be undertaken whose goal is to present a holistic picture of the development of the Indian child today: child-rearing practices, preschool cultural and social experiences, school experiences, and an interpretation and evaluation of the totality of these experiences in a well-coordinated and focused perspective.

In addition to basic research, there is a great need for operational or action research aimed at the assessment of the various educational, social, and health projects developed for American Indian children.

2. *The explicit and implicit goals of Indian education must be examined, defined, and appraised.*

It is singularly important that the Indian people themselves make the real decisions as to what should be the educational goals for their children. All too frequently in Indian history have well-meaning white specialists and professionals set the ends and limited the means of social and economic planning for Indians. The Indian communities must be brought into the school experience at all levels; the parents must be brought into full participation in planning curriculum and in administrative affairs, or else it will always be "the white man's school."

Cultural conflict in education is but one significant area of the greater general question of the nature of Indian identity in today's world, and of acculturation versus assimilation. If we would hope to cultivate good mental health in all of its dimensions among Indian people, they must be allowed to make their own free choice of alternative modes of cultural accommodation. They must be given their rights of ultimate decision making in every area of their life.

3. *We recommend that alternative modes of participation in American society be investigated as to their appropriateness for Indians.*

If it is possible to find areas of participation so that the Indian may become a part of American society, we may thus find that his value patterns and personality structure may begin to be altered. But it is in the finding of these alternative modes that we address ourselves here. We must investigate *white* society to answer this question: Where may the Indian *now* fit so that he may begin his rewarding participation in American life?

There are undoubtedly occupations in this country which could be suited to Indians. Most professionals, for example, do not adhere to rigid time requirements that demand punching time clocks, nor do taxi drivers or craftsmen. We cannot answer the question we raise without careful research into the opportunities offered by white society. But we urgently recommend that such research begin immediately.

4. *We recommend that the school be used as a development agency.*

The BIA has committed 60 percent of its budget and as much or more of its effort to education because it is thought that education is the one institution which can contribute most to the development of Indians. Certainly, the educational institution is the most important agency to the Indian child. And it is our contention that the school can be reformulated into an instrument for social change which may reach the overall goals established above.

What is needed is an entirely new approach to the educational system. It is not enough to take the schools now attended by Indian children and "dress them up" with special classes here, new textbooks there, a psychiatrist or social worker added to the staff, or a few faculty seminars once in a while. Rather, the entire structure of the school must change if it is to be a development agency.

The new school must be built, not for Indians, but by Indians. It must reflect the culture of the tribe which it serves; it must teach the skills which that particular tribe needs and desires. If the goals and alternative modes of economic participation, which have been outlined above, have been adequately defined and determined, then these goals become the goals of the school. As the only existing case in point, Rough Rock Demonstration School could be used as a model to be assessed.

Some specific principles which should guide the reorganization of the Indian school can be borrowed from Goodenough (1963) who compiled a list of procedures which have proved successful in developing nations. Among his recommendations he urges that development agencies, in this case the schools, must:

a. have a thorough knowledge of the main values and principal features of the client community's culture;

b. take the whole community into account;

c. have goals which the client community itself desires;

d. take the client community as an active partner in the development process;

e. start with what the community has in the way of material, organizational, and leadership sources;

f. *not* allow its agents, who represent Western culture, to become the indispensable men in the development process, thus creating a dependent community.

5. *A cooperative body of interested agencies and tribal leaders could be organized on the national and local levels to facilitate communication and promote more efficient services for Indians.*

The body could coordinate community activities in order to obtain the greatest amount of service from the available energy and resources by promoting cooperation and high service standards and by reducing duplication of services. The body could serve as a clearinghouse of materials on American Indian affairs and sponsor orientation and training programs for agency personnel concerning the particular problems of Indian people relocating to urban areas. The body could bring to the general public knowledge about the Indian population of the area, thus stimulating communication and relationships between Indians and non-Indians.

This body could form the basis of a political "pressure group" which would represent to governmental bodies and agencies the needs and wishes of American Indians. In addition, such a cooperative body could foster a public image of the American Indian for both whites and Indians. Indian children badly need models of Indian success and pride to resolve their identity problem.

6. *New forms of community organization need to be explored.*

Recent OEO programs have served as catalysts for organizational structures on reservations and in urban areas which have later served purposes other than those for which they were organized. The school could be used as a rallying point for organization of the community, as it has been used in time of crisis at Rough Rock Demonstration School.

One important component of community development should be the training and use of indigenous personnel in service capacities. There are many ways in which indigenous persons can be used in education and health programs. Aides can be employed productively in classes, and especially in boarding schools and dormitories, to provide the "surrogate parents" and models that psychiatrists have stated are lacking in these institutions. Aides can be used by public health nurses and doctors as translators, facilitators, and technicians.

Since education and health are two permanent service areas, the training will enable these persons to have jobs for as long as they care or are able to work. Thus, this constitutes career training that adds permanent vocational and economic strengths to the community.

Community organizational techniques can be developed to aid families in mobilizing their resources to provide stability for their children. One of the major difficulties in Indian life at present is the lack of centrality in policy decision affecting their own social and economic well-being. Every effort must be made to organize Indian communities for Indian dignity and progress.

7. *Demonstration mental health facilities should be established for Indian children.*

POSITION PAPER ON MENTAL HEALTH NEEDS OF NEGRO CHILDREN

An opportunity package for Negro children is indicated. We cannot continue to approach a problem of such great magnitude and such deep and complicated historical roots with an uncoordinated, piecemeal, Band-Aid approach. We must acknowledge that the problem is more than poverty —indeed it is the result of long-standing racism, abuse, and denial. A program must be developed which enables Negroes to gain representation within the political and economic structure commensurate with their numbers. The community must have the opportunity to protect itself against political and economic exploitation and abuse. The long-standing dependency and sense of helplessness must be remedied through a program which permits group development and an equitable amount of power and control.

The Opportunity Package

1. Guaranteed employment or annual income plan with a minimal wage level which will enable a decent standard of living.

2. Impacted area funding for health, education, and welfare programs at the local level.

3. Negro higher education fund for facilities, salaries, and scholarships.

4. Public school, business, government, and industry cooperative planning, manpower development, and employment programs.

5. Special education and training programs.
   a. Compensatory and "bridge" programs.
   b. Parent participation and training.
   c. Different and deviant child programs.
   d. Multicultural appreciation programs for students and practitioners in the helping and service professions.

6. Black community development programs.

    a. Federal funding for technical assistance selected by the people developing their own communities.

    b. Creation of a high-level government unit for coordinated research, planning, monitoring, and administration of programs—HEW, HUD, Labor, OEO, Agriculture, Commerce—in the area of black community development.

    c. Elements of community development program.

       i. Cooperative housing programs.

      ii. Cooperative business programs.

     iii. Credit union and consumer protection programs.

     iv. Community-sponsored law enforcement and legal aid programs.

      v. Community-sponsored parent-child centers with health, education, cultural, and recreational planning programs.

     vi. Community-sponsored employment, training, and service referral centers.

7. Information and communications.

    a. Federal Communications Commission development of voluntary guidelines for balanced and fair presentation of news, multiethnic performers, and program content.

    b. Federal Communications Commission regulations for fair broadcasting of racial news in all sections of the country.

Discussion

Through little fault of their own, it is clear that a growing segment of the population is unable to earn the amount of money necessary to provide adequate, indeed even minimal, standards of living for their families. Thus, some form of guaranteed annual income appears to be indicated. In addition, many cities are plagued by decreasing industry necessary to finance social services and a disproportionate number of people in need of special services. Here some forms of impacted area spending by state and federal government are indicated. There is already a precedent for this approach in that many areas with a large number of military or government personnel, even when those areas are quite wealthy or the personnel are permanent, receive federal impacted-area funds for education.

The desire of the Negro community to gain power and representation commensurate with its numbers cannot be ignored—indeed, must be facilitated. Otherwise Negroes are forced to go outside established procedures to bring about needed socioeconomic changes. To achieve this end, better trained and educated leaders are needed at every level.

Massive amounts of money must go into higher education for Negro professionals. The vast majority have received their training at Negro institutions and will continue to do so for some time to come. Higher education for Negro colleges and universities is greatly underfinanced. Since these graduates will train the vast majority of future Negro students at the primary, secondary, and college level, it is urgent and of highest priority to adequately finance Negro colleges and universities. While consolidation of existing schools, improvement of faculties, and other changes are indicated, adequate financing is the first and foremost need. White institutions of moderate means are demolishing facilities which are in better condition than major structures at some of the best-financed Negro institutions.

A great number of capable people live in abject poverty in the rural South and urban North. Because of family conditions few can afford higher education. Special scholarships in which the students are able to work with other Negro poor during vacation or part-time during the school year are indicated.

Traditionally, noncollege education has received inadequate attention, although most people do not go to college. This area must receive great attention. There is a need for the major business and industrial groups to develop coordinated and cooperative programs with local schools to develop more realistic programs to prepare students for employment. This would give students an opportunity to know what is available and the kind of preparation, skills, and performance expected of them in the world of work. It ought to be possible for highly motivated high school dropouts to compensate for deficiencies at a rate commensurate with their motivation and ability.

Leadership persons emerging from "grass root" programs should have the opportunity to develop skills they need. People "trapped" in technician or dead-end jobs—orderly, janitor, messenger, etc.—should have the opportunity to move through semiprofessional and professional levels as they develop and as they desire. Pay-while-training programs must be developed.

These recommendations call for a flexibility in the public school which does not now exist. They also require a level of financial support not now available. Public schools serving the Negro community are most adversely affected in these connections. The reduction of class size to that equal to suburban schools is indicated. In addition, personnel with special skills— reading, growth and development, and medical—should be available to the most needful students who sometimes interfere with education of others. Such personnel are now more available to middle-income children than the black poor.

The public school in low-income Negro communities, in particular, should be modified in a way to include meaningful parent participation. As a result of limited educational opportunities, many Negro parents who are quite adequate and well motivated are not as well prepared to give their children the input of information as parents who developed during a less demanding age. Also in the middle-class school, low-income parent inter- action is often a source of misunderstanding and conflict. A self-regulating school organization with school personnel, parents, and students sharing power and responsibility would be helpful.

The problem of teacher training will be discussed elsewhere. It is important here to stress the importance of black and white professionals, educational and mental health, to have some appreciation of the facts and implication of the American racial conflict. Middle-class Negro and white teachers need an opportunity to explore their feelings and attitudes toward low-income Negro children, families, and community problems while still in training. Defensive structure—including "It's cultural," "They don't care," "We can't do anything without more money"—must be understood.

Prior to the past few years only a few child mental health treatment centers worked with low-income or Negro children. Many therapists have little knowledge of the supportive networks in low-income communities. The impact of the social system and healthy adjustments under the circumstances can be viewed as pathology when it is not the case. A greater appreciation of Negro community problems, as well as personal prejudices, should increase the number of Negroes who come earlier and remain in treatment.

Given the much-needed black consciousness development, it is even more important now that the number of Negro early child development specialists, teachers, and mental health personnel be rapidly increased. Likewise, it seems important that a more cohesive Negro community organization be developed to plan, organize, and participate with school and other community groups in the efforts outlined above. Without this there will be limited entree to the most needful segment of the population, and group development will not be enhanced.

On the other hand, local, state, and national government and private business and industrial efforts must be coordinated to approach the particular problems of the Negro community—particularly the hard-core poor. There should be coordinated planning and programming among HEW, Labor, Agriculture, HUD, and other agencies, to meet the current emergency and the long-range goals of adequately preparing and employing the Negro community in a way which leaves sufficient power and leverage in the community. A similar nongovernment black community organization working with government should do the same.

In this discussion most of the emphasis has been placed on Negro community development. This is not an argument against integration of schools, unions, housing, etc. Indeed, wherever racial integration is reasonable or feasible, it should take place. But integration is rapidly becoming an academic argument as major cities turn predominantly black. Moreover, it is through the development of a Negro community that many Negro youngsters will receive structure, guidance, and direction necessary to achieve the personal development needed to cope and obtain a sense of adequacy in the larger society.

Finally, legislation necessary to implement these recommendations will probably not materialize with the present level of societal knowledge and understanding of these problems. In sections of the country, owners or financial supporters of mass media—newspapers, radio, and television— force their personal prejudices on their public with no attempt at making a balanced presentation. Great mobility and internal migration demand that Americans have a common frame of reference with regard to basic, well-documented facts about our society. Without this, it is not reasonable to expect people to respond intelligently to the passing issues of the day. It is important, then, that government agencies protect the rights of the public to be well informed, through voluntary guidelines, regulation of commercial broadcasting, or government-financed radio and television.

MENTAL HEALTH NEEDS OF SPANISH-SPEEKING CHILDREN IN THE
NEW YORK CITY AREA

1. There is immediate need for a directory of Spanish-speaking professional personnel and Spanish-speaking services in the New York area.
2. Provision must be made without delay for adequate Spanish-speaking assistants in situations in which a Spanish-speaking professional staff is not available. Policy and program must be inaugurated to provide this systematically. The haphazard use of clerical or maintenance personnel, the casual use of a child or friend who accompanies the patient, and reliance on other Spanish-speaking patients are not sufficient. Capable and trained non-professionals must be available at all times and on a salaried basis. Provision for this should be made in the budgets of the hospitals where the need is constant.
3. In order to clarify the need, patient load in city facilities should be accurately identified. The effort to avoid disclosure of information according to racial or ethnic identification, lest this be damaging to racial or ethnic groups in the city, is admirable and praiseworthy. Consideration should be given to the publication of statistical data after consultation with representatives of the groups involved. The Spanish-speaking community has a right to be adequately informed of the situation so that they may more accurately evaluate it and be in a position to demand more adequate service.
4. The need to identify promising Spanish-speaking students and to provide professional training for them is urgent. Demographic data indicate that the influx of Spanish-speaking people to the New York area will not only continue, it will increase. Therefore, the preparation of professional personnel to care for them is essential. This must take the form of organized programs in cooperation with professional and medical schools to seek out and train Spanish-speaking personnel.
5. Reorganization of services to bring them into more effective relation-

ship to the Spanish-speaking community is essential. Experimental programs should be carefully evaluated, and where found effective, the program should be applied more widely to areas where Spanish-speaking patients are numerous.

6. The problem of the redefinition of mental illness should be carefully pursued, and innovations in diagnosis and treatment should be evaluated. Where found effective, programs should be made available throughout the area.

7. The fundamental educational problem of reading must be pursued relentlessly in the schools. The relationship between reading retardation, frustration, and behavior disorders in children is universally acknowledged. Mental health services are a poor substitute for the basic remedy of more relevant educational methods.

8. In the movement toward community health services, involvement of the community itself is essential to success. In view of the present social and political climate, there seems to be no convincing reason why representatives of the minority groups should not be named to the Community Mental Health Board of the City of New York.

The Task Force decided to focus on what was considered as the most pressing group of children, those who are diagnosed and known as mentally ill. This included an examination of the literature about rehabilitation, raising the question as to what the needs are and how they are met. For example, they stressed the children's wards in the state mental hospitals and what they were doing as prototypical.

Of the one million or so institutionalized children, about half of these probably can be profitably returned to the open society. This group requires a new mode of care and is essentially a forgotten group in most discussions. The primary reason seems to be the lack of gratification for the professionals who work with these children, as long as they are kept in traditional child care institutions. We recommend:

1. Children who could be rehabilitated in the community should not be dumped into undermanned and poorly financed institutions. It is recommended that these children be given improved foster care and that new foster care models be developed in the community. People should be trained for new careers in specialized foster care, and these programs should be implemented as soon as they can be manned and financed.

2. More attention should be paid to the mentally ill child who can be brought into the community, including the use of planned placement in halfway houses as well as the organization of new kinds of caretaking arrangements.

3. For those youngsters who have families, it is recommended that there be an increased use of the family as a source of caretaking, and that par-

ticular stress be placed on the training of mothers to teach them better ways of caring for children and to help them improve their capabilities and skills.

4. It is recommended that those children still remaining in hospitals be given an improved situation so that separate child and adolescent wards become the rule rather than the exception.

5. Constancy of care should be rewarded, and it should be built into the organizational system that cares for such children.

6. We need research for such areas as the gratification of professionals, that is, how to develop realistic definitions and expectations of outcome, and how to train the kind of people with the maturity to accept modest gains.

7. The Task Force recommends the development of a national screening and consultation service to determine how many youngsters are seriously disturbed and how many more are at risk. A network of referral services should be established as a resource to handle these identified children's problems. Its effectiveness should be continually evaluated and linked to an information and monitoring system so that its programs can be adapted to meet the changing needs of child populations.

8. The utilization of a diversity of professional approaches should be explored in order to increase the range of rehabilitative resources available to seriously disturbed children. It is necessary to examine how these resources can be improved and extended.

9. Different models should be developed to deliver rehabilitative services. These would include special schools for the damaged youngster and the use of personnel in existing schools for special services for those youngsters who can function to some extent in regular classroom settings. It should also include therapeutic groups outside the school system, focused upon some specific problem amenable to treatment in a variety of ways. These would enlarge the social experiences of the youngster who is not developing in a normal way. In general the Task Force felt that these youngsters should be given a chance to be brought back into the mainstream of existence, insofar as they are limited only by their capabilities and capacities. This can be accomplished by realistic services addressed to their incapacities which try to compensate and bring the child to the limits of his capacity and maximize his abilities.

With respect to psychotherapeutic treatment, our deliberations and explorations have led to the following tentative formulations.

1. People involved with therapy should research the possibility of intervening at a broader level of social organization, rather than be restricted solely to the individual therapeutic intervention. Large-scale intervention research would involve epidemiological, social, and political considerations.

In light of this we recommend that NIMH focus its child health activities in the direction of the collecting of literature around the leading edges of treatment and the quick dissemination of this information, so that the most up-to-date information is readily available for the practitioner and the therapist.

2. If the base in treatment is the social-psycho-therapy of the individual, then we should develop a new set of psychiatric criteria which involves an extension of our traditional taxonomic schemes. The concept of indications and contraindications should be made the central core of this process, and rethinking should include at the central governmental level a formalization of the interdisciplinary dialogue, which is now in process. This could also include a recommendation that NIMH explore the experimental mental health programs by using both HUD and NIMH resources in devising new teams to develop evaluation methods. Mental health experiments should be tried in experimental communities. One experiment which might be tried in conjunction with the promotion of an interdisciplinary dialogue would be the development of a demonstration using the new health teams. This would be one way to work toward common goals across administrative lines.

Prevention

The Prevention Subcommittee chaired by Mr. Alfred Buchmueller viewed the prevention area in its broadest sense. Along with Dr. Morris Green and Miss Jeweldean Jones, this group postulated primary prevention as the major strategy and suggested various areas in which programs should be implemented. Mr. Buchmueller's paper incorporated the work of the prevention subgroup as follows.

Traditionally, according to Gerald Caplan,[1] preventive services in the public health field have been conceptualized as primary or secondary:

> Programs of primary prevention have the goal of reducing the risk of mental disorder in a population by lessening harmful influences or by increasing the capacity of people to master such stresses in healthy ways. Mental disorders are conceived as resulting from unhealthy adjustment to burdens in the physical, psychological, or social spheres. Mental health, and its associated capacity for healthy adjustment to life's problems in ways which are consonant with the values and traditions of the prevailing culture, is thought to be based upon providing a person, throughout his life, with adequate physical, psychological and social opportunities.
>
> The aim of a secondary prevention program is to reduce the prevalence of the mentally ill in a community by shortening the duration of illness. This is accomplished by gaining access to established cases, as early as possible, and cutting short their illness by effective treatment. In order to make a significant contribution to lowering community prevalence it is important to find methods of dealing in this way with large numbers of cases; therefore administrative and organizational problems are of considerable importance. It is essential that screening and identification programs reach out into the community in order to gain access to cases which are not spontaneously recognized as mental illness by sufferers or by their friends and relations.

1. Personal communication.

Eli Bower, in *The Protection and Promotion of Mental Health in Schools* (1964), has stated, "Primary prevention of mental and emotional disorders is any specific biological, social or psychological intervention which promotes or enhances the mental and emotional robustness, or reduces the incidences and prevalence of learning and behavior disorders in the population. In this framework, then, we would aim preventive programs at persons not yet separated from the general population, and hopefully, at interventions which are specific enough to be operationally defined and measured."

Primary prevention of mental and emotional disorders, as perceived here, has as its long-term goal the ensuring of continually adequate physical, psychosocial, and sociocultural supplies, which both avoid harmful stress and increase the basic capacity to withstand future stress. It also has the short-term goal of providing current help to individuals wrestling with life difficulties so that they may find healthy ways of mastering them.

In this framework the goals of *programs* of primary prevention would be as follows:

1. To increase the biological robustness of human beings by strengthening those services that deal with prenatal care, postnatal care, and the developmental problems of early childhood, middle years, and adolescence.

2. To increase the area of effectiveness of primary agencies so that they may encompass a greater variety and greater number of persons in the general population. For example, the extension and accessibility of school mental health services for all children, including the emotionally disturbed, may make it possible that some children will not need secondary or treatment services. Again, if health services for mothers or mothers-to-be were located close to their neighborhood and made accessible to them, evidence shows that they would make more use of such services.

3. To decrease excessive or unhealthful stress, or conversely, to work with institutions to build greater stress immunity and manageability into their programs. Community and social action programs are most noteworthy examples here.

PREVENTIVE PROGRAMS

Preventive programs for children can be structured in a variety of ways depending upon their scope and objectives. Because the span of life encompassed by *childhood* covers such a vast diversity of possibilities for prevention, it may be more practical to segment these according to the following:

1. Preventive programs may be organized by age groups, that is, prenatal, the preschool child, the school child, and the adolescent.

2. Preventive programs may also be organized for special populations

at risk, again by age groups or by special population segments, for example, children of migrant workers.

3. Another approach would be to identify gaps in current preventive programs so that action programs may be designed and implemented to correct inadequacies on a priority basis.

PREVENTIVE CONSIDERATIONS BY AGE PERIODS

The following should be considered only as a summary, since each category needs to be elaborated upon, as was done in the Task Force committee discussions. The same is true for the succeeding sections.

PRENATAL

More than any other one factor, prevention of prematurity would result in a marked decrease in infant mortality and in the neurologic sequelae associated so often with prematurity. A recent study indicated that 70 percent of premature births are related to social, economic, or non-medical causes. The premature rate is two times greater (approximately 16.6 percent vs. 8.5 percent) in out-of-wedlock pregnancies. Infant mortality also increases when the mother's age is under fifteen years.

The infant mortality rate in the United States in 1961–63 was 25.6 per 1,000. Infant deaths among lower socioeconomic groups, however, are significantly higher than the national overall rate. In addition, a disproportionately high number of surviving infants among the poor have permanent neurologic damage, such as cerebral palsy or mental retardation.

Although there has been no direct proof that adequate prenatal care significantly decreases prematurity and infant mortality, there are certainly great variations in the availability of medical care in different sections of the country and in different census tracts, depending upon socioeconomic and racial status. Far too few women in the lower socioeconomic groups, especially unwed mothers, receive adequate prenatal care. Out-of-wedlock pregnancies, as compared to pregnancies for married women, increases the mortality rate for the mother five times (21.3 vs. 5 per 10,000) and double the rate for infants (48 vs. 24 per 1,000 live births). There are many gaps in educational and nutritional services to prenatal women and many deficiencies in the care of expectant mothers with such disorders as diabetes, chronic nephritis, urinary tract infections, and toxemia, as well as psychosocial deficiencies. In some cases, maternal-infant blood group incompatibilities or maternal syphilis is not suspected or diagnosed until the mother comes to the hospital at the time of birth.

Another problem currently under scrutiny is the availability of therapeutic abortions for women for mental health or socioeconomic considerations.

Inadequate medical, psychological, and social services for the unwed mother are another factor which needs serious attention in the prevention of repeated out-of-wedlock pregnancies and the promotion of more healthy personality development and interpersonal relationships of such young persons.

Educational and counseling programs, including the use of continuous group discussion approaches, have given promise of being a valuable service, and need adequate evaluation and assessment.

INFANCY

There is inadequate utilization of the lying-in period for educational and other helping services to new mothers. This would be an excellent time to help identify problems, e.g., whether there are adequate arrangements for the mother's return home, and to discuss family planning. (Again, ongoing group discussions with expectant parents and parents of infants under trained, skilled leadership seem to be a valuable educational service.)

There are also many gaps in the access of families to educational help with their infants. While some mothers can turn to relatives, the physician, the public health nurse, the mass media, or the neighborhood pharmacist, in most metropolitan areas there are very limited or no well-organized arrangements for answering parents' questions or routing them to available services.

Considerably more preventive attention should be centered on the birth of the handicapped child. Families of handicapped children should receive help of a preventive nature during the first few days and weeks, rather than waiting until something surgical or traditionally curative can be done. This is largely an untapped area of concern. Some experimental programs of group counseling with parents of children with handicapping conditions (such as those sponsored by Child Study Association of America) need to be developed on a broader scale and carefully evaluated as to their effectiveness. Psychological support and help for such families may also need to include genetic counseling.

The birth of a premature infant also represents a family crisis. More investigation of the effects of the isolation of the baby from his mother and the effects of prematurity on child care practices and on mother-infant interactions is needed.

Another developmental crisis for the infant or young child occurs with separation from the mother owing, for example, to hospitalization of the mother or of the infant. The effects of maternal psychologic illness—in particular, maternal depression—are relatively unexplored, although such maternal incapacity may have profound effects on the developing young infant and child.

Foster care services are often inadequate from the mental health point of view. Emotional problems frequently ensue because children are placed in inadequate homes and moved frequently.

Although much progress has been made in recent years, there still needs to be further basic and operational research in adoptions. There remain an insufficient number of adoptive homes, especially for babies of minority groups and for handicapped infants.

PRESCHOOL

There would appear to be tremendous opportunities for increased prevention during the preschool period. Although much is being done in the prevention of accidents, the leading cause of death and disability at this time, this problem has never received the major attention that it should.

It is the general experience that children in the preschool period are not seen frequently by physicians for routine well-child care although, as indicated by the experience with Head Start, considerable physical health problems both exist and warrant detection—for example, the identification of early amblyopia, dental caries, and other remedial situations.

Day care for normal children whose mothers are working or who are unable to provide for them adequately during the day needs further exploration. Day-care centers should receive maximal attention as one of the ways in which to prevent environmental deprivation. Day-care center staffs, however, need special training to better equip them to function as a preventive mental health service. There is also a crucial and critical need for day care for retarded and other handicapped children who otherwise would have a limited social experience. Centers for the environmentally deprived child, such as Head Start programs, may be able to give needed cognitive tools.

Hospitalization is another fairly frequent experience of the nation's children. Hospitalization should be utilized only if the same services cannot be provided on an ambulatory basis. If hospitalization is unavoidable, then considerably more attention should be given to the mental health needs of children as children in such settings.

Training of pediatricians, general practitioners, nurses, and social workers, as well as paraprofessionals and nonprofessionals, must be considered carefully. New innovative training programs to enable them to use themselves in new ways of role function need to be developed and implemented.

SCHOOL-AGE CHILD

Greater emphasis must be placed on improvement of educational services for *all* children. Although inadequate for many children with normal intellectual development, educational opportunities are tragically under-

developed for children with specific learning disabilities, intellectual retardation, neurologic impairment, or emotional disturbance. In addition,
educational opportunities for young children, sexual education, speech
therapy, and adequate arrangements for school health must be incorporated
into the school experience. Too often there have been "pilot projects"
developed, and then terminated, with little or no thought of replication.

ADOLESCENCE

One of the greatest problems in the adolescent period is the *prevention*
of delinquency and other problems of maladjustment. This, of course, is a
terribly complex psychosocial, economic, educational, and medical problem.
Specifically related is the problem of school dropouts. Their possible
prevention should receive *great priority*. Vocational programs and guidance
for children who are not equipped for or do not wish to pursue academic
programs represent another gap in preventive services. Recreational facilities are also very much lacking for adolescents and almost nonexistent
for the retarded child. Suicide is an increasing problem in need of prevention. Out-of-wedlock pregnancies is another area of possible preventive
action. Narcotics addiction, the use of other drugs, and the increase in
venereal disease are other disorders demanding urgent attention. Finally,
some attention needs to be given to the adequacy of high schools in preparing children more effectively for college entrance, as well as for noncollege careers.

SPECIAL POPULATIONS AT RISK

In addition to the discussion above which relates to preventive opportunities according to age periods, the problem may be approached through
special populations at risk. *Children who live in poverty* are at a special
disadvantage. Of the estimated 14 million such children in this country,
5 million receive almost no medical care and mental health services, while
the rest receive care which is inadequate and episodic. Although *children
who live in suburbia* are frequently considered to be in an advantageous
position, they also face many preventable problems. Unfortunately, we
know too little about the epidemiology of emotional problems in suburbia.
Many of these children and their mothers appear to be overscheduled, some
are taking drugs, others are involved in crime, many live in a relatively
fatherless society, and some do not have adequate schools or have to attend
classes in shifts.

The *handicapped child* (mental retardation, learning disabilities, brain
damage, epilepsy, cerebral palsy, cardiac disease, asthma, hearing impairment, blindness, prematurity, hemophilia, muscular dystrophy, amputees,
and multiple handicaps) needs a vast variety of comprehensive, integrated,

and continuous services. The need for development, expansion, and improvement of these services should be among the high-priority recommendations of the Commission.

Little attention has been given to the effects on children of *physical and psychological illness in parents*. Further research in this area is imperative. Perhaps increased attention should be given to providing support to families when the father is ill for a long period of time.

Marital discord without divorce is an extremely important and frequent problem throughout the country. Special attention must be paid to increasing adequate services for marital counseling and for setting standards and training for quality performance in this area.

The *one-parent family* constitutes another special-population risk. Consideration should be given to further exploration of new institutional patterns of meeting the needs of these families.

Urban children constitute another population at risk owing to traffic hazards, air pollution, lack of recreational facilities, and inadequate schools.

Institutionalized children present another population at high risk, whether in orphanages, institutions for retarded or emotionally disturbed children, homes for dependent children, or training schools for delinquent and predelinquent children. In many ways, these are forgotten children. Careful studies of institutions for children with the point of view of their utilization for prevention of more serious disturbances must be considered.

The effects of grief, particularly unresolved grief, on spouses and on children appear to be extensive. This area has not received much attention from the medical profession or from other helping persons, with the exception of the clergy. This is another type of family crisis for which services should be available and accessible to persons in mild phases of this type of situation. There are, of course, numerous other *family crises* which present opportunities for prevention.

Children of mobile populations (the military, academicians, and corporation executives) may be at some special risk. Although it would appear that their adjustment depends upon that of their parents, not enough studies have been done to determine whether a preventable problem exists. The *children of migrant workers* are another population which receives inadequate medical, educational, and mental health services.

Minority groups at special risk have been discussed by Drs. Miller, Comer, Fitzpatrick, and Gould in the "Rehabilitation and Treatment" section of this report.

Children in families receiving *public assistance* in *welfare programs* are another high-risk population, primarily owing to the variety of inadequacies in the "welfare system." This is discussed in detail by Miss Jeweldean Jones in her paper on welfare institutions and their role in prevention.

Essentially, Miss Jones looks at economic deprivation and inequities as affecting family life and child development adversely, having psychological consequences which promote familial dysfunctions and produce hopelessness and frustration. Such a milieu is obviously inadequate for the growing child, and, what is worse, our efforts to intervene via public welfare measures merely promote poverty life styles rather than enable people to change and move into other economic levels. After a critical review of the welfare system, in which she underscores its punitive and unhelpful modes of operations, Miss Jones points up the equally inadequate health services and poor housing, and the ineffectual role of predominantly middle-class school systems for poor children.

She concludes with several recommendations:

1. Some form of income maintenance, such as a children's allowance, should be implemented.

2. Present federal health and welfare programs, which presently do not reach low-income persons—e.g., mental retardation services to unwed mothers, day care, family planning, etc.—should be expanded and reallocated.

3. Research should be undertaken to clearly articulate the impact of inequities in the major institutions on mental health, and to identify the basic social and economic policies and programs to close the present service gaps; aggressive leadership by the mental health professions is required to obtain the above interrelated services.

In concluding this summary of the Task Force deliberations, we would like to point out that, given the wide range of our charge, it is impossible to assign priorities to competing areas, such as research and service. We would hope that they could be thought of as complementary and reciprocal. Yet, our concern for the economics of family life leads us to reproduce Miss Jones' paper as Appendix A, since it provides some basic information on the kinds of income maintenance or income improvement now being considered.

RECOMMENDATIONS

Prevention is conceived of as primary and is a form of intervention at the broadest level and related to the promotion of normal mainstream development of the child. Prevention intervention has to be looked at in the perspective of evaluation research. There is a need for a continuing view of the population at risk and what prevention has to be tailored to. Programs dealing with prevention should be focused on the following:

1. Pregnant mothers should be given prenatal care as a high-priority preventive program. With respect to the newborn child, programs should emphasize giving help to the family. The programs should aim to minimize maternal depression, child abuse, maternal separation, etc.

2. It is recommended that valuable preventive work can be done with the new mother during the period that she is in the hospital, because during this traumatic period we can lay the groundwork for family planning and child care do's and don'ts when she returns home. Such programs have to be developed along with massive follow-up home programs. One strategic source of manpower here would be the family service agencies, which are now rethinking and reformulating their traditional functions. Also one could use the school as a community agency and locate the planning and usage of new services there.

3. We also recommend the recognition of the changing patterns of medical care and service such as group practice and the reorganization and mobilization of hospital facilities, especially obstetrical and gynecological services.

4. The Task Force recommends that new services must be developed for the one-parent family. These may take the form of day care, after-school programs, parent education, etc.

Institutionalized children should have available to them services which they don't have at present. This would be preventive in the largest sense. In this area a serious shortage of manpower exists, and a program development of needed personnel should be adopted.

5. At the preschool level we could focus, for example, on accident prevention. Here retarded and disturbed children should have programs that enlarge their present limited realm of social experience. All children should be given stimulating and educational experiences which relate to future developmental stages.

6. In adolescence, the programs could be built around the use of drugs. We should also explore the best way to prepare for parenthood, focusing not only on sex education for the adolescent but also on sensitizing the primary physicians who will be involved.

7. Programs to reduce the number of unwanted children, who may in turn account for much of the child abuse syndrome, are also recommended. Family planning programs could be utilized in this connection. This is especially important when statistics indicate that the battered child is usually from large families with children closely spaced in age.

8. Certain research possibilities suggest themselves, e.g., to what extent would the change in the abortion laws operate as a useful preventive measure? What is the explanation of the high proportion of youngsters who show up in child development clinics?

9. In the area of special populations at risk, e.g., poor children (those below the poverty line of $3,000), minority-group children, etc., the Task Force recommends some form of child allowance as a program which is now politically feasible and could be modeled on the Canadian experience. Along with this we recommend that any income maintenance provision should be completely separated from the provision of services. This is

especially true with respect to minority-group populations, who may be doubly penalized by present practices. These groups require a broad opportunity package as a program with which the community could identify as its own.

10. Among all children, we should develop public services of high quality, rather than our present minimal-quality levels.

11. The strategies of dissemination of information on the availability of services should be clearly thought out and rapidly implemented. Such an information program should be a continuing operation, addressing those target groups in need of services.

Appendix A

ON INCOME MAINTENANCE
by Jeweldean Jones

These programs are *public assistance, in-kind programs, social security, negative income tax, guaranteed income or universal demogrant,* and *partial demogrant.*

PUBLIC ASSISTANCE

The income maintenance program with which we are most familiar is public assistance, defined here as the income maintenance program administered by welfare departments. Chief issues: a means test that is degrading, low levels of payment, and so many people are not helped.

The Advisory Council on Public Welfare proposes universal minimum income through a comprehensive reconstruction of public assistance itself—specifically to establish a floor of required individual or family income for each state with need the sole measure of entitlement, using a simple affidavit. This program, a mandatory federal standard of minimum payment, can be achieved only if the federal government is willing to operate public assistance programs, for some states do not have the resources to contribute even a small percentage of cost, and others are not willing.

It is estimated this program would cost $20 billion per year. It would not be constructive for many of the people involved; the problem of incentive—which troubles us so greatly—would be compounded, and in any event, the nation would probably not tolerate such a program. If Congress gave serious attention, conditions about employability and training would be attached and an investigative procedure added—and we would be back to the dismal business of the means test.

Originally, the public assistance program was meant to be *residual*—a safety net for a *few* who fell through all the other protections. This concept is still right, but public assistance does not make a good mass program.

75

IN-KIND PROGRAMS

Medicare, food stamps, and rent subsidies are good examples of these programs which are not currently being proposed as a dominant source of income.

Although there are paternalistic implications in the food stamp program—"They're not able to manage money"—in-kind programs are probably sound as long as they remain a subsidiary type and are not felt as controlling. In some cases the state is in a better position to organize services than the family would be to buy them (as in medical care or rent subsidies). We might seek broad extension of three specific programs—school lunch for children, medical care for those who are not aged, and rent subsidies to broaden supply of low-cost housing.

SOCIAL SECURITY

In principle, social security provides benefits for stipulated risks in exchange for a regular payment during one's work life. This program is both categorical—that is, limited to the aged, the disabled, the orphaned—and directly tied to work. It has succeeded brilliantly exactly where public assistance has failed.

By the federal standard of poverty, almost two out of five who receive benefits are poor.

The issue that must be faced is the degree to which social security is an antipoverty program. The difficult question is how to apportion benefits within the social security system. It may be that we should move by stages to minimum benefits that avoid poverty for most people. The minimum benefit for an aged person is now $44.00 per month—doubling the figure would be a long step toward the desired objective. Wage-related benefits would also be raised.

Apart from adequacy, coverage can readily be broadened. Only something over one million aged people are now uncovered. More radical ways of broadening social security are also conceivable, and we may expect both minimum payment that guards against poverty and complete coverage for categories of population it serves—aged, disabled, widowed, and orphaned. In addition, *medical care* should be extended to all age groups and *unemployment* insurance benefit levels raised, coverage improved, and the period over which payments may be made, lengthened.

NEGATIVE INCOME TAX

A fourth line of development in income maintenance is the negative income tax—a payment related, according to some reasonably simple formula, to the number of persons in a family and their combined income. It is assumed that such a program would be operated by the Internal Revenue Service in connection with the income tax program (really a reverse income tax).

This is an attractive idea which appeals to the principle of equity hard to dispute. That is, a family of four with an income of $6,000 receives a gift of at least $340 (value of four exemptions at 14 percent tax rate) from the government as credit against its tax. With a $2,000 income, such a family receives less, and with no income, no payment at all.

Poor people should receive at least some payment for the value of their exemptions—you and I automatically get $600 for ourselves and each of our dependents; the poor individual doesn't get anything. The concept seems simple to administer and would reach all needy people without categorization. It is efficient, as it gives to the poor without diverting to others who do not need it.

Despite these advantages, it suffers disadvantages. As in public assistance, payments must be scaled carefully to income in order to sustain the feeling that one can improve oneself. The scale is most easily constructed when payments are to be small and would not lift a person above the poverty line. Even a substantial negative income tax would, according to Schorr, like public assistance, provide money payment in a poor-law framework in that it would not be paid for past work, because of childhood or old age, nor for any of the dozens of reasons that have been converted into social rights, but for the one reason we have so far failed to make into a right—*want.*

There are at least nine major forms of the negative income tax,[1] which can be grouped in two major ways: *First,* some of them would set out by providing an initial fixed allowance per head within the tax-reporting unit, against which other income would then be set off at some percentage rate. Others would start from the total value of exemptions and deductions in the unit, instead of an allowance, and again would deduct other income at some percentage rate. All four of Lampman's Plan II variants, together with the plans proposed by Tobin, Schwartz, and Theobald, rest on the allowance method. By contrast, Friedman's approach and Lampman's Plan I both start from the value of exemptions and deductions. *Second,* all nine plans may be classed according to whether they carry a full or a fractional guarantee of minimum income to the reporting unit, relative to the applicable upper income limit, where there is no other income. It is a full guarantee if it represents 100 percent of the minimum amount of income, below which the reporting unit would otherwise be in poverty by current standards, rather than for those applicable in the more distant future. Only Schwartz and Theobald propose full guarantees—all of the others take the fractional approach.

Theobald believes in "divorcing the productive function from the distributive function" in our economic system. To do so, he believes we will need to adopt the concept of an absolute constitutional right to an income. This new right is to be guaranteed to all. Schwartz also believes "the right to a livelihood must be recognized and guaranteed as a constitutional civil right."

Both the Schwartz plan and the Theobald plan would end poverty at one stroke, by guaranteeing free maintenance—a guarantee that would be made effective by a greatly enlarged system of direct transfer from the state to the poor.

Schorr believes that the nation is not ready for this approach. The negative

1. An outline of the discussed plans begins on page 79.

income tax, he believes, is in the poor-law tradition and would, as a practical matter, turn out to be a small amount of money; but even $300 or $400 a year to a poor family and every move toward equity is a move in the right national direction. Negative income tax should be supported as part of tax law reform.

UNIVERSAL PAYMENT

The fifth alternative open is a universal payment to everyone in the country, without regard to income or status—the original definition of guaranteed income. It derives from the concept of a contract between the state and the individual, assuring that the individual will receive income and will give work. As discussed lately in the United States, it has become associated with expectation that work will not be required (Theobald, 1963). For the next decade at least, Schorr (who believes in income by right) believes this is probably a fantasy. In any event, the universal payment, if it provided enough money for decent living, would bring about a sweeping redistribution of income in the United States. It is doubtful that this objective will be reached in one step.

PARTIAL DEMOGRANT

A partial form of the universal payment is the sixth and last alternative. It seems much more nearly practical to extend a payment to specific population groups, without income test or any qualifying test other than age. Two obvious candidates are the aged and children.

The critical group that is omitted in our system of income maintenance is *children*. A demogrant for children—that is, a children's allowance—might correct this long-standing oversight.

Arguments: That it would waste money on children who are not poor that could be spent, in an income-limited program, on children who are poor. A children's allowance designed carefully in relation to the income tax system would waste little money. In any event, that money is well wasted that purchases a sense of its rightness.

That it would increase birth rate, especially among those who really should have fewer children. There is no evidence that this is true.

Apart from the sense of rightness that may be provided by a demogrant, because it is not related to income it avoids interfering with incentive to work. A children's allowance of $50 per month would take beyond the reach of poverty three out of four children now poor. Moreover, family income is generally pooled; a child exits from poverty only when his whole family avoids poverty. If poverty were eliminated for families with children, fewer than a third of those now counted poor would remain poor. It is perfectly plain who the citizens are who require income maintenance. How is it that we turn everywhere else?

SUMMARY

In summary, if we strengthen the existing income maintenance mechanisms and add a couple of new ones, we can assure a decent income to virtually everyone in the United States.

We should seek to improve social security, increasing minimum benefits and reaching all the aged. We should seek to provide medical care and decent housing to all the population. We should seek to right unjust tax laws by providing at least a modest negative income tax. We should seek a program of allowances for children.

Public assistance should be a truly residual program which would deal with hundreds of thousands, rather than millions. To know just who will need this help, individual investigations may, indeed, be required. Quite possibly, these recipients will be troubled people requiring a variety of services which should be close at hand.

A great deal of money is involved in these programs, but not so much as the Gross National Product increases in a single year. That is to say, the cost spread over ten years would amount to substantially less than one-tenth of our *gain* in national production.

This is a pluralistic approach to income maintenance which may assure income for all Americans.

There are two concerns in substituting a general approach to income maintenance. First, it can introduce poor-law concepts into our new programs and even into areas where we have long-established rights. Second, we are a deeply divided nation—we are divided between those who have and those who have not, between slums and suburbs, between those who feel competent and those who feel exploited. The national structure of income maintenance is not a small matter. It can be structured to deepen the schism, or it can help bridge it. In the next two or three years the nation must make a choice, and the nation critically needs our voice in shaping this choice.

SUMMARY COMPARISON OF NEGATIVE INCOME TAX PLANS
BY MAJOR CHARACTERISTICS[2]

1. *Milton Friedman Plan*

Maximum guarantee relative to chosen upper poverty income limit: fractional.
Method of calculating income deficiency: 50 percent of value of unused exemptions and deductions.
Rate at which other income would be deducted from subsidy: 50 percent.
Exclusions from other income to be set off: not indicated.
Groups most likely to benefit: OASDHI beneficiaries, employed poor.
Maximum subsidy payable, family of four: $1,500.

2. *Robert J. Lampman Plan I*

Maximum guarantee relative to chosen upper poverty income limit: fractional.
Method of calculating income deficiency: 14 percent of value of unused exemptions and deductions.
Rate at which other income would be deducted from subsidy: 14 percent.
Exclusions from other income to be set off: OASDHI benefits and PA payments.

2. George H. Hildebrand, Cornell University.

Groups most likely to benefit: OASDHI beneficiaries, employed poor.
Maximum subsidy payable, family of four: $420.

3. *Lampman Plan II-a*

Maximum guarantee relative to chosen upper poverty income limit: fractional.
Method of calculating income deficiency: initial tax credit or allowance of $375 per head.
Rate at which other income would be deducted from subsidy: 50 percent.
Exclusions from other income to be set off: PA payments.
Groups most likely to benefit: those on PA in poor states and the employed poor.
Maximum subsidy payable, family of four: $1,500.

4. *Lampman Plan II-b*

Maximum guarantee relative to chosen upper poverty income limit: fractional.
Method of calculating income deficiency: initial tax credit or allowance of $375 per head.
Rate at which other income would be deducted from subsidy: 75 percent of first $1,000, 50 percent of second $1,000, and 25 percent of third $1,000.
Exclusions from other income to be set off: PA payments.
Groups most likely to benefit: those on PA in poor states and those employed poor who can earn between $1,500 and $3,000.
Maximum subsidy payable, family of four: $1,500.

5. *Lampman Plan II-c*

Maximum guarantee relative to chosen upper poverty income limit: fractional.
Method of calculating income deficiency: initial tax credit or allowance of $187.50 per head.
Rate at which other income would be deducted from subsidy: zero on first $1,500; 50 percent on next $1,500.
Exclusions from other income to be set off: PA payments.
Groups most likely to benefit: families with moderate earning power or property or pension income.
Maximum subsidy payable, family of four: $750.

6. *Lampman Plan II-d*

Maximum guarantee relative to chosen upper poverty income limit: fractional.
Method of calculating income deficiency: initial tax credit or allowance of $500 per head.
Rate at which other income would be deducted from subsidy: 75 percent of first $1,500, and 33 percent of next $1,500.
Exclusions from other income to be set off: PA payments.

Groups most likely to benefit: families on PA, particularly ADC and GA, in poor states.

Maximum subsidy payable, family of four: $2,000.

7. *James Tobin Plan*

Maximum guarantee relative to chosen upper poverty income limit: fractional.

Method of calculating income deficiency: initial tax credit or allowance of $400 per head.

Rate at which other income would be deducted from subsidy: 33⅓ percent.

Exclusions from other income to be set off: PA payments.

Groups most likely to benefit: families on PA, particularly ADC and GA, in poor states; the employed poor; the "nearly poor."

Maximum subsidy payable, family of four: $1,600.

8. *Edward Schwartz Plan* ("FSB"—Family Security Benefit)

Maximum guarantee relative to chosen upper poverty income limit: 100 percent.

Method of calculating income deficiency: initial tax credit or allowance of $750 per head.

Rate at which other income would be deducted from subsidy: 60 percent of first $1,000; 70 percent of second $1,000; and 80 percent of third $1,000.

Exclusions from other income to be set off: not indicated.

Groups most likely to benefit: those on PA; those unemployed poor who quit work; the "nearly poor."

Maximum subsidy payable, family of four: $3,000.

9. *Robert Theobald Plan* ("BES"—Basic Economic Security)

Maximum guarantee relative to chosen upper poverty income limit: 100 percent.

Method of calculating income deficiency: initial tax credit or allowance of $800 per head.

Rate at which other income would be deducted from subsidy: 90 percent.

Exclusions from other income to be set off: not indicated.

Groups most likely to benefit: those on PA; those employed poor who quit work; the "nearly poor."

Maximum subsidy payable, family of four: $3,200.

Appendix B

TASK FORCE IV PAPERS AND CONTRACT STUDIES

A. D. BUCHMUELLER, M.S.W.[1]	"Prevention"
JAMES W. CARPER, PH.D.	"Implications for Mental Health of U.S. Department of Labor and Office of Education and U.S. Office of Economic Opportunity Programs for Children"
JAMES COMER, M.D.	"Position Paper on the Mental Health Needs of the Negro Child"
RAYMOND FELDMAN, M.D.	"Present Status of the Clinical Field"
CARL FENICHEL, ED.D.	"Special Education and Rehabilitation of the Seriously Disturbed Child"
J. P. FITZPATRICK, S.J., PH.D., AND ROBERT E. GOULD, M.D.	"Mental Health Needs of Spanish-Speaking Children in the New York City Area"
VICTOR GIOSCIA, PH.D., *et al.*	"Dimensions and Innovations in the Therapy of Children"
JEWELDEAN JONES, M.S.W.	"Presentation on Income Maintenance"
	"Welfare Institutions and Their Role in Prevention"
SEYMOUR L. LUSTMAN, M.D., PH.D.	"Mental Health Research and the University"
DOROTHY MILLER, D.S.W.	"An Overview of Mental Health Problems of American Indian Children"

1 Morris Green, M.D., provided a working outline on "Prevention" which has been incorporated in Mr. Buchmueller's paper.

82

"American Indian Children: To Be or Not to Be"

"Rehabilitation of Mentally Ill Children: A Position Paper"

OTTO POLLAK, PH.D.

"Mental Health Goals in Relation to Mental Health Manpower"

"Mental Health Goals in Child-Rearing and Child Care"

"Suggestions for Alleviating Manpower Shortages in the Child Mental Health Manpower"

"Position Paper on Elements of Mental Health in a Corporate Society"

OTTO VON MERING, PH.D.

"Needed: Mental Health Manpower Development and Training Patterns"

"Outline for JCMHC-WPIC Reports"

"Toward an Understanding of Manpower Pools, Their Training and Development in Relation to Populations with Different Mental Health Risks"

"Feedback on Joint Commission Priorities"

"Considerations Regarding Manpower Study" (Memos 1, 2, and 3)

"Focal Concerns of Task Force IV"

JOSEPH F. WHITING, PH.D.
JAMES CARPER, PH.D.
RAYMOND FELDMAN, M.D.

"Mental Health Services for the Community: Process, Requirements and Solutions"

"Needed: A Scientific Base for Manpower Utilization in Mental Health Services"

JOSEPH F. WHITING, PH.D.

"Community Functioning, Manpower Utilization and Impact-Evaluation: Foundation Stones for the Delivery of Effective Child Mental Health Services"

References

Abelson, P. H. "Congress and Research," *Science,* 139 (Jan. 1963), 305.

——. "Government Support of Research," *Science,* 139 (Feb. 1963), 377.

Anthony, E. J. "The Developmental Precursors of Adult Schizophrenia," *Journal of Psychiatric Research,* 6 (Dec. 1968), 293–316.

——. "A Clinical Evaluation of Children with Psychotic Parents," *Journal of the American Psychiatric Association,* to be published.

——. "The Influence of Maternal Psychosis on Children—Folie a Deux," in *Festschrift in Honor of Dr. Margaret Mahler.* New York: International Universities Press, to be published.

Aubert, V. *The Hidden Society.* Totowa, N. J.: Bedminster Press, 1965, p. 33.

Barzun, J. *The American University.* New York: Harper & Row, 1968.

Bower, E. M. *The Protection and Promotion of Mental Health in Schools.* Mental Health Monograph Series No. 5. U.S. Public Health Service, No. 1226. Washington, D.C.: National Institute of Mental Health, Jan. 1964, 57 pp.

Brewster, K. *The President's Report.* New Haven, Conn.: Yale University Press, 1967.

Burgum, M. "The Father Gets Worse: A Child Guidance Problem," *American Journal of Orthopsychiatry,* 12 (July 1942), 474.

Caplan, G. *Principles of Preventive Psychiatry.* New York: Basic Books, 1964, p. 108.

Cohen, M. B. "Personal Identity and Sexual Identity," *Psychiatry,* 29, 1 (Sept. 1966).

"Department of Mental Health Reports," Connecticut District Branch, *American Psychiatric Association Newsletter* 8, Aug.–Sept. 1967.

Erikson, E. *Childhood and Society.* New York: W. W. Norton, 1950, pp. 219–233.

Fanon, F. *The Wretched of the Earth.* New York: Grove Press, 1963, pp. 29–74.

Fein, R. *The Doctor Shortage: An Economic Diagnosis.* Washington, D.C.: Brookings Institution, 1967.

Freud, S. *The Complete Introductory Lectures in Psychoanalysis.* New York: W. W. Norton, 1966, p. 15.

———. "On Romain Rolland," *Gesammelte Werke,* Vol. XIV (1948), p. 533, as quoted by Mabel Blake Cohen in "Personal Identity and Sexual Identity," *Psychiatry,* 29, 1 (Sept. 1966), 14.

Gioscia, V., *et al.* "Dimensions and Innovations in the Therapy of Children." A report prepared by the Research Department of Jewish Family Service of New York for Task Force IV, Joint Commission on Mental Health of Children, 1968.

Gladwin, T. "Social Competence and Clinical Practice," *Psychiatry,* 30, 1 (Feb. 1967), 30–43.

Goodenough, W. H. *Cooperation in Change.* New York: John Wiley, 1963.

Grinker, R. R., Sr. "GAP's Next 20 Years," *Archives of General Psychiatry,* 16 (Feb. 1967), 133.

———. "What Are Professors of Psychiatry For?" *Archives of General Psychiatry,* 16 (Mar. 1967), 261.

Grünhut, M. *Penal Reform.* New York: Oxford University Press, 1948, pp. 95–135.

Halmos, P. *The Faith of the Counselors.* New York: Schocken Books, 1966.

Hartmann, H. *Ego Psychology and the Problem of Adaptation.* New York: International Universities Press, 1958, p. 121.

Haskins, C. P. "Evolution or Catastrophe?" *Science,* 159 (Mar. 1968), 1055.

Hutchins, R. M. "Remarks on the Inauguration of President Edward H. Levi," *University of Chicago Magazine,* LXI, 3–5 (Jan.–Feb. 1969).

Masserman, J. *Current Psychiatric Therapies,* Vol. 2. New York: Grune & Stratton, 1962, pp. 14–15.

O'Hara, W. T. *John F. Kennedy on Education.* New York: Teachers College Press, Columbia University Press, 1966.

Oppenheimer, J. R. "The Need for New Knowledge," in D. Wolfe, (ed.), *Symposium on Basic Research.* Washington, D.C.: American Association for the Advancement of Science, 1959.

Perlman, H. H. *Social Casework.* Chicago: Chicago University Press, 1957, p. 200.

Pollak, G. K. "New Uses of a Family Life Education Program by the Community," *Social Casework,* XLIV, 6 (June 1963), 335–342.

———. "Family Life Education for Parents of Acting Out Children: A Group Discussion Approach," *Journal of Marriage and the Family* (Nov. 1964), 489–494.

Pollak, O. *Integrating Sociological and Psychoanalytic Concepts.* New York: Russell Sage Foundation, 1956.

———. "The Social Dynamics of the Negro Revolution," *Voices,* II, 1 (Spring 1966), 186–189.

———. "The Outlook for the American Family," *Journal of Marriage and the Family* (Feb. 1967), 193–205.

Rapoport, R. N. *Community as Doctor.* London: Tavistock Publications, 1960, pp. 27–28, 302.

Rieff, P. *The Triumph of the Therapeutic.* New York: Harper & Row, 1966.

"The Sexual Future of Man." Conference Telephone Dialogue. Moderators:

John Warkentin and Tom Leland. Atlanta, Georgia, *Voices,* 3, 1 (Spring 1967), pp. 16–26.

Shearer, M. L., et al. "Unexpected Effects of an Open Door Policy on Birth Rates of Women in State Hospitals," *Journal of the American Orthopsychiatric Association,* 38 (Apr. 1968), 413–417.

Sorensen, T. C. *Kennedy.* New York: Harper & Row, 1965, p. 392.

Strecker, E. A. *Their Mother's Sons,* Philadelphia: J. B. Lippincott, 1948.

Swain, D. C. "The Rise of a Research Empire: National Institute for Mental Health, 1930–1950," *Science,* 138 (Dec. 1962), 1233.

Theobald, R. *Free Men and Free Markets.* New York: Potter, 1963.

Waelder, R. *Basic Theory of Psychoanalysis.* New York: International Universities Press, 1960, p. 230.

II

ORGANIZATION, ADMINISTRATION, AND FINANCING OF SERVICES FOR EMOTIONALLY DISTURBED CHILDREN

REPORT OF TASK FORCE V

Edited by Harold Visotsky, M.D., Donald Schon, Ph.D., and Frank Rafferty, M.D.

The discussions of Task Force IV have pointed to many vital needs in research, manpower, and services in the field of child mental health. Task Force V provides another view of these issues, dwelling mainly on the problem of the organization, administration, and financing of services for emotionally disturbed children.

—EDITOR

Task Force V

NIMH LIAISON REPRESENTATIVE

MORTON KRAMER, PH.D.

CONSULTANTS

WILLIAM M. BOLMAN, M.D.
Department of Psychiatry
University of Wisconsin Medical
Center
Madison, Wisconsin

JAMES J. GALLAGHER, PH.D.
Associate Commissioner
Bureau of Education for the
Handicapped
Washington, D.C.

JAY G. HIRSCH, M.D.
Chief, Division of Preventive
Psychiatry
Institute for Juvenile Research
Chicago, Illinois

HARRY C. SCHNIBBE
Executive Director
National Association of State Mental
Health Program Directors
Washington, D.C.

DONALD A. SCHON, PH.D.
Organization for Social and
Technical Innovation
Cambridge, Massachusetts

ALVIN SCHORR, M.S.W.
Deputy Assistant Secretary for
Individual and Family Services
Department of Health, Education,
and Welfare
Washington, D.C.

BEN B. SELIGMAN, PH.D.
Institute of Labor Relations Research
University of Massachusetts
Amherst, Massachusetts

JACK C. WESTMAN, M.D.
Director, Child Psychiatry Division
University of Wisconsin Medical
Center
Madison, Wisconsin

Foreword

The prodigious problem facing Task Force V was to design a system for responding to the mental health needs of children. From the inception of our considerations, it became apparent that to improve a unit of mental health care within a larger nonsystem would be economically as well as programmatically unfeasible. The many variables represented in the ecology affecting the child's development mandated a reorganization of all the institutions and services dealing with children. This consideration meant that Task Force V had to address itself to the design of a total system for the care of children. The "sick child" had to be dealt with within this system in order to diminish the mere labeling of illness. Further, economic problems required attention to programs of preventive care, early detection, and corrections of dysfunctions found among our various child populations.

In order that this final report may be viewed in perspective, we shall here summarize the major issues and obstacles that arose and the choices that we made.

1. The first task was to define the population for whom we were planning. That is, should we focus on those who were already diagnosed as having disorder, or should we consider those either with unrecognized disorder or at high risk? We concluded that the second alternative was clearly preferable.

2. In planning for children at risk, we had to consider whether it would be better to orient services toward improved methods of detection and treatment of episodic illness, or toward the maintenance of health, including the maintenance of healthy capacities in mentally ill children. Present trends in psychiatry, pediatrics, education, and social welfare support a health-oriented priority; hence we chose this approach.

3. Next, we faced the question of whether we could focus mostly on the child (either ill or at risk) or whether it was necessary to include his parents, school, and other significant aspects of his life space as integral parts of planning. Again, present knowledge overwhelmingly favors the second approach. Our Task Force struggled at length with the problem of where to set the limits within which mental health issues were predominant, and concluded that this approach was self-defeating. In its place we chose a model that takes into account the *relationships* between environmental forces and the child's mental health, that is, one that views the overall system of services to children.

4. Given the need to develop a delivery system that takes into account the developmental differences in children from infancy through adolescence, that attempts to maintain health while treating illness, and that concerns itself with the significant (pathogenic or healthful) social environment, we were then concerned with how this might be accomplished. We thus considered the following types of questions:

a. What are the needed types of helping institutions?

b. What are the best kinds of organizational structures for these institutions?

c. Where should the institutions be located?

d. How should they be staffed and financed?

e. How should they be evaluated and monitored to permit necessary adaptation and change?

5. In approaching these issues we followed five basic premises.

First, that children in their course of development should be kept within the mainstream of social institutions, whenever possible. When circumstances require that a child be separated and differentiated, any necessary measures should be as brief and temporary as possible. The system of developmental and helping services, in short, should be biased *against* any avoidable labeling and isolation of youngsters.

Second, provision for early case finding, assessment, emergency aid, and other such services related to mental and emotional deviations or problems should be located therefore in the "normal" institutional contexts wherever possible; for example, in child health stations, child development assessment centers, school, day-care, and community centers.

Third, when preliminary screening and assessment in the "normal" institutions indicate the need for comprehensive evaluation and planning of remedial measures, this assessment should be undertaken in a *broad* framework, that is, it should be multidisciplinary and provide a maximum of perspectives and options. The system thus would be guarded against professional bias and premature channeling in the provision of services to children who are thought to be at risk.

Fourth, the community psychiatric system per se would be utilized as a possible aid for children only where the screening and assessment indicate a need for this type of specialized service. Other alternatives would include socialization resources, general medical services, corrections, education, and so on.

Fifth, when psychiatric interventions are needed, they should be family-based wherever possible, until at least adolescent age, and should be integrated into an overall medical service system.

6. Various dimensions of our planning were elaborated in a series of working papers, as follows: "Use of Psychiatric Facilities by Children: Current Status, Trends and Implications," prepared by the Office of Biometry, NIMH, and expanded by Alex J. Hurder; "Introduction to the Presentation of Organization of Services," by Alfred J. Kahn; "A Comprehensive Model for Planning for Children," by Frank T. Rafferty; "Planning for the Mental Health of Children: A Milestone Approach," by William M. Bolman and Jack C. Westman; "Family and Society: Implications for Action," by Vera D. Rubin.

7. As our study progressed, we became increasingly aware that one of the first major obstacles to be overcome lay in implementing what was already known. Reports of the other Commission Task Forces indicate that this gap between action and the application of present knowledge is enormous. For example, it was pointed out that the White House Conference on Children and Youth had made numerous valuable recommendations over the years that have yet to be applied. Even such a goal as universal kindergarten attendance has not yet been achieved! The very fact of such a social lag emphasized for us the futility of presenting an idealized set of recommendations.

8. Therefore, we were forced to identify goals that might be influenced by attainable policy and to recommend approaches that were consistent with developments in other areas. Our conclusion, supported by the previously mentioned stepwise set of programmatic choices, was to adopt the best current administrative approach to planning, organizing, and monitoring a complex set of services, that is, one that utilizes a "systems" approach and stresses economic analysis and feedback. Such a procedure not only makes the form of this final report consistent with current U.S. Department of Health, Education, and Welfare practice, but also provides an overall "map" by which people looking at various aspects of the system, professionals and legislators, can understand the overall relationships and plan accordingly.

Introduction and Summary

At the request of Task Force V of the Joint Commission on the Mental Health of Children, the Organization for Social and Technological Innovation (OSTI) has attempted to develop for the Commission a conceptual framework concentrated around the following three areas:

1. Problems of organizations involved in direct contact with disabled or disadvantaged children and with "normal-stream" institutions.
2. Problems of the interaction and relationship of these organizations.
3. The role of fiscal, administrative, legislative, and other policies governing the service system affecting the well-being of children.

The products of our study can be summarized as follows:

1. A description of the current system of services related to the well-being of children that, hopefully, is better than any currently available.
2. A formulation of critical problems confronting the system and issues of policy related to those problems.
3. A formulation of programs related to the problem areas outlined above, where such programs have been formulated and can be spelled out. Rough estimates of dollar and manpower resources required to carry out these programs will be provided.

Recommendations for change, emerging from the study, will fall into these categories:

1. Establishment of a system of data gathering and analysis designed to permit a more effective management of service systems.

94

2. An outlining of the directions of change in existing service systems which should set the ground rules for a broad program of experimentation and demonstration in the development of new technologies of service and new patterns of organization.

3. Directions for further research into the problems and patterns of operation of the current service system, and the means by which improved service systems can be brought into being.

4. Establishment of a new institution designed to deal, on a long-range basis, with the problems of children and services to children and to assist, on a continuing basis, in the implementation of the recommendations of the Joint Commission on Mental Health of Children.

OSTI's work in examining the feasibility of such an institution was supported by a grant from the Stern Family Fund. The results have been incorporated in this report.

In all that follows, we have tried to confront issues dealing with service systems related broadly to the well-being of children rather than limit our efforts solely to those concerned with mental health, as narrowly defined. We have dealt relatively little with short-term improvements in existing service agencies, on the assumption that these will be covered by other Task Forces, and have concentrated instead on more central and long-term directions of change.

We have profited in our work from the views of the members of Task Force V, particularly those of Dr. Harold Visotsky, its chairman. Mr. Israel Gerver and Mrs. Florence Jacobsen of the Joint Commission staff have provided a great deal of background information, as well as useful criticism and reaction.

Members of the OSTI team for this project were: Dr. Ben Seligman and Dr. Stanley Young, of the University of Massachusetts, who concentrated on economic and management analysis; Dr. Frank Rafferty, of the University of Maryland, who contributed particularly to analysis of new forms of data gathering and analysis and new modes of organization of systems of services; Mrs. Murray (Margaret) Frank; Dr. Sanford Kravitz; Dr. Evelyn Murphy; Susanne Albert; Catherine Gores; Dr. Donald Schon. We have also had the benefit of consultation with Dr. James Kelly of the University of Michigan and Dr. Robert Weiss of Dartmouth.

We have used four complementary approaches. Each analysis has provided us with a different insight into the problems and potentialities of the system of services to children.

Our first approach concentrates on the existing system of services. We examine the level of the problems that agencies encounter in their attempts to meet children's needs as currently diagnosed, and the implications of those problems for policy and action.

Our second approach consists of a gross economic analysis of the flows of children and resources in and out of the service system; an estimate of the matches and mismatches between child demand and service supply; and a rough estimate of projected demand and supply for services.

Our third analysis concentrates on the developmental cycle of the child in an effort to formulate the characteristics of a child-centered service system. We describe illustratively, for given population clusters, environmental determinants of development from the prenatal period to post-adolescence. We attempt then to match these determinants against relevant services and to explore the implications for restructuring service systems.

Our fourth analysis deals with the characteristics of a system of data gathering, monitoring, and analysis, as a basis both for operation of a child service system and for management and policy making at various levels of the system.

Finally, we outline the characteristics of an institution designed to aid in the implementation of recommendations which have emerged from the work of the Commission.

Our findings about the existing system of services are drawn from some 50 interviews with persons in various administrative and field positions in different spheres of the child service system, and from a more detailed analysis of four problem areas. Although there is nothing in our great society which does not in some way affect the well-being of children, our task was to conceptualize, in a systematic way, those agencies and social institutions that have the most direct and crucial bearing on child development. In this context, we found it possible to outline a system of agencies and institutions along the following lines:

If we conceive of development as a continuum stretching from the prenatal period through to the beginnings of work and adult life, we are able to identify critical points and periods of development as well as certain values governing child development at each of these points. We are able to delineate the groups and institutions (mother, family, school, community, and the like) which critically affect the well-being of the child in the "normal stream" of his development. We can also identify the institutions which deal with the crises that arise at various points in development (such as disease, handicap, mental illness, juvenile delinquency, illegitimacy, and the like). Each of these institutions is connected "vertically" to a hierarchy of agencies. Each is related "horizontally" to other agencies providing services to children.

There are, in addition, the organizations that train manpower for this system; the policy-making apparatus associated with government; the organizations, both public and private, which influence policy and legislation; and the clients for services who represent, more or less effectively, the interest of users in the system.

The system is confronted with several outstanding problems. We find it useful to think in terms of the following categories:

1. The first-order problems of children themselves, including those that arise for children in the "normal stream" as well as those crisis problems faced by youngsters who experience disability and disadvantage.
2. The second-order interpretations of these symptomatic problems, including questions of disability, problems of family, and the deprivations of poverty.
3. The problems of institutions which provide services directly to children.
4. The "systems" problems relating to the interaction of agencies providing services to children.
5. The problems of the system's "self-knowledge," that is, those revolving around evaluation, information gathering and processing, and the generation of relevant data.
6. The problems of formulating coherent policy governing services to children.
7. The problems of effecting change in the system and of mustering resources for the implementation of policy.

The following are some of our principal conclusions concerning the problems and characteristics of the present service system:

1. The system tends to be oriented to the needs of professionals providing services rather than to the needs of the children being served.
2. Services tend to focus on correcting crisis situations rather than the affected environmental determinants of crisis.
3. Only a small fraction of the eligible population (as defined by professional diagnosis) is actually served.
4. Service agencies, in their intake procedures, tend to select those most easily treated or most likely to be "cured," and to screen out the hard-core populations. Fashion, not research, often dictates who is deemed the best service risk.
5. There is great variety of service goals and objectives: often these are overlapping or conflicting.
6. A small amount of money is spread over a large number of programs; no one program has enough "critical mass" to be very effective.
7. There is little follow-up or disciplined evaluation of programs.
8. Programs suffer from fragmentation and lack of coordination, both horizontally and vertically.

9. Programs labeled "innovations" are often only marginal upgradings of the existing system.

10. The inability of the formal service system to meet a large proportion of children's needs often results in the growth of a compensatory informal system, which the formal system, in turn, either ignores or represses.

Underlying all of these problems is a series of "second-order" problems relating to management and policy making at agency, neighborhood, city, state, and national levels. These problems are reflected in:

An oversupply of fragmentary, confused data, and an almost total absence of usable operating and management data.

An inability to clearly define pressing problems in the system and to establish meaningful priorities.

A lack of responsibility for a central overview of services affecting the well-being of children and an inability at national levels to devote sustained attention to policy questions of long-term importance.

A tendency for research to be disconnected from operating practice.

When we attempt to put quantitative dimensions on the system of services for children, we encounter the inadequacies of the current data system. Our strategy has been to move from extremely hazardous statements about the total system to somewhat less hazardous statements about specific parts of the system in which data—although inadequate—are more plentiful.

We begin with the year 1965. Our guess is that a conservative estimate of the total expenditure for all services to children in 1965 would be in the order of $60 billion. In that same year, the total number of children was estimated at 79.8 million.

If we concentrate now on what we have called nonnormal-stream services, and divide these roughly into groups under the headings of mental health, social welfare, physical disability, and corrections, we generate the numbers shown in Table 1. Our estimates of children who were "at risk" or "in need" or considered "potential target populations" in 1965 are drawn from a series of independent estimates cited in the text.

Estimates of children in need and serviced contain some double counting. Children may receive service more than once within a particular category as well as across category lines (see Table 1). It is not possible to eliminate such double counting using existing data. Moreover, presenting the numbers of children as counted by the various subsystems of service reflects the way in which the total service system currently operates.

We conclude that the current service system, if it were to meet current conservative estimates of need for service as structured above, would have

Table 1.—ESTIMATED EXPENDITURES ON MENTAL HEALTH SERVICES TO CHILDREN, 1965, COMPARED TO ESTIMATED NEED FOR SERVICES[1]

	Mental Health	Estimated Cost	Social Welfare	Estimated Cost	Physical Handicap	Estimated Cost	Corrections	Estimated Cost	Total Number of Children	Estimated Cost
Number of children estimated served	.5	4.31	7.4	6.71	5.6	9.25	.3	3.74	13.8	24.01
Number of children estimated to be in need (or "at risk")	7.0	6.03	17.6	15.98	7.6	12.55	1.0	12.46	33.2	47.02

[1] All figures estimating number of children are in millions, and all figures estimating cost are in billions of dollars.

incurred for 1965 a dollar expenditure of $42 billion. The estimates indicate, however, that only slightly more than $20 billion was spent for children served by these nonnormal institutions.

When we turn to manpower requirements, data are even more fragmentary and unreliable. However, taking a particular category for which some data are available (public social welfare services at state and local levels), it is apparent that the strain on manpower resources, if the current system were extended to meet conservative estimates of need, would be much greater than the strain on dollar resources. Manpower is the *first* major constraint the existing system would face in its effort to respond to need.

If we extrapolate to 1985, the current system, operating under the same categories outlined above, would need to expend $45 billion in order to serve 35.5 million children *in need*. Manpower requirements in the one area we have examined would move from 460,000 to 490,000. These projections are based on a conservative population estimate.

The burden of this analysis is not, we believe, to argue for massive increases in dollar and manpower resources. Our analysis can be useful only if it is applied to what is realistically possible. Considering manpower alone, it would be impossible to meet the requirements within the near future. Thus, the burden of our argument leads to the contention that the current system, on its own terms (that is, given its present structuring of services, resources, and organization), cannot respond to conservative estimates of current need and will be swamped by requirements levied on it by 1985.

A series of implications follows. There are requirements for:

Restructuring current service organizations.

Development of new technologies for providing service.

New approaches to manpower, related to restructuring of jobs; new uses of what are called nonprofessionals; further reliance and encouragement of the informal system of services; and planning for expansion of professional manpower.

These requirements derive from a rough economic analysis of supply and demand within the current system, and reinforce findings cited earlier concerning inherent problems of the current system.

These are the conclusions that emerge from our analysis:

It is necessary to reconceptualize the importance and standing given to the well-being of children on the agenda of national priorities, as well as the strategies involved in setting priorities.

If the existing service system were extended to cover the total population in need, the system would be strained beyond its capabilities, even if it represented an optimum response to the problem. A radical restructuring of services is therefore indicated.

In order to create any new system of services, it is necessary to create an impetus toward such systems through the formulation of performance criteria for service to children and to evaluate ongoing services against those criteria. We envision generating a national data-gathering system responsible, first, for developing indices against which to measure the performance of the system that provides services to children; and, second, for providing monitoring and evaluation of that system on a continual basis.

From an analysis of the developmental cycle of the child, it may be possible to state a number of the characteristics that a new service delivery system would have to have in order to move from the present problems of operation to a satisfactory delivery of service to different population clusters.

We have sketched out such a developmental analysis, building on descriptions others have undertaken. In this analysis, we see a child's life as divided into segments: prenatal, infancy, toddlerhood, preschool, ages four to eleven, and from eleven to the end of adolescence. At each stage it is possible to formulate criteria for normal or desirable development along the dimensions of physical health, cognitive development, and interpersonal competence. We can ask, then, what are the environmental determinants of these criteria of development at each stage of life.

The answers, of course, will tend to vary for different population clusters—for center-city poor, for example, as against rural poor or suburban middle-class children.

Thinking in terms of health in infancy, for example, subcriteria for development become: adequate nutrition, freedom from disease, ability to cope with disease, and freedom from environmental hazard. If we take the first—adequate nutrition—and ask what are its environmental determinants for the infant in an impoverished center-city context conditions such as the following emerge: the presence of a mother or mother figure in the home; her knowledge of dietary requirements for the infant, and her willingness to act on that knowledge; disposable income available for food; accessibility of a full range of foods at stores within reach; adequacy of equipment for preparing and storing food.

If we ask what, in turn, affects these determinants, we are led quickly to consider: employment, income maintenance, transportation (particularly in relation to public housing projects), consumer and health education, store location and pricing policy, policies of the housing authority, and the like.

If we wish to have an effect on these deficiencies, the range of programs needed, depending on the strategies considered appropriate to deal with various issues, will include day care, development of new transportation services, consumer education, income supplements, food supplement programs, manpower training and employment, tenant strikes and demonstrations, and the like.

The single factor of nutritional adequacy in infancy quickly engages many other aspects of community life and opens up possibilities for a wide variety of strategies.

When the analysis is carried through, illustratively, across the consecutive stages of child development, we encounter a number of implications:

1. Child-centered or broadly preventive services for children must engage a variety of other services which are not normally considered to be part of child welfare or child mental health systems.

2. An effective attack on the problems of child-centered service systems design implies, then, that we need to create a network of related services and oversee these from the point of view of their effect on children. The network must include services now considered outside the system of services to children.

3. There are certain constants—such as employment, income, the presence of the mother in the home, family stability—that appear to be central and crucial at all stages of childhood and for nearly all dimensions of development.

4. The stages of vulnerability or opportunity in the life of the child may or may not correspond with the points at which the child is most easily accessible to agencies.

These points, together with earlier discussions, suggest some of the criteria for development of child-centered, broadly preventive service systems:

They must find ways of linking together apparently unrelated services affecting crucial environmental determinants of child development.

They must find points of access to this network of problems and services which are politically and economically feasible—as well as related to periods of vulnerability and opportunity for the child—and which can be built on or "parlayed" to include other central services. (For example, it would be possible to build an appropriate day-care program linked with job training for mothers, diagnostic work with children, health and consumer education, and the incorporation of research on early learning.)

They must find vehicles for providing continuity of overview and service (such as those shown in the proposals of Dr. Rafferty, pp. 192–230).

They must provide ways of giving clients some significant continuing power over the character of services delivered and over the service delivery system itself—so that the system, in spite of pulls to the contrary, remains responsive to children.

The variety of options for approaches to these goals (some of which are suggested in the text) represent an array of possibilities for the development of more effective child-centered service systems.

From the point of view of the larger issues of service systems design, key questions remain to be explored:

What are the characteristics of service systems appropriate to different population clusters, to nonhomogeneous as well as to homogenerous population areas?

What are the kinds of service functions best performed at varying levels of the system—for example, at municipal, county, state, and national levels—as well as at community and neighborhood levels?

Similarly, where should resources of dollars and manpower, facilities and equipment, be located—what strategies of centralization/decentralization of resource-location control should be used?

These are questions that might be categorized under a macro-service design. They depend in a critical way upon the approach taken to systems for data gathering and analysis which might permit more effective overall management of child service systems.

From the discussion to this point, it is apparent that there is a series of functions, relating to the problems of the current child service system and to desirable directions of change, which existing organizations are unable or unwilling to fill. These include:

The modification of the current service system and the provision of information about the important events in the system.

A clear delineation of the goals of service subsystems—such as day care.

The formulation of optional strategies for attaining and delivering these goals, including those which go beyond boundaries of existing professional service systems.

The formulation of a range of community-based child-centered experiments in service systems, along the lines outlined above; the identification of strategies for initiating these experiments; means for relating these experiments with the desired criteria and for providing an overview of experiments that can be analyzed and used as a reference in planning.

The analyses of requirements for management information systems and the development of model management information programs, to be undertaken at city and state levels.

These functions could best be performed by a new institution which would be limited in duration but devoted to the implementation of the Commission's recommendations.

Such an institution would consist of a small core group, working within a limited series of networks of "temporary systems," each of which would be related to a principal function of the institution. The missions and operating characteristics of this institution will be further elaborated upon in the text of this report.

The analysis of guidelines for a child-centered system of services leads us directly to the support of management data and analysis, and the system for providing and using them. We assume that such management information systems would be conducive not only to effective functioning of the children's system, but that their existence would lead to continued adjustment by permitting public assessment of the relationship between service goals and performance.

We are concerned with several kinds of data and analysis:

1. Data required for cost-benefit and cost-effectiveness analysis, at all governmental levels, in order to permit:

    effective establishment of priorities for investment of scarce resources;

    effective program control.

2. Operating data, consisting of measures of development for chil-

dren and measures of performance for service systems. The purpose of this data system is to:

> identify periods of vulnerability and opportunity in the lives of children and relate them to appropriate service resources;
> monitor performance of service agencies and feedback information in order to modify agency performance.

There is a link between the two kinds of data. Operating data of the kind indicated in item 2 would provide information related to both benefit and cost of children's services. The system for gathering such data would be essential to a management information system related to cost-benefit analysis.

Our treatment of these subjects represents only a beginning and, in effect, spells out criteria for such systems and lays the groundwork for further inquiry.

Our discussion proceeds along the following lines:

> The utility of cost-benefit analysis at various points in the child service system—for determining priorities within the children's system and in relation to other systems, for program control, and for economical management of the system.
>
> A conceptual approach to benefit-cost analysis based on the question: Benefit for and costs to whom? We discuss children, society, and professionals as "client groups," and suggest some measures of benefit and of cost.
>
> Discussions of measures of child development and of agency performance along a series of dimensions—these are in elaboration of the dimensions of health, cognitive development, and interpersonal competence, discussed in the previous sections. These will be discussed as the conceptual framework underlying a possible child-monitoring system.

In the course of these discussions several issues of value and methodology arise. In this field, the very possibility of cost-benefit analysis and of measurement of agency performance has been called into question. We attempt to note some of the obstacles to these forms of analysis, as we encounter them, in the text.

Analysis of the Current System
of Services to Children

Definition and Boundaries of the System

In a sense, there is *no system* concerned with the well-being of children, and that is one of the central problems.

There is not an interconnected, integrated set of organizations and institutions, committed to a set of clear, shared, and self-consistent objectives and managed, under carefully worked-out policies, to achieve the objectives necessary to the optimal development of children.

There is, nevertheless, a complex of individuals, organizations, agencies, and programs which affect children and the environment in which children live. Some of these are formal organizations like the Children's Bureau and welfare agencies; some are informal, like families, peer groups, and neighborhoods. Some, like schools and child guidance clinics, organize themselves around the category *"children."* Others revolve around other categories, such as public housing projects and transportation, but affect children nonetheless. These organizations are both public and private and operate at national, regional, state, metropolitan, county, and community levels. There are, in addition, a variety of subsystems organized around functions such as education, welfare, health, and employment.

The system and subsystem are more or less concerted or fragmentary, isolated or overlapping, complementary or conflicting. Regardless of the intent of particular individuals and particular agencies within the system, these individuals and organizations interact *as though* the system had certain objectives, which are in some cases very different from stated intent.

Institutions related primarily to the normal stream of development (schools, hospitals) and those related to disabled or disadvantaged children (child guidance clinics, day care, mental hospitals) have vertical linkages to other institutions at higher administrative levels. These make resources available, set standards for performance, and evaluate programs. They organize around different but related categories: health, education, housing, delinquency, welfare. They may or may not center on children.

Other institutions relate to the people who work in such institutions—by way of training, professional associations, and unions.

Still others, public and private, affect policy governing the system as a whole. Some set formal policy concerning goals, programs, and resources, as, for example, the Congress and the federal bureaucracies. Others are interest groups or lobbies seeking to change policy or to keep it from changing. Some formulate and set in motion critical issues, such as "child abuse" or "foster care," which are later embodied in action.

Some, among them certain private foundations, seek to improve, challenge, or develop alternatives to some parts of the system.

Throughout, it is important to distinguish the formal, open system and the informed underground networks of people who either effect or prevent change.

The boundaries of the system are necessarily arbitrary. Children are part of our society. Nothing occurs that does not in some way affect their well-being. But it is also possible to distinguish those institutions, programs, agencies, and individuals whose effect on children is more direct and specific.

We will have occasion later (pp. 139–166) to attempt some quantitative description of the system outlined above. With this in mind, it will be useful to specify now more formally what are meant by "normal-stream" and "nonnormal-stream" institutions.

By normal-stream institutions, we mean primarily:

Educational institutions, public and private, which affect children from early childhood through late adolescence.

Health-care institutions, ranging from those providing perinatal care to the full spectrum of pediatric and related health services offered to children in the normal course of growing up.

Institutions, public and private, which provide recreational and learning opportunities for children not usually included under the heading of education.

These do not include, of course, the informal systems of peer group, family, neighborhood, and the like. Nor do they include institutions—such as mass media, transportation systems, housing systems—which exercise significant though indirect effects on the lives of children.

By nonnormal-stream institutions we mean primarily those that can be grouped under the heading of:

Child welfare institutions, e.g., foster homes, homes for unwed mothers, and adoption agencies.

Public and private institutions concerned with mental illness, e.g., emotional disturbance, mental retardation, and severe mental illness.

Institutions concerned with physical disability.

Institutions concerned with corrections, such as juvenile courts, detention homes, and the like.

These categories are neither exhaustive nor mutually exclusive, but data tend to be gathered in these forms. Naming them here is intended to provide a link between the discussions that follow in this section and the quantitative descriptions which will follow.

It should also be kept in mind that this category scheme for the current system does not represent what we propose as a desirable way of organizing services. Suggestions toward a very different scheme of organization are made on pages 176–192.

What De We Mean by "the Well-being of Children"?

Structuring the discussion of the problem around an age cohort, "children," rather than around categorical problems of children provides a more coherent basis for planning services for children.

The focus on children stems, in part, from the fact that there are professionals, organizations, and policies already defined in terms of children. We may be falling into the trap, then, of defining problems around existing services.

But the focus stems, too, from belief and ideology—particularly the belief that our children are our future and their well-being should be a matter of explicit national concern, one that should be given the highest priority.

Even if certain problems are best approached from a categorical view, such as "poor families" or "poor people in cities," there is still reason for looking at problems, programs, and policies from the point of view of the well-being of children.

But the meaning of this phrase has been shifting over the last twenty to thirty years, and there are signs that the operation of the system has been shifting too, although at a lagging pace.

There appear to be three principal views of the well-being of children:

1. Our concern is with the disabled, the disadvantaged, the deviant. We organize around problems like physical handicap, delinquency, mental illness, drug abuse, illegitimacy, dropouts, abandonment, child abuse, foster care. We deal with crises. The problem is to learn how to treat

these crises, to find remedies for them, and to prevent them; and then to muster the resources of dollars and manpower to do these things. The rest can be left to ongoing institutions, to the market place, and to private initiative.

2. The outstanding issue is the gap between the quality of environment and the options available to the children of the poor, and the environment and opportunity available to the children of the rest of the nation. Basically, we know what to do. The problem is to shift national priorities and muster the necessary resources.

3. We must beware of foisting middle-class values on the poor. Slum kids often have resilience and vitality absent in middle-class kids. There are great inadequacies in the systems of education, health care, employment, and recreation available to all children. We are inattentive to these problems because they do not express themselves in crises, and because of our own middle-class views. We need to restructure the systems of education, health care, employment, recreation. We need to develop new kinds of professionals capable of carrying out this revolution. We need to root out exploitation of children and to find ways of recognizing the rights of children. And again, we need a shift in national priorities which will make this possible.

The three views are still to be found throughout the field. It is perhaps not too inaccurate to say that the first is the traditional orientation of those concerned with providing service to children. The second began to be enunciated loudly in the thirties and to take the center of the stage in the last two Presidential administrations. The third is still a front-running view, frequently enunciated and seldom acted upon.

It is important to differentiate these three ways of looking at the well-being of children. They are, in effect, three different statements of objectives for the system concerned with children.

They are not mutually exclusive. We may be more or less committed to one or more of them, depending on the particular problem with which we are concerned, the kind of activity in which we are engaged, and the long-range or short-range view we take. The level and mix of commitment to them will be critical for our views both of the problems of the system and of the nature of an institution designed to deal with those problems.

What are the Outstanding Problems of the System Concerned with the Well-being of Children?

A conference chaired by Dr. Reginald Lourie on January 26 and 27, 1967, revealed a large number of problems relating to the well-being of children.[1] There was considerable agreement about these, particularly about problems relating to the operation of the system itself.

But there is still the need for a more or less systematic view of these problems which would permit us to examine them in relation to one another and to discuss their relative priority.

We have drawn statements of problems from the transcript of the conference referred to above; from the literature (particularly, two White House Conferences on Children); and from some 50 interviews with persons at various administrative levels and in different spheres of the children's service system. We have tried to learn how individuals who function at varying levels and points in the system perceive and attach priorities to these problems.

The following breakdown derives from the schema of the "children's system" outlined earlier.

1. *"First-order" problems of children themselves.* These are problems of disadvantage of disability: abandonment, drug abuse, delinquency, etc. Or they are problems of normal-stream development, e.g., the popular phrase: "Children suffer from the inadequacies of public education."

2. *"Second-order" problems, which are in effect redefinitions or interpretations of first-order problems.* For example: the problems of broken or inadequate families, or the dehumanizing physical and social environment of public housing projects.

3. *Problems of the institutions* directly involved with children; for example, child guidance clinics, elementary schools, and day-care centers.

4. *"Systems" problems:* problems in the interaction, horizontal or vertical, of organizations and agencies within the system.

5. *Problems of innovation and change.* These relate to research on children, to the use of research results, to the difficulties of experiment and learning from experiment, to the diffusion of innovations.

6. *Problems of policy formation:* the difficulties of establishing clear, sustained national policy relating to the well-being of children, and the problems of making that policy effective.

1. *"First-order" problems of children themselves: the disadvantaged and disabled.* The following categories of children represent offshoots from the normal stream of development: the illegitimate child, the abandoned child, the dope addict, the abused, the mentally retarded, the slow learner, the physically handicapped, the mentally ill, the malnourished, the delinquent, the unwed mother, the school dropout, and the unemployed. The following problems are illustrative of these groups:

1. Conference in Washington, D.C., on Strategy and Planning in Child Health and Mental Health.

1. There is a lack of positive self-image which often shows up in socially undesirable behavior. This holds for:

school dropouts, especially young, nonwhite men and women;

young drug addicts who often turn to drugs in search of self-image and relationships with family and peer groups;

unwed mothers, who often seek maternity as a way of finding a useful role.

2. Problems of deviant groups are sometimes reactions to pressure to conform to social standards of the majority, for example:

unwed mothers continue to have illegitimate children although they know about and have access to contraceptive devices;

delinquent behavior tends to stem from frustration of unrealistic aspirations implanted in disadvantaged youths through mass media and education geared to middle-class pocketbooks.

3. Certain kinds of deviancy tend to be family, not individual, problems:

studies show that parents who take drugs—e.g., sleeping pills, tranquilizers—tend to have children who also take drugs;

welfare families sometimes represent a third generation on public assistance and show a marked absence of a father in the home; both problems are often promoted by AFDC;

studies on abused children indicate that in many families a sibling of the child reported has been previously abused.

4. Some kinds of deviancy which become a life style for individuals are forced upon them by a system which is unresponsive to their needs and leads to a manipulation of the system for better payoff. For example:

a small proportion of mothers on welfare may have more illegitimate children to increase their welfare checks;

a small number of Job Corps trainees use the training programs as a cover for hustling, since this brings more lucrative gains than they can expect from the job for which they are training;

young working-age males, particularly nonwhites with poor educational credentials and previous criminal records, may turn to or stay in delinquency because the way into and up the employment structure takes too long, requires too much conformity and regimentation, and is simply uninteresting.

5. Disability, disadvantage, and delinquency may be aggravated by inadequate services:

services for prenatal and postnatal care tend to be disproportionately distributed to white, middle-class mothers; many disadvantaged receive no care;

abandoned children shunted from foster home to foster home often develop severe emotional problems.

Problems of the normal stream. If we look, in contrast, at the problems of children in the normal stream of development, it is clear many of the problems of the disadvantaged and disabled are also problems of the normal stream. But there are differences:

The problems tend not to be as visible (cheating in school in contrast with looting).

They do not involve one-shot or short-term service to the child; rather, children in the normal stream tend to develop long-term involvements with institutions providing them service. The problems of these institutions are, again, of a comprehensive and continuing character.

In medical care problems revolve around:

the provision of comprehensive care, with diagnosis and treatment differentiated to meet the total needs of the child;

continuity of care; in a system of specialists, who replaces the general practitioner?

certain critical shortages: for example, child psychiatrists.

In education:

problems of orienting education toward problems of the future, such as the use of leisure time, future rather than current occupations, occupational mobility, and personal development;

increasing curriculum flexibility and encouraging creativity, which means reformulating and rethinking old standards of measuring learning and educational development;

increasing opportunity for children to exercise responsibility.

In employment:

job opportunities to maximize skill development and promote occupational mobility;

breaking down discriminatory hiring practices;

continuing educational development within occupations.

2. *"Second-order" problems: interpretations of the problems of the individual child.* There are several ways of interpreting problems such as those outlined above. Under one view, we see groups of children as *clusterings of disabilities*—physical handicap tends to be associated with emotional handicap; drug addiction tends to be associated with emotional problems; juvenile delinquency tends to be associated with poverty, with drop-outs, with unemployment, and the like.

Under another view, we see problems center around *sick or broken* families—the abandoned child, the illegitimate child, the abused child, the malnourished child, the delinquent, the school dropout. Almost every category identified earlier is often associated with poor family structure and relationships among family members.

Under a third view, the problems are seen as consequences of *poverty*. Most disadvantaged and disabled children live in an environment of poverty. This view advocates income supplements to the poor, services located in poorer communities, and the involvement of the poor in making their needs clear to those seeking to provide them service.

Each of these views represents an interpretation of "the real problem" underlying symptoms or crises. Each view suggests a different focus for remedial action.

3. *Problems of institutions directly involved with children:* Examples of such institutions are child guidance clinics, schools, day-care centers, hospitals, well-baby and sick-baby clinics, preschool centers, child-family clinics, etc. Each of these institutions encounters problems relating to shortages of money and skilled manpower, development of effective guidelines for service, and the use of research.

There is fragmentation of effort within many agencies along the following lines:

Separate departments within a single agency may conduct their own diagnosis, yielding multiple diagnoses of a single child. Staff members at a neighborhood health center, for example, speak of the family which encountered five different department teams each seeking to diagnose and provide a particular service.

Record keeping tends to be unsystematic; as a consequence there is duplication of information gathering, gaps in data in some areas, and conflicting data in others.

The provision of service is uncoordinated and seldom designed to provide service in light of total client need and continuity in service. There are severe problems in coordination of follow-through services. City welfare agencies, for example, provide compartmentalized services with little awareness of what is happening next door—for example, in the city schools.

Research undertaken within service agencies tends to focus on the problems of a particular department rather than on the total agency or relationships between agencies.

There are shortages of trained professionals in almost every major service category; particularly, probation officers, public health officers, juvenile judges, juvenile practitioners, trained social workers, teachers, doctors, and skilled administrators.

Attempts to bring in subprofessionals have been met with resistance on the part of professional staff. A number of neighborhood health centers report resistance by doctors and nurses to the introduction of paramedical staff.

Problems in training subprofessionals have slowed down the rate of their inflow and acceptance, as, for example, in the experience of training street workers, neighborhood aides, case aides, and medical aides in Montifiori and Lincoln hospitals, Harlem Storefront Academy, and community health projects in Boston.

There are problems in attracting dollar resources. These are reflected in the following kinds of phenomena:

Shortages of facilities (classrooms, day-care centers, local comprehensive satellite clinics, juvenile delinquency facilities) and supplies (teaching materials, audio-visual aids).

Levels of investment are often seen as inadequate to meet minimal requirements, particularly in mental health clinics and juvenile courts.

Agencies tend to screen out the hard-core disadvantaged or multiple handicapped, who are at high risk and require great investment of available manpower and money. There is emphasis on those who "fit" the services provided currently by the agency. Agencies concerned with crippled children tend to emphasize response to children whose *only* impairment is their physical paralysis. Maternity care clinics in large cities tend to emphasize acceptance of white, middle-class, suburban mothers. Later, we will need to examine clusters of tasks and the implications for an institution built around them.

4. *Problems relating to the interaction of organizations and institutions within the system.* There is a mismatch between the organizational structure of agencies concerned with children and the nature of the problems of children. This mismatch takes two forms. First, the problems of disabled or disadvantaged children tend to be multiple. Moreover, they involve many different, interrelated aspects of the lives of children. But agencies concerned with children tend to specialize in particular disabilities and in particular functions (e.g., health, housing, education). With few exceptions, the agencies find it difficult or impossible either to step outside of their specialties or to team up with other agencies so as to respond to the whole child and the whole problem.

For example, welfare departments in many cities provide food stamps to poor families. However, the welfare recipients often find food stamps of only partial use. The stamps do not provide buying power for soap, meat, and other items which are essential.

An instance of the conflict between agencies which curbs their capabilities to cooperate in filling the need of the client as contrasted with carrying out the specifics of the individual programs was encountered at a neighborhood health center. The center cannot convince the Housing Authority that refrigerators are too small to store enough food for large families and that fixing up the roofs on half the houses in the public project would substantially improve health conditions.

The second form of the mismatch between organizational structure and the problems of children relates to the time dimension of these problems. Problems of disabled disadvantaged children tend to endure for long time spans and to be developmental in nature. Agencies, however, are designed to respond to crises and to remain in contact with children only over a relatively brief period. Hospitals respond to medical crises; courts respond when the delinquent is arrested; guidance clinics may respond when the child or family is referred or seeks aid.

In short, there are few *ad hoc* links among such groups, although each may be dealing with the same child. It is difficult to provide *continuity of care* and to respond developmentally. *The tendency is for different agencies to respond disconnectedly to a series of discrete crises which arise in the development of the child.*

Examples of this and tactics used by clients to counter this sporadic treatment appeared throughout our fieldwork. Day-care centers, Head Start programs, prenatal and postnatal clinics, are all examples of agencies which deal with children over a relatively brief, quite defined period of time. In response, families have learned to agency-shop. They may request child welfare services from several different agencies in order to get continuity which is not forthcoming from a single agency.

Problems arise in the relationship between agencies at higher administrative levels in the system and those in direct contact with children. In addition, there is a series of problems which arises in the relationship between agencies and their clients. Local agencies in direct contact with children tend to *distort the intent of programs and policies formulated at higher levels.* This is, at least in part, a function of the field of force in which local agencies operate and their resulting tendency to:

1. define client need in terms of existing services (as seen in the previously mentioned food stamp program and in many child guidance clinics);

2. mold clients to services, and socialize clients to those services;

3. select those clients likeliest to succeed, in terms of agency measures of success, rather than to select in terms of client need; and

4. fight for and compete with other agencies for jurisdiction or power to the detriment of clients.

Several illustrations illuminate the dimensions of the sometimes constructive and sometimes destructive distortion of national policies and programs which we see at the local level. A new neighborhood health center views comprehensive health care as a means of building the political base of the community. Competition for clients has been seen among comprehensive mental health clinics, agencies for the blind, and welfare agencies.

Higher-level administrators and policy makers tend to be cut off from the problems of the field and from the views of children and their families. They are usually more concerned with the planning needs of the agency, the day-to-day administrative matters, and the political fields of force operating within and around their area of coverage. Political savvy is seen by them as critical for their survival and the survival of their agency.

We observe that there is a lack of in-service activities which might bring administrators and fieldworkers together. The need for such interaction is clear. Ways to do this need to be examined and developed.

Children tend to be relatively powerless in relation to agencies, unable to speak for themselves. They often respond through what agencies regard as deviance, or by attempting to "work the agency system" to their own ends, which are different from those of the agencies.

In Boston, the Mothers for Adequate Welfare will not work through fieldworkers. Instead, they go directly to supervisors or to the director when they want action. They insist on educating welfare recipients on federal and state regulations which provide otherwise unknown benefits, and then organize the mothers to demonstrate for these benefits.

5. *Problems of innovation and change in the system:* While there is a great deal of research on children, there is a *lack of research judged as relevant* by those involved in work with children. There is a feeling that too much emphasis has been placed on research in health. Instead emphasis should be on general practice and administration.

Research is done *in laboratory terms* and the *terms of the professional.* This frequently tends to make research unresponsive to real life problems.

Needs for research were itemized as follows: (1) concentration on the *relationship of poverty to various disadvantage and disablement categories;* (2) study of the *total child* and nature of his changing needs through a developmental process; (3) delineation of the *assumptions underlying current actions;* and (4) *identification of ways to intervene at the troublesome or warning spots* which unattended may tend to heighten the degree of the child's problem, so that he becomes delinquent.

There is a tendency to *leave research unused* and to fail to capitalize on the opportunities opened up by research. Researchers often uncover, hidden in unpublished files, studies similar to those they propose. More significantly, those undertaking research tend not to be well connected with administrators who are in a position to implement research findings.

Four Problem Areas

In order to test the view outlined above of problems in service systems which affect the well-being of children, we have taken four specific kinds of problems and related services and examined them in greater detail from the viewpoints of both a local community and the national policy. The areas chosen are day care, juvenile delinquency, nutrition, and compensatory education. Except for their inordinate prevalence among the poor, these problem areas appear to bear little conceptual or organizational relationship to one another. In the case of day care, we looked at national statistics and programs and then in greater detail at how the need is addressed in Boston. We did the same with the problem of nutrition and compensatory education. In the case of juvenile delinquency, we used as our basis for micro-level data the recently issued and very detailed report of the District of Columbia Crime Commission on juvenile delinquency in the District.

1. *Day care—the national scene:* In 1965, there were approximately 24 million children under the age of six in the United States. An estimated 2 million of these children received some form of formal preschool care. Of this group, 76,000 or 3.8 percent were in licensed day-care facilities and were children of working mothers. During this same year, there were an estimated 3.8 million children under six with working mothers. Of this group 1.1 million lived in families with an annual income of less than $3,000.[2]

We have been able to count 26 separate federal programs that can be used in some way to produce day care. Only one is specifically designated for day care. This is the Welfare Administration-administered Title V-Economic Opportunity Act program for children of mothers in Title V training. There has been no concentrated federal effort for construction or development of facilities and training of manpower. A number of the sources of funds are for research and demonstration. Labor Department and Health, Education, and Welfare (HEW) funds can be used for training of day-care aides, but these are not fitted into an ongoing day-care manpower development program. Head Start is the closest approximation to an effort to tie manpower development to the needs of the program.

In the HEW, day-care funds are available through the Office of Education, the Public Health Service, the Children's Bureau, and the Social Rehabilitation Service. In the Office of Economic Opportunity (OEO) funds are available through the regular Community Action Program, the Migrant Program, and Head Start. The Department of Labor has funds for training in several programs, and the Small Business Administration (SBA) provides assistance to private entrepreneurs who wish to start centers. The SBA loan program is modest and does not appear to be coordinated to larger system needs. A system has evolved which is confused and compounded by the lack of clear-cut federal policies.

The city of Boston and day care. There are an estimated 64,700 children under six in Boston. Three thousand children, or 4.6 percent of all chil-

2. *Working Mothers and the Need for Child Care Services,* U.S. Department of Labor, Women's Bureau, May 1967.

dren under six, in Boston were in "licensed" or community-sanctioned day-care services; the national average appears to be 8.3 percent. The licensed services in Boston range from smaller units serving 8 to 12 children to large units serving up to 100 children.[3] The program services offered under the heading of day care range from simply baby-sitting with a snack of milk and crackers to intensive preschool education with psychiatric and health services.

Included in the statistics are programs which function for half a day, twice a week, only during the school year, to those that cover a mother's full working day, five days a week, year round. The reasons for day care range from the mother's need for full-time employment, children with special problems, a temporary place for mothers to leave children for relief, to the rehabilitative purpose of a Head Start program aimed at bringing children to national normal achievement levels.

Eighty percent of the licensed agencies in Boston were private, profit-making groups. Many had initially been started during World War II. They generally reported that the business was highly competitive, and one respondent reported that with an enrollment of 58 and a $495 per capita tuition she had trouble making a profit. Prices ranged from $3,200 per school year to virtually nothing, with most services asking between $200 and $600.

Of the 3,000 children receiving day care in Boston, about 1,200 were from families below the poverty guidelines.[4] They were enrolled in Head Start programs, in United Fund Associated Day Care Services, or in the State Department of Mental Health's guidance centers for mentally retarded children. These organizations tended to run the larger, better-financed, and better-staffed programs with an emphasis on rehabilitative education instead of baby-sitting. The size of their programs fluctuated according to their budget for the year.

Other government agencies were indirectly involved in providing day-care services. The State Division of Child Guardianship and the City Welfare Department were responsible for referring parents to appropriate agencies. The State Department of Welfare had a division in charge of planning family day-care services (the legislature approved such services two years ago but has yet to authorize staff or funds). The Boston Housing Authority provided liaison to other agencies for eight local tenant-run programs. The only agency with any overview was the Community Health Services Division of the State Department of Public Health. This agency inspects and licenses all approved facilities not covered by the educational system. It has no coordinating powers.

3. From listing given by Boston's Community Health Services.
4. Interview with personnel in ABCD Health Services, in Associated Day Care Services of State Department of Mental Health.

Every agency interviewed had sizable waiting lists. Head Start, for instance, had 514 children who qualified under poverty guidelines waiting for places. Welfare mothers had a 60 percent probability of enrolling their children in licensed facilities in September; the rest of the year they had virtually no chance of placing them. Thus, of the 7,600 children under six on Aid to Families of Dependent Children (AFDC) in Boston, about one-sixth received some sort of formal service. Last year, before Head Start expanded, one-twelfth of them would have been served inside the institutional network.[5]

There is also an underground system of unlicensed facilities. Estimates on the number of children served in Boston by the underground system varied from almost none to "a huge number." There are some data available. The City Welfare Department has scattered information on where the mothers using unlicensed facilities send their children—but there has been no attempt to centralize and analyze this material.

Other problems with the formal day-care system are: high costs for private business of providing staffing for the intensive early education, health, and mental health services—there were despairing cries that day-care centers can't break even if they provide good service; lack of public funds to implement existing legislation, such as that passed in 1965 to provide for family day-care services; geographical mismatch between services available and populations needing those services; lack of qualified professional staff.

The lack of definition. Day care was initially defined as any nonfamily educational or caretaking service for three or more children under the age of seven.[6] This definition did not distinguish between nursery or pre-school care for middle-class families and full day care for children of working mothers, nor did it include the latchkey child whose parents are not home to care for him after school is out and who may be temporarily left with neighbors or relatives. Each of these problem "types" raises different questions about the need for and adequacy of institutionalized day care.

There has been a tendency to treat facilities and/or service categories as the major problem—"We need more licensed day-care facilities"—instead of considering alternative approaches to the problems which day-care services attempt to treat, such as:

mothers who must work to support their families;
children who cannot be managed in the home because of emotional or physiological malfunctioning;
children in need of rehabilitation for medical or cultural reasons;
mothers who need temporary or occasional baby-sitting.

5. Interview with John Sharpe of Head Start.
6. Lena E. Cochran and Caroline W. Robinsen, Day Care for Children in Massachusetts, Massachusetts Committee on Children and Youth, Boston.

Is institutionalized or formal care the solution for all of these problems? In some cases, with some ethnic or socioeconomic groups, formal care may be a disservice. Alternatives to institutional care might include: providing mothers in need with income supplements adequate to support their families; carrying Boston Welfare's implicit policy of support for the informal system further and improving the informal service system, e.g., by recognizing and legitimizing it through funding and staff; or by changing licensing requirements so that they measure performance instead of the physical plant.

Each approach appears to stem from a different ideological complex.

One view holds that mothers receiving welfare should work; therefore the problem is to provide full-time institutional care to the children of poor working mothers. If this is indeed the problem, the knowledge and technology for coping with it already exist (e.g., the standards promoted by the Children's Bureau). The necessary resources and commitment remain to be mustered.

Another view stresses the integrity of the family: the child should remain at home with his mother. Here the solution is income support: again, commitment and resources are needed. There are also theories that all children should receive earlier education (as do Russian and Israeli youngsters): do we know how to provide these kinds of services, and which segments of the population respond best to them?

There is a larger view: What is the national concern for children between conception and age six? How adequate is medical care for this population? What role should family counseling play?

Is research on early learning ability discovering new tools to which all children should be exposed at a very early age?

Why do some forms of day care, i.e., Head Start, catch on and become a national cause when other forms of day care have limped along for decades?

How can programs and standards be made more adaptable to changing times and needs?

The licensing issue. Much of the federal concern around day care, in the Children's Bureau for example, has been focused on the issues of standards and licensing. Model standards are offered to the states, and certain matching funds are available only upon the development of satisfactory state licensing laws.

In looking at the microcosm of Boston we learned that many people saw licensing as the main obstacle to entering the formal system. Agencies in Massachusetts are licensed through either the educational or the public health system. Both systems, according to respondents, are outmoded, irrelevant, and extremely difficult to pass through. The building code, designed years ago for public schools and nursing homes, is especially difficult for services which cannot afford the costly "necessary" remodeling.

Actually, licensing is a stumbling block only for those who don't know how to play the system. Of the 56 facilities licensed by the city of Boston in September 1967, only 16 had regular licenses. (One hospital day-care center and 3 run by the State Department of Mental Health were not licensed at all.) The others had provisional or temporary licenses enabling them to operate indefinitely without meeting full requirements. Why some groups get provisional licenses and others get screened out is a question that should be probed.

This appears to be a clear case in which efforts to secure the safety and well-being of children within a relatively narrow definition of day care have served to provide obstacles to program development in this field and to contribute to an informal system of care that goes on in view of and generally outside of the range of interest of authorities and those responsible for official systems of care.

2. *Nutrition*: The material gathered about nutrition can be divided into three areas: (a) the problem definition; (b) the solutions offered; (c) the process of implementing solutions.

Problem definition. There is not in the United States a *widespread* problem of clinical malnutrition, if malnutrition is defined by diseases (such as rickets, beriberi, kwashiorkor) directly related to nutritional deficits. One tends to find these diseases in isolated pockets of deprivation, such as among the Indians, the poor whites in Appalachia, and migrant workers. Essentially, then, obvious clinical malnutrition is limited in incidence and essentially invisible to the general population.

Borderline malnutrition is characterized by the nutritionists as substandard diet. Data show that this is prevalent in the inner city, where children tend to receive less than the required amounts of vitamins A and C and proteins. Similar findings are reported in a few rural studies. Interestingly enough, this is also true in higher economic groups, but the deficit is less dramatic. The difficulty in problem definition here is that the substandard diet causes no direct medical problem that can be attributed to the diet. For instance, one finds infants in the slums dying of pneumonia which may be caused initially by the greater susceptibility to a disease because of a bad diet, but the diagnosis of the disease is pneumonia and not malnutrition. Second, anemia which is present in slum groups to a larger degree than nonslum groups can be attributed to poor diet, but it can also be caused by a number of other medical nondietary reasons. Third, poor diet can be caused by a number of reasons other than the simple availability of money, eating habits, and the knowledge of how to shop and how to prepare food. Thus we see a widespread concern among the nutritionists about a nutrition problem in terms of the fact that inner-city people do not eat the desirable amount of the required food. But it is difficult to make the case dramatic, since the diet is not reflected in obvious medical indicators and the diet may be only one of a number of factors causing poor health.

Multiple solutions. The services brought to bear on nutritional problems reflect varying degrees of confidence in the family's ability to choose foods properly and varying ideas on the processes for influencing changes to improve family diet habits. The problems are threefold: (1) the simple dispersement of food and/or money; (2) education and information dissemination; (3) the organization of the community to press claims for more resources.

1. The first area, the direct dispersement of food and/or money, represents the largest program in the area of nutrition. It is estimated that on the federal level, close to $2 billion is spent on the disbursement of food via the school lunch/milk programs, food surplus programs, and food stamp programs.[7] One could look at this area as illustrating varying degrees of confidence in the family or individuals in purchasing food.

The largest program in this area is the school-lunch school-milk program. In effect, this gives prepared food directly to the recipient, in this case children, and in effect bypasses the family entirely. While this program is large, the coverage is not nearly complete. For instance, in Boston we find only 20 percent of the schoolchildren receiving the school lunch. It is estimated that about 90 percent of the schoolchildren in the Boston area receive milk, but this is a maximum figure; it is based on the pints of milk distributed each day against the total school attendance, which may mean that some children take more than one milk and others take none at all.[8] Another problem that occurs here is that children do in fact have the fifteen cents a week in their pocket, but they may instead buy a Coke or potato chips, which seems to be the snack diet in the ghetto. There are also the OEO experimental breakfast programs. These, however, are limited in number, and we did not find any breakfast programs in Boston. We found one experimental pilot project in Wellesley.

The second program is the food surplus program. This allows some discretion to the family in that the food can or cannot be used by the family. There are problems related to teaching people how to prepare food and also to use food which might not be in their particular diet pattern.

The third program, the food stamp program, allows still further discretion on the part of the recipient. In this case food stamps are sold to designated poor populations for a certain amount of money, allowing them to purchase food worth a larger amount of money. Thus we find that while the recipients are restricted to purchasing food, they have a far wider choice of which food they buy.

The fourth alternative is the simple disbursement of money as it

7. Dr. Ogden Johnson, U.S. Public Health Service.
8. Based on lunch statistics supplied by John Starker, Boston School Department, Boston School Lunch Program.

comes through welfare. This, of course, allows the recipient to buy or not to buy food.

Thus we see in the disbursement of talk resources for nutrition the varieties of initiative allowed on the part of the recipient and variety of initiative taken on by the government. The choice of program is influenced by conflicting federal policies about what the recipient is capable of managing on his own as well as by the Agriculture Department policies concerning what foods are in surplus.

2. Another view of the way to obtain better nutrition is not simply the disbursement of money or food but, rather, teaching the recipients how to buy their food and stretch the dollar, how to plan shopping lists and how to prepare the food. One finds nutrition education components in various poverty programs. Beth Israel's program components in Boston and the Columbia Point Neighborhood Health Center both have nutritionists. It is said that some HUD model cities programs will have nutritionists. Some of the settlement houses and family services provide a nutritionist-home-maker type of service. This is in response to a need to help mothers plan meals better and to learn how to shop. In Boston the coverage of nutrition education programs is very limited. For instance, the Martha Elliot Clinic in Jamaica Plain holds family meal-planning classes for mothers, but they have only about 10 mothers in their classes out of a possible population of 1,700 families.[9] Among the nutritionists interviewed, most mentioned their traditional role had been to accept referrals from doctors for patients who were on bad diets. However, they noted that there is a trend for nutritionists to move out in the community and there is a sense of the need to hold classes or individual counseling with mothers. As with a number of other new programs, there was a sense of a need, but there was some confusion about how best to reach these mothers. It is also clear that the budget for nutrition components in poverty projects remains small. For instance, in the Beth Israel program, the budget for the nutritionist comes to $7,000 out of a $300,000 budget, or roughly 2 percent of the total budget.[10]

In addition to the fact that the money input to the nutrition component of poverty programs is small, there is also a confusion about how to involve mothers in nutritional education and how to spread the knowledge of the nutritionists to a much wider segment of the population.

3. A third area seems to fall under the definition of community organizing activities. The activities here are buying clubs, comparative shopping, and picketing of businesses believed to be cheating consumers. These seem to try to make business more responsive and more responsible in the ghetto.

9. Dr. Irving Silverman, director of Child Care Project, Beth Israel Hospital, Boston, Massachusetts.
10. Miss L. Cutter, Martha Elliot Clinic, Boston.

Questions that come up here are the fact that one hears frequently that the prices in supermarkets in the ghetto go up on the first and fifteenth of each month—days when welfare checks are distributed. Reports of this come from Watts and Roxbury.

We find several examples of this kind of activity under several OEO programs. In Boston, for instance, ABCD (Boston's poverty agency) organizes buying clubs in which they eliminate the middleman. They started out by purchasing large amounts of eggs outside the city and then distributing them to members of the clubs. They claim to have had participation of about 7,000 families out of a total possible 120,000 families in the areas which they serve.[11] MAW (Mothers for Adequate Welfare) publishes comparative shopping lists of different supermarkets that serve the ghetto areas. There is also a Buyer's Coop in Chicago which lists all the prices per ounce so that the patrons can more easily do comparison shopping, and they also provide counseling on nutrition and food planning. OEO has funded a major demonstration project in consumer action and education in the San Francisco Bay area, which has both consumer education and the organization of consumer groups as its goal.

In the area of community organization, as in the education area, development is still in a very early stage. The number of participants is small. Programs are described as good or successful, but still remain in a very tentative "demonstration" state.

The process of implementing solutions. In the area of nutrition there are the usual "process" or "institutional" problems. They fall roughly in six categories: (1) the vertical problems between federal intent versus local and state discretion; (2) the data problem; (3) the knowledge of the client-group problem—What are his values? How do you motivate him? (4) the mismatch between programs developed and the need; (5) the facilities and manpower problems; (6) the lack of overview of policy.

1. With respect to the *state and local problem* we find that the federal legislation allows the states and the cities to implement or not to implement programs as they choose. South Carolina, with a large poor Negro population, did not implement the food stamp program until picketing and local demand put the pressure on. MAW claimed that in Boston the city welfare department dragged its feet on implementing the food surplus program.

2. *The data problem.* There is a lack of adequate data on the numbers of severely malnourished children. In the South one may find that the people who suffer from the medically diagnosed malnourishment may not reach a hospital. The white doctor may not want to report that a Negro died of kwashiorkor or related nutritional diseases. Second, border-line malnutrition is hard to separate from other causes and may not be

11. Interview with Don Newey of ABCD.

recorded in official diagnoses on death certificates, as noted previously. And on the other hand, borderline malnutrition is also hard to separate from cultural causes. For instance, some Indians will starve a female twin; the solution to this problem clearly is not giving food, but dealing with culture. So the question is: Is this a nutrition problem or is this a cultural problem? Even anemia may derive from a complex of causes, which makes it extremely difficult to identify and pinpoint the number suffering from borderline malnutrition. One has to rely on diet intake. These studies are very expensive and very difficult to administer. Finally there are no broad surveys of nutrition habits in the United States. The Agriculture Department has done some food-eating studies, but these are unsatisfactory. They are designed mainly to find out the overall eating habits of large segments of the population and do not have a medical focus. There are some small studies done in Roxbury, Louisiana, Mississippi, New York, and Ohio. These are felt to be very specialized and difficult to generalize. There is currently in the planning stage a large study of selected persons from the lowest socioeconomic quartile in the United States. This may provide some answers to questions for which we have been unable to obtain answers: (a) What is the percentage of malnourished children in a large population sample? (b) What is the percentage of children receiving deficient diets in a large population sample? (c) Finally, what types of services are being offered to this population?

3. As with the other programs, there is a mismatch between the programs available and the need. For instance, if the pattern noted in the Roxbury study is true for other areas of the country—namely, that the diet of children gets markedly worse as they leave the control of the mother —then one finds a lack of programs to meet the problems of the deteriorating food habits of teen-agers. There is, of course, the school lunch program which is available to them. But as children grow older, they apparently eat breakfasts and dinners which are less sufficient nutritionally. This problem is more pronounced in the slums than in the suburbs. The second area of mismatch is that the well-to-do take advantage of the federal programs that are designed for the poor communities. For instance, the breakfast programs which are designed to meet one of the nutritional lacks of schoolchildren has been implemented in the Wellesley school system while the Boston school system has no breakfast program.[12] Nationwide, in 1967, 4 million children—two-thirds of all impoverished schoolchildren—either paid for their lunch or went without.[13]

4. There is also a facilities and staff problem. One reason given for the fact that Boston schools do not participate as fully in the lunch

12. Calculated from statistics supplied by John Starker, Boston School Department, Boston School Lunch Program.
13. *Hunger, U.S.A.* A Report by the Citizens' Board of Inquiry into Hunger and Malnutrition in the United States (Washington, D.C.: New Community Press, 1968).

program is that, of the 187 schools in Boston, only 37 have lunchrooms. So we find that 140 schools have no lunch program at all.[14] They are experimenting with a pilot project of shipping package lunches to 10 schools which have no cafeterias. There is a study currently under way by the Buildings Facilities Department in Boston to look at ways in which lunches might be developed for the schools which do not have lunches—whether to have a central kitchen or whether to add cafeterias. It is not the lack of federal funds, however, that is holding back the expansion of the lunch program in Boston, but the lack of building space in which to prepare these lunches and adequate staff to educate community members in their use.

5. The fifth area one encounters is the cross-cultural problem, i.e., what are the values—what are the motivations—involved in reaching the hard-core people on insufficient diets? One example of this particular problem is how to get the best value for the shopping dollar. The federal government has responded to this need by publishing a comparative shopping list with detailed instruction on how to evaluate the cost of different products. Clearly, this is a response to a need; however, this list is so complicated and requires so long to work out that the people who would profit from it most simply would never cope with it. Further, taking advantage of cost reductions often requires immediate cash resources which the poor seldom have. The question remains, given the need, what kinds of programs will the target population participate in, what kinds of information will they work from?

6. Again, it is quite clear that no one agency has an overview of the problem in nutrition. The largest input, in terms of money, comes from the Agriculture Department, which is primarily oriented toward maintaining the agricultural section of the economy. We see examples such as a large push for a milk program being undertaken when there was a milk surplus.

Nutrition groups participate very marginally in programs. There are advocate groups which represent the spectrum that is usually encountered. There are the various church and YMCA groups who advocate increased lunch programs. Whether or not they have examined other alternative ways to increase the nutritional input in children is hard to say, but our guess would be that they have not. At the other end of the spectrum, there is a national commission which has examined malnutrition and hunger in the United States. Their activities range widely, from encouraging community organization, holding regional hearings to inform state and local officials and allowing the poor to speak, encouraging Congressional hearings pushing for federal grants for nutrition studies, to planting articles in magazines. When members of the commission were asked what they viewed as their

14. Interview with Don Newey of ABCD.

ultimate goal, they were unclear. They were aware of a large-scale need for action, but they were unable to say where the most effective points of leverage were or to specify the nature of the major part of the problem.

3. *Juvenile delinquency*: The problem of juvenile delinquency differs from that of day care services and improved nutrition. Juvenile delinquents or predelinquents are screened into a system which purports to rehabilitate them for wrongs they have committed or are likely to commit against society. Day care and malnutrition programs, on the other hand, are designed to prevent or treat problems, not to deal with them after indications of distress have already been noted. Juvenile delinquency is a more obvious problem in today's society and represents something close to a crisis situation to which we have yet to develop an effective response.

The longer view. The national government has a variety of different programs aimed at combating juvenile delinquency. OEO works through the Job Corps, Upward Bound, and neighborhood antipoverty programs. Labor provides work-training and placement programs under the Bureau of Work Programs, the Youth Employment Council, and the Bureau of Employment Security. In HEW, there are various rehabilitational programs under the Office of Education; Welfare runs work-training programs under AFDC and research and demonstration projects under the Office of Juvenile Delinquency and Youth Development. It also provides technical assistance through the Children's Bureau. In the Department of Justice, the Bureau of Prisons has a division for juvenile and youth institutions, while the Board of Parole has a Youth Corrections Division. The President's Committee on Juvenile Delinquency and Youth Crime works on coordinating the various federal agencies involved in the well-being of the nation's youth. There is no separate juvenile court system; its structure, status, and degree of independence vary from state to state.

These programs represent a substantial effort to reduce the incidence of juvenile delinquency. The effort, unfortunately, has lost much of its impact because of its lack of focus. Each subdivision works on its view of its part of the job, but few work with other sections to provide a coordinated, concentrated program with explicit talks and responsibilities.

On the national level, the existing system for formal treatment has not been able to cope effectively with juvenile offenders for some years now (if the objective is to rehabilitate them and return them to society) and is becoming increasingly less capable of handling the problem while the proportion of juvenile offenders to total population between ten and seventeen steadily rises. In 1960 there were 514,000 nontraffic cases brought before the juvenile court, involving 443,000 youths, 1.8 percent of the youth population. In 1966 the proportion of American juvenile offenders (nontraffic) had risen 18 percent to form 2.1 percent of the youth population: 745,000 cases involving about 641,000 children between ten and seventeen came before the juvenile courts. The current estimate is that

1 out of every 9 children nationally will appear in court by the time he or she reaches nineteen.[15]

A significant proportion of serious crimes are committed by juveniles:

In 1965, persons under eighteen referred to juvenile court constituted 24 percent of all persons charged with forcible rape, 34 percent of all persons charged with robbery, 52 percent of all persons charged with burglary, 45 percent of all persons charged with larceny, and 61 percent of all persons charged with auto theft. The figures appear in the 1965 FBI Uniform Crime Reports (23) and are quoted by the President's Task Force on Juvenile Delinquency and Youth Crime.

Many youthful offenders do not enter the formal treatment system. Often they are never reported to the police; of those that do come in contact with the police, roughly half are never brought to court. Although studies show that most high school and college youths also engage in delinquent acts at some time, both those reported by the police and those brought to court tend to be members of lower-class and minority groups. We have more extensive data on the children referred to court: they tend to be male (1 out of every 6 in the country), especially urban Negro males. Nine out of every 10 urban Negro males will be arrested for something more serious than a traffic accident during their lives. Many of them will come from low-income, broken families, have brothers who are already criminals, and be uneducated or mentally retarded.

Thirty to 40 percent of the children appearing in juvenile court have been there before, about half of them during that same year. Of every 100 children brought before the court, 21 are put on probation: 4 of them violate probation before discharge; 9 of the original 100 are committed to an institution; 3 of those 9 have been institutionalized as juvenile offenders before; 4 of the 9 are committed for such offenses as smoking, drinking, truancy, and being "unmanageable"; 1 out of 9 runs away before a year has passed. The institution spends an average of slightly more than $3,000 a year to rehabilitate each youth. A sizable number of these juvenile offenders graduate to the adult penitentiaries, where they compose half of the inmates.

In 1963 there were approximately 2,230 judges presiding over juvenile courts. Most of them viewed the job as a low-status rung on the way up a career ladder. Seventy-two percent of those who were full-time judges spent

15. *Task Force Report: Juvenile Delinquency and Youth Crime.* Report on Juvenile Justice and Consultants Papers, The President's Commission on Law Enforcement and Administration of Justice (Washington, D.C.: U.S. Government Printing Office, 1967); President Lyndon B. Johnson, Message on Welfare of Children, Feb. 8, 1967; *Federal Programs Assisting Children and Youth,* U.S. Department of Health, Education, and Welfare, Social and Rehabilitation Service, Children's Bureau, Interdepartmental Committee, Committee on Children and Youth (Washington, D.C.: U.S. Government Printing Office, July 1967); *Statistics on Public Institutions/or Delinquent Children.* Statistical Series No. 81, U.S. Department of Health, Education, and Welfare, Children's Bureau, 1965; *Ibid.,* No. 86, 1966.

less than a quarter of their time on juvenile matters. Each judge averaged 269 nontraffic juvenile referrals that year. Each juvenile hearing averaged 3 to 15 minutes in length. One-third of the courts had no probation officers or social workers. Four-fifths did not have psychiatric or psychological services available on a regular basis. If such services were accessible, they were usually for diagnosis only, not for treatment.

In 1966, 223,800 children were under probation for periods ranging from 3 to 36 months at a cost of $75,916,000, or an average of $335 per child for that year. One-hundredth of 1 percent of them were in case loads of fewer than 20; 10.6 percent of them were in case loads of more than 100. Most were in case loads of from 70 to 80. Probation workers were paid from $1,500 to $11,000 a year, receiving a median salary of $5,500. There were few opportunities for promotion. Resignations were frequent, and staff vacancies tended to remain open. Few social workers train for the juvenile courts, since they can find better-paying jobs with better futures elsewhere.

Although lack of suitable detention facilities was frequently cited as a problem, both nationally and on local levels, two-thirds of the juveniles apprehended in 1965 were put in detention facilities. The average stay was 12 days at a cost of $120 per child. The total cost was more than $53,000,-000. Forty-four percent of the children were kept in county jails for lack of other space, although these facilities had often been declared unsuitable even for adults.

For the most part, the overloaded detention facilities were not used for children who threatened the community or had no home of their own, but as a form of psychological deterrence. There were other, more effective, preventive methods available. Rational distribution of staff and resources has not been characteristic of the juvenile courts. Intake workers research juveniles to recommend dispositions according to class, race, residence, and age, not type of delinquency and background of alleged offender—nor, at times, truth of allegation. Probation officers do case studies the judge cannot find time to read. Courts refer youths to facilities that will not or cannot accept them—and the child remains in limbo while the agencies argue about jurisdiction.

In 1965 the number of nontraffic arrests of juveniles in Washington, D.C., had increased 64 percent over 1960. The number of referrals to juvenile court increased 74 percent between 1960 and 1966, while the number of commitments to the two principal juvenile institutions increased by 33 percent and 60 percent. We do not know the increase in population between ten and seventeen for this period: we are told it is far less than the increase in juvenile crime.[16] (We have no information on the changing

16. *Report of the President's Commission on Crime in the District of Columbia* (Washington, D.C.: U.S. Government Printing Office, 1966).

composition of the city: How much of the crime rise can be correlated with, e.g., a growing number of Negro poor?)

The juvenile court system in D.C. is roughly similar to the national one described above. In 1965, 11,700 nontraffic juvenile offenders were reported to the police; 54 percent (6,264) of these reports resulted in arrest; 50 percent (5,913) of them, involving 3,467 individuals, were referred to juvenile court. When all referrals were combined, 6 out of every 100 youths between ten and seventeen in D.C. had been referred to court. Sixty-one percent of these youths (2,115) had been to court at least once before; 42 percent (1,456) had been to court at least twice before; 58 percent (2,017) of those referred to court were placed in temporary detention at the Receiving Home, where 56 percent of the children are repeaters. Of the 9,780 *1966* court dispositions on delinquents, 6.2 percent were referrals to residential institutions (compared to 8.5 percent nationally); 4.9 percent of the referrals were to the Children's Center, where 33½ percent of the inmates are repeaters; 1.3 percent (125) were to the National Training School, where more than 40 percent of the inmates had previously been committed to the Children's Center. The cycle continues: more than 50 percent of the population of adult criminal institutions in Washington had records as juvenile offenders; more than 31 percent of them had been committed to juvenile institutions.

This high degree of recidivism in a relatively small population (6 percent of D.C. youth) suggests two things: (1) there is a group of "repeaters" who pass from one subsystem to another; once a child is screened into the system, he has a fair probability of remaining in that system all the way through to the adult penitentiaries; (2) the delinquency treatment system as it now operates is not effectively rehabilitating juvenile offenders. Those who are initially screened out of the system remain in society; those who are brought into the system tend to move further away from society's norms. (We do not know if those children committed for minor offenses, such as truancy, drinking, running away, etc., form part of the group that go on through the system. If they do, the system not only fails to rehabilitate offenders, but also turns nonserious offenders into criminals.)

One possible reason for the ineffectiveness of the system is the shortage of facilities. The Children's Center and the National Training School have a total physical capacity of 907 youths: they often serve more than that capacity. The Receiving Home frequently doubles its capacity (discrepancy between capacity and number of referrals is due to length of commitment: a child may well stay more than one year). Lack of adequate facilities may result in no action at all, as when children are detained in the Receiving Home for six months while the court's intake section decides what to do with them; or, the lack can lead to diverting children out of the system that was assigned to serve their needs and into other, separate systems. Several children were referred to the adult criminal court directly; others were referred to adult penitentiaries when the Children's Center found them unmanageable.

Not only are there too few physical plants, but also there is a serious lack of trained manpower. Cedar Knoll at the Children's Center has one part-time psychiatrist for an average population of 485 children, many of whom are emotionally disturbed. Maple Glen, also part of the Children's Center, has three caseworkers for an average population of 227.

The limited data available indicate that money is also a problem in D.C. and that where there is money available, it is not always used in the most effective manner. In 1966 the welfare department ran the Children's Center on a budget of $7,058,758. Including aftercare clients, they served at least 3,250 children that year at a cost of $2,170 per child or less. The population served included 1,200 mentally retarded in the District Training School. The District of Columbia is now building a $4 million maximum security institution for 150 youths—spending $26,667 apiece on each of the most difficult cases.

The information available indicates that in 1966, D.C. spent roughly $11 million on treating juvenile delinquency, compared to the $8.7 million it spent on prevention programs between 1961 and 1966. The total for prevention is a rough figure: it includes expenditures by incentive programs for misdemeanants, Neighborhood Youth Corps and similar programs, halfway houses, the Cardozo demonstration project, day-care services for the socially deprived, group foster homes, recreation, services for unwed mothers, employment counseling, discussion groups, and outreach comprehensive youth programs. It excludes programs run by the Boy Scouts, Campfire Girls, and public school system: special social adjustment classes, classes for returned dropouts, a special school for pregnant girls, and a special junior and senior high school for youth presenting the worst behavior problems.

Most of these programs share such common features as: (1) isolating the potential deviant from the normal population (the Boy Scouts have a special troop of boys under juvenile court jurisdiction); (2) low funding ($94,550 to provide fidelity bonding for 300 people with court records: $315 per person); (3) low staffing (the ratio of counselors to pupils within the school guidance and counseling programs is 1 to 738); (4) serving a small proportion of the total potentially delinquent population (the Neighborhood Development Youth Program Centers had a $242,505 grant for five and a half months to serve 160 children at an annual cost of roughly $3,125 per child).

Most of the D.C. prevention programs are aimed at combating the effects of poverty, evidently based on the assumption that juvenile delinquency is usually a symptom of poverty. Certainly there is a high correlation between poverty and juvenile delinquency: whether that is because the poor commit the most juvenile crimes or because the poor get screened into the juvenile crime system is still a subject of debate. More data are needed on the various "causes" of the different "kinds" of juvenile delinquency and the best treatment to remove or alleviate these causes. Attacking the symptoms of poverty may not be the best or the only answer.

We need answers to questions like: How many of the juvenile delinquents who come into contact with the police force are poor? Why don't all poor juveniles get picked up by the police? Is poverty the most significant characteristic delinquents have in common or is the more commonly shared feature an attribute of such variables as race, broken family, poor-quality schools, discrimination, mental retardation, or emotional disturbance owing to any one of the above-mentioned factors? What kinds of prevention methods have been the most successful (measured in return to the values of the majority of society) in cutting the delinquency rate of a given population, a given ethnic group, a given local area?

The existing prevention and treatment programs do not form a system in the sense that a number of defined components serving discrete populations or discrete needs of overlapping populations interact in a set pattern. There may well be informal linkages between different agencies, but formally there is little coordination of service or client. We have no information on which agency serves which clients (and which clients it rejects, perhaps a more important piece of data).

We have no information on what happens to a child before and after a particular agency screens him in. How many youths are being served by several prevention programs at once, each supposedly helping a separate population? How many different programs in both prevention and control have any idea of what is going on in other programs in the same area serving the same need? A child is picked up by the police, delivered to a separate intake system at the juvenile court, released to a court probation officer who has no time to keep track of him, or turned over to a welfare department institution which assigns a new worker to follow him through treatment and aftercare. Each system has a separate set of records and separate personnel. Records may be so poor that a child is detained six months while court intake checks him out.

The linkages between the prevention and treatment systems also lack coordination. How much feedback is there between systems? Does the juvenile court know what happens to the children on probation in prevention programs, and what effects the court has on those children who are still only potentially delinquent? Do the prevention programs follow up the children they have served who get referred to the court by the police, by the schools, by the welfare department, and by their parents?

4. *Compensatory Education*: A brief survey of the compensatory education programs in Boston and on the national level reveals characteristics similar to those noted in our survey of nutrition and of day care. There are

competing definitions of what compensatory education is "compensating for." Even when definitions with their implied goals have been decided upon, it is difficult to isolate compensatory education from other factors affecting the child. Finally, current programs serve only a limited percentage of the target populations, and attempts at innovation are limited and difficult to generalize; at least, people in the established agencies have a very fragmentary sense of the attempts at change within their field.

Problem definition. One finds many measures or indicators in general currency which are used to pinpoint the need for improved education. To list a few: the school dropout rate; underachievement; falling below national norms on the standard tests; failure to receive "a rich and full educational experience." With these varying definitions one finds varying programs for differing target populations. For the dropout there are programs such as Job Corps camps and Neighborhood Youth Corps. For the underachiever there are tutorial programs and Upward Bound-type programs. For children who are achieving below national norms there are the Title I programs designed to beef up the ongoing educational system. Finally, as a response to "full and rich educational experience for the child" there are attempts to revitalize the whole educational system. In this case compensatory education might consist of experiments from the New School in Roxbury all the way to Exeter or Andover and any number of private schools which are trying to provide a fuller educational experience than is currently available in the public school system.

Change and innovation. All four levels of activity listed above take place in Boston, and again our findings relating to coverage and innovation are similar to those in day care and nutrition. Despite the activity, the coverage is extremely limited and there is not a large amount of innovation apparent.

By far the largest program in terms of money and people involved is the Title I project in Boston. It involves 36 school districts, approximately 20,000 pupils out of a total pupil population of 93,000, and has a budget of $3.6 million. Its intent is to be compensatory, but much of the feedback on the Title I project in Boston is that it provides more of the same old thing. Looking through proposals, one sees that some of the budget money went for increased salaries of teachers who were already on the staff. There was, however, an addition of 150 teachers so that the class size was lowered. A number of specialists were also added, among whom were music and art teachers and 50 teacher aides. The school department claims to have increased the test scores of the students involved, but their study was not felt to be innovative enough by a number of education people outside the School Department.[17] The interesting fact is that the Boston school

17. Source requested not to be identified.

system, in attempting to provide compensatory education within the formal system, follows the pattern of most professions which are reforming from within. They tend to upgrade what already exists.

Somewhat more favorable reports were given about the subsystems set up within the Title I project, that is, the Bordman School and the Lewis Junior High School, which take up about $1 million of the Title I funds. Here the classes were very small, and one hears talk of a less totalitarian atmosphere in the schools.

The largest program (Title I), involving the most people and the largest amount of money, seems to have made no significant impact on the system as indicated by the testimony of people who have done work through Harvard or ABCD.[18]

Programs which are more comprehensive, such as Job Corps, Head Start, and Upward Bound, also work in the Boston public school scene. Here, although the programs themselves may be thorough and innovative, they are extremely limited in coverage. For instance, the Job Corps received only 275 youths ("youth" being defined as the age span between sixteen and twenty-one). In this age range there are over 66,000 children in Boston. If one calculates on the basis of the fact that 17 percent of the families in Boston earn less than $3,000, this is a very small proportion of the target population. The Neighborhood Youth Corps, which also attempts to reach this particular age group, accommodates only 800 youths a year in Boston at a cost of almost $900,000. Head Start covers only 1,200 children.[19] The figures for Upward Bound no doubt are also very small in relation to the target population, but the total figure for Boston was not available.

Several characteristics of these programs are:

a. They are all extremely expensive. Job Corps runs from $10,000 to $15,000 per year per trainee. The Neighborhood Youth Corps runs about $1,000, even though it involves part-time work and no residence expenses. Upward Bound runs in the neighborhood of $1,500 a year per trainee, even though it is primarily a summer program.

b. All programs share similar problems in recruiting. They tend to cream in their own way. Job Corps receives applicants primarily from state employment agencies; Upward Bound frequently from high school counselors who send their star pupils. And it has been suggested that juvenile court and other places might provide more challenging clients.

c. These programs also have problems retaining their clients. Job Corps loses 50 percent of its trainees in the first 90 days; most of them are the rural whites.

18. ABCD Evaluation of Title I Programs in Boston.
19. Robert Coord, Department of Statistics, ABCD.

Similarities

Despite the many differences in the four problem areas—day care, nutrition, delinquency, and compensatory education—these programs do share a set of similar problems and patterns.

1. In each field there is a large unmet need. Without even addressing the question of how to innovate or change, there is simply not enough of what already exists. In day care, for instance, if one takes the most well-known and best-financed program, such as New York, only 4,000 of a potential population of 60,000 are reached. In nutrition one finds that the best-financed program in the field, the school lunch program, reaches only about 20 percent of the children in Boston. Institutions for juvenile delinquents are overcrowded, and judges select the less severe cases in the potential population.

2. In each field there is a mismatch between the population served and the population in most severe need. In day care, working middle-class mothers have a greater chance of obtaining day care for their children than do poorer working mothers. Private facilities are expensive; free facilities have long waiting lists. Licensing and standards, lobbied for by day-care associations with the intention of protecting children from bad care, have proven so prohibitive that they have made it impossible to set up a legal day-care center for children under three in Massachusetts.

As a result those who find day care are more enterprising at locating an underground day-care group or forming an informal cooperative. This group probably is only a small portion of the population in need. In New York, Head Start centers are located where there are classrooms. As a result some centers have waiting lists and others have vacancies. In the field of nutrition one finds that the school lunch programs are more fully exploited in the suburbs than they are in the ghetto. The facilities, regulations, and availability of cafeteria space determine the extent to which a school can take advantage of a lunch program. The federal government disperses close to $2 billion in various food programs, but only $2 million of that is earmarked for facilities expansion.

Juvenile courts and the police tend to provide service to youth not on the basis of type or severity of problem, but on criteria of residence or race.

Programs in all four areas are biased in the direction of client populations that have money, facilities, information, and/or connections. Programs do not meet hard-core need.

3. In each field there is an informal, underground system. Most mothers in Boston's Title V program send their children to unlicensed day-care centers. The federal government does publish comparative shopping sheets to help consumers get more for their food dollar, but they have

proved unworkable; it is grass-roots organizations in Boston who publish comparative prices of the supermarkets in the ghetto. Police may let a youth go because the detention house is overcrowded or the backlog of the courts is long or because the officer feels the youth will not be a repeater.

These informal systems may indicate either that current programs are not extensive enough or that they are inappropriate.

4. In each field there is a multiplicity of agencies involved at federal, state, local, public, and private levels. Thus, it is not surprising that there is confusion, lack of overview, and inability to set priorities. It is still unclear in Boston whether the health department or the welfare department will be responsible for the new family day-care centers. In nutrition, at least six federal agencies are involved; however, the major portion of the money for various food programs is dispersed through a department whose interest is not focused on children, that is, the Department of Agriculture. The multiplicity of activity is also reflected on the city level. Even in the same city, people are completely unaware of what their counterparts are doing across town, let alone aware of activities in similar programs in other cities, or of research and program innovation.

In each field, then, it is difficult or impossible to provide an overview or set priorities.

5. In each field there are problems of definition. It is difficult to determine how many children need day care. The nutritionists say they cannot estimate the number of children suffering from malnutrition, though they feel there is a problem.

The data are based on the definition of what one means by terms such as day care, juvenile delinquency, and nutrition. In each field there are competing definitions of the same problem which result in different estimates as well as in different programs. For one person, day care is for the working mother, and its function is custodial. For another, day care is enrichment for the child, and its function is educational; for yet another, day care is supplemental for the child, and its function is to fortify the child so that he can face a hostile future. Nutrition can be measured on a scale from what is necessary to avoid starvation to what is desirable for optimal health.

While the analysis of similarities among these four areas could be carried much further, enough has been said, perhaps, to indicate that the kinds of problems outlined earlier continue to show up in these four areas when they are examined in some detail.

Problems in Management and Policy Formation. A series of problems has been implicit in earlier discussions but not yet spelled out—namely, problems relating to the management of service systems (ranging from individual agencies to national systems) and to the formation of policy. One way of formulating these is as follows:

1. *Problems in the availability of data.* There is a paradox about data in the field of services to children. On the one hand, there are a great many data—on numbers of children in various categories, on services provided, on related phenomena of many kinds. Indeed, the welter of available data is overwhelming. But little of this data is usable, and even less is in fact used. One administrator at the Bureau of Vital Statistics points to the great amounts of data which could be used for fairly sophisticated evaluation and analysis, but are not used. Many agencies—neighborhood service centers, for example—have backlogs of data that no one has the time or inclination to analyze; and it is not clear to agency administrators who should analyze them. That is to say, agencies tend not to see data analysis as an internal function. And few outside the agency are aware of what information exists and what might be done with it.

On the other hand, when an attempt is made to come to grips with data from the point of view of management—for example, in order to estimate need or demand; evaluate services; relate dollars and manpower to competing requirements; set priorities; identify problems—then there is an almost total absence of usable data. There is, in effect, an overwhelming data gap.

Data that exist tend to be—

confused, because of the ambiguity of terms, or
because of overlapping categories;
    fragmentary;
    unreliable.

This tends to be true throughout the hierarchy of services to children—from the individual agency, to the neighborhood or community, to the city, state, and federal levels.

Why does such a data deficiency exist? Our attempts to collect relevant data in preparation of this report suggest some possible answers. Current data collection seems to fit existing administrative structure. It does not appear to be relevant to program content, program or agency effectiveness, or service need. Data are collected along hierarchical lines starting with the local agency, going perhaps to the state level, and finally being aggregated at the national level.

Each bureau at the federal, state, and local level tends to collect data to justify existing organizational arrangements. One finds data which indicate the number of children served or treated by each agency, work load measurements in terms of staffing ratios and staffing patterns, and perhaps deviation of staffing patterns from prescribed staffing patterns in terms of numbers of social workers per client. In general, one receives a rough indication of how much was accomplished in terms of how many children were served. For example, in the Children's Bureau one finds data as to the number supported in day care and foster homes, and the number of day-care centers, and also one can get some aggregate cost figures on foster homes and day-care programs. In general, such data tend to justify the existence of the service and to support increased appropriations for the service. In other words, data collection is largely in terms of developing a bargaining package for legislators in order to gain larger appropriations, which in turn will lead to organizational expansion, which in turn will lead to the achievement of occupational interests. The data indicate that more children ought to be served and that more day-care centers are needed. Further, data collected by public agencies tend to accept professional standards of performance; here, one finds an alignment between the public bureaucratic operation and the professional interests of the service system.

What one does not find is either cost-effectiveness or cost-benefit data. It is not clear in terms of child input-output measures just exactly what day-care centers are supposed to produce or, in fact, do produce in a cost-effectiveness sense. Data are not available which would enable one to measure the value of the system in terms of benefit return. Apart from measuring its productivity or even providing data which are sufficiently discrete so that legislators could make certain kinds of choices, to increase the return on public dollars invested, one has difficulty finding data that will even indicate in a rough quantitative sense what the nature of the present system is. We really do not know precisely the nature of the child inputs, how and why they are flowing through the existing agencies, and what happens to them after they come out of the agencies. There is little or no follow-up, nor is there any disciplined evaluation of programs. What happens to children after they become exits from a particular service? Why do certain children get into the system and others do not? Why do certain agencies provide certain kinds of services? Where are these located? In other words, the data do not give us a good description of the existing system. Perhaps such data exist, but at least in this initial effort, we have been unable to find them, and there is some question as to whether they do in fact exist.

The problem of data availability, in turn, underlies the following problems of management and policy formation.

2. *Problems in the identification of problems.* There is, as we have seen, a lack of well-defined problems. Problems of children, and of service systems related to them, get defined from a variety of conflicting views. Symptoms and causes of symptoms are confused with one another. There is a greater wealth of prescriptions for solution than of careful definitions of problems.

One sees this in the conflicting recommendations of the recent White House Conference on Children. For instance, one recommendation stressed importance of family planning; a later recommendation indicated that family planning is irrelevant.

Administrators tend to stress political and administrative problems. Field personnel may stress hard-to-place children or "star" clients. Researchers tend to disregard planning, and planners tend to see little value in research. Internal agency views of the problem are rarely unified. Within an agency, we may hear at any one time staff saying that the problem is the multiproblem child, or hard-core deviant, or the family, or poverty, or race . . .

The same problems get identified, at a national level, over long periods of time. Compare the lists of the White House Conferences of 1930 and 1960. The similarities are striking. Is this because of the ritual nature of these conferences? The lack of resources devoted to the problems? The persistence of patterns of problem, in spite of what has been done? To what extent have the underlying symptoms changed while we still call the problem by the same name?

3. *Problems in establishing priorities.* At all levels within the service system, the issue of priorities arises. Where need, or even demand, far exceeds available resources, how are manpower and money to be allocated? At the level of the individual agency, resources tend to be allocated to the client judged most likely to succeed, by agency criteria, rather than to cases of greatest need, however judged. At the national level, resources tend to flow toward highly visible problems (such as abused children) rather than toward problems of greater magnitude but lower visibility (such as the needs of poor Indian children). At both levels, priorities tend to be determined by the pressures felt by professionals engaged in providing service. We appear to lack the conceptual framework and the techniques for establishing priorities relating to children themselves.

These problems are, in effect, ways of talking about the need for workable systems of management, which consists in large part of identification of problems, allocation of resources through determination of priorities, evaluation of performance, and restructuring of services.

The inability of the children's service system to undertake these functions effectively is apparent at all levels. But the nature of the management issues varies with the level.

At the local neighborhood or community level, for example, there is a lack of network management capable of detecting children with problems, diagnosing whole problems, mustering varied resources, evaluating the effectiveness of what has been done, and modifying the operation of the system in response to what has been learned. For the multiple-handicapped child, many varied crises can be expected over time relating to school, health, etc. Yet there is no central management which coordinates detection, monitoring, referral, teaching, and evaluation. The lack of network management was heard many times in our interviews. But each agency sees the focus of such a network as being around its particular program, policy, or field of specialty.

At the national level, it is clear that it is difficult for those in positions of power over national policy relating to children to:

> devote *sustained attention* to problems of policy;
> be other than *reactive* in policy making;
> develop policy in response to *comprehensive, long-term* issues;
> develop new policy *in response to what has been learned from old programs;*
> face problems of *relative priority* of problems, as against *relative visibility;*
> make good judgments about the *timing of programs;*
> *draw on the capability of those affected to formulate their own ideas of need.*

The formulation of desirable national policy—on the part of those in the field—tends to lack sanctions for nonperformance. It tends not to lead to major reallocation of national priorities in the commitment of resources.

SOME QUANTITATIVE FEATURES OF THE SYSTEM

The System of Child Health and Well-Being as an Industry

To review the economics of the service system for child health and well-being, a useful analogue is to look at it as a child service industry. One sees many separate, autonomous units, both public and private, competing for the public dollar and the consumer dollar.

If we visualize a market for child health service, such a market can be described in terms of the relationships among buyers and sellers of such service. Two broad categories of relationships are particularly relevant to this discussion. One is illustrated by the case of a family that has a child who requires special services and that has both the ability to pay for such service and knowledge of the agencies that provide the desired service. The seller in this particular case might be a doctor or private hospital or private school that takes in the child and provides service. The connecting link between the family and the supplier of service is the price which the family pays for such services. This relationship describes the central features of the private service market.

The second category of relationships among buyers and sellers of child health services includes cases of families unable to pay for such services. Ability to pay is provided through the public dollar; in this case the buyer of the services includes both the family and the taxpayer who provides funds for purchase of service. The seller in this case may be a private agency to which the family is referred or a public service agency.

For purposes of this section and the next, which deals with projections of services and costs for the years 1975 and 1985, we will focus primarily on the public service sector. Even within this we are forced by the lack of comprehensive and detailed data to deal with a limited portion of the public service system, namely, services relating to social welfare. These include Aid to Families with Dependent Children, adoption services, Veterans Administration payments for support, services for dependent neglected children and unwed mothers, and support payments to dependents of survivors under Old Age Survivors and Disability Insurance. Where it is useful and illustrative, we will look at data relating to other public service sectors such as mental health, physical handicaps, and correctional facilities and selected information from voluntary and private sector services.

Before turning to the public service sector exclusively, we will present a brief but instructive overview of the total system. While statistics are not available to present a good quantitative picture of the total child health industry, there are some trends in the industry's mode of operation which require little statistical support. These correspond to common wisdom about the service system. In this regard, the interactions among public and private sector service agencies, groups, and institutions are particularly interesting. For instance, the capabilities of the private sector to bid away manpower from public services have important implications for the quantity, type, and quality of service provided in each sector. Wages offered in fields like psychiatry and speech therapy draw a large portion of practitioners into private agencies. As a consequence of wage differentials, one finds substantial shortages in manpower in public services for certain categories of trained manpower.

Another dimension of trade-offs between public and private services in the child health industry relates to manpower training. Traditionally, the public sector has assumed financial responsibility for training manpower for the industry and for providing facilities for training. After such training, professionals have sought the private sector in large part; however, the sole reason is by no means the pull of more attractive wages in the private sector. Investment in training has not paid off for the public sector because this sector has not provided public facilities with resource pools for filling staff positions with new, trained manpower upon completion of training. In recent years, as the demands for training have increased, so has the tendency for recent graduates to enter private institutions upon terminating training. Public monies have been channeled into private facilities for training, since public training facilities have been close to capacity. Under these circumstances, trainees have simply remained in the private sector after completing training without even having to make any transition between sectors.[20]

Another factor which has tended to reinforce the growth of the private sector at the expense of public growth comes in response to the increase in family incomes. As family incomes increase and a greater percentage of family income is devoted to private health services, an increase occurs in private markets for these services. This tends to reinforce the ability of the private market to offer more attractive wages, which, at the same time, increases the cost of providing services. Indications are that medical care prices have been increasing more rapidly than the overall costs of living and will continue to do so for the next ten years at least.[21]

Given this overall view, we turn now to look at one subsystem—the

Table 2.—CHILDREN AND YOUTH IN THE UNITED STATES[1]

AGE GROUP	ESTIMATED 1960	ACTUAL 1965	PROJECTIONS 1970	1975
	NUMBERS IN MILLIONS			
Under 5	20.4	20.5	20.0	24.3
Ages 5–13	33.0	35.9	37.2	36.7
Ages 14–17	11.2	14.1	15.8	16.8
Ages 18–20	7.2	9.3	11.0	12.3
Total (Ages 0–20)	71.8	79.8	84.0	90.1
Total Population	180.7	194.6	207.3	223.8
	PERCENTAGE OF TOTAL POPULATION			
Under 5	11.2	10.5	9.6	10.9
Ages 5–13	18.3	18.5	17.9	16.4
Ages 14–17	6.2	7.2	7.7	7.5
Ages 18–20	4.0	4.8	5.3	5.5
Total (Ages 0–20)	39.7	41.0	40.5	40.3

[1] Estimates are for July 1 of each year and include all population, including Armed Forces overseas. Sources: Bureau of Census Publications, 1965 from Series P-25, No. 321, Nov. 30, 1965; 1970, 1975, 1980, and 1985 from Series P-25, No. 359, Feb. 20, 1967, with adjustments between age groups based on estimates of staff of the Bureau of the Census. The Census Series B projections for 1970–85, which assume fertility rates approximating those in calendar years 1964 and 1965, have been used.
SOURCE: U.S. Department of Health, Education, and Welfare, *Mental Health and Child Care Programs,* Oct. 1966.

20. American Association of Psychiatric Clinics for Children, "AAPCC Preliminary Analyses of Survey Data of AAPCC Member Clinics," 1967, Section J: Staff Government.
21. U.S. Department of Health, Education, and Welfare, "Trends," 1965 ed., Part 1: National Trends, Annual Supplement to the Monthly Health, Education, and Welfare Indicators (Washington, D.C.: U.S. Government Printing Office, 1965).

public social welfare service system for children—to explore the numbers of children being serviced and the costs of providing these services.

The Numbers of Children in Need of Social Welfare Services

Any analysis of welfare services starts with a count of the population to be served. Unfortunately, there is no census that can indicate the total number of children receiving welfare and related services in institutions and out of institutions in the United States. The best one can do is to attempt an estimate, utilizing data from a variety of sources.

Necessarily, one starts with a total count of the child population. The census data in Table 2 show the total child population broken down by age groups, in terms of recent estimates and future projections.

If one considers the total number of children *needing* social welfare services, the magnitude of the problem becomes evident by the estimates shown in Table 3.

Sources and Bases of Assumptions for Tables 3 and 4:

1. *Unwed mothers.* Approximately 50,000 of the total 291,200 unwed mothers of all ages were known to public or private social agencies in 1966.[22] Roughly 40 percent of the total or 116,500 of all known unwed mothers in 1965 were between the ages of fifteen and nineteen.[23] Assum-

Table 3.—CHILDREN IN NEED OF WELFARE SERVICES, 1965

TYPE OF SOCIAL WELFARE SERVICE	CHILDREN ESTIMATED TO BE IN NEED OF SOCIAL WELFARE SERVICES IN 1965
1. Unwed mothers	116,500
2. Dependent and neglected children	319,000
3. Adoption	100,000
4. Aid to Families with Dependent Children (AFDC)	13,200,000
5. Old Age Survivors and Disability Insurance (OASDI)	2,635,000
6. Veterans Administration	743,000
7. Services from state and local departments of public welfare	531,200
	17,644,700

SOURCE: See discussion, "Sources and Bases of Assumptions for Tables 3 and 4," pp.142–144.

22. Reports for 1968 on National Health and Welfare Agencies, National Budget and Consultation Committee, New York, N.Y., NBCC, 1967, p. 56.
23. *New York Times,* Mar. 14, 1968.

ing that the same proportion of mothers was served in that age group as in others, we derive a figure of 20,000 unwed mothers in contact with social agencies.

We have been unable to find sufficient or representative data on cost. Since the number of persons involved in this category is relatively small (roughly 0.3 percent), its omission does not have a significant effect on the total estimated per capita cost.

2. *Dependent and neglected children.* 75,000 children were in 1,649 institutions for the dependent and neglected in 1965, 11,100 of them in public institutions and 64,400 in private ones, according to the Children's Bureau.[24] This appears a conservative estimate, since the source cited counts only 1,304 institutions (154 public and 1,150 voluntary) as compared to 1,452 (289 public and 1,163 voluntary) listed in a later publication by the Children's Bureau entitled: "Numbers and Kinds of Children's Residential Institutions in the United States" (1967, p. 26). If we assume the 148 additional institutions serve a proportional volume of children, we derive an estimate of 78,100 children served.

Our estimate of need is based on Dr. Seligman's figure of 300,000 for 1964,[25] updated to 1965 on the assumption that the number of children defined as in need remained at roughly the same proportion of total child population for both years. Joseph Reid, executive director of the Child Welfare League of America, also estimated that more than 200,000 children were in institutions and foster homes in 1966.[26]

The national expenditure for foster care, the bulk of which is provided for dependent and neglected children, was about $1.7 billion. Government sources provided $369 million, $335 million came from state and local funds, and $34 million was provided by federal monies.[27]

3. *Adoption.* Approximately 135,000 children were adopted in 1964, 71,600 of them by nonrelatives.[28] Projecting that number as a constant percentage of the total child population, 143,000 children were adopted in 1965, 75,800 of them by nonrelatives.

According to Reid, 100,000 children need adoption each year.[29] From the context of his statements, the number of children in need of adoption has remained fairly constant for the last several years.

Sixty-six percent of adoptions by nonrelatives were arranged by social

24. *Child Welfare Statistics—1965,* Children's Bureau Statistical Series No. 84 (Washington, D.C.: U.S. Department of Health, Education, and Welfare, Children's Bureau, 1966).

25. *Encyclopedia of Social Work* (New York: National Association of Social Workers, 1965).

26. *Congressional Record,* Apr. 11, 1967: H 3947.

27. *Ibid.*

28. *Child Welfare Statistics—1965,* Children's Bureau Statistical Series No. 84 (Washington, D.C.: Department of Health, Education, and Welfare, Children's Bureau, 1966), p. 3.

29. *Congressional Record,* Apr. 11, 1967: H 3947.

agencies;[30] their costs are thus included under category 7 below. We have no data on the costs of arranging adoptions outside of social welfare agencies.

4. *AFDC.* According to the Department of Health, Education, and Welfare,[31] there were 3,326,000 children under eighteen who received AFDC payments in 1965 at a cost of $1,724,883,000. Of this amount, $956,470,000, or 55 percent, was supplied by the federal government. The number of families receiving welfare payments represents, at a minimum, 25 percent of those in need of such help and 50 percent of those qualified to receive it.[32] We therefore use an estimate of 13,200,000 children in need of AFDC services.

5. *OASDI.* Here, 2,635,000 children under eighteen years of age received payments from OASDI in 1965[33] at a cost we estimate to have approximated $2,731,000,000. We derive this figure on the assumption that children received a proportional share (16 percent) of the payments of $16,997,000,000 which were distributed to 16.4 million people in 1965.[34]

We have no reliable estimate for the number of children in need of OASDI payments per se. We can only assume that at the very minimum those children receiving OASDI support are in need of it.

6. *Veterans Administration.* Dr. William B. Dyess, Office of the Controller, Veterans Administration, Washington, D.C., stated in telephone interviews on April 18 and 19, 1968, that the VA provided $210 million (average annual value) in fiscal 1965 to 742,902 children and that 679,450 of these children, receiving $176 million, were in families supported by pension payments. There were 63,452 children receiving $34 million because of death of a family member.

7. *Services from state and local departments of public welfare.* On March 31, 1965, state and local departments of public welfare were providing child welfare services to 531,000 children. Of these children, 478,-500 were receiving primary casework services; 42,800 were having supplementary services or care purchased for them from another child welfare agency, usually a voluntary one; 7,600 were receiving payment to cover

30. *Child Welfare Statistics—1965,* Children's Bureau Statistical Series No. 84 (Washington, D.C.: Department of Health, Education, and Welfare, Children's Bureau, 1966), p. 4.

31. U.S. Department of Health, Education, and Welfare, U.S. Bureau of Public Assistance, "Trend Report Graphic Presentation of Public Assistance and Related Data" (Washington, D.C.: U.S. Department of Health, Education, and Welfare, Dec. 1965).

32. *New York Times,* Feb. 18, 1968, p. 36.

33. U.S. Department of Health, Education, and Welfare, U.S. Bureau of Public Assistance, "Trend Report Graphic Presentation of Public Assistance and Related Data" (Washington, D.C.: U.S. Department of Health, Education, and Welfare, Dec. 1965).

34. U.S. Department of Health, Education, and Welfare, "Trends," 1965 ed., Part 1: National Trends, Annual Supplement to the Monthly Health, Education, and Welfare Indicators (Washington, D.C.: U.S. Government Printing Office, 1965), p. 34.

board and care only, and 2,300 were in legal custody only. Services were provided at a cost of $352 million in 1965, $34.2 million coming from the federal government, $176 million from state funds, and $141.8 million from local funds.[35]

The Character of Those Serviced by the Child Welfare System

The system of services for the child welfare system includes direct services and income maintenance and support payments. The public agencies which provide direct services are the Veterans Administration, Children's Bureau, Bureau of Family Services, and Welfare Department; for purposes of this discussion we are not including indirect services provided through the Office of Economic Opportunity or the Public Health Service, the Department of Education, or the Justice Department. For example, not until there is a transfer from the courts to a welfare agency is account taken of these cases in the child welfare system, as it is defined here.

The total number of children in the service system in 1965 was estimated at 7,490,000. Estimates for subsequent years suggest a rate of growth in the system of slightly more than 6 percent. The breakdown of children provided service in 1965 by areas of need identified in Section 2 is shown in Table 4.

Table 4.—CHILDREN PROVIDED SOCIAL WELFARE SERVICE, 1965

TYPE OF CHILD WELFARE SERVICE	CHILDREN SERVICED IN THE SOCIAL WELFARE SYSTEM
1. Unwed mothers	20,000
2. Dependent and neglected children	78,000
3. Adoption	75,800
4. Aid to Families with Dependent Children	3,326,000
5. Old Age Survivors and Disability Insurance	2,635,000
6. Veterans Administration	743,000
7. Services from state and local departments of public welfare	531,200
Total	7,409,000

SOURCE: See discussion, "Sources and Bases of Assumptions for Tables 3 and 4," pp. 142–144.

35. U.S. Department of Health, Education, and Welfare, U.S. Bureau of Public Assistance, "Trend Report Graphic Presentation of Public Assistance and Related Data" (Washington, D.C.: U.S. Department of Health, Education, and Welfare, Dec. 1965), pp. 67, 69.

There are several other ways to view the population of children being serviced by the public child welfare service industry. In the next several pages we present the available data describing these children by living

Table 5.—CHILDREN SERVED BY PUBLIC AND VOLUNTARY CHILD WELFARE AGENCIES AND INSTITUTIONS, BY LIVING ARRANGEMENT, MARCH 31, 1965

| | CHILDREN SERVED[1] | | |
LIVING ARRANGEMENT	Total	Primarily by public agencies	Primarily by voluntary agencies
United States estimated total	697,300	483,800	213,500
In homes of parents	254,900	208,300	46,600
In homes of relatives	35,100	32,600	2,500
In independent living arrangements	8,000	5,500	2,500
In adoptive homes	66,900	33,800	33,100
In foster homes	206,000	162,000	44,000
In group homes	1,800	800	1,000
In selected institutions[2]	92,200	13,700	78,500
Institutions for dependent and neglected children	75,500	11,100	64,400
Maternity homes for unmarried mothers	4,700	—	4,700
Residential treatment centers for emotionally disturbed children	6,500	2,600	3,900
Voluntary institutions for delinquent children	5,500	—	5,500
In other institutions[3]	15,400	14,500	900
Public training schools for delinquent children	7,000	6,900	100
Institutions for mentally retarded children	5,500	5,000	500
Institutions for physically handicapped children	800	700	100
Other institutions	2,100	1,900	200
In temporary shelters	3,100	1,700	1,400
Elsewhere	8,600	5,800	2,800
Living arrangements not reported[4]	5,100	5,100	200

[1] A child is counted only once in this table, according to his living arrangement on March 31 and the auspices of the agency responsible for primary service.
[2] Includes all children living in these institutions.
[3] Includes all children living in these institutions who were receiving casework from a child welfare agency.
[4] These are children from whom any agency makes a payment only or exercises legal custody only.
SOURCE: *Child Welfare Statistics—1965*, U.S. Department of Health, Education, and Welfare, Children's Bureau Statistical Series No. 84 (Washington, D.C., 1966), p. 15.

arrangement, by linkages with the mental health service system, and by age, sex, race, and characteristics specific to the institutionalized population.

Table 6.—CHILDREN SERVED BY PUBLIC AND VOLUNTARY CHILD WELFARE AGENCIES AND INSTITUTIONS, BY LIVING ARRANGEMENT, MARCH 31, 1966

LIVING ARRANGEMENT	CHILDREN SERVED[1]		
	Total	Primarily by public agencies	Primarily by voluntary agencies
United States estimated total	741,400	519,400	222,000
In home of parents	282,500	230,000	51,700
In homes of relatives	36,300	33,300	3,000
In independent living arrangements	8,800	6,100	2,700
In adoptive homes	71,600	36,000	35,600
In foster family homes	218,100	171,500	46,600
In group homes	1,800	900	900
In selected institutions[2]	89,500	12,800	76,700
Institutions for dependent and neglected children	72,000	10,200	61,800
Maternity homes for unmarried mothers	5,000	—	5,000
Residential treatment centers for emotionally disturbed children	6,900	2,600	4,300
Voluntary institutions for delinquent children	5,600	—	5,600
In other institutions[3]	15,500	14,600	900
Public training schools for delinquent children	6,400	6,300	100
Institutions for mentally retarded children	6,100	5,500	600
Institutions for physically handicapped children	900	800	100
Other institutions	2,100	2,000	100
In temporary shelters	3,500	1,900	1,600
Elsewhere	8,000	5,900	2,100
Living arrangements not reported[4]	5,800	5,600	200

[1] A child is counted only once in this table, according to his living arrangement on March 31 and the auspices of the agency responsible for primary service.
[2] Includes all children living in these institutions.
[3] Includes all children living in these institutions who were receiving casework from a child welfare agency.
[4] These are children for whom an agency makes a payment only or exercises legal custody only.

SOURCE: *Child Welfare Statistics—1966*. U.S. Department of Health, Education, and Welfare, Children's Bureau Statistical Series No. 88 (Washington, D.C., 1967).

One should note that the emphasis is on care in homes of families and relatives and on foster care. Adoptions remain under 10 percent of the total, although from an economic view this transfers the burden of cost to a private family, releasing resources for alternative use in the public welfare system. Data indicate that adoption rates have gone up, although as a percent of all arrangements, adoptions are fairly static.

From 1957 to 1965, one finds the following: percent of children in homes (parents and relatives) is up from 40 percent to 47 percent;[36] adoptions remain at about 7 percent; in foster homes the percent declines from 37 percent to 35 percent; in institutions the percent declines from 13 percent to 10 percent; elsewhere there is a decline from 3 percent to 1 percent.

Projections for 1970 and 1975 would appear to be: homes: 49 percent in 1970 and 51 percent in 1975; adoptions: 7 percent in 1970 and 7 percent in 1975; foster homes: 34 percent in 1970 and 33 percent in 1975; institutions: 9 percent in 1970 and 8 percent in 1975; elsewhere: 1 percent in 1970 and 1 percent in 1975.

From a somewhat narrower standpoint, children requiring psychiatric

Table 7.—RANK IN PROBLEMS PRESENTED BY THE CHILD

PUBLIC AGENCIES		VOLUNTARY AGENCIES	
Principal problem		*Principal problem*	
	Percent		*Percent*
Neglect, abuse, or exploitation	36	Parents not married to each other	29
Emotional or behavior problem	9	Emotional or behavior problem	18
Illness of parent	9	Neglect, abuse, or exploitation	13
Child in need of guardianship	8	Conflict in parent-child relationship	9
Parents not married to each other	7	Unmarried mother	8
Conflict in parent-child relationship	5	Illness of parent	8
Financial need of family	5	Child in need of guardianship	5
First three problems		*First three problems*	
Neglect, abuse, or exploitation	46	Parents not married to each other	35
Financial need of family	21	Emotional or behavior problem	
Emotional or behavior problem	20	of child	34
Illness of parent	17	Conflict in parent-child relationship	25
Parents not married to each other	16	Neglect, abuse, or exploitation	21
Child in need of guardianship	16	Illness of parent	15
Conflict in parent-child relationship	15	Child in need of guardianship	11
		Financial need of family	10

SOURCE for Tables 7, 9, 10, 11: *Children Problems and Services in Child Welfare Programs.* Helen R. Jeter, Children's Bureau in cooperation with the Child Welfare League of America, U.S. Dept. of Health, Education and Welfare, Children's Bureau (Washington, D.C., 1963).

36. *Child Welfare Statistics—1965.* Children's Bureau Statistical Series 84 (Washington, D.C.: U.S. Department of Health, Education, and Welfare, Children's Bureau, 1966).

facilities represent about 20 percent of all psychiatric patients, including both inpatient and outpatient services.

The increasing severity of the problem is suggested by data on increases in incidence from 1961 to 1965, when the number requiring outpatient services (males, age ten to seventeen) went up 57 percent, or from 95,000 to 150,000, and for females age ten to seventeen such services went up 70 percent, or from 50,000 to 85,000.[37]

The character of mental health problems shows that a substantial percentage of children who have encountered the welfare system services also encounter the mental health system services. Table 7 gives some indication of the extent to which the phenomenon occurs.

FIG. 1—Percent Distribution by Referral Source, Age, and Sex; Adolescent Patients Terminated from 780 Outpatient Psychiatric Clinics, United States, 1962

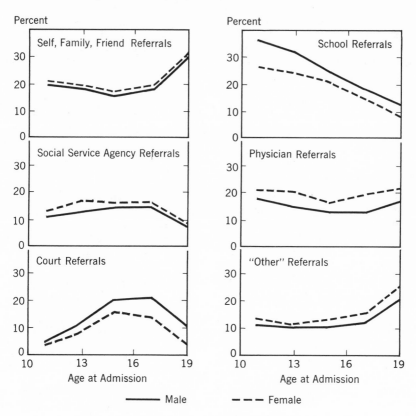

SOURCE: "Adolescent Patients Served in Outpatient Psychiatric Clinics" by B.M. Rosen, A.K. Bahn, R. Shellow, and E.M. Bower, *American Journal of Public Health,* 55 (Oct. 1965), 1563-1577.

37. Source: See Tables 5 and 6.

Some variation is noted in the percentage of referrals to outpatient psychiatric clinics made by both the formal and the informal systems. Figure 1 is reproduced from Rosen, Bahn *et al.* and shows the percentage distribution by referral source, age, and sex, as related to adolescent patients terminated from 780 clinics in the United States in 1962.

Some indication of the auspices of services is provided by Table 8, which indicates the number of institutions distributed by sponsoring body.

Table 8.—Types and Auspices of Children's Residential Institutions in the United States, September 1965

| | AUSPICES 1965 | | | |
	Federal	State and Local	Voluntary	Proprietary
Institution for Dependents Neglected	100	189	1,163	63
Unwed Mothers	—	2	208	1
Delinquents	2	516	108	21
Emotionally Disturbed—Psychiatric	1	123	158	30
Handicapped	4	283	330	447
Total	107	1,113	1,967	562

SOURCE: "Number and Kinds of Children's Residential Institutions," U.S. Department of Health, Education, and Welfare, Children's Bureau, 1967.

Table 9 shows the age distribution of *all* children in the welfare system under study in 1961.

Table 9.—Age Distribution of All Children in Welfare System, 1961

Age Group	Percent Public Agencies	Percent Voluntary Agencies
0–4	22	39
5–9	25	15
10–15	34	26
16–19	17	15

SOURCE: "Children Problems and Services in Child Welfare Programs," U.S. Department of Health, Education, and Welfare, Children's Bureau, 1963.

Among those served by public agencies in Table 9, males represent 53 percent, females 47 percent, indicating a fairly even distribution through the age cohorts. Note that for public agencies there exists a fairly even distribution through the age cohorts.

Tables 10 and 11 show age distribution by "problem areas" for both public and voluntary agencies.

Table 10.—AGE DISTRIBUTION OF CHILDREN PROVIDED WELFARE SERVICES BY PUBLIC AGENCIES, 1961

Age Group	Neglected and Abused	Emotional Problems	Parent-Child Conflict	Mentally Retarded	Unmarried Mothers[1] White	Negro
Under 5	19	5	7	9	—	—
5–9	30	16	18	27	—	—
10–13	24	25	22	24	—	2
14–17	22	40	40	28	31	49

[1] Percent of all unmarried mothers.
SOURCE: See Table 9.

Table 11.—AGE DISTRIBUTION OF CHILDREN PROVIDED WELFARE SERVICES BY VOLUNTARY AGENCIES, 1961

Age Group	Neglected and Abused	Emotional Problems	Parent-Child Conflict	Mentally Retarded	Unmarried Mothers[1] White	Negro
Under 5	17	5	7	16	—	—
5–9	27	17	15	22	—	—
10–13	26	37	26	26	—	1
14–17	23	41	38	26	21	39

[1] Percent of all unmarried mothers.
SOURCE: See Table 9.

A somewhat different pattern emerges when one examines institutional services. Data on the latter are available only in decennial years, but the pattern has remained substantially the same since 1960.

Table 12.—AGE DISTRIBUTION OF CHILDREN IN INSTITUTIONS, 1960

Age Group	Number in Institutions	Percent	U.S. Child Population (% all children)
Under 5	15,022	5.3	29.5
5–9	44,214	15.5	27.3
10–14	90,901	32.0	24.6
15–19	133,811	47.2	18.6
Total	283,948	100.0	100.0

SOURCE: See Table 13.

At age twenty the data indicate a sharp drop. In 1960, the number of children at that age in institutions was 22,400, suggesting movement into adult institutions in the main.

Further detail is given in Table 13. The points to be noted are: (1) the

Table 13.—Children in Institutions, by Age and by Type of Institution, 1960

| | WELFARE | | | | | | CORRECTIONAL | | | | | | | | | |
| | Homes for dependent and neglected children | | Homes for the aged and dependent | | Homes for unwed mothers | | Training schools for delinquent children | | Detention homes | | Diagnostic and reception centers | | Prisons and reformatories | | Local jails and workhouses | |
Age	Number	Percent	Number	Percent	Number	Percent	Number	Percent	Number	Percent	Number	Percent	Number	Percent	Number	Percent
Total	70,892	100.0	2,501	100.0	2,813	100.0	44,366	100.0	9,903	100.0	1,228	100.0	28,325	100.0	17,598	100.0
Under 5	5,965	8.4	294	11.8	1,084	38.5	48	0.1	213	2.1	—	—	42	0.1	33	0.2
5–9	18,191	25.7	473	18.9	79	2.8	428	1.0	572	5.8	8	0.7	—	—	13	0.1
10–14	31,860	44.9	540	21.6	137	4.9	12,209	27.5	4,093	41.3	316	25.7	95	0.3	552	3.1
15–19	14,709	20.7	958	38.3	1,335	47.5	31,316	70.6	4,988	50.4	904	73.6	19,377	68.3	12,535	71.2
20	167	0.2	236	9.4	178	6.3	365	0.8	37	0.4	—	—	8,851	31.2	4,465	25.4

| | MENTAL DISABILITIES | | | | | | | | PHYSICAL DISABILITIES | | | | | |
| | Mental hospitals and residential treatment centers | | Homes and schools for the mentally handicapped | | Homes and schools for the blind | | Homes and schools for the deaf | | Other homes and schools for the physically handicapped | | Tuberculosis hospitals | | Other chronic disease hospitals | |
Age	Number	Percent	Number	Percent	Number	Percent	Number	Percent	Number	Percent	Number	Percent	Number	Percent
Total	21,986	100.0	78,333	100.0	6,246	100.0	11,207	100.0	4,549	100.0	4,699	100.0	1,679	100.0
Under 5	417	1.9	4,473	5.7	54	0.9	160	1.4	767	16.9	1,123	23.9	349	20.8
5–9	1,860	8.5	15,232	19.4	1,945	31.1	2,684	24.0	1,361	29.9	872	18.5	496	29.5
10–14	5,210	23.7	26,564	33.9	2,342	37.5	4,137	36.9	1,605	35.3	812	17.3	429	25.5
15–19	11,682	53.1	27,610	35.2	1,797	28.8	3,997	35.7	739	16.2	1,522	32.4	342	20.4
20	2,817	12.8	4,454	5.7	108	1.7	229	2.0	77	1.7	370	7.9	63	3.8

Source: U.S. Department of Health, Education, and Welfare, Children's Bureau Publication 432, 1965, *America's Children and Youth in Institutions: 1950–1960–1964* (Washington, D.C.: U.S. Government Printing Office, 1965).

age cohort ten to fourteen shows up heaviest in homes for dependent children; (2) the bimodal group in homes for unwed mothers highlights this problem in the fifteen to nineteen age group; (3) the fifteen to nineteen age group is heaviest in the delinquency category; (4) while mental handicaps reveal themselves at an early age, the disabilities show up at about age ten.

The sex distribution of children in institutions appears to be on the average about two-thirds boys and one-third girls. At age five, however, the ratio is fifty-five percent boys and forty-five percent girls. This tends to shift through the age cohorts progressively until at age twenty the distribution is 81 percent boys and 19 percent girls. (For most institutions ratios by race are 80 percent white and 20 percent nonwhite.) Only in correctional institutions is a higher percent found for nonwhite (33 percent), indicating the readiness of society to incarcerate Negroes rather than to give treatment to them.

A breakdown of ratios of institutionalization by race and age in 1960 is shown in Table 14.

Table 14.—Rate of Institutionalization of Children per 1,000 Child Population, by Race and by Age, 1960 and 1950

	1960		1950	
	RATE PER 1,000 CHILD POPULATION		RATE PER 1,000 CHILD POPULATION	
AGE	White	Nonwhite	White	Nonwhite
Total	4.0	6.3	4.8	5.3
Under 5	0.7	0.9	1.1	0.8
5–9	2.4	2.0	3.8	1.8
10–14	5.1	7.4	7.3	5.5
15–19	8.9	19.0	8.6	14.1
20	8.6	21.7	7.8	17.6

Source: See Table 13.

Establishing the length of stay becomes a difficult problem simply because there are no data on the noninstitutional population on which one can rely with any degree of confidence. Further, rotation within the system, that is, repeated returns, beclouds the matter. It seems evident that for the system as a whole, a short stay in the system is the rule. Data on the institutional population also indicate this to be the general case, as shown in Table 15.

Table 15.—LENGTH OF STAY OF CHILDREN IN SPECIFIED TYPES OF INSTITUTIONS, 1960[1]

Length of stay	Homes for dependent and neglected children (Children under age 18)		Homes and schools for the physically handicapped (Children under age 25)[2]		Training schools for juvenile delinquents (All ages)	
	Number	Percent	Number	Percent	Number	Percent
Total	68,975	100.0	22,493	100.0	45,695	100.0
Less than 1¼ years	29,196	42.3	6,699	29.8	37,136	81.3
1¼ years, less than 2¼ years	11,695	17.0	2,664	11.9	4,256	9.3
2¼ years, less than 5 years	15,635	22.6	4,726	21.0	2,536	5.5
5 years, less than 10¼ years	10,857	15.7	6,082	27.0	1,160	2.6
10¼ years or more	1,592	2.3	2,322	10.3	607	1.3

	Detention homes (All ages)		Prisons and reformatories (Children under age 20)		Local jails and workhouses (Children under age 20)	
	Number	Percent	Number	Percent	Number	Percent
Total	10,821	100.0	19,474	100.0	13,133	100.0
Less than 1¼ years	8,705	80.4	15,802	81.1	11,152	84.9
1¼ years, less than 2¼ years	591	5.5	2,500	12.8	526	4.0
2¼ years, less than 5 years	478	4.4	765	4.0	543	4.1
5 years, less than 10¼ years	441	4.1	253	1.3	407	3.1
10¼ years or more	606	5.6	154	0.8	505	3.8

[1] Length of stay refers to time elapsed between the date the child last entered the institution and the date of the census enumeration.
[2] Includes only 491 residents 21 through 24 years of age.
SOURCE: See Table 13.

The data indicate a clear tendency to move away from institutional care, particularly for neglected and dependent children. Emphasis is increasingly being placed on specific social services that offer alternatives to institutional care, with group homes and halfway houses planned to provide the mechanism of transition. Problems of increasing numbers of unwed mothers are met by reducing the length of stay in such homes, a trend visible also in training schools for juvenile delinquents.

Table 16.—HEAD START COSTS BY PROGRAM COMPONENT FULL DAY,
12-MONTH PROGRAM, 1966, 1967

	PERCENT 1966	PERCENT 1967
Recruitment, social services	5.3	5.4
Health (mental, medical, psychological)	3.3	4.0
Nutrition	13.8	14.0
Personnel, equipment, transportation	69.6	68.6
Administration	8.0	8.0
Total cost of program per child	$1,260	$1,380
Cost per child per month	$ 105	$ 115

SOURCE: Bernard Greenblatt, "Planning Models for Daytime Care of Preschool Children."
Background paper prepared for the Joint Commission on Mental Health of Children, Inc.,
1968 (mimeo.).

Data on health care are incomplete for purposes of estimating costs for children. Gross
data on health expenditures are shown in Table 17.

Table 17.—NATIONAL HEALTH EXPENDITURES: AMOUNT AND DISTRIBUTION BY
OBJECT OF EXPENDITURE, 1963

OBJECT OF EXPENDITURE	AMOUNT (millions)	PERCENT DISTRIBUTION
Total	$34,263	100.0
Personal services and supplies	29,391	85.5
Hospital care	11,579	33.8
Nursing home care	825	2.4
Physicians' services	6,867	20.0
Dentists' services	2,369	6.9
Other professional services	890	2.6
Drug and drug sundries	4,335	12.7
Eyeglasses and appliances	1,439	4.2
School health services	150	.4
Industrial inplant health services	298	.9
Medical activities in federal units other than hospitals	642	1.9
Nonpersonal services	4,869	14.2
Medical research	1,195	3.5
Construction	1,566	4.6
Government public health activities[1]	786	2.3
Voluntary health agencies	251	.7
Net cost of insurance	1,071	3.1

[1] May include some expenditures for personal services, such as immunization programs.
SOURCE: U.S. Department of Health, Education, and Welfare, Social Security Administration,
Research and Statistics, Note No. 10–1965. "National Expenditures for Health Care
Purposes by Object of Expenditures and Source of Funds, 1960–1963."

Cost of Providing Child Welfare and Other Child Services

The paucity of data on services to children makes it exeremely difficult to estimate the costs of various services. A micro-view on costs may be obtained by examining Head Start data. The costs of such a specialized program run some 35 percent higher than the costs in the general child welfare system, as will be noted.

However, there is no breakdown for children in this tabulation, so one must again proceed in alternative ways. There are data on mental health costs, given in Table 18.

Table 18.—MENTAL HEALTH COSTS, 1963 (in millions of dollars)

	MENTAL PSYCHONEUROTIC PERSONALITY DISORDERS	DISEASES OF NERVOUS SYSTEM
Hospital Care	2,059.7	684.0
Nursing Home Care	29.7	178.2
Physicians	281.5	508.2
Nursing Care	19.8	46.0
Other Professional Services	11.0	—
Total	2,401.7	1,416.4

SOURCE: U.S. Department of Health, Education, and Welfare, Health Econ. Series, No. 6, May 1966.

Again, there is no breakdown for children. The latter may be estimated as a proportion of the number of children in institutions as follows: (1) number of children in institutions: 114,000; (2) total institutionalized population: 1,462,000. Then, first eliminating nursing home care as applying mainly to adults, one can estimate that out of $3,610,200,000 total expenditure, the children's share is $288,200,000.

Perhaps the best thing to do would be to build on data available in the reports of child welfare statistics. Table 19 shows the statistics for 1965 and 1966.

It should be stressed that Table 19 indicates the cost of the child welfare system as defined earlier. It does not include correctional costs or AFDC. The increase in costs between the two years is in the order of 11 percent. The distribution of source of payments is further delineated by the fact that the original data do not include public institution costs or voluntary agency costs. Accepting these limitations in the data, one finds that state sources provided in 1966 approximately 49 percent; local 39 percent; federal 10 percent; and third-party payments 3 percent.

It would appear that costs are rising more rapidly than the number of children serviced (9 percent as contrasted to 6 percent). The move-

Table 19.—Costs of Child Welfare, 1965 and 1966

	COST 1965	PERCENT	COST 1966	PERCENT
BY SOURCE				
State	$176,000,000	48.6	199,500,000	49.0
Local	141,800,000	39.2	157,000,000	38.5
Federal	34,200,000	9.4	39,700,000	9.7
Third party	10,000,000	2.8	11,500,000	2.8
Total	362,000,000	100.0	407,700,000	100.0
BY PURPOSE				
Foster care	228,900,000	39.5	252,300,000	36.4
Day care	9,200,000	1.4	12,100,000	1.7
Personnel	93,500,000	14.7	108,900,000	15.7
Educational leave	3,200,000	.5	3,500,000	.5
Other	17,200,000	2.7	19,400,000	2.8
Public Institutions for Dependent and Neglected Children	17,200,000	2.7	18,100,000	2.6
Other Public Institutions	18,300,000	2.9	18,500,000	2.7
Voluntary Agencies	250,000,000	39.2	260,000,000	37.5
Total	637,500,000	100.0	692,800,000	99.9
Number of Children:	697,300		741,400	
Per Capita Cost:	$914		$934	

ment of costs is currently exceeding the estimates that may be derived by an extrapolation of trend lines. For example, the latter method suggests that state and local outlays will reach $440 million by 1970; however, estimates for 1967 are actually reaching the $450 million mark.

We have, however, arrived at other estimates which include AFDC and other federally sponsored programs. Using Table 4 (p. 145), which in-

Table 20.—Estimated Costs of Child Welfare Services, 1965

TYPE OF CHILD WELFARE SERVICE	CHILDREN SERVICED IN 1965	COST OF SERVICE (MILLIONS OF DOLLARS)
1. Unwed mothers	20,000	—
2. Dependent and neglected	78,000	1,700
3. Adoption	75,800	—
4. AFDC	3,326,000	1,725
5. OASDI	2,635,000	2,731
6. Veterans Administration	743,000	210
7. State and local welfare services	531,200	352
Total	7,409,000	6,718

dicated the numbers of children being serviced in the child welfare system, we have derived the costs of providing these services. These are shown in Table 20.

A significant portion of these expenditures for programs and services reflects costs for salaries. Some indications of the range of salaries for various professionals and paraprofessionals within the child welfare service system are shown in Table 21.

Table 21.—CHILD WELFARE CASEWORKER SALARIES, 1965

SALARIES PER MONTH	NUMBER
Under–$250	65
$250–$299	120
$300–$349	338
$350–$399	1,373
$400–$449	2,000
$450–$499	1,576
$500–$549	1,191
$550–$599	826
$600 and over	1,135

Median = $463
Modal Group = 23 percent
Some 13 percent earn over $600

SOURCE: See Table 5.

The data in Table 21 are based on what is known of public child welfare workers. These data are so partial that they merit repeating the observations made in earlier discussions. One needs to look at the current service system and focus on relevant categories. Each service category should be examined to obtain the field's view of the appropriate ratio of professional to client in a "best practice" situation. This ratio could then be compared to the actual professional-to-client ratio, and to what that ratio would be if all those eligible for service were actually served.

In Tables 22, 23, and 24, we cite figures for: (1) the median salaries for various job titles in child welfare agencies; (2) salaries for mental health professionals in these agencies; and (3) the educational status of various staff in child welfare agencies. However, a point of up to 20 to 30 percent should be added to all these figures to bring them more closely in line with the salary scales of the late 1960's.

Some agencies employ psychiatrists and psychologists and physicians as well as support personnel either on a full-time basis or at hourly rates. The median hourly rate for non-salaried psychiatrists in voluntary agencies is $20. The data are shown in Table 23.

Table 22.—MEDIAN SALARIES BY JOB TITLE IN VOLUNTARY CHILD
WELFARE AGENCIES, 1966

JOB TITLE	MEDIAN SALARY
Administrator	$12,540
Assistant Administrator	10,976
District Administrator	9,600
Business Officer	10,000
Public Relations	8,125
Manager and Supervisor	4,847 (plus value of maintenance)
Casework Director	10,370
Casework Supervisor	9,430
Case Aide	4,960
Group Work Supervisor	8,500
Group Worker	6,730
Recreation Worker	4,150
Residential Supervisor	8,600 (salary only)
Child Care Staff	4,450 (salary only)
Group Teachers	
graduate degree	7,600
bachelor's degree	5,190
college training, no degree	4,040

SOURCE: "Salaries and Manpower in Child Welfare: 1966." A Report of the
Child Welfare League of America, 1967.

Staffing the Current Child Welfare Service System

Data are available on staffing related to state and local public welfare
services, as well as to voluntary agencies. We will begin with the former
and then present data on voluntary agencies. The material covers several
dimensions, as will be noted. We list first the professional employees in
state and local public agencies, as shown in Table 25.

Table 23.—PSYCHIATRISTS IN VOLUNTARY CHILD WELFARE AGENCIES, 1966

SIZE OF STAFF	NUMBER OF AGENCIES	NUMBER OF PSYCHIATRISTS	SALARIED PSYCHIATRISTS[1]	
			$ 9,500–12,499	5
6–10	10	10	12,500–15,499	5
11–20	33	46	15,500–18,499	2
21–30	31	42	18,500–21,499	5
31–40	14	30	21,500–24,499	5
41–50	8	17	24,500–27,499	3
over 50	32	114	27,500 and over	4
Total	128	259		29

[1] Salaries of psychiatrists in voluntary agencies, January 1, 1966.
SOURCE: See Table 22.

Table 24.—Educational Attainments of Voluntary Child Welfare Agency
Staffs, 1966

NUMBER OF PSYCHOLOGISTS	SIZE OF STAFF	MEDIAN SALARY OF PSYCHOLOGISTS	HOURLY RATE FOR NON-SALARIED PSYCHOLOGISTS
6–10	2	with Ph.D. $10,720	median—$13.25
11–20	14	without Ph.D. 8,850	with Ph.D. 14.84
21–30	22		without Ph.D. 12.86
31–40	8		
41–50	6		
over 50	45		
Total	97[1]		

SIZE OF STAFF	NUMBER OF AGENCIES	NUMBER OF PHYSICIANS	NUMBER OF SALARIED NURSES	MEDIAN SALARY OF NURSES
6–10	4	4	—	$4,380
11–20	20	31	3	
21–30	23	41	10	
31–40	10	18	20	
41–50	7	10	10	
over 50	26	136	81	
Total	90	240[2]	124	

[1] Fifty-one had Ph.D.'s; 46 did not.
[2] Includes general practitioners, pediatricians, and medical specialists. Salaries range from
$9,000 to $25,000.
Source: See Table 22.

Table 25.—Professional Employees in State and Local Public
Welfare Agencies, 1965 and 1966

FULL TIME	1965	1966
Directors	262	280
Director-workers	113	97
Caseworkers	8,511	9,454
Casework Supervisors	1,498	1,619
Consultants	630	——[1]
Specialists	415	564
Other	3,197	925
Total full-time workers	11,429	12,955
Part-time workers[2]	5,033	10,907

[1] Included in "Other."
[2] Full-time workers giving some time to child welfare. In the absence
of data on hours, it is difficult to provide full-time equivalents. One
might assume that two part-time workers equal one full-time worker,
Source: See Tables 5 and 6.

Assuming the equivalency rate suggested in Note 2 in Table 25, there would have been approximately 14,000 jobs in the system in 1965 as compared with 18,400 jobs in 1966, or an increase of slightly more than 30 percent in one year (4,400 jobs).

However, in 1965 roughly 1,600 vacancies were reported, that is, available openings before agency budgeting, mainly in rural, sparsely populated areas, suggesting a most uneven distribution of manpower.

Data on job turnover are given in Table 26.

Table 26.—TURNOVER OF FULL-TIME PROFESSIONAL
CHILD WELFARE EMPLOYEES, 1965 AND
1966

	1965	1966
Accessions	4,043	4,265
Separations	3,022	3,249
Net Gain	1,021	1,016

SOURCE: See Tables 5 and 6.

Table 26 does *not* include part-time workers, so that contrasting Tables 25 and 26 we note two considerations: (1) the increase in *full-time jobs* is in the range of 1,000 to 1,500 over one year; (2) the manpower gap has been filled by drawing in other workers to engage in child welfare servicing. In fact, the latter has more than doubled. There has been an apparent gain of 4,400 jobs.

Manpower quality may be indicated by Table 27.

Table 27.—GRADUATE DEGREES IN SOCIAL
WORK—PERCENT OF EMPLOYEES,
1966

	PERCENT
Directors, director workers	70
Field representatives	76
Casework supervisors	65
Caseworkers	13
Other	56

SOURCE: See Table 22.

However, for *all* full-time professionals the proportion of those with graduate degrees is 26 percent.

In 1960, 23,000 persons were engaged in child welfare; of these, 16,600 were social workers (half of whom belonged to professional associations); 8,000 were in public child welfare full time. But, assuming a con-

Table 28 —DISTRIBUTION OF CASE LOADS FOR FULL-TIME
CHILD WELFARE EMPLOYEES, 1966

NUMBER OF CHILDREN SERVED	PERCENT CASE LOAD
1–24	18.8
25–29	29.5
50–74	30.3
75–99	11.4
100–149	7.3
150 and over	2.7

SOURCE: See Table 5.

Table 29.—STAFF SIZES AND TYPES OF SERVICE RENDERED
IN CHILD WELFARE SERVICES, JANUARY 1, 1966

SIZE OF STAFF	NUMBER	PERCENT
5 or less	2	1.0
6–10	31	14.9
11–20	56	26.9
21–30	41	19.7
31–40	20	9.6
41–50	10	4.8
over 50	48	23.1
Total	208	100.0

SERVICES RENDERED BY PARTICIPATING AGENCIES
(DUPLICATED COUNT)[1]

TYPE OF SERVICE	NUMBER
Adoption	149
Family day care	15
Foster care	165
Group day care	16
Group home	41
Homemaker service for children	46
Institutional	40
Maternity home	7
Residential treatment	40
Unmarried parent's service	142
Child services in own homes	121
Protective	21
Total	803

[1] This indicates that agencies in general have more than one
program.

stant proportional increase, the need for personnel by 1975 would be 33,000.

It seems evident that given existing training capabilities, need will have to be filled by utilization of paraprofessional personnel.

An alternative indicator of manpower needs may be derived from the number of man hours per 100,000 population supplied through outpatient psychiatric clinics in 1965. For the total United States the figure was only 221 man hours per 100,000 persons. Only 16 states and the District of Columbia exceeded the national average. For example, the District of Columbia supplied 758 man hours per 100,000 persons whereas Massachusetts supplied 626. One may assume that a similar pattern holds in other welfare service areas.

Yet the present distribution of manpower will in all probability continue. About 89 percent of the child welfare population served is located in 66 percent of the 3,200 counties that are served in the United States. That is, 34 percent of the counties receive no service. Only 60 percent of the rural counties are served. The distributions run from a low of 3 percent of the child population served in Idaho to 100 percent for 15 states.

The burden of work is indicated by the percent distribution of case loads for full-time workers shown in Table 28. It may be that the salary situation contributes to the shortage (see Table 21).

Supplementary data on manpower and services are provided in the report of the Child Welfare League of America cited earlier. This report related to member and provisional member agencies of CWLA and includes 193 voluntary and 15 local public agencies.

Manpower gaps in this area are revealed by Table 30.

Table 30.—NUMBER OF UNFILLED POSITIONS IN AGENCIES PARTICIPATING IN STUDY, JANUARY 1, 1966

| Size of Staff | Unfilled Positions—All Budgets[1] | | Unfilled Positions | |
| | | | Agency Budgets—Full Time Staff Only | |
	Number of Agencies	Number of Positions	Number of Agencies	Number of Positions
5 or less	1	1	1	1
6–10	16	33	15	30
11–20	32	56	31	44
21–30	24	57	23	42
31–40	15	26	13	21
41–50	6	20	6	17
over 50	39	410	39	357
	133	603	128	512

[1] Includes full-time and part-time staff agency budget; full-time and part-time staff, grant budget; and full-time staff, both agencies and grant budgets.

As with other data, information on manpower appears to be fragmentary. A more detailed study seems essential.

Table 31.—REPORTED EDUCATIONAL STATUS OF CHILD WELFARE WORKERS, JANUARY 1, 1966

| | (Percent Distribution) | | | | | |
	No College	Some College	B.A.	Some Graduate	M.A.	Ph.D.
Administration		2	3	5	87[1]	3
Caseworkers		1	12	10	76[2]	
Group worker supervisor		1	5	1	22	
Group worker		2	3	4	14	
Recreation worker	9	72	34	14	12	
Residential supervisor	13	21[3]	11	10	42	1
Child care worker	50	31[3]	14	2	2	
Education supervisor		4	9	4	17	
Group teacher	10	40	60	15	22	
Assistant teacher	24	26	4		1	

[1] Ten cases with master's degrees in fields other than social work.
[2] Seventy-four reported graduate social work degree.
[3] Includes 1 percent foreign trainees.

Services and Costs of Service in Other Categories

So far, we have focused on the social welfare system. In this section, we will highlight the characteristics of mental health, physical handicap, and correction services. Data for these groups are more incomplete and fragmentary. The derivations of the levels of service and costs in Table 32 are described in detail on pages 166–168.

Table 32.—ESTIMATED COSTS OF CHILD MENTAL HEALTH, PHYSICAL HANDICAPS, AND CORRECTION SERVICES, 1965[1]

	Mental Health	Estimated Total Cost	Physical Handicap	Estimated Total Cost	Correc- tions	Estimated Total Cost
Number of children estimated served	.5	4.31	5.6	9.25	.3	3.74
Number of children estimated to be at risk or in need	7.0	6.03	7.6	12.55	1.0	12.46

[1] All figures estimating number of children are in millions, and all figures estimating cost are in billions of dollars.

The figures in Table 32 yield per capita cost for: mental health: $8,620,000,000; physical handicap: $1,652,000,000; corrections: $12,467,000,000.

Highlights of the Existing Service Systems

The features of the existing system as they have been described in the preceding discussion can be summarized by Table 33.

Table 33.—CHILDREN RECEIVING WELFARE SERVICES AND CHILDREN IN NEED OF SERVICES[1]

	Mental Health	Estimated Dollar Cost	Social Welfare	Estimated Dollar Cost	Physical Handicap	Estimated Dollar Cost	Corrections	Estimated Dollar Cost	Total Number of Children	Estimated Dollar Cost
Number of children estimated served	.5	4.31	7.4	6.71	5.6	9.25	.3	3.74	13.8	24.01
Number of children estimated to be in need or at risk	7.0	6.03	17.6	15.98	7.6	12.55	1.0	12.46	33.2	47.02

[1] All figures estimating number of children are in millions, and all figures estimating cost are in billions of dollars.

The per capita costs for each category in Table 33 are: mental health: $8,620; social welfare: $908; physical handicap: $1,652; corrections: $12,467.

Looking at the gaps between service and need we observe:

19.4 million children need service which the system is not able to provide.

Given the current state of technology and means for providing service, it would cost the system more than twice as much as it spends now to provide service to those in need.

The cost of meeting need in the several subcategories is not evenly distributed. In all of our models, the systems providing service for social welfare and physical handicap are far closer to meeting defined need than those providing services for mental health and corrections.

Estimates of manpower for the public child welfare service system come from state and local welfare agency data. They indicate a staff-to-client ratio of 1 to 38. From this we estimated that the manpower required to supply service to children needing social welfare services would be approximately 460,000. This is more than twice as many people as are estimated to be working currently in the social welfare system as defined here.

SOURCES AND BASES FOR ESTIMATING NUMBERS OF CHILDREN SERVICED AND COSTS FOR MENTAL HEALTH, PHYSICAL HANDICAP, AND CORRECTIONS

1. Mental Health

a. Numbers of children in need of mental health care were derived by adding the total of children estimated to be mentally retarded in 1965 (2,440,000: U.S. Dept. HEW, "Program Analysis: Maternal and Child Health Care Programs," Oct. 1966: II-10) to the estimated numbers between ages five and nineteen years of emotionally disturbed children (4.6 million: *ibid.*) for a total of 7 million.

b. Numbers of children receiving service were derived from the numbers of inpatient and outpatient service administered to persons under twenty-five in 1964 (632,000: "Utilization of Psychiatric Facilities by Children and Youth," Alex J. Hurder: 7, Table 32: Paper prepared for Task Force V, Joint Commission on Mental Health of Children, 1968). The figures given for birth to age fourteen were added to one-half the number given for ages fifteen to twenty-four in order to derive a rough and somewhat inflated estimate of children served under age twenty. This number, 455,000, was then multiplied by 1.15 to represent the increase in service between 1964 and 1965.

c. Cost of servicing children in 1965 was derived in the following manner. State mental health service spent $125 million on services for 150,-000 children. 270,000 children received outpatient care (Hurder, *op. cit.*); using Dr. Nicholas Hobb's estimate of $25 per day ("Helping Disturbed Children, Psychological and Ecological Strategies," *American Psychologist*, 21 [1966], 1105–1115) for an estimated treatment length of 300 days, the cost figure is $2.03 billion. The remaining 100,000 children receiving inpatient care at $60 per day for 360 days cost $2.16 million. Our total cost estimate is thus $4.31 billion.

2. Physical Health

a. Number in need of service was derived as follows. The number of severely visually handicapped was calculated by dividing the budget for service to severely visually handicapped children of the American Printing

House for the Blind, Kentucky, by their figure for cost per child in 1965. Since the American Printing House affirms it serves all children diagnosed in need, we considered this a reasonable method of ascertaining need. Other estimates of need ran up to 18 million children (see "Program Analysis: Maternal and Child Health Care Programs," *op. cit.*), depending on the definition of visual handicap.

b. The number of children with severe learning problems, congenital disease, orthopedic handicap, epilepsy, and cerebral palsy, speech defects, and rheumatic fever were all derived from "Program Analysis: Child Health Care Programs," *op. cit.*

c. Number served was derived from "Program Analysis: Maternal and Child Health Care Programs" for all physical handicaps except visual problems and hearing difficulty. Visual care was derived from the budget of the American Printing House for the Blind as indicated above. Hearing care figures come from "Acute Conditions, Incidence and Associated Disability—United States—July 1965–June 1966," National Center for Health Statistics, Series 10, No. 38, 1967, using the assumption that the percentage of children treated remained constant through 1965.

d. Costs for physical handicap are rough estimates. We added to that part of the budget of the American Printing House which is relevant to children a figure derived as follows. The total public and private cost for health care in 1965 was $38,441,300,000 ("Trends," 1965 ed., Part I, U.S. Department of Health, Education, and Welfare. [Washington, D.C.: U.S. Government Printing Office, 1965]. See Table 2, p. 34). From this figure we subtracted costs which apply to adults only (industrial payments, insurance benefits, and the like) and costs which apply to children only (maternal and child health, school service, etc.), so that we had an estimate of expenditures for children and adults together. We took 41 percent of this figure, since children formed 41 percent of the total population in 1965 and the overloads at each end (under five and over sixty-five) tend to balance each other out. We then added back in the child-only expenses to derive a total figure of $9,252 million, which is the estimated cost for the physically handicapped, shown in Table 32.

3. Corrections

a. Number in need. Various sources estimate the number of children arrested by the police for juvenile offenses at about double the number that appear before the court (see *Task Force Report: Juvenile Delinquency and Youth Crime*. Report on Juvenile Justice and Consultants' Papers. The President's Commission on Law Enforcement and Administration of Justice [Washington, D.C.: U.S. Government Printing Office, 1967]; A. J. Kahn, *Planning Community Services for Children in Trouble,* 1964). We have used the number arrested as indicating a conservative estimate of those actually in need of service.

b. Number served. If one adds the figures shown in Table 13 for children committed to training schools and detention homes in 1960, one arrives at the figure of 54,209. In 1965, 223,800 youngsters were under supervision[38] (*Task Force Report: Corrections.* The President's Commission on Law Enforcement and the Administration of Justice [Washington, D.C.: U.S. Government Printing Office, 1967]).

c. Cost. Representative Roman Pucinski estimated that in 1966 the national cost of delinquency was $4 billion (*Congressional Record*, June 28, 1967. A 3336). The number of children in court that year totaled 745,-000 ("Juvenile Court Statistics—1967," Children's Bureau Statistical Series No. 93, U.S. Department of Health, Education, and Welfare, Children's Bureau, 1969, p. 10, Table 5). We have scaled this figure down for 1965 on the assumption that the cost of serving the child was the same for both 1965 and 1966. Since 697,000 children went through the courts in 1965, we have estimated the cost at $3.74 billion.

PROJECTIONS OF SERVICES AND COSTS FOR 1975 AND 1985

Projecting Child Populations in Need of Service

This section looks at projections of demand in 1975 and 1985 for services for children and the dollar and manpower resources needed to meet that demand.

Projections of total population under age twenty-one in 1975 and 1985, shown in Table 34, are derived by using two different sets of assumptions about fertility rates. Population A is calculated on the assumption that the average fertility rate between 1964 and 1965 will continue to 1985. (This is Census Series B.) Population B is based on the much lower fer-

Table 34.—NUMBERS OF CHILDREN UNDER TWENTY-ONE,
1965, 1975, AND 1985 (IN MILLIONS)

	1965	1975	1985
Population A	79.8	90.1	107.51
Population B	79.8	81.8	84.6

38. Supervision includes both "vesting the legal custody of the child for a specifically designated period of time, preferably not more than 3 months, in an agency for the specific purposes of observation, study, diagnosis, and making recommendations to the court" (William H. Sheridan, "Standards for Juvenile and Family Courts," U.S. Department of Health, Education, and Welfare [Washington, D.C.: U.S. Government Printing Office, 1966]).

tility rate of the early 1940's (Census Series D). In fact, the actual fertility rate in the past few years has been below the rate for the 1940's.

Using as a base the number of children estimated to be at risk or in need, as discussed in the preceding section, the following estimates or risk populations are made for 1975 and 1985. These estimates assume that the risk population will remain a constant proportion of the total population, as calculated in Model 1 above.

Model 2. This theory holds technology constant but assumes a 6 percent yearly growth in the service system coverage of those in need of service. This reflects the growth rate in the public child welfare service system as observed in the preceding section. It will be referred to as the "6 percent growth model."

Model 3. This model assumes an S-curve growth pattern, once again holding technology constant for the twenty-year period. The pattern of growth looks like this:

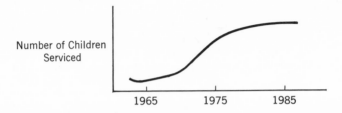

For purposes of illustration, we chose 1965 as the take-off point. At this time the service system started to grow at an increasing rate. In 1975 the system turns to growth at a decreasing rate. In the calculations, we chose straight-line representations of the average growth rates over five-year intervals as follows: 1965–70, a 2 percent rate of growth per year; 1970–75, a 7 percent rate; 1975–80, 3 percent; 1980–85, 2 percent.

Table 35.—NUMBERS OF CHILDREN ESTIMATED TO BE IN NEED OF SERVICES, 1965, 1975, AND 1985 (IN MILLIONS)

	MENTAL HEALTH SERVICES	SOCIAL WELFARE SERVICES	PHYSICAL HANDICAP	CORRECTION
1965	7.0	17.6	7.6	1.0
1975				
Population A	8.1	19.8	8.6	1.2
Population B	7.4	18.0	7.8	1.1
1985				
Population A	9.0	23.7	9.5	1.4
Population B	7.6	18.6	8.0	1.1

Projecting Growth in Service Systems

We will match these projections of need for service against three models of growth in the children's service systems. These models reflect commonly held theories about rates of growth. The models, the theories they reflect, and the assumptions tied to them are as follows:

Model 1. This theory holds technology constant and projects the numbers of children serviced if the system provides services to the same proportion of children as are currently serviced. For purposes of reference in the ensuing discussion, this model will be called "the 1985 version of the existing system."

Using the 1965 levels of service provided in each of these categories (see preceding section), the projections for the numbers of children serviced in 1975 are shown in Table 36.

Table 36.—CHILDREN SERVICED IN 1975
     (IN MILLIONS)

	MENTAL HEALTH	SOCIAL WELFARE	PHYSICAL HANDICAP	CORRECTION	TOTAL
Model 1					
Population A	.6	8.5	6.3	.34	15.7
Population B	.5	7.6	5.7	.31	14.1
Model 2	.9	13.3	10.0	.54	24.7
Model 3	.8	11.5	8.7	.46	21.5

In 1985, the projected numbers serviced are shown in Table 37.

Table 37.—CHILDREN SERVICED IN 1985
     (IN MILLIONS)

	MENTAL HEALTH	SOCIAL WELFARE	PHYSICAL HANDICAP	CORRECTION	TOTAL
Model 1					
Population A	.7	10.1	7.5	.41	18.7
Population B	.5	8.0	5.9	.32	14.7
Model 2	1.6	23.8	18.0	.97	44.4
Model 3	1.0	14.7	11.2	.59	27.5

When we compare the projected numbers of children in need with the numbers which will be serviced, we observe the following mismatches between those in need and the supply of services:

1. Taking the conservative projections of population in need of serv-

Table 38.—Comparison of Children in Need and Children Served, 1975 and 1985 (in millions)

	1965					1975					1985				
	Total	Mental Health	Social Welfare	Physical Handicap	Corrections	Total	Mental Health	Social Welfare	Physical Handicap	Corrections	Total	Mental Health	Social Welfare	Physical Handicap	Corrections
Population B No. in need	33.2	7.0	17.6	7.6	1.0	34.3	7.4	18.0	7.8	1.1	35.3	7.6	18.6	8.0	1.1
Population B No. served Model 1	13.8	.5	7.4	5.6	.3	14.1	.51	7.6	5.7	.31	14.7	.53	8.0	5.9	.32
Population A and B No. served Model 2	13.8	.5	7.4	5.6	.3	24.7	.9	13.3	10.0	.54	44.4	1.6	23.8	18.0	.97
Population A and B No. Served Model 3	13.8	.5	7.4	5.6	.3	21.5	.8	11.5	8.7	.46	27.5	1.0	14.7	11.2	.59
Population A No. in need	33.2	7.0	17.6	7.6	1.0	37.7	8.1	19.8	8.6	1.2	43.6	9.0	23.7	9.5	1.4
Population A No. served Model 1	13.8	.5	7.4	5.6	.3	15.7	.6	8.5	6.3	.34	18.7	.7	10.1	7.5	.41

ices and looking at the 1985 version of the existing system, we see an over-all demand for services from 35.3 million children while total supply reaches 14.7 million. That says that even though the system is serving the same population that it did in 1965, in total numbers, the mismatch is greater in 1985. The difference between those in need of service and supply of service in 1965 was 19.4 million children; in 1985, this figure grows to 20.6 million. Taking the higher estimate of 43.6 million children in need yields a residue of 24.9 million children demanding service which the system cannot supply (see Table 38).

2. Taking Model 2, the 6 percent growth model (i.e., the 6 percent growth in services delivered), we see that the total number of children served (using the conservative population estimate) would be 9.1 million *larger* than the total number of children in need. The nature of mismatch between service and need within subcategories is different than it appeared in Model 1 above. The categories—social welfare and physical handicap —are now overserviced, while the others still demand services which the system is unable to supply: 6 million children with mental health problems and .13 million juvenile delinquents remain unserved. In Model 1 the numbers of those in need were consistently larger than those serviced for all subcategories of service.

Viewing Model 2 in terms of the larger population estimate, a total need population of 43.6 million children can call upon a supply of services for 44.4 million children. The categories of social welfare and physical health appear more adequate than mental health and corrections, which will be receiving considerably less service than required. 7.4 million children with mental health problems and .43 million juvenile delinquents remain unserved.

3. Looking at the S-curve growth rate (Model 3) in the service system, we find a residue of 7.8 million children in need of service which the system cannot supply when we use conservative estimates of need, and 16.1 million children without service under more liberal estimates of need. This mismatch appears similar in character to that of Model 1; however, the size of the gap between need and service is substantially lower in this case. Here, the gap is 7.8 million as compared with 20.6 million for Model 1, using conservative estimates of need.

Costs of Providing Service

In the last section we derived estimates of costs for the current service system and costs for providing services to those currently in need of service. Using these estimates as a base, we turn now to costs of providing service to those projected as serviced and in need in 1985. Table 39 presents costs only for conservative estimates of need.

Table 39.—Costs for Service in 1985 (in Millions of 1965 Dollars)

	MENTAL HEALTH	SOCIAL WELFARE	PHYSICAL HANDICAP	CORRECTION	TOTAL
Model 1	1,029	7,263	9,748	3,989	22,029
Model 2	3,107	21,607	29,739	12,093	66,546
Model 3	1,942	13,345	18,504	7,355	41,146

Costs in Table 39 are calculated in 1965 dollars. If we assume no inflation over the twenty years and a 3 percent per year real growth rate, the costs to the service systems are seen in Table 40.

Table 40.—Costs for Service in 1985 (in Millions of 1985 Dollars)

	MENTAL HEALTH	SOCIAL WELFARE	PHYSICAL HANDICAP	CORRECTION	TOTAL
Model 1	1,842	13,118	17,606	7,205	39,771
Model 2	5,612	39,024	53,712	21,841	120,189
Model 3	3,507	24,102	33,420	13,284	74,313

On the other hand, if we project how much it will cost to service those in need in 1985, the costs in Table 41 appear.

Table 41.—Costs for Servicing Those in Need, 1985

	MENTAL HEALTH	SOCIAL WELFARE	PHYSICAL HANDICAP	CORRECTION	TOTAL
Population B (millions of 1965 dollars	14,759	16,886	13,217	13,710	58,572
Population B (millions of 1985 dollars)	26,656	30,498	23,871	24,762	105,787

Manpower Requirements in 1985

We can say little about the manpower requirements which costs imply. Data which we used in the preceding section relate to a part of the social welfare subcategory. We observed that the ratio of staff to children serviced in state and local public welfare agencies was 1 to 38. This led to the projection that, if this ratio was viewed as representative for the entire social welfare service system, then the system required 460,000 staff to service 1965 need. Using that same ratio, for social welfare only, in 1985,

Model 1—the 1985 version of the existing system—would call for 110,000 people to maintain that rate of growth; Model 2—the 6 percent growth rate—would call for 630,000; and Model 3—the S-curve growth rate— would call for 390,000. In contrast, the numbers of staff called for to meet the social welfare needs in 1985 would be 490,000.

What this indicates is that, for social welfare only, the system must double its present staff loads to meet current needs; and by 1985, staffing must expand by 150 percent to meet conservative estimates of population needs.

FINDINGS FROM THE ANALYSIS

From our analysis up to this point, we can draw certain broad conclusions.

1. *The state of data available in the field is such as to permit no reasonably accurate quantitative analysis of the state of the nation's service system for children at the present time.*

2. Focusing on what we have described as the system of services to nonnormal-stream children, there is a dramatic mismatch between the character of these services and the needs and demands of children. The system is in need of drastic restructuring, in terms of both the technologies for providing services and the organizational apparatus for delivering them.

The reasons for this are varied. In part, the cause is due to the fact that these service systems display certain pervasive, inherent inadequacies, the more critical of which are as follows:

    a. The system tends to be oriented to professionals providing service rather than to children being served.

    b. It is concerned largely with remedial services for crises in the lives of children rather than with broadly preventive programs affecting the conditions underlying crises.

    c. The system is fragmentary, in the sense of serving a very small fraction of its potential target population—those in need, those at risk —even on very conservative estimates of need.

    d. It is selective and tends to choose clients on the basis of capability to perform; that is, it tends to select those candidates for service most likely to achieve success on the agency's terms.

    e. It tends to select as points of entry into the lives of children those situations which are easiest of access rather than those in which the child presents greatest vulnerability or opportunity for change.

    f. It tends to ignore or to repress the underground, informal service systems which do respond to large numbers of those in need.

    g. It tends to be disconnected organizationally, both in horizontal and in vertical terms, in ways that prevent it from providing either comprehensiveness or continuity of care.

h. It tends to be highly conservative, even in the programs it labels innovations.

These problems begin to suggest directions of change in the system. Even on their own terms, agencies within the system would be swamped by the requirement that they meet conservative estimates of existing and projected need.

The swamping effect would be apparent first in the dimension of manpower (where the system is already most deficient) and then in dollars required. Response to this situation, alone, would require:

the development of new technologies of service which permit greater effect or benefit for a given expenditure of dollars and manpower;

new approaches to manpower problems: restructuring jobs, use of so-called nonprofessionals, and linking to informal systems;

selection of service goals on the basis of more rigorous priority ranking;

and, most likely, a combination of all the above responses.

3. One of the crucial requirements for effective restructuring of these service systems is the development of new techniques and systems of management and of management information, at all levels of the system.

Toward a More Responsive System

of Services to Children

CRITERIA FOR A CHILD-CENTERED SERVICE SYSTEM:
NORMATIVE FUNCTIONAL ANALYSIS

Introduction

Since existing institutions serving children direct their efforts primarily at problems which already exist in the child population, an analysis of the matrix of these institutions focuses, of necessity, on remedial procedures. There is little room in such an analysis either to question the definition of the "problem," which all too often tends to be defined by the service institution, or to view services designed to ensure the well-being of children through prevention.

What, then, would a system of services to children look like if it were based on the developmental cycle of the child, having definite criteria for development at each stage as well as procedures for identification of the environmental determinants of development and the firm goal of providing services which systematically affected those determinants? In short, what would be the characteristics of a truly child-centered service system?

It is clear that many people in the field of services to children are currently groping for answers to these questions. The work of Bolman and Westman represents one such effort within Task Force V. The work of Dr. Frank Rafferty at the University of Maryland represents another. Many outside sources could be cited as well. The following pages present a view which is not the one right view, but one, out of a number of potentially useful views, which serves primarily to identify criteria for broadly based, preventive, child-centered systems of services. These criteria, in turn, may serve as guidelines for broadly based programs of experiment and demonstration in the development of new service systems.

Normative Functional Analysis

We are here concerned, as discussed earlier (p. 105), with the factors which could prevent or reduce the flow of children from the normal-stream to the nonnormal-stream services. With full recognition that a remedial system of services must be continued, albeit with greater effectiveness, the normative approach provides several advantages:

1. The understanding of the major factors influencing normal development in children can serve as a backdrop for a view of the current service system and will serve to highlight the gaps in the present array of services. One can anticipate that these gaps will appear in relation to problem areas and optimal ages for intervention.

2. Second, if the picture of a system of services designed to prevent maldevelopment can be drawn finely enough, one should be able to weigh (in cost-manpower terms) the relative expense, in certain areas, of a preventive as opposed to a remedial service approach.

Definition of Prevention: It is important to distinguish between two levels of prevention:

1. *Basic prevention* refers to those measures taken to *ensure* the well-being of children.

2. *Secondary prevention* refers to those interventions responsive to *early warnings* or symptoms. While remedial in nature, these interventions are designed to prevent the compounded and complex problems in children which are the target of most of our present-day remedial services.

Our concern in this section is with basic prevention.

Method of Approach to Basic Prevention: We have raised the question, What is required for healthy growth and development in children? We chose to view the developing child in three areas of functioning: health, cognition, and development of interpersonal relations. These divisions of the developing child are artificial, created for clarity of analysis.[1] We have tended to view each division separately while, in fact, they are highly interrelated. We know that emotional well-being is influenced by physical well-being. In the same way cognitive development is related to the course of physical and emotional maturation in the growing child. We define each area, in turn, below.

1. A more elaborate version of a similar division is presented graphically in Figure 2 (p. 181), drawn from Dr. Rafferty.

Definition of Areas of Development:

1. Health: Under health, our concern is with those factors which serve to provide optimal physical development in the child. We considered proper nutrition, freedom from and adequate coping with disease, and accident prevention (see subheadings under Health) as factors crucial to optimal physical development.

2. Cognition: Under cognition, we attempted to locate the major influences in the optimal development of the child's cognitive capacities. Cognition refers to the many processes of learning to know and perceive. These processes precede and extend into the years of formal academic learning.

3. Development of Interpersonal Relations: Under development of interpersonal relations, our concern is with those factors which serve to enable the child to develop into a "social being" relating to and gaining satisfaction from the society around him.

Stages of Development: Again, necessarily artificially, we have broken the continuum of growth and development into six stages: prenatal; infant (birth to one year); toddler (one to two); preschool (two to four); school age (four to eleven); adolescent (eleven to eighteen). These classifications, widely held by people who study child development, represent points of major change in the developing child. The toddler is to be distinguished from the infant by virtue of his increased motor ability. His needs and the demands he makes on his environment are to be distinguished from his younger and from his more mature self.

To view the developing child in these stages enables us to refine our original question. When we ask: What factors influence optimal development in each stage of a child's life? we are able to locate points of optimal influence on the course of development; or, negatively, we can see when the child is most vulnerable in the absence of these factors.

With the areas and stages of development designated, the next order of analysis is to determine the factors (called primary determinants) which impinge on the original influences; for example, if adequate nutrition is important to the health and development of the infant, then availability of dietary knowledge and cost and availability of food are important primary determinants.

Once we gain a view of the primary determinants, we should be able to locate those determinants which have the widest range of influence. This panoramic view might, for example, point to adequate family income as a factor greatly affecting the well-being of children in every area of their development.

1. *Health:* We have chosen to view the health of a child as comprised of adequate nutrition, freedom from and proper coping with disease, and

freedom from physical harm through accidents. We must next ask what factors influence adequate nutrition and freedom from disease and accident.

A. *Nutrition.* Four factors emerge as primary determinants in the provision of adequate nutrition:

1. cost and availability of food;
2. dietary knowledge;
3. cooking and food storage facilities;
4. size of family and availability of money for food.

When these determinants are viewed in terms of their relative importance at the different stages of development in the child, they appear to remain qualitatively at the same level of importance.

Prenatal: The physical development and well-being of the child *in utero* is dependent on the mother's nutritional well-being. All of the above-noted determinants are influences of import.

Infant, toddler, preschool: In these stages of development all four determinants are again seen as primary influences on nutritional health.

School age, adolescence: For the school-age child and adolescent there is a slight shift in factor 2. Heretofore, responsibility for adequacy of nutrition has been totally parental. Now the responsibility is shared partly by the child and his knowledge, and partly by the educational institution.

The view of factors of influence can be extended even further to what might be called secondary influences: What are the forces which impinge upon factors 1, 2, 3, and 4?

1. Cost and availability of food are determined in part by:
   a. location of retail stores;
   b. stocking and pricing policies of retail stores;
   c. transportation from production site to retail stores;
2. Dietary knowledge is determined in part by:
   a. educational level of parents;
   b. availability of information through adult education programs, mass media, public health, etc.
3. Cooking and storage facilities are influenced by:
   a. family income;
   b. adequacy of housing.
4. Size of family and availability of money for food are determined in part by:
   a. labor market conditions;
   b. knowledge of and use of contraceptive devices.

As the concentric rings of determining factors are drawn and extended further away from our original focus on the nutritional well-being of children, the interrelatedness of the larger factors can be perceived (See Figure 3).

B. *Disease Prevention.* A second category under health relates to those factors which ensure the child's freedom from disease. Of equal concern is the question of adequate coping with transitory childhood diseases (secondary prevention).

C. *Phases of Development.*

Prenatal: general maternal health (including nutrition) protection from exposure to diseases which would affect embryo.

Infancy: nutrition; housing conditions—warmth/cold; sanitation; facilities to sterilize; shots for prevention of specific diseases; alertness to early signs of disease, detection; seeking medical care at warning signals; ability to carry out medical requirements if disease is contracted; home care.

Toddler: All of the above conditions needed in infancy remain important for this phase of development, except that a sterile environment is not necessary past infancy.

Preschool and school age: Freedom from disease is also dependent on the above conditions (except sterile conditions). In regard to alertness to disease, the responsibility for detection extends from the home to school.

Adolescence: The adolescent child's freedom from disease continues to depend on the above factors cited for infancy. Home care is less dependent on parents. The older child can see to his own medication, bed rest, etc. Detection of disease is partly the child's own responsibility.

As one looks at the above list of conditions for freedom from disease, several factors stand out as primary determinants of these conditions:

1. knowledge (to detect and give care);
2. availability of medical consultation;
3. income: purchase of medicine;
        travel to medical facilities;
        personnel to supervise home care.

D. *Accident Prevention.* In this area our concern is with factors which create environmental safety for the growing child and freedom from physical harm through accidents. One must look, therefore, to both home and neighborhood as "environment."

Prenatal: Concern with this stage of development again focuses on the mother's health and well-being. Our focus is on her home and neighborhood environment, protecting her from rat bites, falls due to poor construction, fire, traffic accidents, etc.

Infancy through preschool: Responsibility for environmental safety is with the adult, and the environment of greatest concern is the home. Freedom from the dangers of fire, rat bites, falling parts of the building, and leaking gas are crucial to the infant. Once the child has developed motor ability, the adult must be alert to potential burns, falls, and cuts. With increased mobility, concern with environmental safety is extended to the neighborhood, where traffic, attractive nuisances, and people (molesters) are added to the picture.

School age and adolescence: Unlike his younger self, the school-age and adolescent child develops responsibility for his own safety, depending upon his knowledge (and impulse control).

FIG. 2 —Rings of Factors Determining Nutritional Well-Being of Children

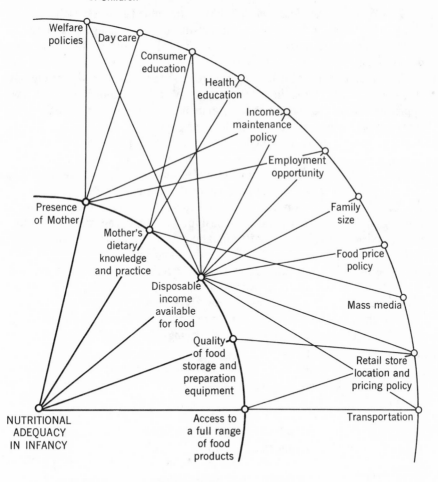

Factors of Primary Importance in Determining Environmental Safety:

    1. housing conditions and income;
    2. neighborhood conditions and income;
    3. knowledge;
    4. time to supervise and train younger children: income and family size;
    5. community concern:
        housing code enforcement;
        traffic;
        street and alley cleaning;
        garbage removal.

    2. Cognitive Development: We have determined that the well-being of children is ensured by optimal circumstances influencing their physical (health), educational (cognitive development), and social (interpersonal) development.

    We have noted the artificiality in treating these factors separately and stressed that their true interdependence must be acknowledged. As we approach the area of cognitive development, this interdependence intrudes into our discussion: one must say, "Given physical well-being of the child, cognitive development is influenced by a number of factors."

    Infancy: (1) development of basic trust (via mother-child relationship); (2) environmental stimulation (sound, tactile, and visual)—the order and intensity of this will increase as the child matures.

    Toddler: (1) development of capacities to sublimate, arising from toilet training and the mother-child relationship; (2) encouragement to explore with provision of safety so that traumatic experiences do not damage curiosity; (3) environmental stimulation, the range of which increases with age. The infant is stimulated primarily by sounds, touch, and visual inputs in which he is essentially a passive recipient. The toddler, by nature of his physical and motor development, needs to be actively involved in touching, manipulating, seeing; (4) encouragement to master, "do for self," balanced with readiness to "do for," strivings for independence balanced with longings for dependency.

    It should be noted that we are discussing conditions which influence optimal cognitive development, not learning, which occurs even in the absence of optimal conditions.

    By viewing these conditions, it becomes evident that, from infancy up to school age, the precursors to "formal education" are greatly determined by the mother-child relationship. In turn, this relationship is influenced by the mother's psychological and physical ability to provide these conditions for the child. Here the range of secondary influences is enormous: income, marital status, family size, knowledge, and cultural patterns are but a few of the more important factors. One tends to separate socioeconomic groups, remarking that psychological factors are the strongest influence on the middle-class and upper-class mother's capacity to provide the optimal conditions; whereas the lower-class mother's psychological and environmental states both influence her ability to provide such conditions.

School age: In considering the school-age child, most of the responsibility shifts to conditions provided by our educational systems. It is our belief that when education is supported by positive parental attitudes the process is enhanced. Note should be made that we have shifted from mother-child to parent-child. As the child matures, the father becomes increasingly influential in the following ways:

1. his attitude toward learning;
2. the role model he provides;
3. his emotional relationship to the child—if mature, he encourages identification and enjoys and is enlarged by the child's accomplishments; if immature, he is rivalrous, forbids identification, is jealous of the child, and discourages accomplishments on a level with or beyond his own.

3. *Interpersonal Development:* The significance of a developmental approach is particularly evident in this segment of our analysis. Interpersonal well-being in the growing child is relative and cumulative; at any point in the child's life, his well-being (or absence of well-being) is dependent upon and derives from his earlier experiences.

Let us consider the interpersonal aspects of the end point of the child's development—adulthood—and then examine the factors that facilitate or handicap the child's progress toward that stage. We can define three functional areas of well-being in the adult:

1. *Friendships:* The ability to establish, maintain, and experience satisfaction from close relationships with other human beings.

2. *Work relationships:* The ability to function with satisfaction vis-à-vis other people according to the demands of the job, whether those call for independence, submission to greater authority, or leadership.

3. *Heterosexual relationships:* The ability to establish, sustain, and gain satisfaction from heterosexual relationships, with acceptance and enjoyment from a biologically determined sex role.

These three areas of functioning cannot be applied to the developing child. We are, however, able to locate in each stage of development important precursors to later interpersonal well-being. The progression takes the form of a fan: each time we advance a stage, the number of precursors increases.

Infancy: The establishment of basic trust is crucial to the later development of interpersonal well-being. This trust is developed in the first year of life through the mother-child (or a mother-surrogate-child) relationship. A steady, responsive, dependable mother creates in the growing infant a sense of well-being or trust that his needs will be met.

What, then, are the factors which influence the mother or enable her to fulfill the role we have defined? The following appear particularly significant:

1. presence of husband for psychological support;
2. sufficient income so that the mother can stay with her child;
3. sufficiently pleasant physical home environment so that the mother isn't driven to escape it;
4. size of family vis-à-vis other demands on mother's time and attention;
5. culture and family tradition.

The above determinants are of a primarily situational nature. Psychological factors become the crucial variable—for example, if we could provide optimal situational circumstances, we could still observe some poor mother-child relationships owing entirely to the mother's psychological states. Conversely, the woman who is able to give, and attend and respond to the infant's needs, often does so under adverse situational conditions. From the point of view of program strategies, however, we are aware that the mother's capacity to attend to the infant's needs is enhanced as the negative "situational influences" decrease. The obvious exception is the emotionally incapacitated mother.

Toddler: As we move to the toddler stage, the importance of the nourishing responsive mother is retained, while several new elements of the mother-child relationship assume significance.

Toilet training now becomes important. The quality of the mother-child interaction here is a primary determinant of several aspects of personality development that have a direct bearing on interpersonal well-being. This interaction establishes the groundwork for:

1. impulse control;
2. self-image;
3. personality characteristics—degree of conformity or rebelliousness.

Again, it is the mother who must make a series of emotional responses and actions if healthy development is to take place:

1. acceptance of the child's resistance to becoming controlled;
2. firm expectation and demands that control will be accomplished;

3. the absence of punitive responses in the face of failure or defiance from the child;

4. the readiness to offer love and approval (or encouragement and rewards).

Once again, the mother's emotional and situational existence influences her ability to provide the responses cited above. Her emotional disabilities, if long-standing and internalized (i.e., not responsive to her situation), are the proper concern of remedial mental health programs. When we examine the situational factors affecting her, the same determinants discussed in the section on infancy emerge:

1. presence of husband to provide psychological and financial support;

2. income;

3. physical environment of home and neighborhood facilities, e.g., laundromats;

4. size of family—vis-à-vis other demands on mother;

5. culture of family—especially attitudes toward cleanliness and control.

Preschool: The child now enters into the process of finding an identity. If the psychological equipment he developed in the earlier stages of life is adequate, he enters into active mastery—gaining a sense of ability and capability. He also steps toward forming a sexual identification (resolution of Oedipal phase).

While still important, the mother now shares the influential role with the father. Both parents need to encourage, guide, and support the child's explorations. Both parents are crucial to the resolution of the Oedipal and early sexual identity formation.

The situation determinants remain important although the reasons shift slightly:

1. *Presence of husband* now is important directly to the child instead of as support to the mother.

2. *Income* takes on greater significance. One might design a subcategory of *job satisfaction.* A father's view of his occupation can strongly determine the kind of object of identification he provides for both sons and daughters.

3. *Physical environment of home and neighborhood* can greatly influence the parent's ease in letting a child explore.

4. *Size of family* now must be considered in terms of demands being made on both parents.

5. *Culture of family:* at this stage of development, families often

have to contend with differences between mother's and father's attitudes toward child-rearing.

School age: Reiterating that each stage of development evolves from its predecessors, we note that the emotionally well-equipped school-age child begins to unfold as a social being. While the influence of both parents remains important, the quality of available peer world now becomes crucial. Here we find further work on identity with age mates offering support and an arena for trying on different roles. The child's sense of himself is less dependent on parental response. He now needs a reflection of himself in his peer's eyes.

The quality of the influence of situational determinants shifts with the maturing child:

1. *Presence of husband:* Both parents are important as cushions, comforters, translators of the "harsh real world." They provide support and nurturance as well as room to experiment and move away from the home.

2. *Income:* In earlier stages of the child's life, income influenced the mother's ability to remain home and the father's satisfaction in his job. At this stage it takes on special meaning, since it defines the child's peer life. The quality and availability of neighborhood peers, schoolmates, after-school activities, and skill-learning activities differ greatly according to income level. The slum child is surrounded by similarly disadvantaged peer groups who will shape his social role almost regardless of earlier parental handling. This stage is one of high vulnerability, and in it programs for children could be instituted on a preventive level. Unfortunately, most formal social groups gather together children of similar situational and emotional backgrounds in which the *social* learning potential is low.

3. *Family size:* The size of family has less important influence on the school-age child. If great demands are made on the parents' attention, it can mean that less comfort and guidance are available when the child touches "home base." As a result, the child might demand from peers more than is realistic to expect, or he could withdraw from peer life to "get his due" at home. But if the earlier years have been adequately nurturing, he will not be deeply affected by family size.

4. *Home environment:* Until this stage of development, we have viewed the home environment mainly as an influence on the mother. At this stage we can consider the home as it influences the child's freedom to "invite friends in." Space and attractiveness become important factors.

5. *Family culture and activities:* Again, at this stage the child in his newfound peer life can be supported by or be in conflict with the family cultural teachings about peer behavior.

Adolescence: The adolescent stage represents a "final" working and reworking at a level of greater maturity of all the previously mentioned precursors to interpersonal well-being. Biological, physical, and emotional development converge in the adolescent. We observe familiar struggles over impulse control, conflicts between dependency strivings and the quest for independence, and attempts at reaching a new level of identity as a total being, specifically as a sexual being. Assuming an adequate inheritance from his earlier years, the adolescent, like his younger self, is affected by situational determinants as follows:

1. *Presence of husband:* The husband's presence is again crucial, both as a support to his wife and as father to the adolescent.
2. *Income:* Income level now affects parental functioning and greatly determines the quality of the adolescent's peer life.
3. *Family size:* The size of the adolescent's family remains important as it influences the availability of his parents. It also directly affects (somewhat dependent on family expectations) his freedom to "live his own life." The adolescent of a large family is often given a parent role to younger siblings. For many, this is a positive learning experience; for others, it involves a too early assumption of responsibility and requires that the emotional tasks of adolescence be skipped.
4. *Home environment:* Size, available space (related to family size), and attractiveness are again crucial to parent and child. The adolescent needs privacy and a place to entertain.
5. *Family culture and attitudes:* The family culture takes on particular significance in this stage as a potential for congruence or conflict with the child's peer life.

Implications: We have attempted to trace developmentally those aspects of personality which have bearing on interpersonal well-being; while noting that at each stage the emotional state of the parents and child is a crucial variable, we have observed a number of situational circumstances which also have a direct bearing on development. Remedial programs rightly direct their energies toward malfunctions in parent-child relationships. This normative view implies that services which ensure income level, adequate housing, and mental health education could play an important role in prevention.

Conclusions

A number of crucial issues emerge from the normative or developmental approach which have important implications for service delivery that is concerned with the well-being of children.

Introduction of services at optimal age of influnce: While the vast majority of existing services to children are remedial rather than preventive, issues arise from the normative analysis which are pertinent to those services concerned primarily with prevention. One has to do with the consideration of the optimal age for introducing preventive services.

A review of existing services highlights the fact that most prevention services are introduced when children can be reached through an institution which has easy access to them. (See Table 42, "Health Services Related to the Well-Being of Children.") While access is an important concern, it should not overshadow the question of ages of optimal influence.

The school is an institution which has access to large numbers of children and consequently has become the major vehicle for preventive programs.

Following the areas of development delineated in our normative functional analysis, we can observe programs attempting to influence each of these areas: health, cognition, interpersonal development offered when the child begins to start school. Yet, when we review development we observe that the child is most vulnerable to healthy development or maldevelopment at ages prior to the commencement of formal schooling.

This observation suggests that new vehicles of access must be envisaged by planners of service delivery, through which children can be reached at a time when their future development is open to the greatest influence.

Institutions with multiple purposes: Programs like Head Start appear to us to offer a model, at least in theory, for the kind of institutions that should be created anew or from the old to answer the concern of access at an optimal time. Ostensibly designed as a program to influence cognitive development, Head Start also can offer dental, nutritional, and interpersonal aids to the development of the children in its program. As a newly created organization, it was free from the struggles which are inevitable when an "old" institution enlarges or shifts its goals of operation. Despite these struggles, it would seem to us that existing programs—well-baby clinics, maternal and child health programs, day care—would do well to try to envisage how their service could be extended beyond their original contract.

Factors influencing the well-being of children: Perhaps the most important issue arising from the normative functional analysis was an enlarged view of those factors which influence the well-being of children. It has been traditional to view and try to influence those factors *close* to the problem or area of concern. Thus, when concerned with nutrition, our programs of prevention have directed themselves at feeding: milk programs, free lunches, etc. When accident prevention has been the goal, we have educated parents and children about potential hazards in the home. Programs concerned with cognitive development have focused on enrichment.

The normative approach has highlighted a view of influences on the well-being of children which are not ordinarily seen as relevant to normal development—family income, housing, neighborhood conditions, transportation, trash collection, etc. The latter are factors which have consistently emerged in this analysis as having an important influence on the well-being of children.

With these larger determinants in mind, we can envisage programs concerned with nutritional well-being of children attempting to influence food pricing, or concerning themselves with the question of availability of food, transportation to markets, etc.

Likewise, accident prevention programs would have to reach beyond knowledge and conditions in the homes to the neighborhood—to garbage removal, to concern with "attractive nuisances," to proper playgrounds. Or, programs designed to influence cognitive development in children would try to retain the mother in the home in the early years of the child's life and would offer parent education about the factors involved early in life which influence later cognitive development.

A New View

The major question which follows from this is: How are we to modify and redefine existing categories of services to include these determinants? It appears to us that shifts in existing services and the creation of new patterns of services can take place only when the implications of these findings are thoroughly understood and envisaged by planners and practitioners alike. What is needed first is a new perceptual set, the ability to move from a traditional view of problems and their causes to this enlarged overview.

A new management: Following from this enlarged perception there must emerge a new kind of management of services which envisages, sanctions, and administers a complex of activities. On the microcosmic level the director of a day-care center, for example, would envisage the wide range of potential influence in his operations and would seek to offer a variety of services:

DAY CARE

1. custodial—physical care of children
2. nutrition
3. disease prevention
4. enrichment program
5. transportation to industry for parents
6. transportation to markets for food purchases

Table 42.—Health Services Related to the Well-being of Children

EXISTING PROGRAMS OFFERING SERVICES RELATED TO NUTRITION	AGES OF CHILDREN WHICH PROGRAM COVERS				
	INFANCY	TODDLER	PRESCHOOL	SCHOOL AGE	ADOLESCENCE
1. Maternal and child health					
2. Head Start					
3. School milk, lunch					
4. Food stamps					
5. Food surplus					
6. Mass media—TV, newspapers, magazines					
7. Consumer education					
8. Food purchasing; transportation groups					
9. Food cooperatives					
DISEASE PREVENTION					
1. Maternal and child health					
2. Well-baby clinics					
3. Inoculation programs					
4. Comprehensive medical care programs					

SERVICES RELATED TO
ACCIDENT PREVENTION

1. Mass media _____

2. School education (of child) _____

SERVICES RELATED TO
COGNITIVE DEVELOPMENT

1. Day care _____

2. Playgrounds _____

3. Head Start _____

4. Nursery _____

5. Schools _____

INTERPERSONAL

1. Play group[1] _____

2. Clubs _____

3. Settlements _____

4. Discussion groups _____

[1] Many group programs designed to influence interpersonal well-being of children are neighborhood-bound and thus are formed of children with similar problems whose potential for negative reinforcement is great.

Moving from a single service to the larger community, to city, state, and federal government, we are envisaging management that seeks to create multiple uses throughout the system.

Implications for Manpower: We are already confronted with severe manpower problems—shortages on every level and in every area of service. The approach suggested by our study places another burden on the manpower concern not in terms of quantity but in terms of *quality* of manpower. To date, programs of higher education have been training practitioners in a single service—the doctor, nurse, teacher, social caseworker, psychiatrist, nutritionist. While the expertise of these specialists must be retained, we see the need of enlarging their education to the point where they can understand and try to influence the political and bureaucratic matrix that characterizes the system of service delivery. It is not enough to train a group of planners and community organizers alone to do the job. This is presently and painfully being experienced by psychiatrists who in their move into community mental health programs are learning that they cannot remain naïve and unaware of the complex ebbs and flows of community, state, and federal government.

CRITERIA FOR A MANAGEMENT INFORMATION SYSTEM:
APPROACHES TO DATA GATHERING AND ANALYSIS

Introduction

Analysis of guidelines for a child-centered system of services leads us directly to the support of management data and analysis, and the system for providing and using them. We have stated our assumption elsewhere that these systems would be conducive to effective functioning of the children's system.

We are concerned with several kinds of data and analysis:

1. Data required for cost-benefit and cost-effectiveness analysis, at municipal, state, and national levels, in order to permit:
    effective establishment of priorities for investment of scare resources;
    effective program control.
2. Operating data, consisting of measures of development for children and measures of performance for service systems. The purpose of this data system is to:
    identify periods of vulnerability and opportunity in the lives of children, and relate them to appropriate service resources;
    monitor performance of service agencies and feedback information in order to modify agency performance.

There is a link between the two kinds of data. Operating data, of the kind indicated in item 2, would provide information related to both benefit and cost of children's services. The system for gathering such data would be essential to a management information system related to cost-benefit analysis.

Our treatment of these subjects represents only a beginning and, in effect, spells out criteria for such systems and lays the groundwork for further inquiry.

Our discussion proceeds along the following lines:

The utility of cost-benefit analysis at various points in the child service system—for determining priorities within the children's system and in relation to other systems, for program control, and for economical management of the system.

A conceptual approach to benefit-cost analysis based on the question: Benefit for and costs to whom? We discuss children, society, and professionals as "client groups," and suggest some measures of benefit and of cost.

An illustration, at the state level, of an organization for such a management information system.

Discussions of measures of child development and of agency performance along a series of dimensions—these are in elaboration of the dimensions of health, cognitive development, and interpersonal competence, discussed in the previous sections. Here they are discussed as the conceptual framework underlying a possible child-monitoring system.

In the course of these discussions several issues of value and methodology arise. In this field, the very possibility of cost-benefit analysis and of measurement of agency performance has been called into question. We attempt to note some of the obstacles to these forms of analysis, as we encounter them, in the text.

The Use of Cost-Benefit Analysis for Child Service Systems

In the organization and administration of the child-centered services, there are certain fiscal aspects that legislators and administrators have to consider. These might broadly be categorized into: (1) priorities, both external to and within the child service system; (2) legislative control; and (3) economy of scale.

Analysis of Priorities: As to the priority question, legislators have to make a judgment as to the aggregate public expenditures relating to child mental health services. Since there is a variety of demands being made at the national, state, and local level as to the manner and direction in which public expenditures should be made, legislators have to make a judgment as to the relative priority or importance child mental health services may receive vis-à-vis other demands. Obviously, a variety of demands exists— to support agricultural prices, aid in redevelopment of foreign countries, exploring outer space, building additional highways, etc. How shall these and others be ranked as to their relative importance, and once ranked, how will decisions be made as to expenditures to support such programs? There are a variety of criteria that one might utilize, for example: (1) need; (2) return; (3) equity; (4) political determinants; and (5) collective value judgment. We might look at each of these in terms of priority setting.

First, as to need, one might postulate that public expenditures should be dispersed in such a manner as to satisfy those who need a particular service both in terms of their numbers and in terms of the seriousness of the need. Of a child population from birth to age twenty, of which in 1965 there were approximately 79.8 million, between 11 million and 15 million constitute what might be considered a risk population. Of the 33.2 million children needing services, only 13.8 million received any service at all.[2] Thus it would appear that on the basis of the number who require services and the number who actually were rendered services, children with special problems receive a relatively low priority.

The question that has to be asked is: To what extent could client groups forgo the program if it were given relatively low priority or if the program did not exist at all? Thus one could raise a question about highways: If a significant expenditure were not put into highways, to what extent would individuals be deprived of transport service? Obviously, there might be a certain measure of inconvenience, driving time might be lengthened, but one would have difficulty finding a serious deprivation on the level of the individual. On the other hand, when we look at children who are emotionally disturbed, abandoned, or mentally retarded, if services are not provided there is a strong possibility they will not become stable, adjusted, productive adults. It is not a question of inconvenience. Yet on the basis of need, in terms of number, the vast majority of children are not currently being served.

One might look at priorities in terms of the dollar return on public expenditure (this is an investment criteria which we shall look at more closely later on); if this is done, then certainly cost-benefit analysis indicates that investments in the development of more productive children have a positive return. Society always receives back a greater economic return than the amount invested. The best indication of this is funds invested in public education. As part of the investment picture, also (and

2. If corrections and social welfare are excluded, the number at risk reads 14.6 million; the number served, 6.1 million (see Table 33, p. 165).

this question will be reviewed later) one has to consider what would be the consequence of minimal investment. That is, if both preventive and rehabilitative measures are not taken, and emotionally disturbed and mentally retarded children requiring assistance do not receive it and subsequently enter society, what additional costs are incurred in the form of public assistance, increasing crime rate, etc.? That is, the absence of expenditures may have consequences which may not be true insofar as other governmental programs are concerned.

Another criterion that one might use relates to the question of equity or the relative distribution of public expenditures vis-à-vis the source of their contribution. Is the taxpayer receiving back in public services the relative amount or value of services that he is contributing? We are discussing a population in need constituting approximately 41 percent of the total child population.[3] Assuming that such a population roughly constitutes 20 percent of the families in the United States, are these families receiving back in the form of public health services for their children an amount of service which is relative to the amount of tax dollars they are contributing? While this report has no hard and fast data on this issue (surely this is an area that could be investigated), there may be reason to believe that on the basis of tax dollars contributed these families are not receiving their fair share in the form of services. Certainly they are contributing much more than the millions per year which are provided for such services. Simply in terms of the public expenditure, there is reason to believe that for total child services more funds are expended on what might be considered the normal child and particularly the above-normal child. For example, in terms of higher education, which is largely supported by public funds, it is the relatively low-income families (contributing to state revenues in the form of sales taxes) whose children are unable to attend state universities and who pay a disproportionate share to the support of state universities. Further, there is reason to believe that the educational system is, to a large extent, geared to the average or above-average child. The child population we are considering, that is, the risk population, is that which has difficulty adjusting to the normal school situation and for whom the schools only recently have begun to provide services, at least in a referral sense. Thus, while we have a public education system in which something like $50 billion a year is currently invested, it would appear that an inadequate amount of funds is being used to support the nonnormal-stream children, who most need the support. At any rate, risk-child families are not receiving back in services the amount that they are contributing in the form of taxes.

Another criterion that might be used in establishing priorities relates

3. This figure includes some double counting, e.g., children who may be both in court and on welfare.

to the political factor. Here one faces the obvious fact that the child population with which we are concerned cannot vote. Nor does it appear that families of these children constitute a distinct and organized political group who in the past have been able to bring their problems to bear at various political levels.

Still another guide which might be used is the collective value judgment of American society. There is every indication that a very high priority has always been placed on the development of the child to his fullest potential. This is demonstrated by the expenditure on public education. Unfortunately, we are dealing with a segment of the child population who does not seem to be falling into this general social objective. It would seem that with respect to the criteria that one might employ, child health services should receive a relatively high priority vis-à-vis other public services which are offered, yet they are in fact currently receiving a low priority.

Another aspect of the question of priorities is the manner in which public funds are to be allocated, given both the limited funds which would appear to be available and the child needs that exist. Given even the most optimistic of predictions as to growth in public expenditures over the next five years, only a small portion or percentage of children will be able to be served. Out of a risk population which by 1972 approximated 38 million children, it is unlikely that funds would be available to take care of more than 24.7 million. Thus the problem that legislators and administrators face is the question of which children shall receive services and subsequently the specific services that shall be rendered.

How are extremely limited resources to be allocated so as to maximize some set of social objectives? What decision strategy should be followed?

There appear to be various allocation problems. At the federal government level, even with a reasonable growth factor, its future contribution would appear to be minimal. This would suggest that if expenditures should be restricted, they need to be limited to one or two programs which perhaps are not currently being offered at the state or local level and which have the possibility of high productivity payoff. The alternative would be to spread the federal dollar over the gamut of existing programs and services. Such a course would have little or no impact in terms of the child-need situation which exists. At the state and local level, assuming that existing sources are going to be maintained, the discretion which state and local legislators have would be restricted to the marginal growth dollar. A question arises as to the discretion that legislators have concerning new services or programs. It appears that these would be fairly restrictive. It is hoped that at both the state and the local level some delineation will be made between the amount of expenditure that must be directed to maintaining existing programs and the marginal dollar that can be used to inaugurate new services or improve the productivity of existing services.

It should be noted that the legislative input is essentially an economic or dollar input. Obviously, legislators do not provide direct services for children; this is done by public and private agencies. The essential problem, then, faced at the legislative level is a decision-making one: What specific services are to be purchased, or how are we to allocate the tax dollar in the child service system?

And while it is assumed that such an allocation would be subjected to the normal legislative processes—committee hearings, appropriations, recommendations by administrative bodies of both state and federal government—*serious questions arise as to whether legislators are currently presented with data that would facilitate such an allocation process*. There is some question as to whether the existing public child service agencies are presenting proposals and data to legislators so that best choices can be made. *There is a need for data models at federal and state and local levels that would stipulate the amount and types of information that legislators ought to have to assure allocation of tax dollars in the most productive manner*. Presumably, such allocation will be based on some form of cost-benefit or cost-effectiveness return.

Legislative Control: Another economic or fiscal dimension that legislators have to consider is the use of public expenditures as a control device to assure that agencies operate in a fashion which is consistent with the social objectives that legislators want to achieve. Legislators can assure this consistency of agency activity with public objectives by insisting that the continuity of public expenditures be contingent upon performance as stipulated by legislators. Thus, whatever performance standards legislators ultimately stipulate, one can be reasonably certain that the efforts of agencies will attempt to achieve such standards if their own future support rests on such an achievement. Another dimension requires that, at least in part, certain expenditures have to be made for control and data collection purposes. What data have to be collected to assure that legislators are receiving the expected return on public expenditure?

Economy of Scale: The last economic dimension that legislators have to be concerned with relates to economics of scale. This is largely a question of the appropriate size of operations to minimize cost of the operation. Given the technology of health care for children, what is the appropriate size of operations to minimize cost of the operation? Given the technology of health care for children, what is the appropriate size of organization to render services and minimize costs? This is largely a question of whether the existing public and private health agencies are efficiently constituted. As already noted, "There is no interconnected, integrated set of organizations and institutions, committed to a set of clear, shared, and self-consistent objectives and managed under carefully worked-out policies to achieve these objectives.

" . . . There is, nevertheless, a complex of individuals, organizations, agencies, and programs which affect children and the environment in which children live."

There is a fundamental conceptual difficulty here. While the particular set of agencies and services has been referred to as a child service system, organizationally we do not have a system. Rather, what we seem to have is a service industry or a service structure. One of the conceptual problems is treating this set of public and private agencies as if they constituted a system. It would appear at the conceptual level that one of the major tasks of the Joint Commission is to convert what seems to be either a service structure or industry into a system in order to provide the needed integration and coordination of service to the child population. To refer to a set of activities as a system does not in a normative sense make the activities a system in fact.

When we view the set of child health agencies as an industry, what we find is a set of voluntary private and public agencies functioning as separate and autonomous units and competing with each other for either the private consumer dollar or a government budget dollar. Presumably each agency attempts to develop a set of services which will meet either a private or a public market demand of a sufficient size that supports that agency. The question of both efficient size and administration from an economic point of view has always been resolved on the basis of competition. That is, as public and private agencies competed for the consumer dollar, the more efficient agency would drive out of the market the less efficient, so that in the long run only the former would survive. Moreover, it was assumed that at the agency level managers would act in such fashion as to make their agencies more efficient. As to the private nonprofit agency, is there any reason to assume that viewed as an industry it would operate in such a fashion as to encourage the more efficient producer and discourage the less efficient? While no data are available, a first impression indicates that reliance on the competitive model will not assure an efficient agency operation and that some form of public or private intervention will be necessary.

In public agencies, one finds dollars allocated and expended and activities administered along bureaucratic lines. Again one cannot view public agencies as a system but rather as a public structure. Characteristically, an attempt is made to organize services along hierarchical lines. At any governmental level, agencies tend to take on an autonomous existence, again for survival purposes, and to compete with one another for the public dollar. The tendency is to submit to legislators programs and data which tend to expand the activities of the agencies and increase the well-being of agency staff. Such an effort frequently leads to duplication of effort, absence of coordination, inefficient operation, and other problems already outlined.

The problems are typical of a public service organized along bureaucratic lines. And if we temporarily ignore the private segment of child services, what the Joint Commission should seriously consider is a view of child services organized along *systems* lines. This should be done to assure that services are rendered in an effective and efficient manner. By effective, we mean that the agencies will actually do whatever it is that has to be done, and by efficient, we mean that they will accomplish their objectives at minimal cost. The task is how to convert a bureaucratic child service into a set of activities along systems lines. It seems fairly apparent that until this conceptual problem is solved, ineffectual services will continue.

At the present time there appear to be neither economic determinants (vis-à-vis market pressures) nor legislative determinants (vis-à-vis analytical devices and controls at the legislative level) which will assure that the most efficient organizations in terms of providing required services do in fact exist.

A Conceptual Approach to Cost-Benefit Analysis for the Child Service System

The Joint Commission may wish to recommend that proposed legislation for child services should incorporate cost-effectiveness, cost-benefit data so that legislators and administrators may make more effective choices. This is currently being adopted at the federal level under the general direction of the Bureau of the Budget, and there is significant interest at various state legislative levels in this general approach.

In performing a cost-benefit analysis at the outset, it is necessary to delineate those respective groups of clients who may be expected to receive some set of benefits from the operation of the child health service system. It would appear there are at least four: (1) the taxpayer; (2) the children; (3) the producers of child health services, the professionals; and (4) various voluntary charitable interest groups. The total benefit output of the child health service system would be some aggregation of the benefits which these respective groups receive. We might look at each of these in turn.

If we begin with children, and society as affected by what happens to children, we can assert that children who return to what we have called the normal stream will in turn be more productive individuals and will produce a stream of benefits to society—psychological, sociological, political, and economic.

Economic benefit is most easily ascertained. Such children will not only earn more over their work life, but contribute more in taxes. In addition, society has a reduced cost in the form of maintaining nonnormal children and adults. If one knew both the economic return of those normal children and the cost of making them economically productive, one would have an investment criterion to serve as a guide in decision making. To illustrate: utilizing cost figures based on nonvoluntary (public) services and at proportionate charges based on current levels, the following formulas are suggestive of some modes of analysis:

1. $$\frac{E\ yG}{E(cL)}$$ where

E = no. of exits from system
y = average no. of years of working life after exit
G = net earning gain per capita per annum
t = taxes, and may be considered a proportion of G
c = per capita cost of stay in system
L = length of stay in system

2. $$\frac{E(cL)}{EG}$$ = no. of years it would take to recapture cost of system for all E in terms of net gain (contribution to gross national product)

3. $$\frac{E(cL)}{E\,t\,G}$$ = no. of years it would take to recapture cost in terms of tax revenue—where t is proportion of G, i.e., taxes

4. $E\ yG - E(cL)$ = social gain

5. $E(yGt) - E(cL)$ = federal revenue gain

Exits from the system at age nineteen can be estimated as follows (on the basis of earlier assumptions):

	Cost	Age cohort 15–19 in system	Exits
1970	$276 million	122,000	24,400
1975	$315 million	143,000	28,600

The foregoing are rough estimates that can be refined by the method of least squares. Of course, exit data need to be based on single-year age cohorts. Data can then be obtained to project occupational structures in estimating average annual earnings after exit. Assuming that without passing through the system, earnings will be at the poverty level, earnings beyond that level would represent net gain. For example, if total earnings after exit on the average would be $6,000, the net gain could be estimated at $3,000 per annum per client after exit. If a thirty-year working life is projected, the net gain to society in terms of GNP would be $2.2 billion.

Taking the above estimates, the cost of the system per "exitee" could be estimated in terms of length of time in the system. Alternatively, cost-earnings data could be used to estimate the length of time the system can afford to hold on to a client.

Once these costs are classified, the manner in which such data can be processed or analyzed will be suggested. For example, it may be desirable to project manpower costs in terms of program requirements and training capability. Some dimensions of the problem can be deduced from the following:

In 1960, 23,000 persons were engaged in child welfare; of these, 16,600 were social workers (half of whom belonged to professional associations); 8,000 were in public child welfare full time.

Assuming constant proportions, the need for personnel by 1970 would be 28,000; by 1975 it would be 33,000.

In 1962 full-time student enrollment in accredited schools of social work was 6,000; the number of M.S.W. degrees awarded was 2,600 for all fields of social work.

It is possible that minimum levels will be maintained, but no expansion of manpower seems possible at this level. Need is demonstrated by the fact that half the counties have no full-time public child welfare worker, and the ratio where services are available is 1 worker to 1,000 children.

Return analyses: Benefits or output of existing services will also be identified and classified. When a program returns the child to the normal stream, what benefits does he receive and, in turn, contribute? There is, for example, the benefit of psychological health to the individual, improvement in social adjustment, family harmony, and economic self-sufficiency.

Given both benefit and cost data, one can begin to calculate return per dollar expenditure on each child treated. An example has already been provided of this type of analysis, in which calculations are estimated as contribution to the economy, in general, and tax revenue, specifically. One may want to calculate economic return by type of illness, program, type of organization (public vs. private), overtime, etc.

It is much more difficult to make even rough estimates of noneconomic return per dollar expenditure. For example, suppose a certain capability is postulated to achieve a certain educational attainment; then calculations could be made as to the required dollar expenditure per illness, program, time period, type of patient, to achieve such an attainment, and so forth.

In this context, as we will indicate later in this section, one can assume certain minimal combinations of standards of development which we would want all children to achieve. At least we can postulate certain standards in terms of biological, emotional, social, intellectual, and communicative categories—along some continuum in terms of well, average, and vulnerable.

Let us shift our attention from children and "society," as beneficiaries of services, to the professional producer group—that set of individuals which deals directly or indirectly with the child to provide services. These are the service personnel, psychiatrists, psychologists, social workers, agency staff, administrators, and supervisors.

In looking at the child service system as it currently operates, one receives the impression that systems performance criteria frequently are structured in terms of professional interest. Professional standards have to be directed toward restricting the supply of manpower into a field and increasing the demand for work for those already in the field. The result is to create increasing income, job security, reduced work load, and other occupational objectives which characterize any occupational group. Here one is not necessarily being critical of the professional group in the child service system. It is not unique in these respects, and its particular standards characterize most professional groups. This would be true of teachers, professors, engineers, lawyers, doctors, etc. It would be unusual, given the opportunity, for any professional group not to substitute its own set of professional objectives as constituting the objectives or performance standards of the particular system with which it is concerned.

We might look at some examples of professional standards. One is a high client- or patient-staff relationship: one professional standard considered desirable is to minimize the number of children any professional has to deal with. A consequence of this, of course, is to increase the demand for labor or the number of professionals that is required. Another standard for the system frequently postulated is high educational requirements: only those who are professionally trained can perform certain activities in the agency context. Obviously, such requirements will restrict the supply of manpower to the system. Low case load is similar to high client-staff relationship. If one looks critically at professional standards which have tended to emerge as the basis on which to evaluate health services, one finds their essential thrust is to increase the demand for manpower and to restrict its supply—the consequence of which, of course, will be to increase the occupational benefits for professionals.

What is being suggested is that (1) occupational benefits are inappropriate as standards of systems performance, and (2) such benefits should be viewed as constituting a specific output of the system for a specific group. Indiscriminate use of so-called professional standards will not increase systems effectiveness but will result in higher cost and greater benefits for the professional component of the system. When we suggest that legislators should consider cost-benefit analysis, or that legislators should consider the system from the point of view of the child, we simply observe that there are multiple interest groups; systems performance standards should be derived from the total set of benefits in all interested client groups. As has been found by the Budget Bureau and prior to that by the Defense Department, one can expect the professionals to oppose any restructuring of the expected benefit output of the system and the systems standards. Obviously such a restructuring may threaten their existing and future expected occupational interests. This poses a serious implementation problem: if the Joint Commission suggests a more total cost-benefit analysis and a re-analysis of the standards of systems performance, how does one secure acquiescence from the professionals?

In designing two new systems, the Joint Commission has not only to consider all client groups and their benefit sets, but there has to be reasonable assurance, particularly on the part of the professional, that the redesign will result in an increase in occupational benefits. Thus the question is not one of selecting among alternative client groups which group is to receive the primary benefit from the system, but rather it is a question of redesigning in such a fashion that there is an increasing aggregation for all groups.

Measures of systems performance: One way of looking at measures of performance for the child service system is as follows. It borrows its approach and language from the concept of a child service "industry."

The basic system has as its input a child with a set of nonnormal characteristics. The process of the system eliminates these undesirable characteristics—this is the system transformation—and the output is a child with normal characteristics or a predisposition to behave in a socially desirable manner. The system, then, can be measured in terms of the cost to change a set of child characteristics. Thus, in funding a program or a service, a plan would exist which would stipulate the expected number of children, their input characteristics that were going to be processed, and in what given period of time. There would be a description of the transformation function, that is, what particular technology was going to be used or what particular services would be rendered and what the effects of these services were going to be on the children who were going to be processed through the system. Also, it would be provided with an output measurement in terms of the expected number of children to be processed and their changed characteristics. From this plan, then, one would have the expected cost per characteristic change per child. Also, such a program would include measuring devices of the system itself that would indicate whether program objectives were in fact achieved. That is, such measuring devices would measure the number of children served and the extent of change in the child's characteristic. If actual output of the systems differed significantly from expected output in terms of both numbers of children and expected changes in the characteristics of children, this would indicate a serious program deficiency, and program modification would be indicated. Or it would indicate to the legislators and administrators that the system was not meeting the performance standard that they have funded.

On the local level, one can expect considerable variation in services rendered. This would derive largely from variations in child characteristic input mix. That is, from locality to locality, we can expect the numbers and mix of characteristics to vary. Children from a ghetto area would exhibit need in greater numbers than children from a relatively high-income suburban area. Moreover, in some parts of the country nutritional deficiences may be higher than in other parts of the country. Further, the concentration of children will vary; in the rural areas they will be dispersed, whereas in the metropolitan areas they will be concentrated. Ideally, it is hoped that the child welfare system will be sufficiently flexible to adapt its services to the variety of input mixes in a given community situation. Further, if the system or the set of services is sufficiently adaptive, we can still expect a fairly uniform output.

The current system seems to require that the children adapt to the set of services of the system that exists rather than adjusting the system to fit the needs or the characteristics of the children. Data indicate that agencies both search and screen for children in their population to fit the kind of services they have to render. The consequence is that many children are not adequately served. If legislative bodies would insist that the evaluation of such programs and services be done in cost-effectiveness measures, or if cost effectiveness becomes the standard of systems performance, this will force agency operations to adjust to child needs, which in turn will lead to a more effective system in that we will be concerned with what is actually happening to the child as he flows through the system.

The great deficiency of using professional standards, such as low case load or best practice, is that it does not provide a specific performance standard to measure what is actually occurring to the child.

Measures of Costs: In terms of cost identification, certainly for budgeting and planning, and program choices and evaluation, it would be ideal to know, either in terms of the total system nationally or in terms of any community setting, what the preventive, corrective, and underground costs are and what these are over time. We might briefly define what these cost dimensions are. Preventive costs relate to cost of those services that prevent the child from becoming part of the risk population as defined previously. It has been estimated that something on the order of 11 million to 15 million children constitute the risk population which potentially may require corrective measures. A broken home family situation or illegitimacy may result in ultimately placing the child in a foster care home. This is turn will incur a dependency cost over a significant period of time. However, child planning services may prevent illegitimacy and would reduce the risk population or increases in the cost of foster care. In one case we have a preventive measure; in the other we have a corrective measure.

Cost correction relates to those children who enter the system with a certain type of health deficiency and the cost of the services that are required to eliminate that particular deficiency so that they can return to the normal stream. Here one would like a detailed cost breakdown of the cost of health deficiency, whether biological, social, emotional, intellectual, or any set or combination of deficiencies, and in respect to both a given child and a given population of children. One would like to have some idea of the costs of alternative services in terms of correcting different types of deficiencies. This assumes, of course, that agents in the field use a variety of technologies in handling a deficiency. The same analytical data would be helpful in terms of preventive measures. Thus, if one had an array of preventive programs per child characteristic, one could evaluate these programs in terms of their relative cost, given the budgetary constraints of the system.

An additional cost dimension has been referred to as an underground cost. This is the cost to society that results if neither preventive nor corrective measures are taken with respect to the risk population. Assuming that a child incurs certain deficiencies and is not treated and does not return to the normal stream, what costs are incurred in terms of both his life as a child and his life as an adult? One can postulate certain cost consequences. As an adult he may be less productive economically and thus reduce his contribution to the Gross National Product and the subsequent tax revenues he could have generated. Further, as an adult, he may incur certain costs for society in terms of an increased crime rate which in turn generates greater cost for police protection, prisons, court systems, lawyers, etc. Also, one may develop a dependency cycle in that dependent children who are not adequately cared for may in their turn produce dependent children whom the state will have to support. As a child, certain costs may be incurred on the educational level in that either the child is not as productive as other children or the school systems have to devote an extensive amount of services and energy in attempting to cope with such children. Such children may present disciplinary problems in the classroom and detract from the educational process, or present other problems, such as excessive truancy. And certainly, there are psychological and social costs insofar as the family is concerned. It will be desirable also to have some idea as to the cost trends of the three classifications we have noted, preventive, corrective, and underground. Also, one would hope to project some of these costs into the future.

At the legislative level, the objective is to minimize costs, particularly given budgetary constraints over time. Thus, if one had data as to preventive, corrective, and underground costs, one might be able to calculate trade-offs between these three general types of programs or activities. Thus, if one in fact knew that preventive costs were much less than corrective costs, one would invest in such measures. If one, for example, projecting into the future, knew that the risk population was going to increase and postulated that under present conditions a significant number of children will not be treated, the consequence of this would be then an increasing underground cost, which society will have to support in some fashion. If one had some idea of the dimensions of both corrective and underground costs, there could be a deliberate legislative attempt to shift such costs from the underground to the corrective area. The significance of attempting to delineate the full cost dimensions of the risk population is to sensitize legislators as to appropriate public expenditure investment programs. One wants to avoid a short-term attempt to minimize costs, or being "penny wise and pound foolish." Thus legislators may think that they are saving money by not investing in either preventive or corrective measures insofar as the child risk population is concerned. What they may, in fact, be doing is increasing underground costs.

The fact that the service system services only a minimal number of children does not mean that the children are going to go away or disappear. Rather, it means that children merge into some other system, both as children and as adults. Thus, one faces a problem of shifting the costs, or the costs will shift as the children shift. A full analysis of the present system in terms of total child flow should indicate the total cost of the present system.

Still another dimension in cost analysis concerns direct and indirect costs. Direct cost relates to the amount of labor, material, and overhead at the agency level incurred to provide a specific service. Indirect cost relates to development costs incurred to assure that the system ultimately is able to operate. Some of the latter are the training of professional personnel, an educational cost that must be incurred to make professional employees available for the system. Another cost dimension is the creation and introduction of new technology into the system. This relates to current research efforts to invent a new service system. The diffusion of such new research and its introduction into the system may disrupt the existing system and require retraining of existing personnel, thus incurring other costs.

New technology can be thought of as being classified into at least two broad categories. One relates to the child services themselves, specifically how child deficiencies should be responded to, and the other relates to the organization and administration of the system with which this report is concerned.

It is fairly obvious that until one has a full analysis of the total cost of the existing system and a full analysis of any proposed modification in the existing system, it would be difficult to make the appropriate investment decisions. Nevertheless, we are proposing that cost of the existing system can be viewed from an investment point of view. That is, we are concerned with the general problem of the investment in human capital, from the point of view of society and the individual.

In a gross sense, we have now delineated at the conceptual mapping level some of the cost-effectiveness and cost-benefit dimensions of the child service system.

Conclusions based on an example of a cost-benefit analysis system at the state level:[4] It appears to us that the real crux of the cost-effectiveness, cost-benefit thrust is to force administrators to plan in such a fashion that they must delineate by way of their programs an expected cost-effectiveness output.

While it may be inadvisable to attempt to substitute an entirely new administrative structure for the existing one, what may be feasible is to require the existing administrative staff to postulate performance standards for their service systems. Since we have an essentially voluntary, fairly fragmented system, it is unlikely that a process of centralized direction can be instituted. However, if existing administrative staff is required to set standards and to modify programs to achieve these standards, we should then have a self-generating and self-effectuating system with a minimum of external intervention.

Nor would it be unreasonable to expect that at the governor's level and legislative level we could aggregate the planning and programing of the various departments. Of course, there could well be deficiencies in such a planning process, but until some of the initial data as to performance standards are introduced, we cannot take the next step of attempting to devise a more integrated program that would bring together operationally the various departments.

What is being suggested is that primary reliance be placed at the state level on existing agencies to establish specific performance standards in terms of cost effectiveness, program content, expected inputs, etc. Once

4. Editor's note: The original OSTI report contained an example of a cost-benefit analysis for the State of Massachusetts Child Welfare System. For the sake of brevity, the actual analysis has been deleted here. What appears are the overall conclusions from this analysis, as they might apply at any state level.

such planning is completed, this would be done in such a manner that the appropriate data-collecting devices would be part of the overall planning process, which would facilitate each service agency's ability to collect its own data. There may be a consulting or advisory unit which would assist in how to plan such a system; presumably such a unit would be similar to what is currently being done at the federal level with the Bureau of the Budget and within the Department of Health, Education, and Welfare. Such an advisory unit would not actually establish a cost-effectiveness system, but would advise existing administrative staff on how this could be done and assist in devising the appropriate paperwork or computer programing. Once such planning had been completed, copies of operating plans would be received by both the governor and the legislators. Through time such plans would represent the context of expected performance. When state agencies request appropriations, these would be evaluated in terms of previous planning efforts, and both the governor's staff and the legislators could then evaluate appropriation requests in terms of plans and programs and expected performances that agencies were required to submit previously.

The question of who will receive what particular data, in what form, and how often, at least in terms of cost-effectiveness, cost-benefit data turns on the question of the decision-making responsibilities of the various planning and programing centers in the system. Until one delineates what the planning responsibilities are of various administrators and legislators in the system, one is unable to determine their information requirements. If one redesigns some aspects of the decision-making system, then as part of that redesign one can include the information requirements. However, in terms of the foregoing analysis, it may be assumed that the legislature and the governor's staff would have expected programing and planning and performance standards, etc., and that a data system would exist that would feed back to them information as to how well existing service systems were performing in terms of expected performance.

What all of the above suggests is that movement toward a child-centered service system requires undertaking the enormous job of designing new criteria of systems performance and new decision-making procedures. There would need to be a commitment to establish such a system. We are only at the initial stages of examining the problem. Creating a child-centered system that is feasible and directional would be a long-term undertaking.

Conceptual framework for a system of operating data for child-centered services:[5] The efforts toward planning, organizing, and financing programs of delivery of services to children must be viewed in terms of

5. This portion of the report was written by Dr. Frank T. Rafferty, Task Force V.

short-range and long-range goals. These operations, in turn, derive logically out of thorough appraisal of present programs and goals, and realistic weighing of the state of knowledge, manpower, and economic resources expected to be available.

This section is directed to the long-range purpose of planning a program of delivery of children's services that can be organized, financed, and implemented in locally appropriate phases during the next ten to twenty-five years. Planning is a process of thinking ahead in order to anticipate difficulties and to seek reasoned solutions. Solutions must be based on a systematic analysis of information available now. The staggering difficulties and previous discouraging failures of the planning process must be confronted directly. Though all would prefer to believe in an easy, enthusiastic, rapid, unswerving march to utopian goals, history has not been supportive of this perspective. A characteristic of democratic process has been the difficulty in arriving at collective decision about long-range, intensive, comprehensive plans for coordinated policies. Such plans are obscured by the rhetoric of political party platforms, compromised in the seeking for political consensus, forgotten in the urgency of episodic crises, and in general considered suspect because of the association with greater governmental control and bureaucracy.

The problems of planning and budgeting in a democratic society have been of considerable interest to social scientists and program administrators for more than thirty years. Economic planning was placed on the road to respectability by the Employment Act of 1946, but only since the early 1960's has the entire field of social planning come up for serious consideration. Several different groups of scientists both within and without government have addressed themselves to this task as expressed by the co-chairmen of a Social Indicators Panel organized within the Department of Health, Education, and Welfare:

No society in history has, as yet, made a coherent and unified effort to assess those elements in the society which facilitate and which bar each individual from realizing to the fullest extent possible his talents and abilities in order to allow him to find a job, or establish a career commensurate with his talents, to live a full and healthy life equal to his biological potential, to establish the conditions for an adequate standard of living which allows him to live in a civilized fashion, and which provides a physical and social environment which enhances his sense of life. We believe that these are aims implicit in the American purpose. We believe that the means of realizing these are possible (Gorman and Bell, 1967).

As Gunnar Myrdal stated, ". . . planning should not be attempted in an airy optimistic mood. It must imply strivings against heavy odds . . . what we need today is not a deceptive hopefulness that success comes easy, but the will to grapple with staggering difficulties. We need not the courage of illusory optimism but the courage of almost desperation" (Myrdal, 1967).

The strongest enduring motivational force in the United States is the drive toward a maximum of freedom of each individual to seek equality of opportunity to realize his unique biological and social potential and the drive of each individual to seek for himself, his family, and his children the maximum participation in the privileges and resources of the society. The socialization of these individualistic drives comes from two major sources: (1) a capitalistic economy consisting of market forces of supply and demand, a price system based on the relatively freely operating effects of supply and demand, and a labor market theoretically based on freedom of selection by employer, employee, and a freely mobile labor force; (2) a social, political, and governmental system that assumes that most individuals desire a minimum of government with systems of checks and balances so that no major concentration of power can develop at the expense of others. As the country has grown more and more complex, government has developed an increasing number of regulatory agencies to assure the rights of the many against the power of the few.

Until recently there were few ways of measuring the success or failure of these forces. The obvious success of the United States in business, science, war, and population growth was enough, but in the past thirty years the Depression, the international competition with Soviet Russia and Communism, and the concerns with understanding, assisting, and measuring economic progress in developing countries and at home have led to the development of instruments to monitor the economic forces and to modulate undesirable fluctuations. More recently has come the realization that there are skewed distributions of wealth, jobs, occupational skills, education, and access to health services that effectively block large groups of individuals from the freedom of self-development and self-determination. Social indicators are less well developed than economic indicators, but promise to become indices of the development, utilization, and conservation of human resources. The challenge to America is no longer simply one of developing the power to produce. Problems of participation and the quality of participation of all members of the society have become paramount. These are problems of man himself rather than the material objects with which he deals. As John Dewey wrote thirty years ago, "Democratic institutions are no guarantee for the existence of democratic individuals . . . individuals who prize their own liberties and who prize the liberties of others; individuals who are democratic in thought and action are the sole final warrant for the existence and endurance of democratic institutions" (Fadiman, 1938).

The rate of unemployment has been a primary indicator of the level of participation in the material resources. Now, the rate of unemployment has reached 3 to 4 percent, and there are signs that this is a level in which there is a balance of supply and demand of labor. With this rate of unemployment, there are large areas of labor demand, e.g., professional, teachers, nurses, nonprofessionals in the health areas, household services, engineers, clerical, skilled craftsmen, etc., going unmet to the point that the unmet demand is forcing salaries up and contributing to an inflationary spiral. Furthermore, the rate of unemployment does not accurately reflect the partially unemployed, the discouraged worker, or those who would seek employment if it were available. Unemployment is known to be distributed in such a way that the young adult, the Negro, the Indian, the Spanish American, and the uneducated are highly represented. Americans in institutions such as prisons and hospitals are not counted.

Perhaps a more informative measure of adequacy of participation is the statistic that more than 11 million families, containing one-sixth of the nation's children under eighteen, were living below the threshold of poverty in 1966. More than 15 million persons were barely over the subsistence level of participation (Orshansky, 1968).

A monetary figure is only one means used to gauge the level of participation in our society. A more crucial measure would be one that reflected the informational requirements of full participation. The United States is technologically and pluralistically oriented. Strength and willingness are no longer sufficient. Education, technical skills, social aptitudes, and physical and emotional stability are not only desired but absolutely necessary. These are the informational requirements of participation. Some beginning indications of their complex distribution are being developed. One interesting comparison is provided by the Manpower Development and Training Act programs; these can be divided into the institutional programs of training, in which the trainee is chosen by the U.S. employment service, and the On Job Training program, in which the enrollee is chosen by the private employer. In 1966, two of every five institutional enrollees were nonwhite, while among OJT trainees one out of five was nonwhite. Half of institutional enrollees had less than a high school education. Only one-third of the trainees of OJT had less than a high school education. One out of nine in the institutional programs was a welfare recipient, while only one out of eighty was in the OJT program (Levitan, 1967).

Not only do educational skills determine the employment of an individual, or the placement in a training program, but one of the basic impediments to use of the Manpower and Development Training Act has been the lack of basic education, preventing even the testing for potential of candidates. The figures of the Armed Services are most precise and reveal that a third of these young men are physically and mentally unfit for military service. These figures tell us that in a society of abundance, 20 to 40 percent of our population live in a subsociety of social, economic, and educational deprivation. These figures reveal the plight of millions of individuals, but it must be recognized that the despair of individuals may lead to the destruction of a political system. A political system is not a static, permanently molded fixed entity. Especially a system with the range of freedom possessed in this one will respond to pockets of despair and desperation. Not only are these discordant individuals dependent on the economic and political system, but the system is dependent on them in a variety of significant ways: (1) the productive manpower of the United States must be maintained at effective levels; (2) the professional and service manpower must be expanded manyfold if our citizens are to enjoy the fruits of their economic productivity; (3) the electorate of the United States and its elected officials at all levels must be fully informed if democratic process is to lead the way in a complicated international society; (4) the family, held primarily responsible for the training and enculturation of our children, is now a complex administrative unit and requires informed democratic leadership by parents.

The problems of the economically disadvantaged have become more visible in the past decade, and the special relationship of racial discrimination to poverty has been disclosed, but it would be a gross and fatal mistake to think of the problems of participation in the society as being limited to the poor or the black. Some individuals have inadequate information in the form of education or occupational skills. Other individuals have distorted or defective information about themselves and their world and suffer from mental illness, mental retardation, or criminality. The statistics of the poor, the black, the sick, the mentally ill, the delinquent, and the criminal are highly correlated, but statistics of all of these groups also indicate that problems of participation occur in every economic, racial, social, and ethnic group in American society. The school dropout is an easily definable example and furnishes visible statistics. The youngster of lower socioeconomic groups is several times more likely to be recorded as a school dropout. But the school dropout is found in all socioeconomic groups and controlling for poverty and color the following characteristics are found: the dropout comes from a family with more children than the parents can control, has received inconsistent affection and discipline, and has an actual or psychologically absent father. The family of the dropout is more isolated and has fewer social contacts and sources of information and support than the family of the graduate. In school, the dropout is characterized by a two-year deficiency in reading and arithmetic, failure of one or more school years, irregular attendance, behavior problems, and a feeling of not belonging. Dropouts characteristically seek unrealistic emotional satisfaction in early marriages to the neglect of educational and occupational goals (Cervantes, 1965).

In pursuing the purpose of the United States—the right to life, liberty, and the pursuit of happiness—there has been the assumption that each individual is responsible for his own health, housing, education, choice of occupation and spouse, income level, and style of life. Given individual freedom of choice, it is assumed that market forces of supply and demand will result in an equitable distribution of the privileges and resources of the society. This ideal of equality of man is limited by accidents of birth, inherited wealth, sex, race, geographical location, etc. The two-century history of the United States is the account of the struggle to bring about a social structure to put the ideal in practice as much as possible. Today, the citizen of the United States has greater individual freedom than ever before and greater individual freedom than the citizen of any other country. Despite this, citizens are aware more than ever of the inequalities within our society. Citizens of different sex have unequal access to certain occupations or to positions of authority. Citizens of different ages have unequal access to sex, liquor, or the privilege of self-determination. Citizens of different color have unequal access to education, housing, employment, social position.

It is known now better than two hundred years ago that each individual is a unique organism and that the principles of individual responsibility and self-determination are the best guides in the seeking of life, liberty, and the pursuit of happiness. It is also known now better than two hundred years ago that there are unique individual variations in biological, emotional, and intellectual potential that will ensure relative inequality of access to the privilege and resource of participation in any society. The market forces of supply and demand will always determine that some individuals will be more important, more valued, and more rewarded than others dependent upon how they are productive and effective in the social system. The unique, the exceptionally talented, and the valued will and should be rewarded. But this kind of inequality is not resented by others. This kind of inequality is accepted, appreciated, and encouraged.

What is resented is the inequality of opportunity for an individual to realize his own biological and social position in our society free of the arbitrary constraints of sex, creed, race, or age. This strong tendency to realization of the biosocial potential of each individual is in itself limited. Man is not an omniscient or omnipotent being. Built into each individual are limits of performance, limits of achievements, limits of virtue. Equally important to the cohesiveness and morale of the society are the mutual protection and security that are offered to one another in time of weakness, of need, of disability, of cupidity, of ineptness. Many of the features of our political system are checks and balances designed to protect against ineffectiveness, greed, or the corrupting effects of power. Other aspects of our political system are to offer services to those groups who have been identified as having special positions or special problems. The roll call of federal executive departments and agencies identifies the areas the democratic system has identified as requiring special attention: State, Treasury,

Defense, Postal, Justice, Interior, Agriculture, Commerce, Labor. The newest departments are Health, Education, and Welfare, and Housing and Urban Development.

The problems confronting many of these departments have to do with the general issues of individual and group deviancy from the social, emotional, biological, intellectual, and communication norms of the society. The problem of deviancy presents the reciprocal phenomena to the issue of participation. Who can participate? Who is allowed to participate? What are the dynamic forces within the group and society that specify certain forms of participation as dangerous to the group? Some of the distorted, ineffective, or distractive efforts at participation are defined as dangerous and require punishment to deter or confinement to protect the society. Other failures, ineptnesses, awkward or unpleasant efforts to participate, stimulate less resentment but more sympathy and efforts to help. Whether to punish in anger or to help in sympathy, the institutionalized response is to move the individuals to the periphery of the society and to further restrict their threatening participation. These forces are only partially counteracted by efforts at treatment and rehabilitation designed to restore full membership in the society.

The United States, despite its egalitarian philosophy, remains a stratified society. There is a dynamically determined, changing, diffuse, difficult to concretely delineate but terribly real line between one set of social positions considered relatively effective, relatively productive, and relatively autonomous, such as management personnel and skilled craftsmen and another set of social positions that are relatively ineffective, nonproductive, and dependent. These would include the socially dependent and criminals.

A given adult may move from one category to another, with time, or may occupy more than one category at a time. But taking a cross-sectional statistical approach to the large numbers represented in our society, the ratio of prevalence of the one set to the other becomes a rough ratio of participation to nonparticipation present in the adult population of the society. A high index of participation is, simultaneously, a major goal of our political-economic system and a major means of achieving other goals of the system.

The fact that this is an index of goals achieved as well as a means has been a confusing factor in evaluating the growth and success of the United States. For the most part, the cost of maintaining adequate nutrition, housing, health, education, etc., has been treated as a consumer expenditure. The items of the good life have been viewed as goals to be bought by effort. The economic effects of investment in the development, in the maintenance, or in the conservation of human resources have been neglected. But now "it has become evident that the concept of investment in human resources (as constituting an important segment of the stock of capital) is essential to analytical efforts to account for the economic growth and productive achievements of technically advanced countries such as the United States" (*Federal Programs for the Development of Human Resources*, 1966, p. 4). "The national income has been increasing at a faster rate than national resources and productive efforts. . . . These trends and the large increase in real earning of workers can be explained only by recognizing that there has been improvement in the productivity of the human component. A man hour of work today is generally more productive than was a man hour of work in 1900, because the workers today are typically more skilled, healthier, and less fatigued than were their grandfathers" (*ibid.*). The educational level, the products of research, the organizational skills, managerial techniques, attitudes toward work, etc., are also part of the same picture of the value of investment in human capital. The variations of the index of participant/nonparticipant become a rough index of the capital investment status of the adult population. The fact that the ratio can vary is an indication that capital investment in human resources can also deteriorate or depreciate. A skilled craftsman, trained for one job, is no longer part of capital if his job changes to the extent that the man's skills are rendered obsolete.

The ratio of participant/nonparticipant was restricted to the adult population. It is necessary to consider the special position of childhood that has been evolved by modern society. Considering the positions in the nonparticipant section, it is evident that children are in those categories. They are unemployed, they are socially dependent, they are not producers, they are frequently sick, retarded, delinquent. Yet, they are the future. Expenditure to support children represents one of the greatest consumer items of the Gross National Product. No single statistic can represent this cost. As illustrative charges, one can point out that the social welfare expenditures under public programs for 1965–66 were estimated at $87,578,000. Of this, $33,775,000 was allocated to maternal and child health, school health, school lunch, child welfare, and education. Other items such as public housing, rehabilitation, and public assistance contain large expenditures related to children, leading to a conviction that at least half and probably more than half of public funds in social welfare goes to children (*Federal Programs,* Table 2, p. 14, 1965–66). Another illustration is given by noting that child feeding constitutes the nation's single largest market for food, approximately $1.33 billion a year, expanding at the rate of some $50 million annually. The school lunch program alone employs some 300,000 nonfederal workers (*Ibid.*, p. 41).

Historical analysis of the social position of children reveals that childhood as we know it is a modern institution. Until recently the child was simply an incomplete adult. The concept of a psychological and moral homunculus survived long after the biological thesis was displaced by knowledge of the developmental processes of embryology. In fact it is still fair to assume that the average adult is unaware of the complex psychological, intellectual, social, communicative developmental processes that occur in childhood. The changes in size and body configuration are more obvious.

However, there has been a steadily accumulating body of knowledge about children, a changing of attitudes toward children, and the development of social institutions devoted to supporting, supplementing, or replacing the family in rearing children. These changes have taken place in a fluid, shifting culture. Like other accumulations of knowledge, whether about transportation, energy utilization, chemistry, or nuclear physics, the body of information about children leads to both positive and negative results. With survival rates in childhood increased manyfold, parents not only have affection for children, but, indeed, treasure them and protect them as precious objects, sometimes to the detriment of the child's maturity. For more than fifty years we have assiduously protected children from the inhumane abuses of child labor, but we now face the problems of alienation of the adolescent from meaningful participation in the society. The acquisition of information became the specific task of childhood, and the child is protected from influences that interfere with education. But the amount and nature of information now imparted in education requires of the child great endurance, unswerving attention, ability to transcend short-range satisfactions in favor of long-range goals, and freedom from more immediate needs and fears of survival, nutrition, sex, and social status.

Thorough analysis of the problems of children reveals that they are deeply enmeshed in the major social and economic issues of the present while representing the human resources of the future. The resolution of the broad issues of dependency of children, the health, nutritional, and emotional requirements, and education of children would require a complete restructuring of the ways in which services are organized and delivered. Discontinuities of health, education, and welfare services as presently constituted not only result in the failure to reach goals of child care but make a substantial contribution to the pathologies of childhood.

The definition, analysis, and description of the present problem with all the complicated interchanging of biological, social, psychological, political, economic, individual, and professional ramifications is tedious, frustrating, and overwhelming, but the following major issues must be abstracted and given consideration in developing guidelines for future planning effort.

1. The prevalence of mental illness, retardation, learning disability, delinquency, etc., in large numbers of individual children represents the cumulative product of thousands of multiple transactions of individual, group, and social institution variables over the long time span of a given

child's growth and development. Indeed, the history of the child's parents, his extended family, and the historical structure of his culture are also determinants.

2. There has been no dearth of individual, public, or professional concern about the prevalence of these problems. Discussions are found in our national publications, the professional literature, the deliberations of legislatures, the informal conversation of every aggregation of people. Unfortunately, this concern is frequently guided by incomplete or un-integrated information and consequently leads to proposals that may be attractive but are likely to be inadequate, simplistic, or unachievable. These include the following widely discussed positions:

a. Problems in children are the result of inadequate, misguided, or defective supervision of parents. Correction is achieved by re-proaching, insisting, or legislating that increased attention, love, and supervision be carried out.

b. Problems of children are corrected by the direct application of professional expertise. Correction of large numbers will be achieved by mammoth expansion of budgets and of the programs as now struc-tured.

c. Problems in children are caused by: the war in Vietnam, vio-lence on television, bad schools, living in cities, poverty, overindulgent parents, racial discrimination, etc. Each cause suggests a desired direction of change. While such suggestions may be correct, they represent only a part of the problem and suffer seriously from lack of means to implement.

d. Problems in children are the result of the social institutions that care for them. Consequently, we must reorganize the schools, the child guidance clinics, the welfare departments, etc. Like the other solutions, the problem described may be real enough, but the correla-tive solutions quickly fade away.

3. For sixty years an impressive body of scientific information as well as clinical practice has been accumulating with respect to correcting emotional disturbance, mental illness, or behavioral deviations. The scientists and clinicians who have been most responsible for this effort are also the ones who are most thoroughly acquainted with the limita-tions of theory and practice. Because of the recognition of these limita-tions the ethical, competent professional has been conservative in his claims, careful in the selection of his patients, meticulous in application, and fundamentally reticent and modest about results. It is now rather frightening for this body of informed professionals to be confronted by a total population seeking the inalienable rights of security, safety, long life, happiness, and prosperity from the health, education, and welfare services. It is regrettable even though understandable that when these

professionals offer what their experience has taught them, they are confronted with angry denunciation as being interested only in the wealthy, the middle class, the white. Causing even more consternation is the accusation of failure to reach goals that were never embraced or sought by the professionals and their organizations.

4. It becomes even more understandable that the ethical, competent mental health clinician clings stubbornly to his hard-learned techniques of controlled individual or small-group therapy with carefully selected patients in the context of the private patient-therapist contract when he views the failure of public health, sociology, or urban planning to solve the riddles of mental illness, urban blight, poverty, criminal behavior, or civil disorder. Presumed etiological factors are not hard to find, but to date it has been virtually impossible to transform study findings of correlations with social class or other demographic variables into a viable public health program. It has been said that:

If public health were to act upon the information thus obtained, it would among other things, have to upgrade social class, eliminate status incongruity and occupational stress, selectively control geographic and social mobility, make cities into country farms, improve family incomes, shepherd groups through cultural change, maximize the individual's acceptance of his life situation, prevent social isolation, and provide a value basis for choosing whether one's parents should or should not be church going people. It is no condemnation of public health to note that it simply is not up to such tasks. Indeed, no existing social program of any kind would be (Rogers, 1968).

5. Contrasting the problems of the private therapist who must be selective to be effective with the problems of the social engineer who cannot implement his insights highlights the difficulties of the planning task. The private therapist selects children to treat who have their major dependency needs at least potentially satisfied, whose families have the minimum requirements of energy, money, and information, and whose biological, intellectual, and communicative skills can support the treatment process. On the other hand, the social engineer finds himself confronted with sets of variables that will not stand still for corrections. It is impossible to narrow the behavioral field. If he focuses on health services, ill-advised or defective education defeats the effort. If he tries for a measure of control over education and racial segregation, inadequate family income or value conflicts sabotage the effort. If he supports the family income and establishes jobs for parents, deficient health and education turn temporary support into the permanent dole. The private therapist solves these issues by selecting only those individual patients who can present or achieve enough control over biological, social, intellectual, and communicative factors. The social engineer

committed to the total population in all its diversity, with its plethora of uncontrolled, continuously transacting variables, can only envy the private therapist while steadfastly striving for some new means of getting all the data under control.

6. The contrast between the goals, techniques, and success of the private clinician and those of the social engineer are extremely instructive to policy and decision makers. National policy makers cannot justify programs that are selective, i.e., favor one economic, intellectual, racial, or diagnostic group. On the other hand, if they are committed to a universalistic program aimed at the optimum in mental health for all children, they commit themselves to deal with the full range of significant variables. No previous goal of the society has ever approached this degree of complexity—will have ever sought to control as many variables—and in particular, will have ever tried to deal with values, causes, rights, etc., so intimately associated with each citizen. Obviously, such a goal has to be the goal of the society as a whole. It cannot be the goal of a professional segment such as education, medicine, psychiatry, social work, or psychology. Neither can a single science such as biochemistry, sociology, or physics achieve this. Such a goal will be more difficult than fighting World War II, more difficult than the Manhattan Project to produce the atom bomb, more complex than the Marshall Plan or the space mission.

On the other hand, the goal of a universalistic program aimed at the optimum in mental health for all children could merge with many other social targets that have been sought, usually with less than full success. These include such diverse programs as housing, comprehensive health, full employment, poverty, aid for dependent children, Head Start, riot control, crime control, etc. If the society deliberately chooses to commit itself to a goal of such complexity, a major information and education program for citizens, parents, government workers, professionals, students, etc., must be the first order of business. Conceptually the issues are not so difficult to understand as they are to grasp in all their complexity and multiplicity. A different habit of thought is required. Simple Newtonian-type physical equations in which one force acts on another is the habit of thought comfortable to most of us. Required is a mode of comprehension that can conceive of the resultant state of events as being the culmination of hundreds of significant forces mutually influencing one another at multiple levels of integration. As yet, there is no readily accepted way of simultaneously illustrating or describing the thousands of variables, hundreds of systems, and many levels of integration involved. Two representations are offered here to convey that the longitudinal history of a specific child as an emerging core or spiral depends on the adequacy of complex systems, multiple variables, and plural levels of integration. If one conceives of each level as a wheel in constant circular motion, some appreciation of the dynamics can be attained. The second representation is that of a cross section of the cone illustrating the various levels of integration as wheels within wheels. See Figures 3 and 4.

An interesting facet of people's attitudes toward people and to children in particular is revealed by contrasting an engineering problem of the usual type with the social engineering task of delivering health, education, and welfare services to children. If the Department of Defense sought to build an atomic submarine, it would be decided upon only after detailed studies of need, mission, feasibility, alternative courses, etc. Once the decision was made and a prime contractor was sought, each aspiring corporation would

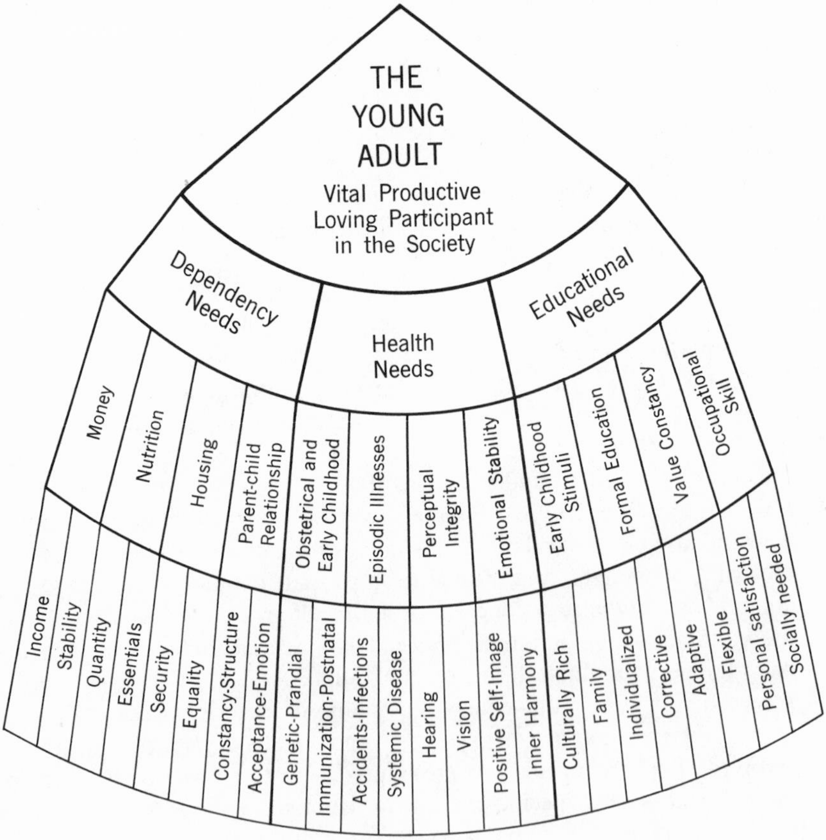

FIG. 3—Dynamic Representation of Systems Impacting on the Growing Child

be required to submit project proposals, to demonstrate its special competence, and to document its manpower capability, financial stability, and administrative competency, and to establish clear performance criteria. The same procedure is followed in placing a contract for a road, or building a bridge or a house. After extreme care was taken in letting a contract, there would be a schedule of inspections, deadlines to meet, and rigid performance criteria checked. But in delivering health, education, and welfare services to children, characteristically the problem is defined in its most superficial aspects. There will be a statement of good intentions and the task will be assigned to an official, monopolistic agency. The agency is not required to submit proof of its competence to do the job. Indeed, the very feasibility of the job will not be questioned. Since end result is not established and

FIG. 4—Cross Section Showing Integration of Systems that Impact on the Growing Child

neither feasibility nor competency is questioned, budget will have no relationship to anything. Having proceeded in this way, it is no surprise that results are seldom checked for performance criteria.

It seems reasonable to suggest that such naïveté about human problems and human problem solving in a scientifically and technologically sophisticated culture is an indication that there is considerable reluctance to consider the mechanisms of human behavior and behavioral systems with scientific dispassion. Achievement of mental health of children on a population basis is a qualitatively different task than medical or paramedical treatment of individual illness. A demonstrably different number of variables must be integrated. Intervention to change one or more sets of variables requires a different order of complexity. Policy decisions can no longer be left to professional judgment, but become goals of the body politic. It is crucial that this distinction be grasped if the task of this Commission is to be accomplished. It is crucial that this distinction be communicated to the American people, their elected representatives, and their civil servants if the Commission activities are to be other than moralistic statements of the desirability of some forms of behavior and the undesirability of others. Presumably the need for a commission on this subject as well as recent related commissions on crime, juvenile delinquency, civil disorder, comprehensive health care, income support, medicine, etc., reflect a real and growing interest in the quality of life within this society. Concern with the mental health of children becomes identical with a concern for the fullness of life for the entire society.

The major issue may well be the recognition that the quality of life of the various populations within the total society must be the concern of all. The unwritten assumption has been that concern for the quality and style of one's life is the concern only of family members. One of the most firmly established findings of the Commission has been the changing patterns of family responsibility. Taking the four major categories of dependency, socialization, education, and health needs as pertain to all members of the family, it becomes clear that these are frequently controlled from outside the family. The job market, changes in economics, need for two wage earners, mobility necessary for employment, obsolescence of some jobs, etc., are all noted reasons why parents cannot adequately fulfill the dependency and socialization needs of the family. Educational needs are equally dependent on the quality of the public school system, the tax base, the training and attitudes of teachers, racial segregation, etc. Health needs may well not be available because of distribution of physicians, cost of care, shortage of facilities, mismatch of facilities and need.

Correlative to the general view that families managed the style and quality of their life was that elected officials, bureaucratic managers, employers, etc., did not. Elected officials have been constrained to view their office in the narrowest possible manner. At its worst, the officials are simply brokers between the collection of tax monies and the distribution of these monies to crisis-oriented agencies of police, fire, roads, health, and schools. The bureaucratic officials of these administrative agencies, in turn, have a narrow area of responsibility and are so constrained from presenting an overall appraisal of the situation.

As an alternative to the above, it can be suggested that the resolution of the social problems of the family, the community, and the nation will depend on three well-delineated sets of processes that are sequentially related, equally necessary, and often widely separated by barriers of time, distance, and personal responsibility. These are: (1) detection; (2) evaluation; and (3) corrective response. Figure 5 helps illustrate the relationship.

The problem-solving model in Figure 5 is an abstraction of the well-proven model used in many individual and professional problem-solving

FIG. 5—Sequentially Related Processes Needed to Resolve Social Problems

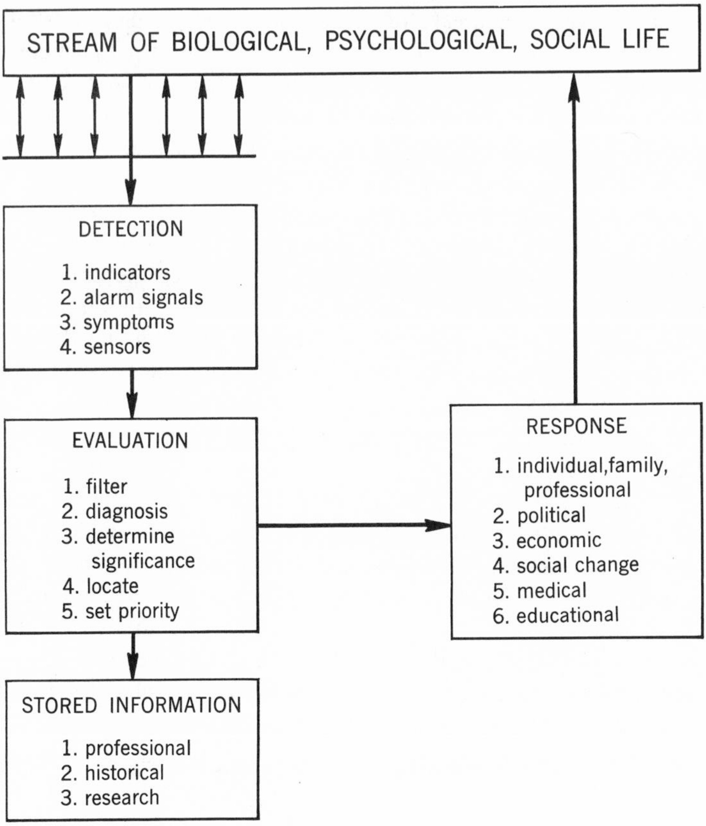

events, e.g., medical diagnosis and treatment; the trouble-shooting maintenance work of the plumber or electrician; the detective work of the
policeman; physiological homeostasis within the biological organism, etc.
Although the model is well proven, the increase in complexity as described
above moves the implementation to the entirely different order of group
political behavior. The chain of events from detection through evaluation
to corrective response may involve tens or hundreds of individuals and
numerous agencies related only by their commitment to the goal, participation with the data, and the behavior of individuals carrying the data.
Because of the length of the problem-solving sequence and the multiple
steps taken by many anonymous people, special provisions must be taken
to assure that detection is followed by corrective response. Each segment
of the problem-solving sequence must be thoroughly analyzed, organized,
and energized. The coordinating informational system will require major
attention.

At first view, this suggested operation may appear overwhelming and
impossible. But another perspective can provide hope. Consider that what
is suggested is not a new process. The rearing of children has been so much
with us that many are unaware of the extent of effort, money, skill, etc.,
that is already devoted to the operations. Perhaps the fact that nearly half
of the nation's population is children is not fully appreciated. Few of the
other half escape direct involvement in the child care or the support of
child care. None of us as a nation can escape the implications of the quality
of this care for the future. With or without planning, this particular half of
the population will become the adults of tomorrow. What is suggested is
the evolution of performance criteria with respect to the growth, development, socialization, and education of each child. Since the child grows in
time, the primary process must be one of longitudinal monitoring of the
individual child and secondarily of specific populations along the tortuous
route to maturity. Monitoring the growth process must then be accompanied
by a continuous process of filtering, evaluating, checking for significance,
etc., and this must be followed promptly by corrective or conserving
responses.

Immediately, the question of whether the professional and scientific
disciplines have sufficient skill, knowledge, and manpower to engage in
this set of operations must be raised. The answer is a clear, concise, certain,
"No, of course not." Scientific knowledge and professional manpower must
be utilized whenever possible to assist, to lead, to guide, to catalyze, to
stimulate, to respond to, and to research the basic democratic political
processes involved. At the present time, many communities in the nation
are well on their way to developing plans adapted to their resources and
needs. Each of these differs, and flexibility at the local level must be a
feature of any project. On the other hand, perhaps a majority of com-

munities have not yet begun to recognize their problems, much less to plan solutions. As a beginning projection of a national child care system integrated by an information utility, the following abstract model is given in outline. The reader must read into the outline the longitudinal process of following an individual child. The three essential components of each problem-solving unit—Indicators, Evaluation, Response—are the keys to the model. The Information Utility is illustrated at the two major interfaces, although it obviously must be present at all. In practice, then, the model has four distinct sections: I. the individual child and his individualing variable systems; II. the total child care system with the family as central agency supported, supplemented, or replaced by other social agencies; III. the supporting, developing, maintaining, conserving, or corrective responses available; and, IV. the Information Utility serving, modulating, evaluating, and correcting the movement of the total system. Each of these must be explicated in more detail.

I. The Individual Child.

The key to the content to be monitored is inherent in the multiple system complexity of the individual child. The major conceptual lag influencing the organization of the present child care system is the shallow connotation given to the word "individual." Phrases such as "treat the total child," "provide individual education," "allow 35 square feet for each child," etc., ascribe individuality to the visible uniqueness of the skin-boundaried child. Actually, within the organic boundaries of the child are a number of subsystems, each capable of varying with respect to many functions. However, the biological complexities are only the beginning of the individuation of the child. There are emotional, social, and intellectual and communication systems that transcend the skin boundaries, e.g., membership in a particular family, ethnic group, social class, or language group. At any given point in the child's life, these factors may vary in dimension and importance. Considered as individual variables, there would be thousands of discrete items to account for. Professional disciplines and service agencies have developed various classification or diagnostic categories to deal with the embarrassing wealth of significant variables. Each of these classification schemes has been useful and valuable, but unfortunately, each classification scheme presents difficulties in that something must be left out. Some classification schemes have been the private property of specific professions, have been built into legal restrictions, legislative actions, and budget structure. Some categories have become the subject of considerable emotional and financial investment, and others have become synonymous with second class citizenship. These classification devices and the psychological and emotional impediments which they have accumulated cannot be abolished, since they do serve important junctions in our state of incomplete knowledge. But they can be of little use in a national system of child care built upon the concerns of an entire polity and dependent upon integrated operation of a variegated manpower pool of many disciplines and many levels of educational preparation.

An Information Utility must seek a management technique to account for at least hundreds of potentially significant variables. The significance of a variable is a relationship to be determined by evaluation and research. Obviously, any simplification of reporting of hundreds of variables can legitimately be called a classification device. Classification is a basic mental and scientific process that permits thought to move from a number of specific concrete items to an abstract concept. The result of this process is given a name which then acquires an existence, meaning, and value of its own that may outrun the significance of the delineation of variables built into the original definition. Examples of this are found in the terms *mental*

FIG. 6—The BESIC System

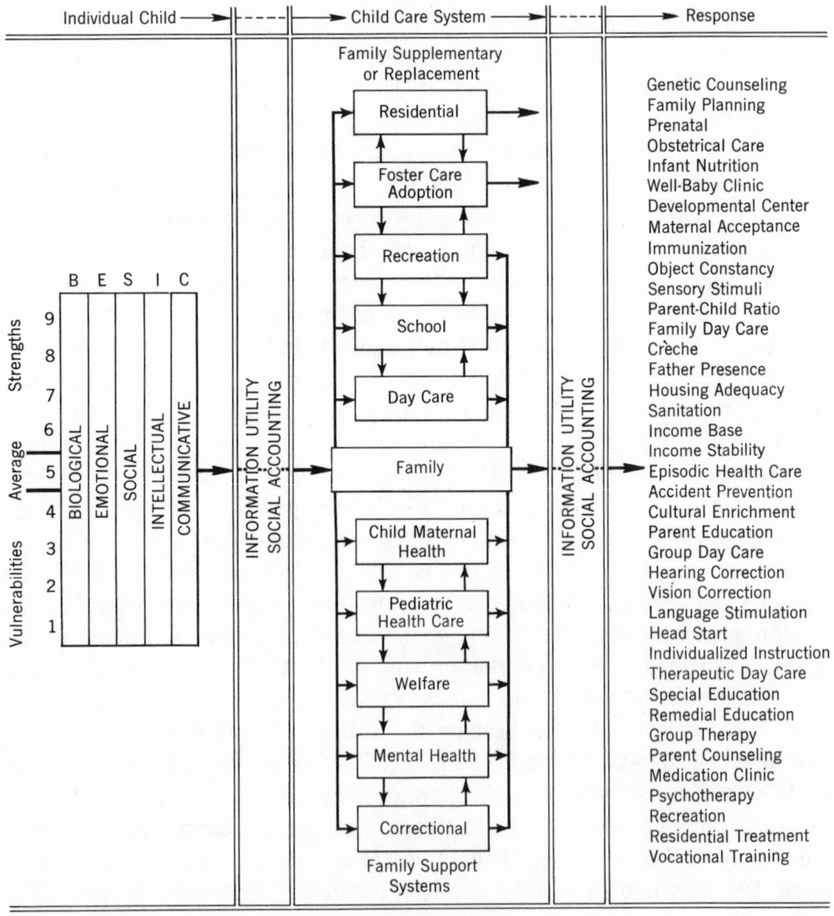

illness, schizophrenia, mental retardation, minimal brain damage, slow learner, remedial reading, vocational education, counseling, treatment, etc.

Fortunately, new developments in data processing equipment, electronic networks, computer time sharing, etc., now permit us to dispense with the naming process to a great degree. Computer equipment is capable of processing discrete values of multiple variables in time brief enough to be simultaneous without having to give the constellation a name and adding meaning of its own. The meaning can be derived by appropriate statistical techniques to test significance of relationship. As yet, the techniques for utilizing this equipment for the procedures of a national child care system are not available. The problems of developing these techniques and the development of a national child care system require simultaneous solutions.

As a tentative suggestion of a possible direction in which to search for a solution the following "nonclassification profile" is presented. The criteria sought may be listed: (1) maximum unique individuation of the child is to be represented; (2) each child can be represented as varying within the major systems of variables currently under study; (3) each child is represented as a composite of strengths as well as vulnerabilities; (4) association or ownership of the "nonclassification scheme" by any specific professional discipline or service agency is to be avoided; (5) on the contrary, each agency or discipline should be provided with a device to correct for narrow professional training; (6) suggested solutions and/or prognoses are to be avoided as much as possible in the informational data. These are to be results of the evaluation process.

The "nonclassification profile" is a rating scale of strength and vulnerability of the individual child in five major systems—biological, emotional, social, intellectual, and communicative. Its purpose is to emphasize multiplicity of significant variables rather than to smooth out differences as within diagnostic categories. The use of five systems is almost but not quite arbitrary. It can as easily be three, seven, ten, or twenty-five, since each system must be the container of a list or multiple lists of variables. Each number of sets would present its own particular technical problems. Three may not be enough for adequate delineation. The higher numbers may provide difficulties deciding variable membership in a particular set. Five is a convenient informational span for the human brain and perceptual system as well as offering a convenient acronym—BESIC.

The actual content of each set of variables, measurement, weights, standardization to extent desirable, etc., must be the product of future effort. But each of these five sets is in widespread current use. Unfortunately, each set is likely to be more efficiently used by only a portion of the personnel of the child care system. For example, pediatricians are most comfortable with biological variables; some psychiatrists with emotional; sociologists and some social workers with social, etc. As indicated in

Figure 6, only three ratings are used to indicate strong, average, or vulnerable status. Theoretically, this three-point scale could be extended to five, seven, or nine as major groups reached consensus on a standard. This discussion will only indicate examples of each set:

Biological: height, weight, muscular control, reaction time, vision, hearing, nutrition, developmental deficiencies, proneness to illness, metabolic disease, pathological sequelae.

Emotional: stability, lability, range, depression, withdrawal, autism, expressiveness, body image, self-concept, anxiety, confidence, self-esteem, control, anger, fear, phobias, compulsions.

Social: family per capita income, parent-child ratio, housing adequacy, stability of parent income, two employed parents, intact family, parent education, race, neighborhood, peer group structure, school expenditure per child, teacher training, number of children in class.

Intellectual: attention, concentration, cognition, similarities, pattern recognition, memory, abstraction, synthesis, analysis, deduction, induction, animism, IQ, identity, discrimination, sensor-motor, conservation.

Communication: smile, crying, prelinguistic vocal sounds, gestures, frequency of vocalization, babbling, jargon, first words, vocabulary, sentences, pronouns, verbs, grammar, phonemes, dialect, imitation, comprehension, receptive aphasia, expressive aphasia, semantics, syntax.

II. The Child Care System.

One of the most significant contributions of social science in the past decade has been the clearer delineation of the structure and function of the American family. The average person in the community has been more inclined to bemoan or malign the presumed loss of family integrity than to describe and understand the shifts in function, problems, composition, and resources of this complicated administrative social institution. The naïve view considers the family as the environmental unit that is the other side of the nature/nurture interface. There is some doubt whether the family was ever the intact, sacred, independent unit that we nostalgically remember. In any event, observations of family function and structure lead to a series of conclusions germane to the organization of a child care system.

1. The nuclear family structure is and will remain the major institutionalized means of providing dependency needs, socialization, early education, and health support to the individual child.

2. Even the best families, however, are increasingly dependent on extra family systems for:
    a. economic support and stability;
    b. value system;

      c. comprehensive health monitoring;

      d. infant and preschool care;

      e. early childhood education;

      f. education;

      g. recreation.

3. The family, despite its long history and great responsibility, is a fragile organization sensitive to economic and social factors. At this time, we must recognize that many families are in serious difficulties and require more supportive and supplemental assistance than has been officially recognized. These difficulties are directly related to economic and social factors which the entire nation is participating in and responsible for. They include:

      a. urbanization;

      b. changes in women's social role;

      c. employment requirements for men;

      d. geographical mobility;

      e. transportation;

      f. increase in population;

      g. effect of electronic communication media on value systems;

      h. economic pressure for women to work;

      i. change in educational requirements for political, social, and economic life;

      j. effects of automation;

      k. effects of racial discrimination.

4. Official recognition must be given to the fact that child-rearing is no longer exclusively a family responsibility. Instead there is a complicated, poorly coordinated, formal and informal child care system that contracts and expands with reference to family variables, individual child factors, economic and social mores of the community, etc. Perhaps the ideal remains that the family has the primary responsibility for child care, but to a considerable degree this is becoming a brokerage or distributive responsibility. The family sees that the child gets to the doctor, to the recreation center, to day care, to school. The parents do not have the time, money, expertise, or social reinforcement to provide the total child care experience. The child's dependency on his parents and membership in the family system is greatly attenuated. This holds particularly for many adolescents who literally do not live in families. An almost completely informal peer group structure provides the major socialization experience.

5. Figure 6 represents the complicated individual child's BESIC system's boundary with the equally complicated array of social institutions. The family is presented as the primary system relationship. But the great volume of movement to and from other systems is obvious. Each

of these social systems is engaged in the process of meeting the dependency, socialization, educational, and health needs of the child. There is a continuous process of sensing the child's status, evaluating, and responding. Necessarily much of this is intuitive and automatic. An unfortunate amount is inadequate and ineffective. Some of the systems, such as health, welfare, mental health, and courts, are clearly support systems that respond to indicators of obstruction to the desired flow of behavior, e.g., health problems, behavior deviations, etc. Other systems are more supplemental or even replacements for actual family life. The child's propensity for problems follows him into these systems, and the system response, like that of the family, may be more or less adequate.

III. The Response Mechanisms.

Theoretically the entire process of child care could be conceptualized as an energy and information exchange—an output-input matrix between the multiboundaried child organism and the plural-system environment. In practice, this is not only impossible at this time but not necessary for the purposes of this Commission. Fortunately, biological evolution has provided a rather full set of automatic and intuitive stimulus and response patterns between adults and children. These automatic patterns carry the major behavioral load. However, in the past half-century, specific techniques, corrective devices, enrichment procedures, scientific expertise, etc., have been developed to meet specific needs and problems of children. An incomplete list in rough chronological order is provided in the "Response" column of Figure 5. No priority or logical order is implied. No other mechanism is excluded. These responses are simple or complicated behaviors that may or should be utilized by any of the child care personnel in any or all of the child care systems. When, where, to which child, by whom, for how long, and what were the results are just some of the questions that must be answered by the Information Utility.

AN INSTITUTION TO DEAL LONG RANGE WITH
THE DELIVERY OF SERVICES TO CHILDREN

Analysis of the problems of the current system of services to children suggests a number of gaps in the system—functions of analysis, experiment, and action which need to be carried out but are not or cannot be carried out within existing organizations.

We have outlined some of the features of child-centered service systems at the community level, and of management information systems for children's services at city, state, and federal levels. But these are only the beginnings. Further, extensive analysis is required, as well as concurrent programs of experiment and demonstration. If the Commission chooses to recommend such analysis and experiment, its recommendations will require continued energy and attention if their implementation is to be successful.

It is suggested that the Commission recommend, as part of its legacy, the establishment of a new institution whose function is to undertake certain activities both in relation to the present system of children's services and in the implementation of the Commission's recommendations.

Our analysis of the existing system, and of desirable directions of change, has definite implications for the form of a new institution concerned, in long-range terms, with the well-being of children. Two kinds of functions emerge as important. One is traditional—that is, the gathering and synthesis of information, the undertaking of analyses, policy formulation, and the like. But these do not address many outstanding problems relating to: vertical and horizontal interaction of agencies, the need for affecting mobilization in the services of existing agencies, and mustering resources where directions of action are clear.

If the new institution is to deal with the kinds of problems outlined above, it should undertake, directly or indirectly, the following activities:

1. *Map the field.* It should determine the full range of agencies and programs operating outside the system and under legal or licensing sanction. Sampling or census techniques should be used to map what these agencies and programs do, where they operate, how they are funded, and the range of overlap in their operations.

2. *Identify alternative objectives.* In each problem area, we found a number of implicitly inconsistent objectives. It would be important to identify the actual and presumed goals toward which each subsystem is aimed.

3. *Assess the problems of the system.* This would consist of an extension of the analysis of the first part of this report, undertaken on a continuing basis. Among the key problems to be addressed would be those related to manpower, its allocation and training, and the interaction of subsystems of the children's system, as reflected in what were earlier described as horizontal and vertical interactions.

4. *Examine analogies with other systems.* The new institution should explore experience gained in other service systems in the United States, such as the blindness system, and in other countries. Sweden, Israel, and Russia, for example, have developed approaches to total service systems for children which are worth continuing study.

5. *Foundation of optional strategies of service.* The new institution should explore alternative strategies for attaining service goals, with particular attention to those not restricted by the boundaries of any given professional service system; e.g., direct payment to mothers as an alternative to day-care services.

6. *Formulate and seed experiments in service delivery systems.* We

have formulated some criteria for child-centered, community-based service systems. Within these criteria, a wide range of community-based experiments are possible and desirable.

These experiments will tend to threaten established boundaries and vested professional interests; they will need continued outside overview and support. A range of experiments should be undertaken, testing out approaches to: network management, bases for continuity of service, points of access to systems of services, matching of services to population clusters of varying kinds, and means of keeping significant control over services in the hands of users.

A problem of great interest will involve choice of sites for community-based experiments. There is, for example, some "unclaimed territory" that offers opportunity for innovation. Head Start is an example of an experiment that began in a relatively open area.

The new institution should formulate and develop strategies for initiating these community-based experiments and then help them to connect to and learn from one another, and provide overview of their conduct.

7. *Formulate systems of data gathering and analogies.* This report began with an explanation of the nature of cost-benefit and operating data systems. This work needs extensive development, leading to the formulation of models of management information systems which can be implemented, in prototype fashion, at city and state levels.

If the new institution is to perform these analytic, intelligence, and experimental functions, it must have:

a critical mass of resources for analysis, data gathering, intelligence, execution and evaluation of experiments, synthesis of results, generation of model programs, and the like;

access to many different constituencies;

ways of handling the dangers inherent in efforts for change.

It does not seem feasible to combine in one centrally organized institution the resources necessary to perform the tasks outlined above. The resulting bureaucratization and rigidity would render such an institution incapable of the flexible, action-oriented program needed. We propose, therefore, the formation of a "core" activity, relatively small but with substantial funding, and a series of "networks," or temporary systems, which the core brings into being to focus on particular problems at particular times, and then dissolves as those problems are met.

The core of the institution is its permanent mobilizing force. The core identifies issues and priorities, then spins off a series of *ad hoc* "networks" to concentrate on studying these issues and resolving them. Core members themselves may direct these networks, or may at times choose to bring in additional personnel to perform administrative and management functions.

The networks should cover the four areas listed below. It should be kept in mind that network boundaries are fluid: members of one network may have to move from one to another as work on a project progresses, although their prime responsibility will remain in terms of their original network. The stage of work and nature of the project will also determine how many networks are in operation at one time, and the scale and scope of that operation. We suggest the following four networks:

1. Intelligence. Basic information on current happenings ("mapping the field," as stated above) on local and national levels will be needed.

2. Data analysis and program generation. Alternative objectives and strategies, utilization of funding, manpower and facilities, and analogies with other systems will need to be examined. New standards of legislation, model programs, and political formats will need to be designed.

3. Experiment and innovation. New programs will need to be tested in specific communities. These can be "seeded" directly, or existing entrepreneurs can be supported and reinforced.

4. Strategies for implementation. In order to move toward implementing its proposals, the institution must be able to place issues on the national political agenda and muster support behind broad new programs at the national level.

Keyed to its success in this connection will be its ability to muster a variety of kinds of support in a temporary way around particular issues without becoming committed to one group at the expense of others and without acquiring a label of political affiliation.

Among the groups to which connection must be made are the following:

business groups, members of the management groups of large banks, insurance companies, and utility companies with special concerns for the problems of the center city;

administrators in federal, state, and municipal bureaucracies—particularly new administrators who want to move with new programs;

connection to the professional middle-management levels and the "young comers" in these bureaucracies;

action-oriented groups concerned directly or indirectly with the well-being of children, such as the remnants of the Child Development Groups in Mississippi, field workers of the CCAP, the welfare rights movement in New York City, the MAW in Boston;

the policy-making centers of political parties;

the Congress of the United States, through both legislators and key staff people working for them;

journalists and writers who, provided with background data and material, can help to place issues before a national public.

The new institution should be capable of producing relevant data and information, background material for programs, model programs, and legislation for Congressional figures as the need arises. It should also be capable of providing political intelligence to new administrators, such as a local welfare administrator or a commissioner of health for a large metropolitan area, on such topics as:

> his potential allies and enemies;
> ongoing projects and persons with whom he can collaborate;
> key persons who can become the nucleus of his staff.

In addition to core group members, some senior members of networks such as those outlined above should be given a guarantee of employment for a set minimum number of days per year to ensure their availability when required. Other senior members, especially those active in experiment and innovation, often use up over a period of time their personal capital or credit in the community in which they operate. These men will need a "nest," to which they can temporarily retire after completing work in one community, where they can plan new fields of action somewhere else.

Younger members can be trained and retrained through internships and small supporting grants, on the model of the long-term program of Dr. Leonard J. Cottrell, Jr., at the Russell Sage Foundation. Junior staff might be available full time and switched from project to project as the need arises. Such job rotation would provide them with the fuller, interdisciplinary perspective that many older professionals do not have.

The maintenance of these related networks will require sustained effort, skill, and effective intelligence concerning the interests and movements of persons within these networks. It will require a continuing effort at communications, both face to face and by telephone. Most of all, it will require the ability to sustain interpersonal as well as bargaining and trading relationships, out of which effective teams, temporary or permanent, are built.

Size and scope of work: With respect to the *number* of problem areas or issues to which the new institution should address itself, it is clear that these should be enough to be significant but not too many to be overwhelming, particularly in the early stages. The new institution should identify problems as discrete problems (in spite of the inevitable connection of all problems to one another when analyzed in depth), and it should be capable of devoting some labor to problems over a number of years and then mounting significant efforts when timing indicates that intensive work is needed. It must have several projects going, in order not to be hooked on the failure or unanticipated irrelevance of any one project, yet it cannot spread itself too thin.

On what basis will the institution allocate its resources to work on issues?

These are among the relevant factors: In the early months of operation, the new institution must establish its credibility. It will need some rapid successes in order to survive. It must, therefore, devote attention to problems which are "ready" in the sense of already being on the national agenda and lending themselves to some kind of visible and at least partially successful attack. Moreover, it should seek those problems which are "open," where positions are not so firmly taken by the various constituencies involved that intense conflict is the only feasible route to solution.

In short, in its early years, the institution should move where the action is and toward relatively manageable pieces of problems. Examples might be as follows:

> child health; in particular, the design of new health service systems for children on the community level;
>
> the cluster of issues surrounding day care;
>
> access to recreation for poor children;
>
> on the level of legislation and national policy, welfare and the well-being of children.

At the same time, the new institution should be devoting attention to other factors governing priorities (such as the numbers of children affected, the intensity of the effect, the availability of approaches and techniques for dealing with the problem under consideration, the relative costs of attack on the problems, the extent to which manpower represents a constraint on such attacks, and the like).

The new institution must quickly identify several issues for immediate and short-range attack, under criteria relating to its own success and survival. At the same time, it must set in motion longer-term, continuing inquiries into issues chosen because of their likely long-term significance to the well-being of children. Concurrently, it must devote attention to the problem of identifying relative priorities in the field.

The institution we have described will need a relatively low level of funding in its first year or two. Once it has established credibility, funding should rapidly increase and then level off within several years. The Appendix provides some estimates for various projects and a sample Core budget.

The creation of an institution such as we have proposed here would bring us one step further toward creating a truly responsive system of child services. We cannot meet the needs of our nation's children until these needs have been realistically determined. The well-being of our children rests ultimately upon our knowledge and our commitment.

Appendix

FUNDING FOR CORE AND CORE-GENERATED PROJECTS

Funding can be divided into funding for Core and funding for projects generated out of Core.

It is estimated that a minimum figure for Core funding should be in the order of $400,000 a year over a minimum period of incubation of three years.

Core funding will involve the following:

1. Sustaining funds for a small number of Core staff, including the director, one or two senior program people, a few bright young junior analysts, and operations and clerical support.

2. Network maintenance, including both communications functions (telephone bills, which will be staggering; meetings; travel) and small guaranteed funding to network members.

3. "Nesting" support for project managers and entrepreneurs in communities who will return to the institution for periods ranging from a few months to a year, between assignments to communities.

4. Training budgets for young interns who are funded either to operate in communities in particular projects or to work with central staff.

A sample Core budget for the first year of operation might be as follows:

a. Central staff	
Director	$35,000
Three senior program people at an average of $25,000	75,000
Four junior staff members at an average of $15,000	60,000
Subtotal	170,000
b. Network maintenance—communications	10,000
Sustaining support for network members at an average of $5,000 each	50,000
Subtotal	230,000

    c. Nesting support
       One in the first year   30,000

    d. Training grants for $10,000   40,000
                        Subtotal   300,000

    e. Overhead, including rent, supplies, clerical support   120,000
                  Grand Total Core $420,000

In addition there should be *ad hoc* project support over the first three to five years. This figure may vary from $1 million to $3.5 million a year. These are funds to support specific projects of analysis, data gathering, advocacy.

References

Cervantes, L .F. *The Dropout: Courses and Cures.* Ann Arbor: University of
   Michigan Press, 1965.

Fadiman, C. (ed). *What I Believe, Revised, Living Philosophies.* New York:
   Simon and Schuster, 1938.

Federal Programs for the Development of Human Resources—Report of Subcommittee on Economic Progress of the Joint Economic Committee,
   U.S. Congress, Dec. 1966, p. 4.

Gorman, W., and Bell, D. Social Indicators Panel of H.E.W. Quoted in B. M.
   Gross and M. Springer, "A New Orientation in American Government."
   The Annals of the American Academy of Political and Social Science,
   May 1967, p. 11.

Levitan, J. A. "Will Employers Be Induced to Train the Poor," *Poverty and
   Human Resource Abstract,* II, 6 (1967), 19–21.

Myrdal, G. "The Necessity and Difficulty of Planning." Washington, D.C.,
   Oct. 3, 1967.

Orshansky, M. "The Shape of Poverty in 1966." Reprinted from the *Social
   Security Bulletin.* Washington, D.C.: U.S. Dept. HEW, Social Security
   Administration, Mar. 1968.

Rogers, E. S. "Public Health Asks of Sociology," *Science,* 159 (Feb. 1968),
   506–508.

III

CLINICAL ISSUES

REPORT OF THE COMMITTEE ON CLINICAL ISSUES

Edited by Joseph D. Noshpitz, M.D.

In the following pages, the problems of research, manpower, and services to children are discussed at length from the clinician's viewpoint, and great emphasis is placed upon the specific and individualized needs of the child. In addition, the Report of the Committee on Clinical Issues addresses itself to many aspects of normal and abnormal child development.

—EDITOR

Committee on Clinical Issues

241

Preface

Childhood in its broadest sense involves the total human life cycle. It begins with birth and carries through to the teen-age years when motherhood and fatherhood are often crowning events of adolescence, and the cycle begins again. The psychological issues of childhood thus involve the full gamut of changes, from infancy to parenthood, with all the mastery and happiness and success that can attend these epochs, and with all the failures and arrests and catastrophes that the clinician so often encounters.

To construe an approach to so vast and complex a panorama of human experience inevitably involves choices. Some landmark issues stand out, and need primary attention. Others, no less important for being more subtle, might still be relegated to the second rank of concern. And still others are in the realm of wish, hope, and fantasy—wouldn't it be wonderful if . . . !

243

Foreword

We of the Clinical Services Committee have labored many months preparing this report. From this work, a certain overall recommendation has emerged that encompasses the many detailed suggestions that appear throughout the text. We would like to make this explicit. We recommend that our country develop a range of mental health treatment services, that these be linked to interventive and preventive programs, and that we thus establish a network of comprehensive services for emotionally disturbed children, and those at high risk of becoming so, that will reach every child in need, whoever he may be and wherever he may be. It is our professional opinion that we cannot plan for the mental health of the children of this country in general, without concrete provisions for the appropriate care of *individual* children and youth who need *individual* diagnostic and treatment services.

As clinicians, we are all too aware of the obstacles to the implementation of such recommendations; it is our daily fare to cope with the problems of scarce manpower, escalating expenses, and the hopes of so many people that provisions of basic services would quickly and magically do away with emotional disturbances in children. Indeed, one of the most serious difficulties that arises today comes from the view that the provision of preventative programs will eliminate the need for treatment services. Much as we applaud the emphasis upon generally supportive services to children, we do not believe that the specific needs of those emotionally disturbed at present, and of those likely to become so in the years to come, can or should be minimized. To slight this aspect of long-range mental health programing, in our view, lacks dignity, humanity, and elementary social wisdom.

There is general agreement that current facilities are grossly inadequate: without emphatic, explicit support of a greatly expanded and diversified treatment network, resources for the emotionally and mentally ill may well

244

decline in quality and number over the next few years. Within the current structure, waiting lists are long and many children are without any possibility of care. Nor should anyone take for granted that the available network will flourish or even continue to exist unless explicit attention and support are given to it. Indeed, at the time of this writing, federally funded training programs for mental health professionals have been warned to expect a 10 percent cut across the board—the direction is toward contraction of services at precisely the moment that demographic pressures plead for their expansion.

The scarcity of child psychiatric facilities and of staff trained in clinical work with children is a reality with which we have lived and worked for many years. Probably no group is more familiar with the number of children needing help and the scantiness of treatment resources to meet these needs. However, we believe that such measures as a determined backing of training for as many professional and paraprofessional persons as the current centers could accommodate, the phased establishment of new programs as personnel become available, the expansion and diversification of existing centers, the full utilization of trained personnel, and the implementation of child development and clinical research findings in collaborative and creative new programs would, within a few years, provide a striking change in the individual treatment picture. In 1967 the United States spent $11.1 billion in the cotton support program; that same year the federal government did not spend more than one-twentieth that amount for child mental health services. We hear this, we read this, but do we, as a people, really ask ourselves the harsh question: In terms of dollars and cents, just how do children stack up against cotton, or oil, or whatever?

Thus, we come to the issue of costs. We do not know what an adequate network of treatment services across the country would cost. Clearly the price tag would run well into billions of dollars. The investment of even $5 billion in treatment services would call for a radical rearrangement of our priorities in the United States. We can support cotton, send men to the moon, spend huge sums for defense, subsidize a supersonic liner for our prestige, spend billions for cosmetics, alcohol, and cigarettes. Few Americans are criticizing the costly programs of kidney dialysis and organ transplants as too expensive, or as helping only a few. We need more research in mental health, as well, and our methodologies will undoubtedly be altered and improved upon as a result of systematic investigation. This state of affairs we share with physical medicine, education, environmental control, and arms control.

On the other hand, the cost of emotional disturbance in children to our society in terms of human waste, economic loss, and custodial and welfare support has never been added up, but it is clearly huge. It is no small problem to which we are addressing ourselves.

We feel it is important to tell our readers that we are recommending not just more of the same, but rather a purposeful, energetic commitment to building a network of clinical services for emotionally disturbed children in this country. We know such a commitment will require a drastic shift in values, a strong motivation based on the conviction that salvaging Mary Jones or Johnny Smith for a productive, gratifying life is worth the investment of time, energy, and money. It will call for the recognition that our best hope of building our society to meet our stated ideals and the demands of a technological culture is to invest in all of our children. The emotionally disturbed child is one of a family, he is a student in school, he is part of a neighborhood. He will perhaps one day be responsible for a family of his own, he is a peer, a relative, and eventually will become employer or employee: effective treatment for him affects the lives of many beyond his own. We challenge our readers to view the information in this report as a call for a genuine reordering of our priorities, and to join with us and others in seeing that our societal responsibilities to emotionally disturbed children and youth are adequately discharged in the years to come.

Introduction

The Committee on Clinical Issues was established early in 1968. It was drawn from members of the Board and added to by a group of consultants. All its members had for many years been engaged in the clinical care of emotionally sick children; they included child psychiatrists, child analysts, clinical psychologists, and a social worker. They viewed their charge from the Commission from the vantage point of the professional person responsible for mental health service programs for children, and for the associated training and research. The committeemen had all borne the weight of much personal clinical experience. They had developed opinions and dreams, watched one fad after another come and go, worried about the limitations of their knowledge and techniques, and seen other approaches to emotional and mental illness in children placed in juxtaposition to their clinical approaches. As they met together, exchanged views, matched recollections, and worried about some new developments (and about the lack of other new developments), certain consensual attitudes emerged, crystallized, and were written down. These comprise the bulk of this report. It seems fair to say that several hundred years of clinical experience have been distilled here. Perhaps it is best to start by asking: What is a "clinical approach"? What is a "clinician" in the mental health field? In the exposition below, and later in this report, we will not preface the word each time by "mental health," but the reader is to understand that we are discussing the group of professional persons working with emotionally troubled children. Certain descriptive terms may apply to physical medicine, or to education in general, or to pastoral counseling. Nonetheless, we have in mind a specific group charged with specific functions and characterized by certain attitudes and proclivities.

The very term "clinical" possesses many connotations and presents multiple facets. It is derived from medical practice and connects most immediately with the area of diagnosis and treatment of the sick. In this sense, the mental health clinician dealing with a client carries on an activity that assimilates large volumes of complicated data, processes them rapidly, and emerges with conclusions about what is wrong and what needs to be done that are skilled, sensitive, practical, and humane. The clinician is one who embraces complexity; the chances are that he will not communicate effectively with those who seek and will accept only simple linear solutions to problems of health and illness. At its best, his work involves the integration of an empathic awareness of the child's current psychological situation, a knowledge of the family history and social status, a thorough knowledge of child development (intellectual, emotional, instinctual, physical, social, etc.), an amalgamation of all this information into a systematic schema of psychopathology, a capacity for honest and knowledgeable estimation of the clinician's own emotions and motives, as these might color his judgment, and a translation of the resulting reflections into constructive activity: making the right diagnosis, saying the thing which will help, and acting in a way to relieve pain and foster development.[1] More than this, basic to any definition of "clinical" is the whole issue of appreciation of and concern for feelings and fantasy, and for the human's fundamental need to defend against threats to his subjective sense of personal security. This is one of the major differences in approach which distinguishes the mental health clinician from people in other branches of medicine and the related professions. Central to the clinician's orientation is his sensitivity to the complexities of communication. Whether speaking as the one who treats, as the one who teaches, as the one who informs, or as the one who consults and supervises, the clinician is aware of the influence of the other person's needs, sensitivities, and problems and how these affect what can be perceived, and understood. This, in turn, maximizes the possibility of a fruitful dialogue in which nonproductive ways of perceiving or reacting to problems can be discarded, and new ways evolved.

In discussing feelings, the bywords for the clinician have been "know thyself." To do his work the clinician has had to learn about himself, about his own reactions, his own suffering, fantasy, and feelings, his own limitations and shortcomings, and his own strengths. Only then has he been able to reach out and do something about others—whether through teaching or through working directly with patients. And he has had to come to understand the enormous force of the irrational in shaping human behavior. He has had to come to grips with his own unconscious yearnings,

1. See Appendix A: Psychosocial Disorders in Childhood and Adolescence: Theoretical Considerations and an Attempt at Classification, by Dane G. Prugh, M.D.

and to learn to recognize and deal with the prelogical factors in his patients' lives. More than that, the clinician has been pressed to go beyond mere understanding and awareness of his own feelings and those of the patient—he has had to develop himself as a clinical instrument.

Evidently, this goal will not always be realized in its ideal state—but in terms of labeling persons as "clinicians," in organizing training programs, in setting ideals and targets for our trainers and trainees, these are some of the elements that need to be included. Among the definitional problems are the wide variety of systems of psychopathology and the equally varied treatment methods currently clamoring for precedence on the public scene. Behavior therapy, family therapy, psychoanalysis, the range of group therapies, the endless variety of psychotherapies, various pharmacological, organic, and mixed approaches, and so on and on, all are before us and all claim usefulness. Some are brand new, capturing the enthusiasm and hope of those who had struggled unsuccessfully with stubborn problems using older methods. They attract us with the promise of the novel, the ingenious, and the clever, and have not yet risked being tarnished by extended exposure to clinical experience. Other therapies are well established and have been the mainstay of clinics and practitioners for years. We of the Clinical Committee do not feel that now is the time to attempt to set bounds to so dynamic and turbulent a field; this is the period for eclectic approaches, experimentation, and opening new possibilities for exploration. We would caution, however, that welcoming the new does not imply abandoning our seasoned and established methods of treatment. Indeed, this is a time when the business of treating the sick child is important as never before. Oswald's behavior was predicted by a diagnosing clinician, and as our population grows, the absolute number of emotionally sick people will grow as well, and in time we will be facing greater hazards rather than fewer. Hence the continued use and application of those methods we do know and have found to be useful over the years are vital elements in any program that the Joint Commission on Mental Health of Children recommends.

The clinician knows that we have no panacea, no universally effective method that applies to all illness. There are cases in which clinic treatment is optimal and the clinics need to be supported, strengthened, and multiplied to give the care and the help they can do best. Many very sick children need residential treatment, and we need to see to it that such services are provided and staffed with the level of skill and competence necessary for dealing with these serious conditions. There are cases in which psychoanalysis is indicated, and for such children we are failing them if we do not strive in every way to make analysis possible.

Now newer treatment techniques and structural modalities are being developed which involve the use of tranquilizers and other drugs, behavior therapies (operant conditioning, behavioral modification, desensitization), day care, evening care, halfway houses, family care, home visits, and a variety of other methods. Older clinicians recall that many of these approaches had been ventured on and experimented with in the past. Today a more intensive, systematically selective, and widespread attempt is being made to have them widely available for use everywhere. The doctrine of a spectrum of services has caught hold, and the Clinical Committee endorses this wholeheartedly, with a particular emphasis on the need for that band of the spectrum that speaks for direct treatment.

What we have seen in our communities is the spotty and uneven provision of services, so that here a residential center has been asked to take cases for which some other placement should have been made, but no other placement was available; there a clinic was called upon to treat a case which needed residential care, only no funds were available, or no bed could be found. In many areas there has been an almost systematic misuse of facilities and the resultant dissatisfactions with the outcome have cast their shadows over the real worth that is in fact inherent in each of the several modalities.

One of the great guiding principles for the clinician is the importance of the individual. The feelings and the worth of the individual person and concern with finding a mode of communication that will reach the individual are central in all his thinking. Clinical responsibility begins with the individual; it does not, however, end with him. To achieve his ends, the clinician must seek understanding and communication all the way down the line, from the treatment of the sick, to the people who deal with the sick, to the people in related areas. The treatment of the individual is the focus, but it is set within an envelope of broader processes—the intrapsychic problem of the child is viewed within the context of the family, the community, and the social system. All of these must be weighed and utilized for an optimal outcome. It is important to recognize that when there is sickness and help can be obtained, it has enormous positive meaning for the family and the community.

Thus, the definition of clinical work becomes: first, the evaluation of behavior within its intrahuman and interhuman contexts from a vantage point of knowledge about child development and about deviations of development; and, second, a planful approach to the amelioration of the problem on the basis of the clinician's particular conceptual approach and professional experience.

The clinician views etiology as complex; he sees emotional disturbances as originating from a variety of sources: genetic, constitutional, developmental, familial, ecological, and so forth. Thus multiple types of treatment can be employed, and many different schools of thought ranging from behavior therapies to psychoanalysis all can have their sectors of relevance.

At the same time, clinical work entails certain qualities that are unique and essential. These include an ability to tolerate the ambiguity that accompanies so much of the effort in this humane area, and the readiness to accept and live with the fact that many life problems cannot be resolved, or can at best find only partial resolution. The clinician is primarily neither an academician nor an experimentalist; he is a healer with all the strengths and biases that implies. Since he lives and works in a society which tends increasingly to emphasize human engineering and computerized solutions to problems, he is likely at times to find himself somewhat outside the mainstream. Rather than hypothesize the main relevance of a few dimensions, or strive for mathematical models of the problem, he insists on embracing the full complexity of the human situations he confronts. He accepts personal responsibility for the sometimes empathic rather than explicitly demonstrable formulations derived from his own filtering of his data. He is as much or more concerned with the unconscious, the irrational, and the implicit as he is with the evident, the obvious, and the straightforward.

Many years of training and experience are required to produce a full-fledged clinician. There is no one discipline of origin for this work. Psychiatry, psychology, social work, education, and the ministry, as well as other disciplines (such as anthropology and sociology), have all been the training grounds for excellent clinical people. Unfortunately, intellectual background alone does not guarantee clinical capacity. Poor clinicians have also been found among those who had been awarded degrees by these same disciplines. Regardless of his origin, the clinician is an end product of a great deal of time, expense, and commitment; he has had to work hard for years in order to learn what he has to know. Once trained, he needs to sort out where he can be most effective as teacher and consultant, and where he must intervene directly.

A further elaboration of the concept of what is "clinical" is the relationship of the clinician to child-rearing. In a very real sense, all childhood psychopathology is developmental deviation of some sort. The clinician sees the effects of slum conditions, overcrowding, and material deprivation no less than the impact of maternal overprotection, excessive enemas, and sexual overstimulation of children. Moreover, individual treatment has regularly led to considerations of how particular symptoms come into being, and a good deal of data has been accumulated around what works—and what fails—in raising children. From all this, certain cardinal principles of child-rearing have emerged, certain do's and don'ts that are basic ingredients of bringing up any children anywhere. These are certainly not ultimate truths about how to bring up a child, and new advances in research and experience will undoubtedly alter some of our views today as they have in the past. Nonetheless, there is a central core of hard-won knowledge that has been amassed and should be a crucial part of any schema of prevention that is contemplated. In particular, certain outside limits of

child-rearing practice have become reasonably well established; for example, information concerning the effects of overpermissiveness, overprotection, excessive punitiveness, the results of sadistic handling, the
outcome of inadequate limits, the impact of neglect (and its differential
effects at different moments in development); the meanings of separation,
of hospitalization, of overfeeding, of surgery, of enemas, and so on and on
for many items—all these have become marked as significant, and are
becoming better understood with the passage of time and the accumulation
of data. There is a genuinely positive contribution to healthy child development available in such compendiums of current knowledge as Dr. Spock's
Baby and Child Care. This is one of the best manuals, but by no means
the only one. New knowledge is constantly being acquired on differences
in constitution among children, and we will undoubtedly be developing
new formulations geared to the typology of the child and the style of
family into which he is born. The wave of the future is for ever greater
specificity; we will one day be able to say that within such a family context, such and such a handling is necessary for this or that particular kind
of infant. But for all its present shortcomings, our current knowledge is
still substantial, and every effort should be bent to making it available on
every level—to parents, to general practitioner, to nurse, to pediatrician,
to welfare worker, to teacher, and to the host of others who impinge on
child-rearing in one way or another.

Thus, over and above his work as a therapist, the clinician has roles
in good child-rearing and in all the varied aspects of prevention, as well
as in the treatment of the sick. But they are different roles, involving
different patterns of activity and different responsibilities. One such area
is to act as guide and supporter for the child-rearers and for those who seek
to help the youngsters past the shoals of the ordinary growth problems.
Only when there is substantial and/or prolonged interference with development or when a major disturbance appears does direct responsibility fall
on the clinician for treatment. For example, in the course of clinical work
with communities, it has been observed that some percentage of the children seen are the product of "surface conflict." The help needed for such
situations will often best be given by recreation people, by volunteers like
"Big Brothers," by special assistance in the school, and by other service
organizations in the community who would rely on the clinician primarily
as adviser, consultant, and back-up resource if other methods should fail.

Inevitably, the clinician's roles will flow into one another, there will
be doubtful, borderline situations, and there will be variations in agency
structure that will require some re-sorting of these categories. Primary
prevention, with its review of large populations of children, be it in well-
baby clinics, Head Start programs, schools, camps, or wherever, inevitably
leads to secondary prevention—sick children turn up who then need treatment. Any such attempt to prevent problems always uncovers problems,

and the clinician will then be pressed to change his role from consultant to therapist.

It is extremely important to underline that regardless of our approach, for the next several decades the brute reality is that we will be finding and facing large numbers of troubled children who will need all kinds of help —including psychiatric treatment—and there will not be enough well-trained people to give the help. In the face of this fact, the task of allotting the available time and skill becomes a major problem for our society. It is therefore crucial in planning new services, and in revamping older agencies, that the clinician be called in as consultant and that a thoughtful ear be turned to his counsel. His judgment about where and how his capacities can best be utilized should figure prominently in developing blueprints. Moreover, his knowledge and experience will prevent many possible false starts and structural errors. Finally, his skills, directly applied, can be of considerable use in the areas of interstaff tensions and the intrapersonal problems that are an inevitable part of managing troubled children on every level.

There is no doubt that one of the most open and available channels to communicate with the poor, the deprived, and the alienated is along the route of health, medical care, disease prevention, treatment, and similar modalities. The needy are usually especially concerned about these areas; they tend to have more problems, to suffer more, and thus to have very significant contacts with health personnel. Hospitals, home-visiting nurses, general practitioners (who on the whole see far more of America's children than do the pediatricians), well-baby clinics, and other such agencies provide major interfaces for contact with children and with their parents. In the hospital alone, adding play, recreation, and education programs to the practice of encouraging overnight stay for the mothers of young children will bring about a major advance in mental health. All such avenues allow for constructive clinical activity.

Ultimately, the clinician's counsel must be needed in setting national policy. In wartime England, Anna Freud's was the deciding voice which established that there was a greater emotional risk in separating children from their families than in leaving them all together in bomb-threatened cities; many other issues about national policies for child care, rearing, and treatment need clinical consultation. For example, the impact of racism, both on the minority populations restricted to ghetto conditions and on the majority populations which ignored, tolerated, or benefited from those conditions, has clinical as well as social ramifications. Concepts such as hostility, guilt, anxiety, projection, identity formation, and the like will inevitably be necessary for understanding this social ill and for the development of constructive methods of intervention in order to relieve it. The impact of segregation has already received some study, but much remains to be done at every level from nursery school on up, and over the full spectrum from the Head Start type of program through that of the posh boarding school with its one black student.

Up to very recently, communication with impoverished minorities has not been a major feature of most training programs for clinicians—a great deal of specialized preparation to deal with such nonmiddle-class populations should be incorporated in the graduate programs, the residencies, and the fellowships that prepare our professionals. Furthermore, more trainees need to be recruited from minority groups; we have a serious dearth of Negro, Indian, and Latin professionals.

THE SICK CHILD

In terms of this report, the gross and immediate problems facing us are those of treating the sick child. For the clinician, this overshadows all other considerations—it is primary and imperative. It is not more important, but it is more immediate than the closely associated problem of preventing sickness. Nor is this less important, although again less pressing, than the long-range matter of giving each child the fullest, richest life possible at each stage of growth.

As we consider this ordering of our material, it is perhaps worth noting that the study and treatment of the emotionally ill has probably been our single most fruitful source of information about the fundamentals of human personality organization and, indirectly, about possible methods of prevention of illness. By this time, many of our treatment methods are seasoned and tested; whereas our preventative techniques are relatively new and untried. We have some idea of what we can do and what we don't yet know how to do in the area of therapy; with most of our preventative programs we have enthusiasm and hope and theory—but no assurance as to how well our undertakings are likely to succeed or whether in fact they will accomplish anything. This should not be construed as an argument against the implementation of preventative approaches; it is rather an affirmation of our need for them, together with the appropriate caution to temper our level of optimism to that which is reasonable with any new approach. It speaks for special emphasis on built-in evaluation methods so that we may more quickly winnow the chaff from the grain and more rapidly come to distinguish the strategy that is fruitful from the method that promises but does not deliver.

As of today, the availability of treatment to the emotionally and the mentally ill child in America is uncertain, variable, and inadequate. This is true on all levels, rich and poor, rural and urban. The problems are more widespread among the poor, as are all health problems, but the fact is that only a fraction of our young people get the help they need at the time they need it.

Furthermore, beyond the paucity and uneven distribution of means of treatment, we must point to the lack of adequate research[2] and of appropriate prophylactic measures and, indeed, the limited supply of all the elements necessary to assure our children of the best care and of the requisite preventive measures for their emotional health.

There is little to suggest that this situation is likely to change in the near future. Up to very recently, there has been no national planning for services for children on the drawing board despite numerous White House Conferences, an active and interested Children's Bureau, and repeated recommendations by a variety of professional and lay organizations. The resistance to such planning and to the implementation of what planning has been done seems to run deep. The existence of the Joint Commission on Mental Health of Children augers well for the possibility of change, but we must recognize that changes will not come easily.

THE GOALS OF THE COMMISSION AND THE DEVELOPMENTAL APPROACH

The Clinical Committee recommends to the Board of the Joint Commission on Mental Health of Children that it pursue three goals:

1. The diagnosis and treatment of the emotionally and mentally sick child.
2. The prevention of illness whenever possible.
3. The achievement of optimal growth and capacity for each child.

To accomplish these ends, services to children or affecting children must be organized along developmental lines. This requirement means that the training of specialized personnel to deal with the characteristic problems of each age period must be organized in this way. The nature of agency types and locations must be governed by similar considerations. It must be part of the thinking, the practices, and the community relations of each individual involved with children.

The range of childhood is such that our planning for children must include the prenatal care of the pregnant mother at one end of the spectrum and the transition of the college-age youth into young adulthood at the other. But again and again our planning must be dominated by the awareness of the child as a person in transition—we deal with the issues of development and arrests of development. We strongly endorse the concept that every child has a right to health, physical and emotional, and, if ill, every child has a right to treatment, physical and emotional.

THE PRIORITIES FOR THE ESTABLISHMENT OF SERVICES AND TRAINING

2. See Appendix B: Recommendations by the Clinical Committee of the Joint Commission on Mental Health of Children on Research.

PROGRAMS AND FOR THE OVERALL DISTRIBUTION OF MONIES SHOULD FOL-
LOW THIS ORDER OF GOALS: FIRST, THE TREATMENT OF EVERY CHILD AS
WELL AS THE FAMILY AROUND THE CHILD WHEREVER DEMONSTRABLE ILL-
NESS IS FOUND; THEN, AND, OFTEN ENOUGH AS PART OF THE SAME EFFORT,
THE ATTEMPT TO PREVENT ILLNESS AND DISTURBANCE BY LARGE-SCALE
PLANNING; AND, ULTIMATELY, THE REORGANIZATION OF SOCIAL STRUC-
TURES IN A WAY THAT WILL ENCOURAGE THE MAXIMUM FLOWERING OF
EACH PERSON'S INDIVIDUAL POTENTIAL FOR SELF-REALIZATION AND SOCIAL
CONTRIBUTION.

In addition to our basic concern with treating the sick, there is another
reason for stating our priorities in this order. It rests on a salient observation that has been made again and again in mental health work—one
noted earlier, and one that will be commented on repeatedly in this report.
Within our current experience, wherever and whenever any program of
preventive character has been initiated, one invariable consequence has
been the discovery of large numbers of disturbed and troubled children and
families needing all kinds of help. It does not seem to matter whether we
talk of well-baby clinics, programs for preschool children, sex education
classes in schools, or adolescent recreation projects—the sick youngsters
are presently there and need to be dealt with. If our attempts at preventing
emotional disorders and improving children's lives are not backed up by
adequate clinical facilities, a very real discontent soon appears within
both the project staff and the people in the community served. Here are
situations for which something needs to be done, and all one has are
waiting lists and referral "elsewhere." *The stark realities are that if we are
to make prevention work, and enhance development, we need to have the
facilities available to treat, specifically, to give the appropriate treatment
for each developmental stage. Otherwise we jeopardize everything we
undertake.*

In keeping with the emphasis on development, we will organize this
report along developmental lines. The sections will thus be titled genetic,
prenatal, infancy, preschool, primary school, and junior high and high
school.

Genetic Considerations

The available data suggest that this will be a target area some decades hence, and that the reports and surveys of the future will be filled with major contributions arising from newfound knowledge. There are many conditions recognized today that are associated with genetic transmission and even with known genetic abnormalities. Some are evidenced at birth, such as Mongolism. Others develop in early childhood, like Tay-Sachs disease, and still others may not appear until late in life, as, for example, Huntington's chorea. Certain conditions, such as diabetes, seem to have definite genetic linkages and may appear at almost any time within the life cycle. By and large, there are no specific therapeutic techniques known to us today which could operate on a molecular or chromosomal level and correct an inborn error of this sort. Such treatment will be a goal of future generations of biological research. When such a level of technical capacity is achieved, this will have enormous implications for the very stuff of our species.

It is important to recognize that many humans who have some level of genetic or congenital deficit do continue to survive, grow, and develop. As they grow, they quickly become aware that they are not like the people around them. There is a great deal of clinical evidence that highlights the importance of psychological stresses associated with the awareness of being different, especially when this means different in a deficient way. We know this is a source of emotional problems and neurotic defenses in these humans, and that it requires the services of mental health professionals and resources. Leland has argued that even constitutionally limited individuals have available certain behavioral potentials that can be brought to a higher

257

level of functioning. Such injured people have emotional disturbances that are exacerbated by, and often organized around, a sense of being inferior, "picked on unfairly," punished for the intense correlated anger, etc. Leland has demonstrated that these conflicts and problems of low self-esteem are as responsive to psychotherapy as are the conflicts of individuals not restricted by genetic (and other) constitutionally determined limits ("Newsletter Section on Clinical Child Psychology," 1969).

In addition, members of the family of the child with a constitutional (or other chronic) deficit, who are trying to live with the retarded, cardiac, diabetic, etc., child, are burdened by all sorts of psychological problems. These can be manifested by intense overprotection or by rejection of the child or by periodic oscillations between these extremes, any one of which is bad for the constitutionally limited youngster. There are possibilities for intense guilts, anxieties, or despair as well as exaggerated defenses against these affects which are destructive to the mental health of the other family members. They often need appropriate kinds of support and psychotherapy. Illuminating studies have highlighted the sheer oppressiveness of the burden placed on parents and siblings by the responsibility of living with and caring for the grossly retarded child. It seems reasonable to generalize the findings to include those living with chronically ill, limited, or otherwise deviant children. Such conditions generate serious psychological problems in other family members. Farber and his colleagues at the University of Illinois demonstrated the intense vulnerability of the older female siblings of the severely retarded child. Their findings showed how the presence of such a child in the home could provide a stress which constantly threatened the integration of the entire family.

In sum, even before our technology develops to the point where a direct intervention (by biochemical, radiation, surgical, or other as yet undiscovered treatment methods) can directly remove factors limiting development, the important psychological problems in the limited and ill child and his family can be identified on the basis of existing knowledge. More to the point, these problems can benefit from the investment of effort by mental health clinicians using the knowledge which already exists.

PREVENTION

With all of our accumulated wisdom, we can still do little more than some probabilistic counseling of prospective parents. We can advise people from lineages of known genetic dysfunction, such as members of families with porphyria, what the probability is of their babies' having this condition. Such counseling may become particularly important when marriage with a relative is contemplated. No legal sanctions currently exist to prevent such people from bearing children, no matter how ill advised we think this to be.

We can detect a number of genetically caused conditions in infancy, such as Mongolism or phenylketonuria (both associated with mental retardation) and, where the genetic problem permits, strive to compensate for the deficiency. It was thought a few years ago that if phenylketonuria were detected in infancy in its full-fledged form, severe mental retardation could be prevented by altering the diet in a way that compensated for the inborn error in metabolism. This attempt has been made in a number of cases with results which are uncertain, to say the least. In sum, we must conclude that thus far our efforts are not too successful. Other conditions currently being subjected to study in this regard are galactosemia, tyrosinuria, and maple syrup urine disease; thus dietary therapies may become more successful in the future than they are today. Vitamin deficiencies can be treated, and enzyme or hormone replacements offered in a few cases. This is an area about which more will be heard in years to come.

TOWARD OPTIMAL GROWTH AND DEVELOPMENT

Perhaps the great breakthrough of the future will lie in changing the species through genetic manipulation. If our culture would be a far-seeing one, we could do well to begin today to consider the ethical, social, and empirical problems and consequences of genetic control. Theoretically, some day—and not at some impossibly remote day but within decades— it might become possible to add specific traits to or delete given genes from a particular pair of gametes by some combination of microsurgery and biochemical effect. We can only forewarn that such developments should not catch us unaware, but should be presaged by major efforts in thinking through how best to deal with the impact of these new possibilities if and as they arise.

The study of genetics is fast becoming a crucial area for research, money, and energy. This should by all means be fostered, but at the same time a substantial effort needs to be made to study the implications of these emerging data. For example, let us consider the recent publicity given to the phenomenon of the XYY chromosome aberration producing the so-called supermale. A number of men institutionalized for violent behavior have been found to carry this particular abnormality. It would seem important to study their offspring—are they different in any way?— or to study large populations of babies and, if some are found to show such a chromosomal pattern, to observe their development. Do they develop as other babies do, or are they unique in some ways? If we can identify children with XYY constitution, how do they study in school? What is their psychological and neurological profile like? If subjected to child psychoanalysis, what are the findings? And so on and on. . . . This one discovery opens a universe of basic research studies with enormous implications for increased understanding of the relationship between constitution and behavior, as well as information and suggestions that judges and juries might use in dealing with the social problems of such men. As things now stand, few controlled studies of this condition have been reported. A major suggestion, then, is to consider the more widespread genetic typing of babies in order to accumulate knowledge about the nature of our population, and in order to do what is possible to detect and to study variations, normal and abnormal.

Prenatal Period

THERAPEUTIC INTERVENTIONS

There are many conditions that are detectable during pregnancy and that are correctable or preventable at that time—so many, indeed, that it can safely be said that no woman should go through pregnancy without medical supervision. This is a medical truism, yet it is violated every day in our country. Large numbers of mothers receive no prenatal care, with a resultant massive infusion into our population of babies born prematurely or with congenital handicaps that will limit them for life and impair the lives of everyone about them. Ultimately, many products of such unsupervised pregnancies will become social and psychological problems.

Certain pregnancies should never be carried through; for example, those of women with German measles in the first trimester or with known exposure to high doses of radiation or dangerous chemicals. The likelihood is too great that the baby will be born deaf or congenitally mentally retarded, or that he will have congenital heart disease, abnormal limb development, or other serious conditions. Medically and socially speaking, abortion is the proper step, and if the law forbids this procedure, it is the law that is wrong.

Other pregnancies can be regarded as dubious ventures at best; for instance, those occurring in a setting of severe emotional or social problems. If a woman has had two psychotic breaks post-partum, is pregnant again, and wants an abortion, she should be able to obtain one. If a mother has a sixth child on the way and is already unable to care for the first five because of a combination of poverty, retardation, and alcoholism, and she wants an abortion, she should have one. There are numerous gross indications for not bringing another baby into a situation that has proved catastrophic for previous infants. Adoption agencies are enormously sensitive to such issues and will investigate carefully and exhaustively, with infinite refinement, before allowing prospective parents to adopt. How, then, as Dr. E. James Lieberman (at the time of the JCMHC study, Chief of Center for Studies of Child and Family Mental Health, National Institute of Mental Health) has posed us the question, can we be so rigid in insisting that once conception has occurred, pregnancy must then continue no matter what?

If we face the issue squarely, a pregnancy, each and every pregnancy, is not merely a personal matter; it is a social issue as well, fraught with immense consequences to the large polity. This sense of social concern and responsibility for pregnancy is a break with our tradition; it would seem from all the data now before us that it is a necessary break.

There are any number of ways of approaching the issue. For example, funds can be made available to each pregnant woman for dietary supplement, medical care, and general hygienic protection regardless of any question of need. If the woman is barely into her teens, is unmarried, is sick, has just been abandoned by a husband, is psychotic, has a handicapped child to care for, or is about to be evicted from her apartment, access to necessary social supports must be available. A sense of urgency, of emergency response, must become the trained-in value precisely because pregnancy is an event of such critical social import.

The value has to be spread to all of our health and welfare agencies— and more than to the agencies, to the entire community—namely, that pregnancy requires immediate mobilization of social action resources such as care, protection, and counseling if we are to protect our generations to come from physical and psychological debilities.

If a reward system is instituted (a regular stipend, or a fee for each clinic visit, or whatever), at some point the newly pregnant woman is likely to be in touch with the funding agency. This opens up an opportunity for helpful intervention. This is an ideal site for indigenous, community-derived, paramedical personnel to become active in seeing that the pregnant woman gets to the doctor on a regular basis and is protected from traumatic events such as having the heat turned off in the winter because she couldn't pay a bill, etc.

The unprotected, uncared-for pregnancy is a primary source of prematurity and birth defect. From society's point of view this is a serious matter. The premature infant is particularly prone to respiratory difficulties, and the underdeveloped nervous system is extremely vulnerable to any lowering of oxygen tension. The end result of this sequence is the all too common appearance of organic brain disease in the lives of such babies as they grow up. This eventually translates itself into learning difficulties, hyperactivity, impulsiveness, and other precursors to later maladjustment. Statistically, prematurity is one of the most frequent causes of mental retardation. The techniques for dealing medically with pregnancy and its complications are well known. The problem is one of social organization— getting contact with the gravid woman as early as possible, setting up a pattern of helpful relationship and supervision, and keeping it alive throughout.

Some of the problems involved can easily be seen if one steps into the waiting room of the average OB-Gyn clinic in a city hospital. The seats available are usually old, worn, and uncomfortable. Sometimes they are merely benches. The people wait for hours at a time, and when called they are herded into examining rooms without dignity and with a minimum of privacy. The entire experience involves delay, frustration, physical discomfort, and, ultimately, alienation.

The basic value issues that are necessary throughout involve, first, individualization and, second, expert helpfulness. This, as we shall see, will be the essence of the clinical attitude throughout.

Individualization is a difficult issue—we are talking of large populations, and it is no minor demand on the resources of a society to deal with each of its members as individuals. It is nonetheless essential in the context of health matters, which so intimately concern the body and the sense of self, that some account be taken of what matters to this particular person, how she sees the world, what frightens or troubles her, and what might drive her away from the help that she needs, and that her baby needs. Ultimately her society itself cannot safely do without this kind of understanding. It is only on such knowledge that effective programs can be built.

Research has shown that women who drop out of prenatal care in the last trimester are "at risk" and should immediately become targets for intensive follow-up and help efforts. They are a highly vulnerable group, and on the average their babies will do less well than they should. All pregnant women in every walk of life need some counseling. To determine who needs what kind of help requires that special training be given to obstetricians, to public health nurses, and to all others who might play an important role in the management of this condition. The professional person needs to be able to explore the emotional status of his patient in at least a general way and to refer those who cause him concern to mental health practitioners for more intensive evaluation.

We do not know all the relationships between maternal mental status and fetal health, but it is likely that the connections are more than trivial. Dr. Edward Mann (1959) has described a psychotherapeutic approach to habitual abortion that helped 80 percent of his cases. In general, a baby born to an unmarried and depressed mother creates a situation calling for very active intervention to preserve and protect both mother and child. Or if a mother has an inadequate husband, feels she has too many children already, and desperately does not want this one, she might need a great deal of active work to help sort out the alternatives open to her; for instance, abortion, placement, or homemaker service in the home.

Obstetrical clinics might usefully add group treatment to their procedures; private practitioners in group practice might add a psychiatrist, psychologist, or nurse trained in mental health to provide discussion groups for the developmental issues involved in pregnancy and the rearing of young infants. The interested obstetrician could well take some specialized training in order to prepare himself to work with this aspect of his patients' lives.

PREVENTIVE CONSIDERATIONS

One major aspect of prevention concerns itself with pregnancy among adolescents. The following quotation from a paper by Maurine LaBarre (1969) gives some details about the dimensions of the problem.[1]

Much concern has been expressed about the high incidence of pregnancies out-of-wedlock among teenagers. A Connecticut study[2] in 1965 estimated that one out of every six 13-year-old girls in the state would become illegitimately pregnant before she was twenty. While many people were shocked and incredulous, health and social agency workers familiar with the extent of the problem considered the estimate too low. No one knows how many youthful conceptions are terminated by miscarriages or abortion; how many girls conceal their pregnancies by assuming a married name or seeking shelter in a maternity home or residence in a state which does not report illegitimacy, nor how many pregnant girls married prior to delivery. What impresses the public is the number, not the rate or proportion of teenagers who bear illegitimate children. The statistics are rather tricky.[3] Actually the rate of illegitimate births per 1000 teenage girls has not increased in the last two and three decades, as it has most rapidly for women in their late twenties. Only two percent of the potential teen-age childbearers deliver illegitimate children. This small percentage, however, results in around 88,000 babies a year, of which 72,000 are born to mothers 17 years of age and under, and it constitutes 40 percent of the total number of illegitimate children. What is usually ignored is the fact that eight out of every nine babies born to teenagers are legitimate.

A review of forty some published obstetric studies of adolescent pregnancies[4] shows that these young patients and their babies are high-risk groups, for complications of pregnancy and delivery, especially toxemia and prematurity. The

1. Editor's note: Footnotes correspond to the references cited from M. LaBarre's paper.
2. "Every Sixth Girl in Connecticut," *New York Times Magazine,* May 20, 1966.
3. Elizabeth Herzog, "Unmarried Mothers: Some Questions to Be Answered and Some Answers to Be Questioned," *Child Welfare,* October 1962.
4. Maurine LaBarre, "Review of 38 Obstetric Studies of Adolescent Pregnancies" (manuscript).

younger the mother, the greater the risk. Of surviving premature infants, there is a four-fold increase in the incidence of neurologic defect and mental retardation. A number of obstetric studies note that these young patients suffer numerous serious socioeconomic and psychological problems, and plead for studies of their needs and special services for them. Many of these young mothers, like their older sisters, are poor, and black, have had inadequate nutrition and health care previously, and suffer the same reluctance and difficulties in using pre-natal clinic facilities, with the inevitable lengthy waiting, impersonal service, examinations by different doctors on each visit, plus the special difficulties of their class and their youthfulness in communication, understanding directions, and lack of means to carry them out.[5] While none of the numerous psychiatric studies of emotional aspects of pregnancy focus on this age group, many of the same experiences and reactions occur among young primiparae and are part of the complex factors related to complications of pregnancy and delivery.

The prevention of unwanted pregnancy, and of some of the complications, emotional and physical, that can come with any pregnancy, must obviously be undertaken before conception takes place. Ideally, a knowledge of sex and reproduction would have been imparted in the home in a natural way from early childhood on. Since in fact this is often inadequately handled or not handled at all, schools have taken over many responsibilities for sex education. This can be helpful, but the school intervention needs to be extended to home life courses in which realistic and carefully presented information about body function, mating, conception, and childbearing are skillfully presented. This, in turn, should be amplified by discussion of child-rearing, the needs of infants, the role of possible illegitimacy in a person's life, the pros and cons of placing a child, the responsibilities of parents who raise a child, the role requirements of father and of mother, homemaking, home maintenance, and the like. If such courses could become universal in junior high and high school, a crucial addition to the acculturation process would have been joined to the equipment of the emerging youngster, and some modicum of preventive preparation introduced into any later encounter with pregnancy.

It is important that along with its benefits, the limitations of such work be kept in mind as well. More than most human activities, sexual behavior and conceiving a baby are overdetermined patterns and at the mercy of powerful unconscious forces. Often enough they take place in defiance of all sorts of set conscious attitudes and intentions. Without minimizing the fundamental usefulness and desirability of adequate education and preparation of youth for the tasks of maturity, we should not create false expectations that illegitimacy and disturbed sexual adjustment will disap-

5. Blanche Bernstein and Mignon Sauber, *Deterrents to Early Prenatal Care and Social Service,* New York State Department of Social Welfare, 1960.

pear in the wake of improved education. It will take a great deal of change in our child-rearing practices all through childhood and adolescence to achieve the results we would like to see on a large scale. Nonetheless, the educational courses will make some degree of difference to all students, and a very crucial difference to some.

Ultimately, people need to be prepared both to make rational decisions and to understand and cope with the fact that there will be irrational components in their way of conducting their lives. Thus, the girl must learn about control of impulse, and if she yields to impulse, about control of conception, and if she does conceive, about the choices she has and the adaptations and services she can turn to for help. If possible, she must learn about all of these well in advance of the event.

We speak of the girl, but it is noteworthy that the role of the father is too often thrust aside in weighing the psychological meaning of pregnancy; clinical psychiatric experience teaches again and again how massive the impact of such events can be on the man. Wild young men have settled down and become steady citizens in the face of fatherhood, and apparently stable men have become depressed and even psychotic when a birth was in prospect. The fathers of illegitimate babies have traditionally been scorned and criticized. They may be forced to pay for the state of their gravid partner. Persons who work with unmarried mothers know how frequently the man is used merely to achieve impregnation and then quickly rejected and devalued, often enough to his intense chagrin and subsequent deterioration. The boy too needs preparation and help around this aspect of life. Generally speaking, both father and mother of an illegitimate child need support and counseling. The most effective intervention would be that obtained in a preparatory way long before sex relations were entered into. For at least some youngsters, adequate preparation will enable them to avoid impulsive sexual behavior or to use appropriate means to prevent conception if they do initiate such a pattern. When pregnancy does take place, the preliminary schooling might give them some picture of their mutual responsibilities and their options.

To speak of such courses in primary or secondary school is to take for granted a whole universe of teacher training, some of which should be the property of every teacher, but much of which will require specialized preparation for certain teachers who will major in this area. A program of this order requires teachers who have themselves been exposed to good clinical teaching, who have worked with clinically sophisticated professionals, who have had small groups of students to lead and have been supervised by experienced group practitioners. Only with such training are they likely to be ready to meet the needs of their young charges in these sensitive and personal areas. Such teachers will inevitably prove to be casefinders as well, since many troubled children will bring their questions and anxieties into this context and the teachers will find themselves looking at rather serious situations and trying to do something about them. The need for back-up personnel for such home-life classes is mandatory. The teachers will need consultation from time to time, and the occasional student will need referral.

Even before this specific program in a school can begin, clinical skills may well be needed to handle the anxiety and defenses of the adults in the community served by the school. No matter how committed a school system and its teaching staff might be to the task of presenting meaningful family, developmental, and sexual educational programs, and no matter how well conceived, carefully rehearsed, and skillfully presented the program is, it will fail if there is not prior and concomitant preparation of the total community. It is vital that parents, clergy, political leaders, and opinion molders accept the goals and content of the program as legitimate.

Recently newspapers carried reports of a vigorous protest against a sex and family life education program by a fundamentalistically oriented religious leader and parents endorsing his views. As reported, this man and parents in his community felt that merely using words such as "sexual intercourse" or anatomical terms such as "pelvis" was inherently bad, and any program requiring their utterance had no place in his community. Obviously the best-prepared teacher or the most knowledgeable education administrator would be sacrificing himself and his school if he initiated the program we advocate without prior careful, clinically sensitive, and in some communities, long-term consultation work designed to change the emotional and attitudinal climate of the community.

It is not surprising that an active dialogue with the community is in order here. These intimate facets of home life constitute culture-connected issues more centrally vital and emotionally salient than nearly any other topic. A teacher who is an indigenous member of the culture to which the majority of the class belong would obviously have a personal reservoir of information, and might be received with an initial degree of acceptance which would facilitate the program. In any event, where the teacher is not an indigenous member of the culture to which the majority of the class belong, he must be able to communicate with that culture, to know and to respect its values, and to support these values and not attack them.

Probably the most important single criterion for such a teacher would be a history of having himself achieved a reasonably effective solution of his own adolescent conflicts in the areas of independence and sexual identity. The ability to deal with adolescents is a direct function of one's mastery of his own adolescent problems. This does not mean that one has passed through adolescence without problems. It does mean that the problems of that time are not the problems of adulthood—that by dint of his own efforts, or with the help of therapy, or by the sheer accumulation of maturing experiences, the person has coped with the issues of his teens and can look back at his own struggles with empathy, with humor, and with compassion. At this point he is ready to help others.

Since the selection and the preparation of such teachers involves sophisticated clinical knowledge, it is clear that psychiatrists, psychologists, social workers, educators with strong clinical backgrounds, and other professionals, similarly equipped, will have to begin giving time to teachers' training programs in order to supply the necessary screening and supervision. For an already overextended professional population, this is no small requirement; the powerful spread of the effects of such preparation (one such teacher can reach hundreds of children each year) should be a strong incentive to engage in such preparatory work. The clinician should join forces with the administration of the training center at every level: curriculum planning, selecting candidates for the program, lecturing, supervising individuals and small groups, and occasionally even giving the commencement address. In short, he must become important in the life of the institution, and he must be a bearer of values: his message again and again will be that human relationships can be conducted with skill, with real expertise based on understanding, and that the end product of all the work must be individual growth and individual happiness for each child.

TOWARD OPTIMAL GROWTH AND DEVELOPMENT

Greta Bibring (1959) has conceptualized pregnancy as a developmental crisis and a major maturational task in the growth of a woman. Ideally, pregnancy should be a happy affair, defining or reinforcing for the woman the richness of her femininity and building up toward a successful mothering experience. The elements that can interfere with this state are legion: marital stress, economic burdens, emotional disturbances, social pressures, physical illness, and all sorts of combinations of these mosaic bits. To the extent that we would improve our future generations, we must commit ourselves ever more intensively to a better social support structure and emotional preparation for this experience, in both young men and young women.

Group discussion and counseling for all high school youth would help; this could include attention to the details of such events on every level; for example, what illegitimacy means to the youngsters themselves, how the parents of the unmarried gravid girl feel, how classmates and teachers react, the effect on siblings of both boy and girl, what goes into giving a baby up versus keeping him, and so forth—all these need full and well-led discussion.

Sheltered situations for many unmarried pregnant girls will be crucial to their achieving an optimum response to the experience. The Florence Crittenton Home provides a network of placement settings in many cities; many other agencies deal with such problems, and it might well be desirable to increase this service manyfold.

Work with pregnant women, married and unmarried, or with couples preparing for the arrival of their first child might do a great deal to intensify the richness and gratifications that can go with this experience. Gerald Caplan (1960) has written of the pregnant woman's relationship with the unborn fetus. This is an area that invites research and that might readily give rise to improved clinical management of pregnancy. His description of the "emotional lag" before the inrush of maternal feeling for the newborn provides another prime site for sensitive observation and appropriate intervention.

Infancy

The next great horizon for psychiatric advance in diagnosis and treatment is the area of infant mental health. Our knowledge at this point is fragmentary and consists of bits and pieces of suggestive research data. Certainly there is no ready body of treatment information, no adequate body of evaluation techniques, no tested and proven methods of intervention, that can be applied generally to remedy emotional ills in the first year of life. But certain syndromes have been recognized, and it is clear that we are on the verge of establishing some kind of classification that will give rise to diagnostic and therapeutic practices.

René Spitz performed a series of classic observations on children reared in environments that were physically adequate but emotionally deprived. From this has come an understanding of the critical need of infants for adequate stimulation, for affectionate "loving up," for regular human interaction as a biologic necessity during this period. Lacking such stimulation, intellectual growth fails to take place, the child loses interest in his environment and withdraws, growth gain and weight gain fall off, susceptibility to infection skyrockets, and mortality is high. The long-range outcome is often stunted intellectual development or psychosis.

A host of other conditions is coming to be recognized as reflecting issues in the child-rearing environment. The colicky baby, the hyperactive baby, the hypersensitive baby, the vomiter and spitter, the failure-to-thrive group, the baby with prolonged sleep disturbance, the passive, listless baby, the baby who cries when he's picked up or when people come near him—these are a few of the emerging syndromes that are becoming more familiar as research data accumulate.

Of central importance here is the matter of "fit," of the meshing of needs

270

and personalities and communication patterns of this mother and this infant at this time. We can illustrate this by imagining a spectrum of "mother-liness," a basic sense of warmth, emotional availability, and affectionate interest in the baby that some women (at one end of the spectrum) may have in marked degree and others (at the other end) may lack almost entirely. Thus a given population of women might range from "warm" to "cold." The babies too will range across a spectrum—some will be cuddly, smile early, adapt to the body of whoever picks them up, and radiate a kind of winningness and joy in closeness from a very early age indeed.

Others, at the other extremity of the scale, will be unrewarding to ministering adults. They will look solemn or anxious most of the time, cry readily, and show every evidence of displeasure when picked up or handled. Thus, the babies too will vary from "warm" to "cold." Now if a "warm" mother bears a "cold" baby, the mother's unusual capacity to nurture and love might overcome the infant's innate difficulty in relationship and evoke from him a relatively good response—the "fit" would be right. By the same token, a "warm" baby might be able to bring out the warmth in an otherwise constricted or depressed woman who would have had great difficulty with mothering at that moment in her life had the baby not brought with him these special attributes.

But if baby and mother are both "cool" people—what then? The fit would not be a good one, and a vicious cycle of unrewarded mother unable to give adequately to an unrewarding infant would soon be in play, to the serious detriment of both.

These are crude analogies, but they serve to illustrate that "fit" is always important and, in extreme cases, can be crucial in the development of the mother-infant relationship, which in turn will have massive force in shaping the fate of the baby's health and personality growth.

When identified early enough, infants showing early signs of decline can be rescued and achieve a full recovery. In a given home where, for example, the mother is depressed and unable to do more than give minimal biologic care to her infant, the assignment of a paraprofessional "grandmother" to serve as caretaker for the baby can be a critical treatment factor in heading off serious pathology for the child.

Such "grandmothers" can be trained briefly in the needs of babies and the meaning of the infant's decline, and perform a crucial service in homes where such care and stimulation would otherwise be absent. A ready pool of older women whose children are grown, who are themselves in need of some part-time gratifying and remunerative activity, and who like babies is to be found in most communities. Their training could be done by public health nurses with some psychiatric back-up, and they could be supervised regularly by the agency of origin or by the nurses who trained them.[1]

1. For more complete discussion of new mental health workers see Appendix C: Utilization of Paraprofessionals in Clinical Settings, pp. 390–397.

Another type of paraprofessional who could serve as a source of such essential infant care is the "homemaker," the woman who is trained to step in where maternal function is impaired and to help with the overall tasks of child care, cooking, cleaning, and in general, carrying a family through a period of crisis or temporary disablement (for example, a family in which the mother has suddenly fallen ill or has abandoned the home or has had to leave to get treatment for alcoholism or addiction, etc.).

As noted above, certain pathologic conditions are diagnosable at birth; for example, Mongolism, cranial abnormalities and birth defects, and certain metabolic diseases like PKU. Aside from the dietary management of PKU, there is little definitive treatment available today for most such conditions. Much clinical skill is necessary at this time, however, to deal with the parental reaction to such tragic events and to help the parents in their orientation to a new and unexpected role: the care of a brain-injured child. For some parents, immediate institutionalization of the infant might be the best answer. For most, this is not true, and the many special adaptations, such as special feeding techniques, careful supervision of activity level, possible drug therapy, and so forth need to be taught to the parents. More than that, their own emotional response, the mourning for the child that might have been, the guilt and self-blame that so commonly attend such events, the rage that sometimes appears and is directed at the other spouse or at the baby itself—in short, the full range of human reaction that is likely to manifest itself in response to corrosive and continuing stress—all these need expert clinical management. The program for treatment must be set by the doctor in charge, and a wide range of auxiliary personnel can be involved, depending on the details of the case. The visiting public health nurse is an invaluable person in such situations, particularly when the want is acute and parental anxiety and grief are keen. Nor is this work the exclusive province of any one medical discipline. A great many pregnancies and deliveries in the United States are probably still in the hands of general practitioners. Certainly by far the large bulk of children are cared for by general practitioners, and the recently created family practice board will undoubtedly mean that still more mothers and children will be cared for in this way. Since brain injury and retardation will be with us for many years to come, it must become part of the training of all physicians and an element in all medical school curriculums to deal with the appearance of such children and with the parental problems accompanying them.

PREVENTIVE CONSIDERATIONS

The leading finding emerging from the research currently under way in the country is that we can now begin to identify mother-infant interactions that will need preventative intervention. Bruno Bettelheim (1967) has raised the question for us: Is not maternal response to the young infant's cues and initiatives the critical factor for the prevention of autism in susceptible babies? Sylvia Brody and Justin Call have taken movies of the feeding process and have begun to try to classify types of feeding patterns with some evaluation of their helpfulness or harmfulness to the infants involved. Margaret Mahler has studied and made films of the meaning of separation to the infant and the details of how individualization develops. In a controlled study of prematures, Kaplan and Mason have successfully predicted parent-child difficulty by counting the number of visits to the premature nursery—a fall-off in the number of visits is an urgent indication for a visiting nurse to go to the home. Indeed one can list tens of researchers who are daily increasing the breadth and depth of our knowledge about the actual exchanges between mothers and babies, and the import of different patterns for later personality growth. Lois Murphy has developed a vulnerability index along which infantile strengths and susceptibilities to trouble can be rated; any number of investigators—e.g., Bell, Chess, Fries, Escalona, Huntington, and others—are working toward some classification of infants and the ordering of their responses.

Among many other fruits of such research, we seek with special interest for knowledge about those inborn constitutional tendencies that might make the baby specially prone to later mental illness. There is much to suggest that many infants are born with vulnerabilities or with subtle differences in their make-up that make the likelihood of later serious disorders especially great. At the time of this writing, controversy about the genesis of infantile autism and childhood schizophrenia is especially intense. The one school of thought emphasizes the baby's constitutional defects and their impact on the nurturing mother, all of whose efforts are frustrated and brought to naught by the inability of her baby to respond to her or to engage in that myriad of nonverbal accommodations and communications that form the critical network of mother-infant experience. The other approach stresses the failure of the mothering adult to provide the essential responses to the tiny buds of emotional reaching out and human responsiveness on the baby's part so that they wither aborning and never come to flower. One investigator (Dr. William Goldfarb of the Ittleson Center) has divided his series of cases of childhood psychosis into two groups—those with evidence of marked constitutional deficiencies and those whose environments seem to have brought about their condition. The final unraveling of such questions awaits further research into the elements of constitution as well as into patterns of rearing.

In general, we are converging on a body of data which will allow a trained observer to perform some tests on the baby himself and then to watch a mother play with her baby, feed him, and talk about him, with a reasonable possibility of emerging with specific suggestions for helping the mother do a better job and avoid possible difficulties. Moreover, we are approaching the capacity of including an analysis of the stress-reducing or stress-enhancing contribution of the husband, the extended family, and other contextual dimensions as they support or interfere with the mother-baby relationship. That we are on our way to this level of achievement is clear; that we have not yet arrived there is equally clear. These are still research horizons, but research that appears fruitful and laden with promise.

What is most cogent at this point is the question of achieving and maintaining contact with new mothers. It would appear in the best public interest that every baby-mother pair be given the benefit of periodic checks by expert observers to note the progress of the baby's personality growth and intellectual development. A number of Western countries are sufficiently concerned about the welfare of this culture-critical pair to subsidize each newborn child. We wrote in the previous section of supports for the pregnant woman. The infant-mother periodic checkup would be a logical extension of the same program and with a similar intent: to ensure the health, mental and physical, of forthcoming generations.

The necessary social organization for such a venture would be extensive: a system of well-baby clinics spread far beyond what now exists would have to be developed: perhaps as an integral part of the existing community health centers, perhaps as one segment of a proposed new type of organization, the child development center, and in some areas, perhaps as an isolated agency on its own. In any case, parents, all parents, would be encouraged to bring their infants there at some regular intervals. A first visit at one week is particularly important, and thereafter, these could be at one month, four months, eight months, and twelve months, for a series of checks and tests. (The one-week visit might better be done by having doctor and nurse go to the home.) These studies would start with pediatric examination but go on to a sequence of interactional studies including feeding, play, separation, napping, etc., which could then be evaluated by the staff and responded to in constructive ways. Some parents will need only encouragement; others will require advice; a few will need intensive work in groups or individually; occasional cases will require a paraprofessional in the home; and rare situations might emerge in which a family or mother should simply not be required or permitted to bear the responsibility of continuing to care for a young child. For such children, foster parent settings which can provide a warm, ongoing adult-child relationship must be available.

The director of such an agency would belong to a discipline that does not yet exist in any clearly identified form—the infant-rearing specialist. This is a type of expertise that may very likely arise from pediatrics; on the other hand, many psychologists and child psychiatrists are inclining toward such an area of work, and, like psychotherapy, it may come to be the common skill of a number of different professional groups. Certainly there is urgent need for further research in infancy and for the introduction of the data thus far obtained into the professional curriculums.

The much-discussed question of the battered child has begun to receive certain consensual agreement and legislative action throughout the country. To some extent, the separation of a child from a home when battering has taken place is a form of remediation. Actually, it is of still more import as prevention. It prevents further injury or death for the child, and it prevents the terrible assault on the growing ego that must be part and parcel of such battering experiences. We do not yet know enough about the parents of such children to be sure whether or not removal of the child is also supportive to their mental health; it would not be surprising if that should turn out to be so. Certainly research to help identify personality and family relationship problems which are predictive of child battering needs to be pursued actively to increase the possibility of intervening *before* the first battering ever occurs.

There are other, comparable situations in which traumatic events are flags of trouble and should be heeded as such by an aware society. Recurrent poisoning of infants, when it is clear that the child was readily exposed to danger; recurrent accidents, when things keep "happening" to the baby; pica, the chronic consumption of paint or sand or other inorganic materials by an infant—all speak loudly for something seriously awry in the life of that infant-mother pair and should be grounds for considering social and psychological intervention.

It is not easy to separate an infant from his parents, but in some of these situations it may be life-saving, and to the parents as much as to the child. Again, the possibility of introducing another person in the home, "homemaker" or "grandmother" or nurse as described above, may be the salvation of some very difficult situations of this sort. Skillful persistent work with the parents may change the home milieu for the other children. In some instances, it might even provide a means whereby the injured child can eventually return to his own home.

TOWARD OPTIMAL GROWTH AND DEVELOPMENT

The basic requirement for optimal development of infants is that they have a stable home with happy, loving, and informed parents caring for them. We cannot at this point in time provide for a larger number of families who can provide all of these criteria, but a great deal can certainly be done to see that people who rear babies are better informed than they now are.

It would perhaps be a most useful change in our educational curriculums if the eleventh grade in high school were devoted exclusively to the science of being a human being: to courses in personality development, child-rearing, sex, marriage, divorce, drugs, society and the individual problems of adolescence and young adulthood, dating, etc. Practicum experience with infant care and dealing with toddlers could be included. In any case, a strong indoctrination in the psychology and needs of the young infant should be a mandatory part of the experience of all parents. They need to know about the stimulation needs of babies, the importance of talking to a baby, the crucial role of consistency in child care, the dangers of over-stimulation in the child's everyday life, the meaning of separation to infants at different points in their development, the emergence of stranger reaction in the second half of the first year, the crucial quality of spontaneity, and so on for many such details. They need to know, too, that children see and hear and are affected by all that goes on about them, and that the self-serving self-deception of so many parents who fight or lie or make love while assuring themselves the little ones "won't understand" is just that: a comforting untruth. And these things can be taught and, to some extent, learned. In brief, the more children are protected from the more massive errors of parenting, the better their chances for optimal functioning later on.

Another site for significant improvement will be in the care of those infants who are left to the mercy of their society by parental disability or outright abandonment. Currently, such infants are likely to meet one or two fates: they will be turned out to foster placement until someone comes along to adopt them, or they will be kept in some kind of institutional setting; for example, in a general hospital, children's hospital, foundling home, etc.

Both our foster home programs and our institutional work very much need revamping and rehabilitation. Numerous studies attest to the fact that infants reared in institutions tend to be subjected to insufficient stimulation and/or noxious stimuli calculated to create lags and distortions of development. This is the more unfortunate because we now are coming to know something of the essential ingredients for healthy growth at this time. The problem of getting our knowledge into the many situations where infants are cared for over the long term is a first order of priority for any future programs.

This applies to the institutions where children may be placed temporarily as well, such as hospitals where a baby might go for medical or surgical treatment and have to remain for some period of time. Here too the management of the situation can be supportive or traumatic for personality development, depending on the skill and understanding of the personnel involved.

To return to the general principles of infant care, we spoke above of the need for stimulation and affectionate handling during the first months of life. This seemingly simple, commonplace element can all too easily be omitted or slighted in an institutional setting. A second vital ingredient is constancy of the management personnel. This is especially important as the baby moves into the middle and the last part of the first year. The stability of the person who acts as "mother" becomes at this point not a desirable factor but a vitally necessary ingredient—if this is not available, a critical moment in learning to be an individual, to have confidence and trust in other individuals, and to see one's self someday as a person among peers, as a separate personality who can join with others in cooperative living, all these potentials will have been seriously, perhaps irreparably, injured. Constancy of a mothering person in the middle and the latter months of the first year is a major guarantor of later possibility of normal relationships; a shifting, uncertain, undependable relationship at this vulnerable time is all too likely to initiate a pattern of later social and personal problems.

This is no peculiarity of the hospitalized infant. It is just as important for parents who care for their children at home to be alert to the possible effects of vacations from their infants during these critical months and to consider enforced separations as significant events to be dealt with by as much compensatory care as possible. Obviously, this is an individual matter. There are times, for example, when it might be important for a parent to have some vacation from an infant, or when father or grandmother or even maid might be better for the baby than his mother. Our general principle here is just that, a flexible guideline, not an absolute dictum. By the same token, the hospitalized infant needs his mother or other close family members sleeping in with him and continuing as much personal care, changing, feeding, playing, etc., as possible. It should be an institutional recommendation that such a pattern be maintained—not merely as a graciously extended privilege but because it is medically available. As such it should be covered by medical insurance.

There is much to suggest that not only institutional practice but foster care too needs considerable reevaluation. Currently, foster parents are typically volunteers whose motives for engaging in such care are sometimes dubious, or they are the product of exhaustive and exhausting recruitment on the part of determined caseworkers attached to various placement agencies. Occasionally, families have been literally dragooned into accepting such a role. In any case, there are always too few of them, so that many homes are allowed to continue as foster placements even when there is real cause to doubt the desirability of this practice in that particular setting. What it boils down to is that some home is so much better than no home that the situation continues.

It is evident that the next step is the beginning professionalization of the foster home—where professionals are in charge of a corps of paraprofessionals who have had some advanced training in infant care and personality growth, and where adequate supervision is available together with back-up consultation as required. The fifth to the eighteenth month of life of the individual baby must be regarded as sacred as far as change of foster mother is concerned—and the paraprofessional must herself be committed to careful advance planning to avoid undertaking the care of an infant if there is any prospect of her having to leave during this period in the infant's life.

Along with foster care, the pattern of day care for the babies of working mothers is clearly necessary, and an appropriately prepared cadre of staff with training similar to that of the foster mother is required for this as well. Such day care is now a spotty, often ill-managed, hit or miss proposition. In a country where so many women work, it becomes a vital social necessity to establish appropriate government-sponsored facilities to give proper care and help to the babies and young children of working mothers.

Such centers should draw children of all races and socioeconomic levels. The working mother can be a career woman with a professional degree as readily as a member of the unskilled labor force—and the same level of expert care is necessary for the babies of one group as for the other.

The care of infants has in general been a low-status, low-reward activity in our culture, with the lowest socioeconomic group being called in to assume this "burden" at a trifling wage in order to allow their higher-income employers to pursue their own unfettered course toward personal gratification. The devaluation of child-rearing is a major stumbling block to paying the professional and paraprofessional a wage commensurate with the social importance of the task of rearing the young infant.

The first year of life sees the development of a sense of reality, a sense of trust, the quality of self-confidence, and the ability to relate one's self to other people in a positive way. Should any of these elements be injured in the making, a major deficit will be present in all future coping efforts.

Preschool

The preschool years, from the end of the first year until approximately age five or six, are a period of immensely rapid growth. This takes place along many axes, intellectually, emotionally, and socially, as well as physiologically. The major portion of the phases of psychosexual development is lived through during these years, and there is much to suggest that a large percentage of all later character unfolding is completed by the end of this period. Events crowd upon one another as the weeks and months go by; one area of cognitive growth treads upon the heels of another as the tantrums and nightmares and habit training and personal body care and language development and impulse controls and beginning social relationship patterns and many other elements all jostle one another and seemingly leap into being or give way to newer patterns in a conglomerate, helter-skelter way that makes the rearing problems of the period extraordinarily complex.

It is impossible to cover all the many details of disorder and practice implied in so rich an assemblage of changing, ongoing psychic events—at best some high spots can be noted. But it is safe to say that the great treatment, prevention, and optimization practices of the future will lie in the increasing refinement of work during infancy and the preschool years.

THERAPEUTIC INTERVENTIONS

Much overt psychiatric disorder is easily diagnosable during this period. The most serious illnesses, the childhood psychoses, are usually discernible from age two onward. These have been variously categorized as childhood schizophrenia, autism, symbiotic psychosis, and atypical state by different child psychiatrists and analysts. These categories are not as clear-cut as one might wish; the need for intensive treatment, regardless of the particular shade or school of diagnosis, is always in order. Three types of treatment are generally invoked for these conditions: outpatient psychotherapy, day care, and residential treatment. Any or all of these might include drug treatment. Every community of any size needs to have an adequate number of facilities of each kind to care for all the children in its bounds who show signs of these grave and life-warping conditions. It is difficult to be certain about the actual number of children suffering from such illness. It is all too likely that many people later diagnosed as retarded were initially victims of a childhood psychosis of some kind. The author would estimate the incidence of such illness as something like 0.5 percent to 1 percent of preschool children, but close surveillance might boost that percentage.

The problem of the parents of such children presents grave and painful difficulties. There is today so much uncertainty and controversy about etiology that a parent who sees a number of different consultants is all too likely to be given to understand (a) that the condition is caused by some deficiency in the parental handling of the child; (b) that no one knows what causes these conditions; and (c) that this is the result of some inborn congenital disturbance in the child's central nervous system that would result in illness no matter how the child was reared. The probability is that in particular cases any one of these explanations could be true and that, in every case, it is likely that more than one "cause" has been at work at once. Thus it is reasonable to presume that only a child with a certain constitutional predisposition will respond to improper parenting by becoming psychotic; other children of these same parents may show other forms of disturbance, or no disturbance at all. The strong feelings generated about such issues make adequate research and assessment very difficult. To illustrate this, let us consider two situations.

A parent brings an autistic child to an outpatient clinic. A skillful, patient therapist begins to see this frozen child weekly; presently, the youngster begins to use words, to show some appropriate feeling, and to begin to build a positive relationship with his therapist. At this point, the parent announces that the treatment is not helping and abruptly discontinues the appointments. After this happens with two cases treated by two different people in the same clinic, there is no use telling the clinic staff that the parents don't want these children to be sick. The staff has gone through the pain of achieving improvement in the face of immense difficulties. This always evokes intense emotion among the treatment personnel, and to see the parents destroy all this because father or mother seems literally unable to endure the improvement is a traumatic experience of shaking intensity.

The other side of the coin is the description given by many a harried parent of a psychotic child, a parent who has literally flagellated himself or herself with guilt, felt entirely responsible for what has happened, tried every means to change what needed to be changed, and found that his best efforts availed nothing. Such parents may have reared other children well. They could not see what it was they did with this one that was any different. They pour in energy, emotion, time, money, whatever they can, and the child continues as before—nonverbal, bizarre, out of reach. Finally, they come to the point of saying, "Surely if it were something we had done, or were doing, it would be altered by now. This makes no sense. Indeed, it is an unjust accusation that is leveled against us by some of these people we have consulted."

And there the matter stands. It is a field that cries for additional research.

A second category of relatively serious illness is that of childhood neurosis.[1] This group of conditions appears with startling frequency in the preschool population. Although this is again an impressionistic estimate, it is the author's belief that some 5 percent of preschool children will show signs of these severe reactions during their development. They may take the form of massive phobias; overwhelming obsessive rituals; childhood depression; paralyzing anxiety with frequent outbreaks of panic; serious inhibition, shyness and fear of strangers; compulsive and even injurious self-manipulation such as hair pulling, head rubbing, or unceasing masturbation; multiple tics, severe lags in language use, and similar evidences of major disturbance. Here the indication for treatment is also very specific— the bulk of such children can be treated with outpatient psychotherapy; for some, child psychoanalysis will be the treatment of choice.

The occasional case will need day care, and a few of the most severe conditions will require residential treatment. Drug therapy is also important in such instances, with the particular goal in mind of making the child better able to use the educational and psychotherapeutic techniques available to him.[2]

Another category of problem to which we are becoming alert is that of the organically injured child, often called the child with minimal brain dysfunction. Although this condition is usually diagnosed later in life, work on recognizing the earliest evidences of this disturbance is now under way, and special remedial techniques are coming into being to help such injured children to adapt and compensate for their deficiencies in alternative ways. This involves taking account of the hyperkinetic restlessness, the difficulty in concentrating, the short attention span, the instability or emotional lability that may be present, the unusual difficulty with controlling or arresting excitement such children may display, and, in short, the excessive vulnerability to impulse or to stimulation that is so often part of their pathology. Special counseling of parents to give help in understanding why

1. More precisely, at this age we would call such conditions "reactive disorders."
2. For a more complete discussion of drug therapy, see Appendix D: Psychopharmacologic Agents, by D. G. Prugh, M.D., and A. Kisley, M.D.

their children act a certain way and how to manage them, the use of drugs, often so dramatic in relieving the driven restlessness such children may exhibit, and early remedial training are all indicated for such youngsters. Appropriate specialized nursery school settings of the day-care type are often necessary for their management.

Yet another category of preschool psychopathology lies in the area of cultural imprinting.[3] Under circumstances involving poverty, hopelessness, emotional deprivation, and cultural stigmatization, children become subject to severe shaping forces at home which require them to achieve a kind of precocious maturity in order to cope with the rigors of their lives. The result is a sort of complete absorption with the concrete details of getting along safely, at the total expense of expanding intellectual interests, symbolic and abstract thinking, and richness of emotional modulation. At three, these youngsters may be hyperalert to the actions of adults about them, unable to play or express themselves emotionally with any freedom, unusually competent in certain areas such as shopping or crossing traffic-burdened streets, and at the same time, seemingly totally devoid of the curiosity and childish wonder and interest that will distinguish the unburdened three-year-old.

Such adaptive patterns are not unusual in the impoverished and socially devalued segments of the population, nor have we as yet developed adequate means for dealing with them. The working out of the necessary techniques for reversing the effects of such premature ego consolidations is a major horizon for therapeutic research. The chances are that a combination of individual therapy, group techniques, and day care will be necessary in many instances; some youngsters may need residential treatment. It is noteworthy that the greatest bulk of cases later diagnosed as mild mental retardation come from such environments; it is all too likely that the developmental sequence described here will in time result in a child unable to learn at school. We are dealing with huge numbers of children in this category, and the research need is therefore all the more urgent.

Another large group of disturbances lies in the area of behavioral problems. This includes the dangerous child, the impulsive child, the self-destructive child, the child whose tantrums, lying, stealing, and destructiveness set him apart from other children from a very early age indeed.

The more severe cases of this type require residential care; day care may suffice for many, and the occasional child will respond to psychotherapy or child psychoanalysis. Drug therapy has to date not been very rewarding with such youngsters, although some are helped. Interestingly, follow-up research on this group has suggested that they do not become the delinquents of the future so much as they do the learning problems.

3. For a discussion of clinical considerations of racism, see Appendix E: Statement on Racism of the Committee on Clinical Issues.

Again, this is an area involving many children in which research is vitally important.

A final group to be mentioned is children with sexual deviations. Transsexualism and various forms of perversion or precocious sexual interest can be observed all during the preschool age range. Some boys, for example, show marked feminine interests from age two or even younger, and driven patterns of sexual activity associated with confusion of sexual identity are well documented at ages three and four. There is no sure and certain treatment for such conditions currently available. Psychoanalysis may benefit certain cases; others might respond only to total removal from the home into a treatment setting. We work here on the frontiers of our knowledge of treatment.

The treatment methods for preschool children have suffered from three major handicaps. First, the tendency in the field for many years was to regard the preschoolers as the primary psychological property of the parents. Any treatment activity, then, was directed toward the parents in the hope that by changing the adults, the effects would express themselves in altered handling of the child and resultant improvement. This mode of approach has, alas, borne limited fruit. For one thing, it is enormously difficult for parents, even interested, cooperative people who expressly wish to change what they are doing in order to help their children, to alter certain deep-seated, emotionally charged attitudes that are often central in the problems of the little ones. A mother who had grown up bitter and unhappy in the shadow of an adored older brother might find it very hard to deal comfortably and positively with a son who somehow evokes all the old feelings of her painful childhood. She might find it hard despite a conscious awareness of what is happening. How much harder, then, will it be for a mother who does not make the connections between her current feelings and her previous experience, who, indeed, denies that there is any problem, because it would hurt too much to know, and even more to know why!

For another thing, children develop far more character structure at an early age than they are usually credited with. A child might well become disturbed because of some specific stress stemming from his home experience. It doesn't always follow, however, that when the stress goes away, the symptoms will disappear as well. Some of the trouble is likely to be built in, and to persist, because the trauma came at a critical period, a moment of heightened vulnerability, something within the child changed, and set, and thereafter the child's make-up has a certain form and substantiality of its own. Thus, once initiated, problems may persist despite environmental change.

Certain professionals, however, have continued to emphasize work with parents and have withheld treatment from many children when some intervention was necessary and would have helped. The result has often been an even more difficult problem to cope with a few years later. In fact, however, this attitude is not confined to the mental health professional. In many ways, it mirrors the ongoing community "set" toward the troubles of small children, and parents are discouraged from seeking diagnosis and treatment by pediatricians, by nursery school teachers, and by the community in general, neighbors, friends, family, not to mention the parents' own inner values and anxieties. In most general terms, we might say that our culture is not really ready to perceive that the little child's troubles are premonitory, and significant.

A second source of difficulty has been the lack of training and professional skill in dealing with preschoolers. The average course of training in child psychiatry or child analysis does not include work with preschool children; and when we examine the rosters of our clinics, we find that many do not accept children of this age. Those clinics which do accept this age group are often making a gesture rather than stating a policy. Their records show very few such cases taken into treatment. It is not surprising that professionals whose training did not emphasize such work would find it convenient to advise the parents rather than treat the child or defer making the more serious diagnosis, and avoid becoming involved in the case as therapist until the child is older and the picture "clearer."

The third problem has been the belief, long held in the field, that preschool children should not be taken out of their own homes. As a result, very few agencies have developed facilities and personnel for accepting such youngsters into residential treatment. That this has deprived many of the sickest children of the only treatment that offers them much of a possibility of help has been an unfortunate outcome of an insufficiently evaluated premise.

If the researches of the last decades are to be believed, for many children their natural homes are the least favorable sites for their growth and emotional health. This possibility must be borne in mind in planning for the future, since alternative placement for younger children does involve special skills and methods, and we are particularly lacking in the trained people to deal with them. The primary focus for change in this area must be in our training programs; this emphasis plus an aggressive pattern of case finding and working with preschoolers should be part of every agency that prepares child therapists.

Indeed, one of the most difficult issues our culture presents us with is this matter of the home unfit for children. Clinicians constantly encounter homes among both the rich and the poor in which the parental sickness and the family atmosphere are such that no child could grow there in a healthy way. Again and again, the mental health workers deal with homes in which this child is battered, that one homosexually seduced; here a father leads a daughter into incest; there a child shares in the family criminality—and again and again, despite vigorous efforts to "do something about it," nothing is done. Nothing can be done.

The sharp and clear criteria for removing a child from such a home are lacking, and there is an urgent need for clinical and legal professionals to join forces and to formulate the guidelines that would help judges and welfare agencies, not to mention the several professionals involved, to deal with these often excruciating problems. We speak here of thousands of homes. Inevitably, it is a matter that tends to be avoided or swept under the rug in professional circles because of the many tense and difficult areas it opens into. Nonetheless, many, many children are harmed by such environments, and it is strongly urged that research be directed toward careful specification of the conditions at which children of each age could be removed from such unfit backgrounds.

From the above it is evident that much of the treatment work with this age group implies the existence of certain minimal clinical facilities. These include the basic triad: the outpatient clinic, a day center, and a residential treatment center. The services provided may also include a home visiting program plus consultation to parents, to nursery schools, to adoption agencies, to foster care programs, or to other agencies that care for young children. The greatest strength of the service, however, will lie in the presence of a team of clinicians with the skill and training to evaluate and deal with such problems. Granted that many varieties of community support can be extended. Lacking that, whatever else is provided may look impressive on paper, but is all too likely to lack significant substance.

PREVENTION

Once we accept the notion of society's concern for the mental health of the individual child, we are led irresistibly to the conclusion that some means of reviewing each child regularly should be provided so that early deviations could be identified and remedial measures attempted.

We have alluded to one suggestion for achieving this goal—the creation of a child development center where normal children could be reviewed at regular intervals and the ongoing problems discussed with the parents. This would imply the emergence of a new type of professional—a child development specialist who would be particularly alert to the range and variations of normality, and who would act as counselor and guide to his community in this area. If a built-in reward system were offered for attendance and participation in the center's activity, the bulk of the children in the community would be under regular review, and case finding could follow automatically.

Such a center could well operate as an independent agency. On the other hand, it could as readily be part of a general hospital, a children's hospital, a community mental health center, a child guidance clinic, a special school, or any one of several other possible auspices. But in any case, its work would have to be closely integrated with that of the more directly clinical agencies described above. It would breed enormous frustration and disappointment both in the community and in the staff of the center to encounter a child who is showing serious deviance, and for whom no help is available. We see enough of this today with schools and juvenile courts unable to find professional help for needy older children; how much more feeling will be generated by a three- or four-year-old whose needs are unmet!

Another device for helping with preschool children is the introduction of early nursery school programs as required schooling in the same sense that grade school and, indeed, school attendance until age sixteen are legal requirements. The Head Start programs have shown us that mass nursery school experience for many children is feasible, although there are many associated problems. (Where clinicians have been connected with Head Start, for example, they have regularly encountered some percentage of sick children in the program—and the question of treatment and help for these little ones, and for their families, has always been posed.) Nonetheless, this is a program that promises a greater margin of help for many parents and many children.

The body of data referred to in the previous section about child-rearing practices, the do's and don'ts that we know something about, need far wider dissemination than they have received. For example, the effects of overstimulation in children have often been described, but somehow one has the impression that the culture has taken no note of this. Yet this is a matter of considerable impact on the lives of people. Patterns of overstimulation take a variety of forms. Parental nakedness in front of the child, sexual teasing, tickling, excessive fondling or handling, sharing a bed with the child (be it the child's bed or the parent's), exposing the child to parental sexual activity, especially on vacations or visits, and the like—the ego-flooding and emotionally disturbing effects of such behavior are well documented. But the public reaction to such information seems curiously muted. This needs study. We are faced with the task of literally revamping some of the child-rearing practices of our culture, a task not lightly undertaken, yet a necessary one if we are to prevent the passivity and character disorders that so frequently follow from this type of childhood experience.

In certain inner-city ghetto areas in particular, the simultaneous occurrence of many social problems—alcoholism, crowding, family breakdown, emotional disturbances, and the like—will produce settings where fighting to the point of bloodletting, overt sexual encounters between adults or between adults and children, or dramatic emotional eruptions of all kinds might frequently occur in the presence of children, and where special kinds of overstimulation are the daily fare of these youngsters. Small wonder, then, that many people emerging from such settings bear the evidences of these early experiences in the form of a defensive apathy and emotional dullness, or of an overstimulated proneness to hyperactivity and to violence in the conduct of their lives. The rare individual will escape from such a childhood unscathed; by and large, these early events groove deeply into developing character.

Obviously, an occasional lecture on child-rearing will have little impact on a situation that needs many kinds of treatment help and social support. On the other hand, even very disturbed parents are often eager to help their small children in any way that they are able to—*sometimes, indeed, this area is the only one around which they can be contacted,* and, as such, might well provide an entering wedge for a variety of additional services to be brought to them. The issues and needs around caring for small children have peculiar emotional force, and skillful help in this area is of very special value.

There are many items of child-rearing practice that might be explored: the question of limit setting versus punishing; the impact of television; the role of body manipulations such as enemas, spankings, excessive lap sitting, and the like; the handling of toilet training and tantrums; the management of the child when he is stubborn and when he is negativistic; his curiosity about sex and pregnancy; his preparation for a new baby and discussions about his feelings; the role of violence and aggression and the management of such behavior; the management of a child in the face of divorce; and so on and on for a host of details about many issues.

There is much that parents need to know about the problems of their children and about the critical areas of concern and reaction—and means should be found in high school courses, in group programs for young mothers, in educational TV beamed at the general public, in the training of general practitioners and pediatricians who could then discuss these points individually with families—in short, in as many ways as possible—to communicate this knowledge to the public at large. Special efforts need to be made with those multiproblem families in which the parents might find survival itself to be too much for them and have little heart left for the niceties and refinements of avoiding childhood emotional problems. The paraprofessional helpers, the "grandmothers" and "homemakers," could then act not only as material assistants but as teachers and bearers of value as well.

The Father

It is a curious and often-remarked characteristic of mental health research that it concerns itself far more with the study of the mother-child interaction than with the role of the father as parent. Yet, the place of the father in child-rearing is of central importance, as almost anyone can attest from his own childhood memories. It might well be pondered how it comes about that our scientific formulations have taken the bias along which they seem to have inclined. This becomes a particularly important question in the light of the radical and crucial changes in the role of the father during the twentieth century. In this connection it seems worth reviewing some of the psychological aspects of fatherhood. Obviously different cultures will structure the networks of child care, parental responsibilities, and other aspects of family life in highly divergent fashions. Nonetheless, the psychological meaning of the father as distinct from the specific mode of functioning of a particular father in a particular home seems vital to the developing child in the following ways:

1. As an important aid for the structuring of realistic thinking. Fantasies wreathe about mother, play and wish cluster around mother, the whole magical universe of symbiotic fusion and subsequent separation and individuation center on mother. Father offers an alternative, an additional increment of realistic consideration, a presence who is less involved in wish fulfillment and more concerned with what is.

2. As a source of limit setting. The classical picture of the development of conscience is the taking in of parental values, of the literal voice of the controlling parent, as part of one's own system of inner controls. In fact, this is a complex process, one that involves a hierarchy of such inner control elements, but the role of father as voice of final authority has been a critical factor in the adequate structuring of the conscience in the lives of most youngsters brought up in the traditional style of child-rearing in the West. The mother who attempts to rear children without a father in the home often has particularly severe difficulties helping her youngsters in this area of impulse control. Where a traditional and intact family functions well, father is the one who finally sets the limit. But it is the internalized image of a father figure that really concerns us—our clinical experience teaches us that, however arrived at, this is an essential ingredient of a well-functioning conscience.

3. As a model for sex differentiation. The commonsense logic of having adult male and female figures in the home as examples for the children of what it means to be a man and a woman is borne out by a good deal of clinical experience. The enormous problem of the boy growing up in a female-dominated household has been highlighted for us with particular force in the inner-city ghetto areas. The need for many boys from such backgrounds to fly into a sort of excessive masculinity in which the accent is on putting people down, on having heart, on maintaining a rep, and the like is in some measure at least a response to the feminizing influence of the commonly encountered mother-led home.

4. As a model for career choice. We no longer live in a day when a youngster is necessarily encouraged to follow in father's footsteps (although in certain subcultures and families this is certainly still an available pattern). But the impact of father as worker and earner and as a model for such adaptive behavior has ramifications that go far more widely and deeply than choice of occupation alone. The sense of caretaking, decision making, supporting, protecting, and the like are all part of this pattern; lacking such a presence in one's growing up confronts the youngster with a serious deficiency in his or her attempt to define an identity and, in turn, become a parent in his own right.

From the clinical point of view, one of the most serious mental health problems in our culture has been the apparent erosion of the quality and definition of masculinity and manliness in the American family. If one opens a file drawer in any child mental health clinic anywhere in this country and selects a case at random, the chances are that the opening sentence will read: "The patient is the product of a marriage characterized by a dominating overconcerned mother and a passive uninvolved father who leaves all decisions about the children in mother's hands. . . ." There are numerous explanations advanced for this, varying all the way from the closing of the frontier through shifts in technology to throwing aside the shackles of the past and entering a new era of unconstrained freedom. In fact, the chances are we don't yet know enough about history and about the dynamics of large populations to speak about causes with any certainty. What does seem evident is that much study and research about the role of the father in the psychological development of children is vitally necessary at this point in order to develop the theory and practice of giving children what they need in these crucial areas in which the role function of the father is central.

Important Issues

There are several theoretical elements that are well worth considering in addition to the points made thus far. *The question of later delinquency, lack of impulse control, violence, and antisocial activity has been frequently associated with events and experiences during the first five years of life.* Psychoanalysts give particular weight to the two-year-old period, the time associated with the anal phase, for the establishment of verbal patterns as control elements in ordering of impulse life. The commonly encountered delinquent is typically a person who responds only to external control, who seems devoid of fantasy, who is totally action-oriented, and who can readily burst forth into violent behavior when frustrated or aroused. In brief, he seems to function psychologically in a manner analogous to the function of a two-year-old. Thus, it is a major frontier for research to seek out the events of this early phase in life and trace the connections between traumatic shaping experiences in the preschool period and the later character structures that emerge. There seems much to suggest that to some extent, at least, the violence in our streets has been preceded by and reflects the failure in the nursery. Adequate intervention at the one moment in development may head off major troubles later on. (Needless to say, this promise would build upon the firmer foundation resulting from improvement in the handling of the child in infancy. Unless the problems of the first year are handled well, work in the second and third years will be far less effective.)

Another theoretical possibility that commands attention is *the relationship of these preschool experiences to cultural, social, and racial identity*.[4] At which point in his development does a child begin to think of himself as a Jew, a kike, a black nigger, an upper-class blue-blood, a no-good halfbreed, a wop, a spic, a dago, or whatever other social role is available? Again, we need to go back to these early years—much that we know suggests that our self-concept is first formed as a result of taking in the parental views plus those of the immediate environment. When parents see themselves, or their offspring, as devalued, or when they devalue others, the children will presently have this attitude as a built-in element in their own make-up.

But the impact of the larger society impinges as well at a surprisingly early age, and even very young children who tend to see their parents in idealized forms will be aware of the labels and contradictions in behavior that establish social identities. It is clear, then, that effects of racial discrimination will first impress themselves on children through the parents' views about race—to the extent that black parents hate themselves because they are black, their children will be all too prone to accept this attitude along with mother's milk; to the extent that nonblack parents fear or hate or despise or devalue blacks, their children will be scarred by the same malaise.

But, in addition to taking in the parents' values, the children will also be responding to how others treat their parents and how their parents act toward other members of society—and the parental fawning or cringing, the parental arrogance or superciliousness, the parental dignity and respect, all will have their role to play in building internal images in the toddlers and preschoolers.

The problem of long-range elimination of discriminatory thinking in contrast to discriminatory practice rests in part on the intensity and skill of the work done with preschoolers. One possible approach might be the use of nursery school programs both for teaching and for unteaching. If such schooling became universal, a situation would be available for some work with children's perception of themselves and others in racial and

4. For a discussion of the clinical aspects of discrimination, see Appendix E: Statement on Racism by the Committee on Clinical Issues.

social areas. This could be both educational and diagnostic. A child who devalues his own skin color or his own subculture at this point in development should be considered as much at risk as a child who wets the bed or who has night terrors—all these children need help, and the family needs help as well.

The direct supportive and instructional material that can be extended by an appropriate program of play school will also be important. It will certainly not outweigh the effects of parental attributes and training, but neither will it be trivial in offering children alternative ways of viewing, valuing, and growing. In any case, the seeds of racism are planted when the self-concept of the child is forming, and when his perception of group differences first becomes acute. That this occurs so early in life offers a tremendous barrier to helping people as well as an especially direct route to influencing them. It is vital to consider approaches toward the preschooler in future research and planning.

Character Traits

For the most part, when we talk of prevention, we concern ourselves with the most obvious and identifiable symptoms of disorder: delinquency, psychosis, neurosis, perversion, and the like. Our culture is far from being at a point where we know how to prevent and to treat all these unfortunate conditions; and we have failed signally to apply even the knowledge that we do have.

It therefore seems almost irrelevant to list some of the more subtle conditions that play a part in many people's lives, yet which are seldom diagnosed and rarely described in mental health work. Indeed, these are personality traits of such diffuse character that it is not easy to define them. However, to the extent that we would strive for richness of living and optimal levels of personality growth for all children, we feel broader professional concern with these conditions will be necessary. By way of illustration, let us confine ourselves to only three concepts: narcissism, passivity, and masochism.

Narcissism refers to a tendency toward self-centeredness, a turning of one's essential love and interest inward, and a readiness to use others for one's own gratification with little concern about these others as feeling people in their own right. It is in a sense synonymous with selfishness, with egocentricity, with a "me-first" or a "me-only" attitude.

In most cases, it is a quality of character and never emerges as a frank symptom of the usual sort; nevertheless, it is connected with a great many of the shadings and modulations of behavior that make for tension in human relationships. It is frequently seen as part of the more commonplace emotional disorders, marital problems, readiness to take offense or to feel slighted, left out, etc., and plays an especially important role in behavior disorders. Indeed, it is a prime element in the emotional make-up of delinquents.

Passivity refers to an attitude that also can pervade an individual's life in ways that can be both subtle and vital. Here we deal with a characterological "set" that expresses itself in a tendency to avoid acting or doing, and that prefers to be acted upon, or to be done to. It can take the form of always looking to be given to, of viewing life from the standpoint of the pawn or the victim, or the helpless object whom others will act upon, rather than studying in what ways one's own activity can produce pleasure or gratification or reward. In terms of its origins, it expresses the wish once again to be the babe in arms, to be nourished, held, supported, gratified, and cared for without having to "do" anything except "be." To the extent that this attitude continues to play a role in life past the time of infancy, it obviously affects the capacity for work, for independence, for creativity, and for maturity in general. In a particular child, it might be seen as laziness, lack of verve and zest and interest in doing things, "sissy" tendencies, a readiness to be led around by others, inability to stand up for oneself, and the like. It is particularly damaging to males, since it is so much at odds with the social expectations of masculinity. Like narcissism, it may be part and parcel of many other conditions, but even where no overt symptomatology is present, passive tendencies can play hob with an individual's social relationships, productivity, sexual satisfaction, and overall adjustment as a person.

Masochism is the name of a recognized sexual perversion. Our concern here, however, is with a somewhat different use of the term. For many people, there is a powerful unconscious need to attract punishment, to act so as to cause oneself to suffer, to deny oneself pleasure. This may never reach the proportions of an evident symptom, but if one lives with such a person, or reviews his life in some detail, it is evident that he must quite unwittingly, and indeed unwillingly, do those things that cause his ambitions to be blunted, his expectations to be disappointed, and all his most ardently expressed yearnings to be frustrated. Such people are often called unlucky, but a deeper exploration into their lives reveals that their "luck" is self-created and that underlying their various misfortunes is a profound need to suffer, a need that eventually turns out to be associated with pleasure. Thus, this unconscious character trait is allied to the perversion called masochism, yet radically different from it because there is no awareness of or wish for the pain as a road to pleasure—there are only the "bad breaks" that seem to keep happening. Many provocative children, or bright youngsters who don't seem to be able to capitalize on their intelligence, or youngsters who are forever falling and hurting themselves, or who are always the scapegoat or the butt of other's teasing, actually are motivated in large part by such masochistic needs. Such covert tendencies can be powerful barriers to successful growth and development, although their presence is not always easily recognized. In adulthood, the nagging, miserable, and misery-creating wife, the self-destructive prealcoholic man who is always passed over for promotion, the many "average" people who live lives of quiet embitterment, all give testimony to the ravages of this condition.

These three rather subtle styles of behavior are only a few of the character traits that can so often injure development. They are very common traits indeed, and so far as we can tell, they are in large measure a product of faulty child-rearing practices. It may, in fact, be true that there are particular proclivities and vulnerabilities inherent in constitution that make a given child especially prone to this characteristic or that. But there is no doubt about the fact that such tendencies have often been connected with specific patterns of management in childhood that have acted to augment and to fix these unwholesome orientations to the great detriment of future growth. Currently, psychoanalysis remains the treatment of choice for attempting to deal with already crystallized character problems. Prolonged analytic treatment has successfully helped change character traits and elicited the early memories and experiences which suggested how the problems came into being. Intensive psychotherapy can also be of great help.

TOWARD OPTIMAL GROWTH AND DEVELOPMENT

Our studies in child development are now proceeding at a rate that should give us additional valuable insights into child-rearing problems in the next several decades. As things stand, we know more about noxious stimuli to avoid than we do about how best to encourage the fullest flowering of each youngster's potential. However, it is likely that even if we did no more than allow development to go on with a minimum amount of baneful activity on our part, it would already be a great boost to the average child. If, in addition, skillful play techniques, group activity patterns, and teaching methods could be developed for this age group—and someday they will be—to enhance the richest elaboration of each child's latent possibilities, a tremendous spurt in healthy growth and consolidation would likely develop. We get hints of these things from the work in the Israeli kibbutzim, or from some unusual observation made in this nursery school or that. In time, we can hope that the winnowing of many experimental methods will produce the balance of individual and group approaches that will improve development at each age.

Thus, again and again, as we consider ways and means to give children the best possible beginnings for their lives, we are led back to the elements of rearing and handling within the home. This should be one of the great frontiers for research in the next decades.

Grade School

In this section, we will cover a wide span from the era at the beginning of grade school when the child consolidates his conscience and begins to encounter his first major out-of-home educator, all through until the prepubertal epoch so characteristic of the transition into junior high. These are fruitful years for personality growth. Although not so basic as the first five years, they are critical times for the training and refinement of the peer values and social group practices that will be of such importance in later life. They are also years of greater accessibility for society in contacting child and family, in which the school, required by law, valued by tradition, and essential by common consent, becomes a major vehicle for acculturation. The parental role is still a highly central one, however, although it strains against the pull of the school, the peer group, the street, the neighbors, and the neighborhood, all of which exert great force as well. In short, this is a time of relative equilibrium in growth, but a period of dynamic tension, nonetheless, with many forces at work to shape the growing, emerging mind.

TREATMENT[1]

The Child Psychiatric Clinic

Until recent years, the large majority of children treated in community child guidance clinics have been of school age. The range of problems leading to their referral has been fairly wide: the symptoms of childhood neuroses, such as morbid fears or compulsions, inability to attend school because of fear or nausea or concern about fainting, soiling and enuresis, learning

1. For a discussion of factors important in planning for clinical services, see Apdix F: A Clinician's Overview, by Meyer Sonis, M.D.

difficulties of various kinds (in the face of normal or superior IQ), tics, rituals, inability to make friends with other children, sadness, and the like make up one considerable group. Of these, perhaps the most frequent source of referrals arises from problems in the school area, in particular, in connection with learning difficulties of various kinds. A few more serious conditions such as borderline psychoses or psychosomatic illnesses like asthma or colitis might also have been found on the treatment rolls of the child guidance clinic. The group of behavior disorders has encountered rather varying acceptability depending on the nature of the clinic, but almost all child guidance agencies treat children referred for truancy, fire-setting, running away, stealing, attacking and bullying others, sexual molestation and perversion, and other evidences of antisocial behavior. However, many outpatient clinics do not attempt to deal with the more severe patterns of antisocial action or with the psychoses of childhood, since the essential supports for such treatment are often lacking in the community: the outlook for outpatient treatment alone is dubious without such back-up services as special educational facilities, day care, material help in the home, adequate hospital care for moments of crisis, and the like.

The child guidance clinic staff was originally composed of members of four professions—psychiatrist, psychologist, social worker, and pediatrician —but within a few years the first three made up the familiar clinic team. There was a rather specific ordering of responsibilities; for example, the social worker saw the families, the psychologist did the testing, and the psychiatrist did the evaluation interview and much of the treatment. Nonetheless, for some years now, members of all the disciplines have been carrying out psychotherapy, and supervised child therapy is now a part of many training programs in psychology and social work. This development has had the effect of increasing the pool of skilled child therapists available for clinic and private practice.

Since the second decade of the twentieth century, when the pioneering facilities were first set up, child guidance clinics have been established under many different auspices. Community clinics supported largely by voluntary groups still make up the largest group, but through the years universities, hospitals, medical schools, clinics, various governmental units, and more recently industries and labor union health services have developed child psychiatric clinics, so that a wide variety of settings, functions, and patterns of service now obtain (American Association of Psychiatric Clinics for Children, 1968). Some became highly specialized, dealing only with one age group or one type of disorder, such as learning difficulties, but most clinics retained a general character.

The range of treatment methods has gradually broadened and widened as the years have gone on, additional personnel have been added to the familiar three disciplines, and now clinics exist which carry out not only the evaluations and psychotherapy, but also family therapy, group therapy, speech therapy, remedial tutoring, drug therapy, and such other activities as the particular interests of the director and the opportunities of the local situation encourage. Earlier practices such as home visiting, parent guidance, and emphasis on mental health education have again appeared. Inevitably, the nature of the activities and responsibilities of the original triad have shifted and broadened as well. All members of the clinic team now work with families (in some experimental structures all of them work with a given family at once!), all team members may carry out psychotherapy, many of them do group therapy, they might all do intake interviewing—indeed, practically the only activity that remains truly exclusive is psychological testing. By common consent, the psychologist is usually the only person who does that. (In fact, however, some special educators are moving into that area as well.) Dr. Jerome Silverman (1968) has remarked that in his extensive study of New York City clinics, there was much to suggest that a diffusion and confusion of professional roles was taking place.

The Day-Care Center

The tendency to increase the range and scope of personnel and methodology has led to yet another development of potentially major significance to the child mental health scene, the day-care center. Although many people have experimented with such programs in small ways through the years, the day-care center has only recently become the focus of a great deal of attention. It provides a combination of school, treatment, and recreational activities integrated into a planned therapeutic pattern for the bulk of the child's day. Several such centers are now springing up, some in connection with clinics, another group as extensions of the range of services provided by residential treatment centers, others related to mental health centers, and still others as unique facilities under independent auspices. Here the professional problems begin to compound. Keeping the original triad of the clinic operating in synchrony has been no minor matter; the task of dealing with so many, and so many levels of professional development and skills as those represented by teacher, occupational therapist, psychologist, social worker, recreation therapist, etc., all impinging on the same child, or the same small group of children, creates very intricate and difficult staff management issues.

The Residential Treatment Center

As complex as the operation of a day-care center with major mental health functions has proven to be, it is far simpler than the ultimate in child treatment techniques, the residential treatment center. Here the child is taken over completely by the therapeutic staff, who attempt to create a whole new life setting to act as the major modality of treatment. For this work, the disparate elements (the psychotherapy, schooling, group work, casework with parents, remedial education, recreation, milieu management) are each a detail in an overall pattern. And it is the pattern that matters. When properly patterned, the program of the treatment residence emerges with a life style peculiarly its own, tailored precisely to the emotional needs of the individual child, and always striving for maximal therapeutic gain.

A few psychiatric treatment residences have teachers of experience; many are being set up for handling the very seriously disturbed child. More than that, this type of facility gives promise of having a seminal effect on the practices of all institutional placement and, ultimately, for providing a laboratory for observation and study of child care and child-rearing practices in general.

By the same token, it is administratively the most difficult and intricate type of treatment to carry out. Here, as nowhere else, staff people live in intimate working contact with severely disordered children over extended periods of time—this exacts a price at the same time that it develops certain capacities to an extraordinary degree.

Private Psychiatric and Psychoanalytic Treatment

Many children are helped by agents other than those described. The standard approach to the psychological treatment of troubled children is child psychotherapy. Both private practitioners and clinic staff employ this technique. It involves child and therapist meeting at regular intervals (usually once or twice a week) with the work taking place in some form of play room. Normally, the parents would also be seen at regular intervals in connection with the child's treatment.

The basis of the method lies in the capacity of the therapist to communicate with the child in his own idiom, to understand the many levels of meaning in the child's language, play, and drawing, and to respond in clinically appropirate ways to this complex of cues. A wide variety of cognitive and emotional issues can be approached in this way. More intricate still is the therapist's capacity to use the relationship that develops between the child and himself as a basic medium of treatment. Careful and skillful exploration of emotional issues and deft therapeutic handling of the interpersonal relationship within the treatment room have been of substantial help to many troubled children. When this is coupled with appropriate supportive help for the parents, a very useful therapeutic impact can ensue.

A very small but important group of therapists is the child analysts who offer the field a unique body of skill and knowledge about treatment. Child analysts have, in fact, provided a basic science of therapy from which most psychotherapeutic practice has derived. They are in the very forefront of research into the intrapsychic components of the psychopathology of child-hood, and into the techniques for their relief. For those children for whom it is feasible, they supply a method for dealing with the developmental blocks and neurotic conflicts, the efficacy of which is unmatched in our treatment armamentarium. Since this treatment calls for sessions four or five times a week with a highly trained clinician, it is obvious that only a small number of children can be reached directly through this means. However, most child analysts participate actively in consultation and teaching programs, so that their contributions to child care cover many more children than they can see in psychoanalytic treatment.

There are various innovative therapeutic techniques now being tried; some which were innovative a short time ago are now becoming standard. Group therapy, for example, has come to be accepted as a useful and, indeed, basic means of dealing with certain childhood disorders. It is an expanding field of immense value, although its limits are still in dispute. Family therapy remains in an experimental status, but it is quite widely studied and practiced and will probably take its place along with more established methods within the next few years. Dr. Jerome Silverman (1968) reports that in the recent survey of mental health clinic care for children in New York City, which he directed, an attempted analysis of data about family therapy was virtually impossible because of the enormous variation in practices that were included under this rubric. In effect, it was a nonspecific designation. In any case, it is already clear that working with an entire family simultaneously has its dangers and contraindications as well as its strengths, and the entire area is currently the subject of much clinical study.

Perhaps most promising of all these methods is the potential for skillful blendings of individual, group, and family therapy techniques that will allow therapists an ever wider spectrum of possibilities to bring to bear on a given case. Thus, an inhibited phobic nine-year-old might meet with an individual therapist for help with the underlying structure of his disturbance, share in group therapy sessions to help with his social problems, and take part in family therapy as well, where the impact of all this on his parents and siblings—and theirs on him—could be approached directly.

Behavior Therapy

In recent years a growing and enthusiastic group of clinicians, largely clinical psychologists, has begun to apply very different therapeutic methods derived from the formal learning theories of academic psychologists to the treatment of the emotional disturbances and symptomatic behavior of children (and adults). A description of the potential contribution of "be-havior therapy" using environmental (stimulus-reward) manipulations and the principles of conditioning was published decades ago (Jones, 1924). However, up until the 1960's a rather complete split existed between theoretical investigators interested in developing and testing "models" of learning theory as such (and often using rats as experimental subjects) and the professional clinician attempting to alleviate the problems of human patients by means of interview methods based on psychodynamic concepts.

As the confluence of these two quite different approaches occurs, today we have the valuable opportunity to study each in terms of the other, to measure the comparative strengths and weaknesses of each method, and to reap the benefits of the interaction of two highly divergent schools of thought. It is a situation rife with possibilities for misunderstanding and pregnant with potentials for increased breadth and depth in our mastery of human suffering.

Terms such as "behavior modification" and "shaping behavior" suggest the difference in focus. The learning theorist is alert to the visible response which is the symptom. Irrespective of the history of the symptom, and the possible unconscious underlying motives, he undertakes to examine the responses of the environment to the symptom and to seek those specific reactions that may serve to maintain it. Thus, it may be that a child is attended to only when he does have a temper tantrum, and the pattern of parent-child interaction, analyzed in learning theory terms, suggests that the mother is reinforcing the very behavior she objects to.

Some behavior therapists claim that in an amazingly few number of "desensitization" sessions the phobic child is able to function normally in a situation he formerly could not enter. Others are less sanguine about rapid results. In any case, when planning a course of a desensitization therapy, the therapist must have a great deal of interpersonal sensitivity and interview skills of a high order. Moreover, psychodynamic understanding of symbolic equivalences and derivatives must be part of his armamentarium no less than it must be part of the skill and competence of a psychodynami-cally oriented therapist.

It is evident that the promise of learning theory does indeed warrant further pursuit. In many instances the presumed incompatibility of be-havioral modification and psychodynamically and psychoanalytically de-rived approaches is illusory; it is more likely that these two theories can lead to therapeutic approaches which can complement each other. Neither one has "the answer."

Drug Therapy

Drug therapy is used by most clinics, many private practitioners, and probably the large majority of residential and day centers. This will be discussed in more detail in Appendix D.

Problems in the Delivery of Services

The problem of bringing therapeutic services to the children who need them has not been merely the variety of treatment approaches. More serious still have been the extraordinary difficulties encountered by the attempt to create an organizational structure which can deliver the service to the child in an adequate way. One of the most serious is the fragmentation of services in almost all communities. Thus, if a child needs at once certain drugs for physical symptoms and individual psychotherapy for behavior symptoms while his mother is receiving casework in a family agency, there may be three different groups involved to provide the three services. If, in addition, some remedial education were necessary, yet a fourth agency might be drawn in. The parents must then engage in a complex process of traveling, history-giving, fee arrangements, and confusing involvement with a number of professional persons. The child is the focus of the ministrations of several pairs of hands during the week over and above that of the school; the problem for him of relating himself to so many people can be overwhelming.

Conglomerate, multipurpose agencies specifically and consciously designed to prevent this experience of fragmentation on the part of the family are one type of answer to this drawback. Another possibility is a central child-caring service that shepherds and accompanies the child through the whole gamut of studies and treatments, remaining always a unitary link between the family and the diverse community resources. Where extensive agency structures exist, it is likely that the child's ombudsman, the caretaker, should be the point of initial contact, and this caretaker should "run interference" for the child and family during the entire process. Such a situation is likely to obtain in a large city where a great many agencies with different functions have gradually grown over the years, so that what faces the troubled family is a veritable thicket of names, functions, places, rules, responsibilities, and expectations; and what faces the child are all kinds of people each of whom seems to want him to do something else with or for him—and none of whom he may understand very well, let alone have a chance to come to feel comfortable with. A guiding, constant, friendly mentor to come along, find the way, stay nearby, carry the burden of the arrangement, help with the transportation, and explain what's happening can be a life saver in such a situation.

Wherever new agency structure is contemplated, then the evident need for simplifying and unifying the experiences as much as possible for the individual child and for each family is self-evident and of central importance.

Many different agency structures have been proposed. A number will be listed, but the list presented here is not and cannot be exhaustive. The limits of the possibilities are the limits of creative social imagination. The point that emerges from a contemplation of the possibilities is that here too the accent should be on variety, on differing methods in different places, on encouraging the spontaneous emergence of new forms, or new combinations of old forms. In time, with a body of social experience to draw upon, we may find that one, or several, modes of delivering services will be optimal, and these patterns can then crystallize and become the national style for some decades. But currently we are not at that level, and the watchword now should best be: Just as the clinician would emphasize the individual handling of each person, he will regard planning as an individual matter for each community. Each agglomeration of people is different, and so each community has its own profile of needs and values, each needs to be individually assessed. All have needs, but what will work well here may be contraindicated there. An individual "diagnosis" needs to be made, and a specific community-tailored plan developed. From the point of view of the Clinical Committee, then, let each community harness its own creative planning to its specific needs, and with a full awareness of what the problems and the dangers are, let it come up with its own formulation. Some will need a great deal more help in doing this than others, but the help should be directed toward getting the people to formulate what they need and to help them plan, rather than to impose a service.

The one generalization that does seem fruitful is this: There should be a center of population, and of population interest, from which the community service plan should stem. In one area it might be a large corporation, in another a labor union. A consortium of factories might pool its resources, or a neighborhood in a large city, or a moderate-sized town, or an entire county. A large university could be the hub, a major hospital, or a community mental health center which might expand its services. Various structures and varying auspices should abound in a conscious search for the type of planning that will best serve particular populations.

Several possible models follow. *The community mental health center* as it is now organized may include children's services but it may not, and in most cases, in fact, it does not. *We recommend that henceforth all new applications for establishing such centers be considered for funding if and only if an adequate spectrum of children's services be included.* This requirement could grow directly out of the current five-facet structure of the center: there should be appropriate emergency services, consultation, and inpatient, outpatient, and day-care programs for all children and adolescents as well as those serving adults. The planning should be along developmental lines, with the appropriate services available for each age group. Our population now includes more than 40 percent of children and youth under seventeen years of age: it is bizarre to establish such major public agencies without a built-in requirement to care for the evident needs of children. However, including child services does not ensure a functional clinical unit: the operation of such services in a child mental health center is a highly complex undertaking if we judge by the limited reports thus far available to us.

Another useful concept is a network of perhaps 15 mental health centers for children to be established on university campuses the country over. These centers would evolve a series of services tied in with those of the community.

The university centers would have a most immediate impact on training in different professions, confront academic researchers with problems not now visible to them, and thereby encourage application of the most advanced theoretical thinking to the development of specialized services for different age groups. These centers would have access to and responsibility for the operation of a field station in or near a city. The impact of the university centers upon professional and paraprofessional training would ensure the preparation of the trainees for work in the urban field station when they finished their training as well as in other types of settings. Diversity would be built in by virtue of the different settings of the centers. They would be subject to continuous evaluation.

Yet another plan is to tie mental health services to a program of overall health planning. Urban health centers could be established where every facet of clinical management, social, psychological, psychiatric, pediatric, medical-surgical, familial, and so forth, could be included under one umbrella. *Again, the school system in a given area could enlarge its function to extend services to children of all ages and with all levels of function and competence*—with classes for genius-level children and provisions for retarded youngsters; with facilities for newborns, and academic-vocational possibilities for teen-agers; with community job services for the mature youth, and clinics and residential treatment for the sick, all combined within one administrative framework.

The concept of the child development center, a clearinghouse for all the children within a given population or locus, and with a back-up of all necessary clinical facilities, merits experimentation. The accent could be on normalcy—all parents and all children need their regular examinations, their questions responded to, their progress assessed, and their problems provided for. Such a center need have no particular clinical facility attached, but it might provide the ombudsman,[2] the health mentor who could

2. Editor's note: The concept of advocate for children emerged as the major recommendation in the Commission's final report. The advocate at the neighborhood level would link the child and his family with *any* type of service needed, whether this be clinical, educational, social, vocational, etc. This neighborhood advocate would be located in any agency or facility designated by the community. This direct advocate function would be backed by an advocacy system operating at all levels of government

arrange for needed diagnostic and treatment services and provide the continuity for child and family as they entered the mental health care system. What must be kept in mind is that provision of consultation or intensifying a mental health approach cannot take the place of needed treatment services.

Since we speak of large agencies, a cautionary note needs to be sounded. A basic principle of clinical work which has been alluded to but which cannot be restated too often is respect for the individual. It is one of the complications of bigness that people tend to become statistics, to be herded and processed and depersonalized, to be assigned numbers by which they are subsequently identified, and to remain fundamentally meaningless and unknown unless they can remember their number—whereupon they are suddenly granted an identity and the agency will now agree to do business with them. To some extent, lower-echelon employees are treated in very similar ways—each has exactly the same size office, with identical furniture and the same type of phone hook-up, etc. These tendencies are antithetical to the mental health of both employees and clients, and must be considered and countered at every level. For example, a large waiting room filled with people waiting for appointments is a beginning step to loss of individuality. Instead, an agency should "think small" in its grouping of people, with a number of small waiting rooms, each furnished in a different color, none harboring more than two families, with comfortable furniture and reading and diversional material for all age groups, with coffee or tea always available, and with a different effect created in each room by the drapes, carpeting, and wall pictures—in short, a set of rooms with individuality and character, each one perhaps decorated by a different community volunteer group but, in any case, designed to convey a sense of respect for the family who waits, and recognition of the uniqueness of everyone who comes—such thinking is basic to the communication of clinical values, and to setting the tone for the kind of work the agency offers.

Expense

It is obvious, too, that such planning will all too readily be vulnerable to the accusation of "frills" and exorbitant budgetary demands. This in turn throws a major responsibility on planners to come to grips with financial issues in a very painstaking and careful way, not by slighting their clinical values, but by documenting them at length and spelling out to legis-

---

—local, state, and federal. These governmental agencies would be charged with planning and funding of needed services for children. Hopefully, this endeavor would lead to the development of a network of comprehensive services—the second major recommendation of the Commission. See *Crisis in Child Mental Health: Challenge for the 1970's* (New York: Harper & Row, 1970).

lators and granting agencies in some detail just why things cost what they do.

For it is a fact of life that child treatment is considerably more expensive than adult therapy. The exact figures are not easy to state categorically, but it is likely that the difference is between 1.5 to 1 and 2 to 1. That is to say, many adult inpatient facilities can give intensive treatment at $10,000 or $12,000 a year, whereas an equivalent child program would cost $15,000, or $18,000. The difference lies in several areas. First, there is the much wider scope of programing facilities children need; for example, a school is a normal and necessary part of a child program and is ordinarily not an element in adult treatment setups. Also children need a far greater concentration of caring adults to look after them, there is much more supervision necessary, much more family involvement, often some additional community or agency involvement such as a juvenile court, welfare, and the like; and finally, the overall level of professional training required to work with children is far greater, and the personnel therefore command higher salaries. Thus, for example, compared to adult psychiatry, child psychiatric training adds at least two years to the time required to obtain one's diplomate; credentials in child analysis often take three to five years beyond the already extensive training in adult analysis, and so on for most disciplines. Child work is harder than adult work, takes longer to learn, and costs more.

The combination of many more disciplines necessary, and more expensive ones at that, gives the entire field of children's treatment a special cost of its own, which is reflected in the higher per capita cost of treatment.

Staff

Given any agency budget, the largest percentage is likely to go for staff. A whole host of disciplines is involved, some new disciplines are implicit, and a great array of various adjunctive, paraprofessional identities are emerging. It might be well to pause here and list some of the more immediately relevant professional groups, with some comments on their functioning and training. The longest training by far is that required for qualification in *child analysis*. This group of practitioners, although tiny in numbers, has been of extraordinary influence in mental health practices with children in this country. All theories of development are in some kind of dialogue with psychoanalysis. Most treatment methods are in some sense derivative from or dependent upon psychoanalytic constructs, and in particular, on the work of child analysts, although drug therapy, conditioning techniques, and some other methods derive from quite different approaches.

As therapists, child analysts attempt to do intensive work on factors retarding or arresting personality development; at best, they can treat only a small number of children. From this enormously close and detailed study of individual children, however, emerges a body of theoretical and empirical skills that make the child analyst an invaluable counselor and resource person to almost any type of agency that deals with children or trains people to deal with them. The major leverage of the child analyst lies in his work as theoretician, teacher, and consultant; agencies as diverse as medical schools, juvenile courts, and residential treatment centers have benefited from his knowledge. More than that, the analytic situation has generated many research ideas of great importance to the field. Indeed, in the hands of certain practitioners every analysis is a research study.

Child psychiatry is another profession of central importance to the field, and again this discipline is one for which it takes many years to prepare. It is now an accredited medical subspecialty, and can be completed only if full training in adult psychiatry has also been accomplished. This heaping of one psychiatric specialty upon another produces a physician of unusually rich background. Added to this is the unique quality of children's work; it is characteristically work done by a team, and the child psychiatrist is therefore given intensive preparation in working with a team, in consulting with a team, and/or in how to be the team leader. He can assume responsibility for all issues involving the mental health of children, and if need be, he can ultimately decide what procedures and what people are necessary for diagnosis and treatment. As the physician-in-charge, he is the one member of the team who can prescribe drugs. Moreover, he is prepared to deal not only with the cases he encounters, but with the community. He is trained to consult with the juvenile court, the school, the group home, the ghetto agency, the community action program, the public health nurses program, and the like. So much emphasis, indeed, has recently been thrown upon the child psychiatrist as community worker that much concern has been expressed that other aspects of his preparation might be slighted to the detriment of his overall contribution. In any case, it obviously takes a long time to prepare a specialist for such central social and clinical responsibility. It would seem desirable to shorten this training time if at all possible in the service of giving society his urgently needed skills more rapidly. At the same time, the increasing range of competencies and services requested of this discipline presses toward even more preparation. As a team leader, interdisciplinary worker, physician, consultant, and the person who is legally responsible for the diagnosis and treatment of the troubled child, the child psychiatrist is of pivotal importance in planning for children, sick and well, and should be included in early stages of any schema for coping with youth of any age.

In time there will inevitably be specialization within this field, with some psychiatrists turning their interest toward infancy, others toward adolescence, still others to delinquency or childhood schizophrenia or whatever. The frontier areas of today are work with ghetto Negroes, the special problem of the poverty groups, work with infants, and work with the severe delinquent. Such areas now receive considerable emphasis in most training programs, and as more skillful teachers become available, such specializations will be more frequent. However, if the child psychiatrist is to continue to serve the many functions listed above, he will more often need to be a generalist, a reality complicating our current plans for training programs.

Psychology, particularly at the Ph.D. level, has gradually come to occupy an ever increasing role in the clinical universe. Alone among the classical disciplines, the psychologist's work is closely wedded to research methodology and experimental and statistical techniques. The measurement of intelligence, the evaluation of perceptual capacities and integrative brain functioning, the objective determination of personality status by standardized means, and many other vital elements in clinical work are the exclusive property of this specialty. Moreover, many psychologists are well prepared in the several types of therapy ranging from psychoanalysis through group therapy to behavioral modification. In short, they represent a field of enormous richness and variety, and within the clinical area they are making major contributions on many levels: research, treatment, testing, teaching, administration, etc. Much of what we today know about cognitive development and learning difficulties has arisen within the bosom of this discipline. It is not surprising that for the school system in many areas, psychologists have become the major source of clinical skills; they counsel and advise teachers and parents, and diagnose and treat a large number of children. Many juvenile courts depend on them for guidance. They are undoubtedly among the leading thinkers in the area of mental retardation. In the child guidance clinic, they are probably the largest single cadre of therapists, as well as the only group equipped to do psychological testing. There is a never-ending need for their services in a great variety of social agencies, and it behooves the universities to respond to this need by increasing the depth and richness of clinical psychology training, by active recruitment of Ph.D. candidates with primary clinical interests, and by creating or linking up with field services which will give adequate supervised clinical experience to these trainees. This point cannot be emphasized too much—it is a vital part of the training of those who would do clinical work to have intensive supervision of actual work with cases by experienced clinicians.

Social workers have long been the chief laborers in the mental health vineyards. By and large, social workers are trained to deal with that critical interface, the site where theoretical knowledge of personality and psychodynamics impinge on the practical empirical issues of how to rear a child, how to get along on the job, how to manage money, how to cope with a difficult spouse, and the like. Standing as they do, midway between the complexities of theory and the intricacies and burdens of everyday living, the social workers have often been the great interpreters of such theory to the public at large, and perhaps the most numerous group of implementers of these ideas in terms of current social practice.

It is evident that social work competence implies a high order of skill and a very specialized and comprehensive preparation. Their orientation toward theory has made some social workers among the best therapists in the clinical field; their inclination toward the empiric elements of living has produced a style of practice ideally suited for counseling, guidance, family support, welfare, and perhaps most important of all, the management of personnel structures and agency operation. Welfare agencies, family service, adoption, and a host of other services and institutional structures are staffed primarily by social workers. They are an essential part of the child guidance clinic, of the residential treatment center, and of almost every variety of therapeutic service. Most social workers in the clinical field now have an M.A., but the number who seek Ph.D. training is gradually increasing. Some of the most sophisticated and experienced child therapists have been social workers—significantly, however, their therapeutic skills have accrued largely as a result of on-the-job training *after* they left formal social work school.

Many different agencies are administered by social workers, and they probably comprise the largest pool of skilled mental health administrators available. This is a vital resource in a rapidly expanding field. The combination of administrative and clinical skills that tends to be built into this discipline is unique and should be counted upon heavily in the future.

It would be desirable if student social workers with the talent and inclination to do therapy could be trained in their clinical skills earlier and more intensively. Schools of social work need to be alert for this capacity among their students and to nourish and nurture it with good clinical supervision and a solid experience in dealing with clients.

Having spoken of these basic mental health disciplines, we may at this point wonder why universities have not attempted to establish an M.A. or Ph.D. in psychotherapy per se. The work of Margaret Rioch and others in training appropriate candidates for two years for certain kinds of psychotherapeutic responsibilities has provided adequate grounds for recognizing that this can be done, and that there is a need for such skills. As things are now constituted, most civil service job descriptions do not have a slot for "psychotherapist" as such; and there is some floundering necessary to attach such people to recognizable positions on public payrolls. But once such a discipline comes to be respected and appears in any appreciable numbers, the administrative changes will follow in due course. It seems an idea well worth pursuing.

Educators are now becoming much closer to clinicians than at any time in the past. They have never been far away; indeed, such people as

Fritz Redl, Erik Erikson, Peter Blos, and many other stellar lights in the clinical universe were educators who became lay analysts. Currently, there are a number of different patterns of integration of clinician and educator. There are combined degrees in education and psychology given by some universities; there is training available in school counseling given within the structure of certain departments of education; sex education trainees are in the nature of things taught some clinical skills; and perhaps most notably, there is a great expansion in the training of special education teachers, a discipline that is essentially clinical in orientation if not in overall methodology. For the preschool child, the really well-trained nursery school teacher is in the very quality of her task a clinician, and the work with the emerging day care centers that are so much built around a core of school structuring means an ever closer blend of educator and clinician. Certainly the teacher in the residential treatment center, in the special nursery school for very disturbed or retarded children, in the day center, and so forth must communicate regularly with clinicians and to some extent modify his own methodology to assume a more clinical cast.

Nonetheless, the techniques and goals of education are not identical with those of treatment, and it is as important that the educator retain his professional identity as it is that the therapist preserve his. The degree of integration and interaction between the disciplines should increase, however, and within the school, the clinician has a very primary responsibility as consultant to the educator and as back-up person to the setting. The teacher in the special education class needs regular clinical consultation; a therapeutic nursery school implies that other skills are present beside that of nursery school teacher—no matter how competent; and so on for all the situations that deal with problem children. More than that, the very proliferation of school psychologists and school counselors speaks volumes for the new-felt need for clinical backing and support for the average school system that caters to normal children, or rather to the mixed population of troubled and untroubled children that comprises any given group of youngsters.

The general principle that emerges from our experience to date is this: child rearing, child training, child educating on any level, with any group, will inevitably bring up problems in approach, management, and response for which clinical consultation is essential. The occasional child will need more than consultation, and direct clinical intervention will be required (in the form of clinic referral, or treatment by a private practitioner, or even placement in a special setting). But the consultant's role will be a central responsibility of the experienced clinicians in any community.

What exists in fact is a hierarchy of skills with a small group of especially skilled people at the top, the elite of the clinical world, who must act as consultants and teachers to the next echelon, the service people in the various agencies. Thus an experienced, fully trained child psychologist, or child analyst, or M.S.W. social worker who has achieved local recognition as a superior clinician may visit a residential center, a home for unwed mothers, a university clinic, a medical school, and a ghetto project, all in the same week. He might never see a patient or a client in any of these agencies, but he would teach and give backing and support to those who do the work with the community, and provide a service of inestimable value to all people involved. The availability of consultation from a skilled psychologist might be the necessary catalyst to keep a whole school system growing by increasing its sensitivity to childhood disorders, by helping teachers recognize the role of their own feelings in dealing with problem youngsters, by bringing staff tensions out in the open where they can be dealt with constructively instead of going underground and wrecking things, and by direct help to principals, to the counseling staff, and to specialized teachers in coping with exceptional situations.

The ancient question of who will watch the watchers thus has a kind of answer: the professional elite will teach and support those who treat, those who teach, and those who rear. The real question in the field is not so much who will do it—the problem is how will you keep him doing it? The easy life for the mature professional is private practice: there he is his own boss, there he can make the most money. He sets his own hours and works at his own pace. Some pretty strong inducements must be provided to lure him away and to harness him to society's needs.

Incentives to keep top people in supervisory and consultant posts will thus have to be developed, on the level of both idealism and income. A contingency that profoundly affects the public welfare is well worth strengthening on both fronts. As matters now stand, a seasoned top professional who wishes to do public work has to function largely on the basis of his values and interests. As a senior person, he carries responsibility for programing and fund raising which can take him far from his earlier and perhaps basic interests. The many abrasive elements of mental health planning, such as collaboration with the community and all its tensions, trying to sort out and adapt to rapid changes in medical care patterns, and student unrest, all of which he must assimilate, put him under considerable stress. At the same time he is expected to provide support and encouragement for others while he manages his own discouragement, anxieties, and resentments alone. The most strident social ills are part of the daily fare of his agency experience; and although being in the mainstream of current life was probably a potent attraction to his job, in time the wearing down of energies, patience, and ingenuity takes its toll. Moreover, in a public agency he is likely to command a salary that is little better than that of his junior colleague just out of training, and a great deal less than he can obtain in private practice. The resultant attrition rate is high.

The nature of training at the professional level has been critically influenced by the shift of interest toward community work. Many of the younger people in the field are far better prepared in community organization than they are in clinical skills. At the same time, it is noteworthy that Dr. Jerome Silverman's (1968) study of clinics in New York City revealed that the operational concepts behind what was called "community psychiatry" were startlingly diffuse. In any case, it cannot be emphasized enough that basic to all mental health work is a thorough grounding in the dynamics and techniques of the individual encounter. To work effectively as consultant, counselor, adviser, or teacher, a strong infrastructure of skill and knowledge in working with individuals is an irreducible necessity. On that framework, any given variety of group, community, family, etc., techniques can be erected. Lacking that, we will have one-sided people who can never understand their problems in a thoroughgoing and fully professional way.

Today the trend in all mental health professions is a return to observing people in their own settings. We need to see them and work with them where they face their everyday challenges and stresses. This means a whole new range of sites for clinical work. Children are now being worked with on street corners, in well-baby clinics, in school corridors, in hospital wards, and in many other informal "natural" locations. However, as we talk about expanding the settings in which we bring our competence to bear, as we learn more about the many places where the problems can become visible and where a variety of experiences can be helpful, it becomes increasingly evident that here, too, the professionals cannot do the job themselves and must work indirectly as consultants. A direct consequence of this fact is that we cannot reduce the need for complex, intensive, long-term training of clinicians; in fact, this is even more important when we realize the needs of the new settings, new approaches, and new ways of evaluation. The experimental program is the one most in need of a seasoned clinician. When we think of training, therefore, we should not think in terms of numbers alone in one field or another; rather we must continue to emphasize quality of training, to advocate maintenance of an elite group with a rich experiential background. These are the people needed as supervisors and consultants.

We must maintain this emphasis on high-level training across disciplinary lines because each such trained clinician will be backing up a great many other people, and lending substance and experience to novel and innovative settings that might otherwise bog down or flounder.

Clinical work can best be learned in clinical settings, whether attached to a university or in the field. Dispersal of training is a highly desirable characteristic to include in future manpower programs. Another essential ingredient is evaluation, a built-in means for measuring the fruits of the clinical work as well as the outcome of the training—this element is so essential that its necessity needs endless iteration and reiteration.

To return to our list of clinical disciplines: there are the teachers of special function such as those who work with speech and reading difficulties, or who teach blind or deaf or otherwise handicapped children. Here the need for some degree of clinical training and for continued consultation is self-evident. Another group is the public health nurses who specialize in the areas of family support, of seeking out target populations (such as the children of hospitalized or ambulatory psychotic patients, or children recently returned home from residential treatment centers, and the like), or of taking primary treatment responsibilities in the home. Such specialized nursing requires a good deal of intensive psychiatric supervision built on a basis of rich clinical exposure during the postgraduate years. Many nurses now seek for M.A. degrees, and the commonest form of training is in nursing education. For the interested candidate, the university centers might well step up their pace of producing nurse-clinicians who would have supervised work with families and children in different settings during their preparation for the M.A. degree—there is a crying need for such personnel to accomplish a variety of essential tasks. One of the important roles of such graduates would be to supervise cadres of paraprofessionals who would be working on the front lines in many of these areas.

Quite a different group of skills is connected with a series of therapies that has emerged in the last several decades: occupational, recreational, art, music, work, drama, dance, etc. These are a somewhat heterogeneous group of clinicians, but where adequate talent and training are present, they introduce an extraordinarily useful element in therapeutic care. The increase in the use of day care and residential treatment that is now in process will mean ever more demand for skilled services in these areas. The occupational and recreational therapists have relatively standardized training; the other disciplines are more a matter of personal election and individual preparation. Here and there an isolated university may give courses, or even a degree in art therapy or music therapy, but it is still rather hit and miss. Nonetheless, these are valuable adjunctive services to holistic treatment programing, and we can look forward to their elaboration and development in the decade to come.

Insofar as sublimation and work are perceived as essential ingredients in the maturation of children and adolescents, it is evident that skilled clinicians working at these interfaces will be enormously helpful to treatment.

If we leave the professional group now, and turn to the paraprofessionals, we find ourselves working with a number of disciplines that have established some foothold in the field, and many others that are new and strange.[3] Much here is in fact brand new, the field is in a state of genuine ferment, and it is hard to say what novel development in role definition

3. For a discussion of new mental health workers, see Appendix C: Utilization of Paraprofessionals in Clinical Settings, by Rena S. Shulman, M.S.W.

and preparation tomorrow will bring. It is clear, however, that we are dealing with a major horizon in professional responsibility—the selection, training, and utilization of such paraprofessionals should be a matter of considerable concern to the field.

The development of a large cadre of such people will inevitably lead to the necessity for creating and maintaining standards. There will be simultaneous impulses to cautious overtraining and to precipitate production of 30-, 60-, or 90-day wonders. The issue comes down to one of built-in evaluation methods to go along with the new programs. Let the planners be as innovative as they like, but let them also build in methods to follow up, to measure, and to watch what happens to the people they prepare, what they do, how well they do it, how long they stay with it, what they got that was valueless and nonproductive, and so on.

The question of too much training versus too little is a critical one for the paraprofessional. Too much training extends the training period and defeats the purpose of supplying large numbers of sadly needed personnel in the shortest possible time. Too little training gives insufficient preparation for the trainee to do a competent job. It will be the task of the evaluation programs mentioned above to help the field toward the optimal channel between the Scylla of too little and Charybdis of too much.

Currently, the average paraprofessional and his charges are the victims of too little. Those who have tried to deal with such groups as child care workers in residential treatment centers have learned all too well the problems involved in selection of such staff and in their education. When attempts are made in the literature to list the necessary characteristics of such personnel, the profile that emerges is of a sort of superman (which only highlights the contrast between who does work with the children and who should). Reduced to its most primitive level, perhaps the single most critical factor in evaluating candidates for such work is the quality of teachability—a trainee needs to be someone who can learn and change. Lacking that, no other virtue means a great deal; granted that, we can begin to add such other requirements as may be deemed necessary.

The selection and use of such staff people, and of indigenous workers for the many community mental health tasks for which they are particularly fitted, should be in large measure in the hands of clinicians—it falls to the clinician to clarify what they can and cannot do.

It is worth noting that not everyone can do everything regardless of his training. Some clinicians work better with individuals; others prefer groups. Some feel more at home with delinquents, others with psychotic children, still others with neurotics. The sorting out of paraprofessionals will follow similar principles. It is important to help people find what they can do best, and then support them in doing it.

It is above all important to train them so they will know what is undesirable, what must be avoided. Willingness without training can lead to highly dubious situations. A foretaste of these problems has already come to light in certain Head Start programs in which some of the indigenous workers sought to give the children obvious gratifications rather than to facilitate learning and help strengthen the children's ability to delay. Clinical involvement in the training and programing for such workers is essential, and the clinician's responsibility to share in these endeavors is clear.

Another area that demands clinical attention is recruitment. Even though openings are available, it is no easy matter to interest minority-group members in mental health careers. Clinicians need to contact the high school, community college, and undergrad students of every socioeconomic level and strive to depict the positive values of such training and such a life's work. With certain minorities whose social deprivation or language difficulties make for unusual problems, special program adaptations should be made as needed. Without strenuous efforts, the present imbalances will continue without change.

Since training is best done early, it follows that clinicians should be directly involved in curriculum planning with high schools and junior colleges—particularly in the core content of what the students learn about behavior. Early involvement is preferable to waiting until students have finished college and then training them from the ground up. We will need many specialized people with specialized training, and the issue is the content of the training and of the core disciplines.

Regardless of how energetic the recruitment and training efforts, it will be years before there will be enough skill available to cope with the nation's mental health problems. While this behooves us to use the skills we have in the most efficient manner possible, it also requires the preparation of more and more paraprofessionals to whom appropriate tasks may be delegated.

It is proposed that the Commission recommend federal funding for agencies which want to develop paraprofessionals. These agencies would have to be involved with junior colleges and community colleges regarding formulation of curriculum, teaching courses, and counseling; there would be additional involvement with personnel through cross ties in fieldwork or placement in the agency. With experience, a formal pattern should emerge for developing people in the paraprofessional disciplines—combining on-the-job training with course training and adding the indispensable formal recognition (with credit given) from an official educational setting. All these elements are important; there can only be disillusionment, bitterness, and a loss to the field when someone is trained and then finds there is no place to go with his training.

It is also suggested that the Commission recommend federal subsidies for graduate and medical students to continue their work in the behavioral clinical fields; there should also be some form of encouragement for bachelor-degree persons trained in an assistant capacity to remain in that capacity. We face the phenomenon of trying to develop a professional technician without too much specialized training, while graduate schools are encouraging just the opposite.

There are many types of career ladders that can be set up. For example, curriculum development for various paraprofessional certificates is currently emerging in junior colleges the country over—this is still inchoate and uncertain, varying widely from one area to another. We would recommend increased federal support for these programs and for a series of periodic, cross-regional conferences to encourage the gradual development of standards and methods. In time, these measures would allow defined subprofessional careers to come into being. A number of plans are emerging. In one approach larger universities would permit individual courses to be taken by nonmatriculated students who can then use these courses toward achieving a high school diploma and, in time, if the student so desires, toward a college degree. A different strategy involves the establishment of special training institutes designed to prepare many types of mental health personnel. These could serve as major laboratories for devising new methods and experimenting with different curriculums for the instruction of promising candidates. Yet another career ladder could be built by adding trainees to judiciously selected segments of existing training programs for psychiatrists, clinical psychologists, psychiatric social workers, and the like. Such programs have already been broadened to include training facilities for psychiatric nurses, and occasional courses and workshops for foster parents, psychiatric aides, and similar groups. Another extension of their facilities could be the addition of permanent ongoing programs for training paraprofessionals in depth.

There are a host of paraprofessional "identities" that are shaping up, and more to come. An account of these roles is included in Appendix C, but by way of illustration, a partial list of available roles is presented here:

Psychiatric technician—there is a state hospital program in which young people, mostly high school graduates, are given a six-month training period followed by ongoing supervision. They work with other youngsters; they know their limitations and do not try to do too much or too little.

Case aide in social work—does not usually try to do therapy but helps in other ways in the social work sphere.

Foster grandmother—used in home settings where the mother is ill or in hospital wards, where her role is not psychotherapeutic but rather supportive (spending time with children and doing things the nurse has no time to do). There is some initial training and ongoing supervision.

Semiprofessional foster parent—a training program for work with individual children is being developed and also one for staffing group foster homes. In effect, the goal is to develop a sophisticated parent role with some understanding of child behavior and the capacity to work with mental health professionals.

Nurse practitioner—training in doing physical exams; some training about anticipatory guidance and counseling for parents, screening—physical, psychological, and in terms of developmental problems. (Denver Developmental Screening Test is used.)

Pediatric associate—college graduate with about two years of additional training. The candidates develop some knowledge in the area of prevention and could work in an office with a pediatrician.

Child care worker—not a formal psychotherapeutic role, but actively involved in milieu therapy in a number of different ways. These workers are intensively supervised; may use the life-space interview type of approach.

Homemakers—now receiving some training in mental health areas; undertake supportive handling of children in homes when mother is sick or family broken. Require mental health consultation and supervision.

It is evident that all of these people need guidance and supervision; many of them will be supervised by recently graduated psychologists and social workers, who will in turn need a great deal of help and support in dealing with their supervisees. The chances are that the more untrained the paraprofessional, the greater will be the degree of clinical sophistication needed to guide and support him.

In effect, the very nature of the roles described suggests the degree of transformation of our society—the tasks once assumed by family, by neighbors, by charitable organizations, and by churches are falling ever more regularly into the province of professional and subprofessional mental health work.

In particular, the indigenous paraprofessional worker is an essential link in what is today an incomplete chain—the series of measures designed to bring mental health services to the deprived and the alienated. Much has been written about the mental health professional's discriminating against the ignorant, the culturally estranged, and the nonverbal segment of the population, against the inner-city, ghetto-reared, poor black, the wary, defensive, deprived Puerto Rican, or the taciturn action-oriented resident of Appalachia. In fact, however, it is not clear whether it is the currently available techniques that are at fault or the many difficulties in bringing those techniques to bear on this target population.

Insofar as the clinician sits in his office and waits for applicants for help to appear, he will do little business with people who feel themselves excluded from the mainstream of national life. They will not come to him voluntarily, and if they are sent, they may be very suspicious of his motives and methods. Their previous experiences may not have been conducive to trust—either within their own subcultural context or in relation to the larger, hostile-feeling culture about them.

As a result, mental health clinicians have not had as rich an experience with the lower socioeconomic groups as with middle and upper classes. For those who have established clinics in ghetto areas and who have made contacts with youngsters there, it has often enough resulted in useful therapeutic work, and it is no exaggeration to say that many bona fide ghetto residents, as well as members of other minorities, can be helped very materially by existing methods.

But it is also true that many people who should be reached are never contacted, and that many who are reached are hard to work with within the conventional framework. There is urgent necessity for additional supports and adaptations of method to meet the unique needs in specific areas.

If we confine ourselves to the Negro ghetto, for example, we face the immediate problem that the black child requires a great deal of reinforcement of his sense of identity as a black. He needs to feel that his skin color is a respectable and positive part of his life, and that it is indeed the skin color of many important people, people in authority, people with responsibility, people who are looked up to. If a clinic is established in such an area, ideally the staff would have a goodly percentage of black top-level professionals. Since in fact the number of Negro psychiatrists, psychologists, and social workers is minute compared to the needs the country over, the clinic should strive to have a black as director. He, in turn, would be able to give that much more structure to the perceptual world of the black child, as well as be in a position to open some doors in the surrounding community that would not as readily permit access to a white.

Moreover, the clinic itself should have a board of directors either totally or largely composed of local residents—it should in a very fundamental sense be the community's own agency, accountable to the people it serves for its functioning and policies and deeply concerned about maintaining open lines of communication with its patients.

The difficulties that might arise from such a policy are likely to be in the area of personnel hiring and firing, and in maintaining proper clinical standards. There is no evading the possibility that conflicts in these areas can readily arise, and one has only the community's own self-interest to rely upon—the chances are that the people will want the best possible service for themselves and their children, and will defer to the clinicians about the competence of a particular person or the appropriateness of a given policy. But there is no guarantee that certain local conditions might not run strongly counter to a given clinician's judgment; e.g., if a board of directors insisted that someone competent and well trained be fired because he is a Jew, or someone unable to fill a certain role nonetheless be taken on because he is a local black, there might be some hard decisions thrust upon the staff of the agency. Nonetheless, the general policy of local control together with an ongoing active dialogue between clinician and community would seem to be the best approach.

The other side of the coin is that a clinician cannot and should not give up his responsibility and authority to be the one to make the clinical decision in the particular case. With all due regard for flexibility, he can never be entirely the creature of any community, be it blue-stocking or blue-collar. There is a body of competence and experience he brings with him, and this must always have a certain solidity and substantiality; there are things about which he must insist no matter what the community —or the administrator—or anybody else says. It is always a matter of judgment as to where to yield and where to stand firm; at times the distinctions may become rather nice.

The same principles would dictate the formation of agency arrangements anywhere, whether it be amid the taciturn people of a bleak Appalachian community or a Spanish-speaking Mexican-American group. These include: local involvement with meaningful representation, a considerable measure of local control, extensive use of indigenous people, plus active dialogue between clinician and community on many levels.

It may be that an entirely new pattern of therapeutic exchange would also have to develop, but this is certainly an open question. At this point, the stampede to find a totally new technology to work with deprived people has not borne fruit. It remains to be seen whether solid and sensitive clinical competence as we now know it cannot find a way to deal with the emotional problems of the individual, be he from whatever cultural subgroup. So far as we can see, the basic flexibility and adaptiveness of experienced clinicians has much more to offer the ghetto dweller or the Appalachian resident than any technique we know.

There is an altogether understandable rush for fads, fashions, and gimmicks, all dignified by noble titles like "innovative," "novel," and "creative." The field is certainly open-ended, and really helpful ideas would be welcomed by all. But the readiness to scrap all known methods and leap aboard this passing bandwagon or that is not in the best service of the many troubled people who need help; we need to temper our yearnings for dramatic breakthroughs, based on new ideas, by a steady application of methods which we know by experience can be helpful. What must be borne in mind is that the range of problems faced by the poor and the alienated is so great that the emotional difficulties cannot even be recognized for what they are until an immense range of material issues has been dealt with. It makes no sense to talk of phobia or impotence when the baby is at home sick, hungry, and uncared for in an unheated room in winter—but at the point that there is some action being taken to get heat, food, medical care, and a baby-sitter, the phobia and the impotence will still be there, and still need help.

On the other hand, the clinician faces his own problems in dealing with treatment issues. Often enough his own biases, his own likes and dislikes, his affinities and his aversions, his culture heroes, and his culture's villains can make for inner resistances and hazards in his address to his work. Many trainees tend to favor people like themselves, verbal people of similar educational background, people who look nice, smell nice, and act politely, people who accept the same value system to begin with and who understand something of the nature of the process with which they are getting involved. People who don't use words readily or freely, who tend to wait for questions to be asked to which they respond with monosyllables, and who understand treatment to mean one or two visits, some pills or advice, and that's it—such people pose major issues for certain clinicians. Yet, ultimately, this is no more than another clinical evaluation and decision: what can be best for this particular person at this time? If the nature of the character structure is such that pills and advice are all that the patient can use at this point, then that in fact is the correct evaluation and disposition. It meets the person's needs in a way he can use. It helps. Another person from the same background may look the same at first, yet have a latent capacity for verbalizing his feelings that needs only to be tapped. If this can be perceived, a very conventional kind of psychotherapy may develop and be most useful.

There are other difficult biases that clinicians have to deal with within themselves, such as racial prejudices, religious prejudices, or feelings about appearance. In a given clinic, the handling of the Negro applicant may be just a shade more impersonal, or the Jew or the Catholic treated a trifle more patronizingly, or the ugly girl passed over on the waiting list a great deal more easily than the pretty girl, and so on, for a variety of human biases, conscious and unconscious. There is no solution for these problems but an active and continuous self-scrutiny. The clinician must question his own motives and feelings about cases all the time—it is an occupational hazard of the profession—and there is no easy substitute for this as an ongoing part of clinical life. Here the role of good leadership can be crucial—this is a point at which the model, the example, the identification figure for the professional team, will have particular force. The biases can be positive as well as negative—too great an interest in a patient or client can be as destructive to treatment as too little—and there is an optimum level of involvement that the clinician strives always to maintain with the subjects of his work. Much of our training seeks primarily to inculcate the need for the means for doing this at all times. One can treat a person whom one likes a little, or dislikes a little. But it will not work to try to treat anyone when feelings of liking or disliking outweigh the commitment to the professional task.

PREVENTION

The prevention of emotional and behavioral disorders in later life is always a major interest of clinical work in childhood. Much of the urgency to treat the young stems from this specific goal—if one can deal with the issues at this early time, what a tremendous amount of grief and disability one could head off in the years ahead. A number of factors, however, combine to make this premise more uncertain than it might be.

To begin with, there seems to be a considerable bias on the part of parents, pediatricians, and nursery school teachers against "labeling" a preschool child as sick or in need of treatment. The constantly expressed wish-idea is that "he'll grow out of it." It is really dubious that many children grow out of anything—what one sees far more commonly than anyone's growing out of things is their growing into new versions of the old problems. In any case, there is a great reluctance to refer these younger children for treatment, even though to the clinician their symptoms might seem rather striking. For example, a child is seen at age four because ever since he began to talk at age two he would talk to no one but his own mother and father. The nursery school teacher, after one year, finally suggests referral for evaluation. The clinician makes a diagnosis of elective mutism, informs the parents that their child has a neurotic reaction of some proportions, and suggests child analysis or intensive therapy. The parents say they can't believe their child is that sick; they make determined efforts to get the youngster to mingle with other children, and indeed, with added pressure, in a few months he does begin to talk to others. The parents are enormously relieved, and in a later chance encounter with the evaluator, they describe this chain of events, adding that although he talks, their youngster is very shy and sensitive now. But, they conclude, they believe it is only a matter of time until he grows out of *that*.

The clinician hears this as an account of a symptom giving way to a character change. Under parental pressure the child gave up his restriction of speech only to replace it by a general character inhibition that to some extent affects all his relationships.

This is a common story, nor is the failure of the pediatrician to be the source of referral unusual. Sometimes pediatricians are not told of certain odd patterns of behavior that children display; more often the pediatrician's training has been woefully lacking in the dimension of psychiatric evaluation and treatment, and unless the disorder is of marked severity, he does not consider it as *needing* referral.

In any case, very many of the school-age children referred to clinics and private practitioners have been in trouble for four or five years by the time they are seen, and the mental health specialist dealing with an eight-year-old is actually faced with a chronic illness, a long-standing condition which he may be able to relieve, but which he cannot "cure." Where the nature of the problem stems from disruptive events in the first year or eighteen months of life, the profundity of the insult might make the attempt to come to grips with it years later a work of immense difficulty (hence the critical necessity of infant psychiatry to begin reparative work before the personality structures have rigidified and set along pathological lines).

Another factor that profoundly influences preventive efforts is the fact that children's personalities grow and change and that one aspect of this growth is the emergence of new vulnerabilities as well as new capacities at each new stage of development. The child relieved of a neurosis at age eight or nine still must encounter the rigors of puberty, of adolescence, and of the approach to adulthood, and a whole new confluence of forces will be at work at these later periods which might precipitate a renewed need for treatment. It seems safe to say that the situation might have been a great deal more serious at this later time had not the earlier therapy figured in the child's life. But the existence of an earlier experience with treatment is in fact no assurance against the possible appearance of new symptoms at a later date. What one can say is that treatment is helpful because it relieves pain, and that treatment is preventative to the extent that it can loosen up blocks and barriers to personality development and allow the child to navigate the difficulties of his particular point of arrest and grow along healthy lines for the remainder of that epoch of his life.

One of the major tasks of child-rearing and educating personnel (we include parents in this group) is to identify trouble when it appears and to get help for it. This is no less true in the grade school years than it was earlier. At this time, however, since most children are in a school, a made-to-order site for evaluating and recognizing pathology is available. This is a precious assist to the process of getting help for children in need or at risk, and many a youngster has finally found his way to proper care because the school recognized his difficulty and initiated a sequence of working with the parents and getting them to seek help. More often than not this is effective merely because a neutral observer has crystallized the suspicions and anxieties the parent has been warding off, by saying in so many words that something seems to be wrong. For many parents this is a shocking and painful experience, but it does break through the pattern of denial that may have hindered their freedom to act. It can then bring the child and family into a helping situation providing that the resources are available. Sometimes the resistance is so great that it requires a threat to eject the child from school before something is done.

It is during the early school years that patterns of mild mental retardation and minimal brain dysfunction are usually recognized. These are areas of considerable current research interest. It is not at all clear why mental health clinicians have tended to disregard or to avoid a concentrated focus on these particular problems in the past; this too might be a subject deserving study.

Minimal brain dysfunction, the current version of what was formerly termed "organicity," is only now settling down into a reasonably recognizable condition with characteristics and treatment methods that show consistency in the writings of different professionals. Mild mental retardation, on the other hand, was formerly considered a constitutional given and is only now coming clearly into view as the final common path of a variety of conditions. It can be the later form of an earlier psychosis, or the end product of cultural deprivation during the formative years, or the consequence of prenatal dietary deficiency or prematurity, and/or lack of appropriate amino acid intake in infancy, etc. In short, it is a condition which requires careful diagnostic evaluation. More than that, the presence of retardation rather typically exposes a child to failure, frustration, teasing, shunning, rejection, and exploiting which are bound to provoke many emotional problems in their own right. Thus, even where the retardation as such will not respond to therapeutic intervention the associated emotional pain can and should be helped. Here, collaboration with educators is a primary requirement for treatment, and the issue of adequate consultation and integration of services should be uppermost in the minds of the planners. The goal is one of constructing a way of life for handicapped children that is at once sheltered and enriched, with a primary focus on the individual child and his specific array of competencies and problems. It should be recognized that the disciplines of psychology and education have provided the workers in these vineyards for many decades; the psychiatrist must come to this area with a full recognition of what has been accomplished thus far against great odds, and with an effort to see how he might contribute usefully to the work of those who have cared for the retarded for so long.

There are a great many situations occurring in the lives of families which require careful handling if children's development is to be protected. Divorce, for example, is a common phenomenon in our society, and disputes over the custody of children are no rarity. The legal system has attempted to adapt to this by establishing a family court with some protection for the privacy of parties involved; it is desirable that professional consultation be included in such issues as a matter of course. Indeed, it would be well if parents who separate or who contemplate divorce could be encouraged (by courses on the subject given in high schools, by educational TV programs, by Sunday supplement writing, by proper training of lawyers and judges, etc.), to have at least one conference with a clinician in order to best deal with the impact of the experience on the children.

Again, the death of an important person such as a beloved grandparent, a sibling, or a parent is always a mental health crisis for a child, and some awareness of how to handle these matters needs to be communicated. What should a child be told about death, should he be taken to the funeral, and so on—many question arise. Clergymen need to be more carefully trained in these areas, since they are of such central importance at moments of bereavement and can be in the first rank of those available to help families.

Severe illnesses, whether affecting child, parent, or sibling, often need careful supportive work for the particular youngster: all the many factors that go into hospitalizing a child, or handling the fantasies about the hospitalization of a parent or a brother or sister—these should become foci of much conscious structuring.

One of the neatest paradigms for the essential nature of neurosis can be seen in the common observation of nursing staff on a pediatric ward; how often they will say: "The children are happy and contented with us —it's only when those parents come during the two-to-four visiting hour that you have any crying and acting up." What happens, of course, is that the child is filled with anxiety and grief about being sick, about being in a strange place, about being abandoned in the hands of strangers—but these feelings are kept out of the ongoing life except in the context of being with the parents, when the dam breaks and the emotions pour out. In effect the child develops a situational neurosis—he spares during most of his waking hours the anxiety and the depression by compressing the feelings into the one point in his life where the pain is felt most keenly, the contact with the parents. This in effect is what any neurosis does: it frees the person from symptoms except when the one symbolic situation arises—when he is in an elevator, or is on a height, or sees an animal— and then the anxiety strikes, or the obsessive thought begins, or the compulsive ritual must be carried out.

Such concepts can be made part of the understanding of the pediatric nursing staff, and the resultant changes in the attitudes toward both children and parents are likely to be very meaningful. There is an infinity of details of this sort that need to be brought into hospital practices for children. The need for recreational and educational activities, for adequate stimulation for the immobilized child with a severe burn, for example, for diversion and interesting craftwork for the more active child, for the chance to learn and be read to, for treats and entertainment, for a chance to talk and be comforted—all this is necessary for any child who is sick and separated from home. These elements of treatment planning are important not just because it makes us smile to see children happy. They are vital ingredients of treatment aimed at the corrosive impact of sickness-separation experiences on children's sense of trust and security, on their feelings of personal worth and body integrity, on their sense of mastery in an active way or helpless passivity in the face of overwhelming threat, on many facets of ego growth and character consolidation—in short, they are necessary if we are to minimize or prevent the adverse reactions and long-range changes that can come with traumatic experiences. They must therefore be prime considerations in our preventative-medical management of our youngsters.

TOWARD OPTIMAL GROWTH AND DEVELOPMENT

One of the difficulties is that all of us are essentially culture-bound—we know the ideal type of our particlar culture, or subculture, but who is to say that it is better or worse than some other? The clinician too, has his own in-group cultural set, and it might be worth specifying here. He believes in maturity—ego maturity, characterologic maturity, psychological maturity—as the measure of mental health and personal fulfillment. This is quite different from success in adaptation. Many highly neurotic people are very successful in certain adaptive ways; a man may make a lot of money, or wield a lot of power, or be loved by many women, and still be very infantile in many aspects of his overall emotional make-up. For the clinician, the task of helping a child achieve a truly mature character, relatively free from neurotic conflict, and utilizing all his ego potentials in a satisfying and pleasurable way, is the basic goal of child-rearing and child treatment.

Given the child's degree of ability to function in an age-appropriate way without obvious conflict, it becomes the function of the school and the community to supply the constant input of idealism and opportunity that healthy growth seems to require. Some means of supporting a child's values is necessary as one element in psychic nutrition; in an earlier day religion dealt with such issues; now this seems often to fall by the wayside. The superego is dependent on some support from without in most children's lives—and it is the confrontation with the negative ideals of the street plus the absence of positive value teaching at home that so often helps blight the development of the ghetto child.

The growth and enrichment of intellectual and sublimatory functions, the contribution made by the school, are by no means a mere addition of information to a child's life—they are a prime source of furthering personality development (or blocking it, if done badly) and fostering ego growth. Hence the school is of incalculable importance to the full elaboration of human potential and is the site for major research efforts in this area of optimization.

Educators are becoming ever more aware of the crucial quality of their impact upon development, and many, many new ideas are coming to the fore. Clinicians too are actively sorting out possibilities and making imaginative suggestions. Dr. Hyman Lippman, for example, has concerned himself with the plight of the great multitude of children who are not academically minded, some because they are dull and others because of the natural bent of their personality. They soon feel that school is boring, and that it shows them up as inadequate; the parents of many of these children are not academically oriented and are not concerned about how their children do at school. Could not such children have tasks presented to them in the first four grades that would be work to be done with one's hands? They could paint, draw, do woodwork, work with metals, play games, own small businesses, carry errands within the school settings, and do many other things. These would promote good work habits, improve memory, and offer gratification. They would not be denied reading, writing, and arithmetic, but these would be used for reading simple directions, writing out brief reports, working out ways of using a ruler and recording costs of materials, etc. The processes would have meaning because they connect with concrete goals. The youngsters could return to their homes stimulated, carrying tangible evidence of work and accomplishment, rather than notes asking the parents to see the teacher because of failure to learn and bad behavior. It could help get the parents to the school that is making their child happy and eager to attend, and the children would see the school as a good place and not as one that destroys their self-esteem. As they get into the fifth, sixth, and seventh grades, their good work habits might help them deal more successfully with the core subjects taught to other youngsters, or they could continue in nonacademic channels.

Junior High and High School

Much of the treatment of the troubled teen-ager has fallen to clinics and private practitioners, but the major unmet need in this area, and a major target for the recommendations of the Joint Commission, lies in the area of institutional care. It is no exaggeration to say that an enormous number of teen-agers pass into and out of state institutions each year, and instead of being helped, the vast majority are the worse for the experience. This is true for the average state training school or state industrial school or state farm for boys or girls; to a lesser extent it is true of the state hospitals in many areas.

The admission of teen-agers to the state hospitals has risen something like 150 percent in the last decade. The number of youngsters in the correctional institutions is also increasing. And few if any of these situations provide anything approaching adequate treatment or rehabilitation.

It is not usually recognized that the state training school (or whatever might be the local term for the institution for delinquents) is a "normal" part of ghetto life. A great many youngsters from deprived areas spend some very significant months in such establishments sometime during their growing up. To the extent that we would understand ghetto life, it is necessary to take a good long look at these institutions.

The usual picture is one of untrained people working with outmoded facilities within a framework of long-abandoned theory (when there is any consistent theory) attempting to deal with a wide variety of complex and seriously sick youngsters and producing results that are most easily measured by a recidivism rate that is often 30 to 50 percent and occasionally higher.

325

What we have, in effect, is a state of quiet emergency, unheralded and unsung, silently building up its rate of failure and disability, and seemingly allowed to go its way with an absolute minimum of attention from the public, the legislators, or the clinical professions. Nor is it difficult to understand why this state of affairs obtains—no one likes a delinquent youth, a bad actor, and when he is sent away the chief wish is just that, that he go "away." Out of sight. Out of mind. We have come past the point where we want only to punish him and make him pay for his depredations; there is at least lip service given to the wish to rehabilitate him. Indeed, the juvenile court was created largely for that very purpose. But the finances and the skills to implement this wish have not been forthcoming the country over, and with rare exceptions, these institutions for delinquents are, at best, of no help, and more often than not, destructive. The youngsters confined to them develop elaborate and sometimes bizarre peer societies in sheer self-defense against the inadequacy of the adult care and interest available. The heroes of this society are usually the most negative and antisocial individuals present, and the overall experience of the teen-ager passing through is then a thorough dunking in this bath of antisocietal hostility.

Having said this, we find it a sad commentary on our society that there are still many youngsters who could be helped in such faulty settings if they could only stay there long enough. Duration of stay is critical. Many inadequate environments could still do some good if they did no more than to provide an alternative to the youngster's home and the ambiance around that home. A bad institution in all too many cases is still better than a dreadful home. What happens to many a youth who is "sent away" is that despite the rigors of the new setting, he quiets down, he behaves himself, and presently he looks pretty good. Sometimes, of course, the improved adjustment is based on "conning" the punisher, covering up the pathology in the service of putting something over on the court and the institution and getting out quickly. More often, however, the youngster is simply in a far better situation than he has ever been before—the untrained and unsympathetic personnel are still kinder and more consistent than the alcoholic, sadistic, antisocial parents; the rough and ready peer life of the institutional cottage is less exploitative and less perilous than the street where the boy or girl came from; there is less stress, less danger, and less privation; and in a variety of ways, there is really a resultant improvement in adjustment. No sooner does that happen in two months, or six months, or nine months—and out she or he goes again, back to the same parents, the same street, and the same inevitable pattern of antisocial response. The swinging door continues to swing, and the character problems grind in more and more deeply. If the institution did no more than keep such youngsters for a long enough time, get them past the shoals of early adolescence into young manhood or young womanhood, it might still contribute immensely to their overall adjustment. But even that is lacking. The institution is inadequate to begin with, but even those youngsters whom it might help are not kept long enough, and so the average institutional program fails there too.

There is a great deal that can be done, that urgently needs to be done, for these settings. The need for intensive skilled clinical work with these many troubled youngsters is crying and urgent, and it is a first order of priority for the work of the Commission to turn Congressional attention toward this shameful and correctable condition.

State hospital programs for teen-agers, albeit less totally deprived than the boys' and girls' schools, are still seldom geared for the special needs of the adolescent population. Many youngsters are placed on adult wards, often a dubious business for them, without benefit of the special sports activities, education, supervision, and group experiences teen-agers need. The result is at best a partial treatment program, with many gaps left in what could be a major assist toward recovery from their illnesses.

The answer to both situations is the conversion of the existing facilities into residential treatment centers or combined residential and day-care centers, depending on the nature of the problems dealt with.

It is evident that we are developing a tradition the country over of converting institutions from one style of child care to another. A particularly frequent example has been the evolution of the orphanage that was once such a common aspect of the American scene. The true orphanage has almost ceased to exist in its original form; and in its place one now finds new establishments that strive to function as residential treatment centers. Another such conversion has taken place here and there in state hospitals. This, alas, is far less common, but there has been at least some tendency to take a unit, cottage, or ward and transform it from a chronic back ward to an adolescent program or a children's program in which some attempt is made to give active treatment. Unfortunately, very little indeed is heard about similar conversions of industrial schools or other institutions for delinquents.

The point at which such conversions come about is often when some long-established director retires. At this juncture, the board or governing agency feels free to look about for more progressive ways of doing things —quite commonly a survey is requested from a private or public body of experts, with instructions that they make recommendations. These duly forthcoming, the next step is usually to hunt about for a new director who will be able to implement the overall plan and the specific suggestions.

When he or she finally arrives, the usual state of affairs he encounters is a confused, frightened, often hostile staff, some of whom have been there many years and have firmly entrenched views and spheres of influence, and a physical plant that was never intended for the use that is now planned. Inevitably, there are dramatic days of change, mutiny, revolution, confrontation, dismissals, complaints, dismay, encouraging adaptations, help from unexpected quarters, betrayal from equally unexpected quarters, a split board, some hectic board meetings, and in time, major staff changes and a new therapeutically oriented program. Essentially, the task of the new director is to teach those who can be taught, get rid of those who can't change and learn, and add new professionals to the existing staff. As surely as fate, he finds that there is never enough money to get all the people he needs, never enough offices to house the people he does get, and too many children applying for the agency to give care to all who should have it. He admits a group of youngsters who are too sick, or act out too badly; there are incidents, someone is hurt, or there is a fire or a riot, he and his staff learn, and presently everyone is agitating for a new plant and better facilities. Often enough there is a happy ending: things grow and flourish, and after a couple of years a valuable new service is available for the children of that area. Sometimes catastrophe ensues: the forces opposing change are too strong, or the personality problems of the new director get in the way, or certain sources of money fail to come through, and the program fails, the director leaves, and things limp along in some totally inadequate way or close down entirely.

But this pattern of conversion of institutions, for better or for worse, is a major social tactic in our approach to the problems of children, and it needs to be studied, made more efficient, and practiced more widely the country over. There are many, many people working ineffectively in badly led institutions who can learn to do wonders if they are given some training and a sense of identity and direction by a good leader—but the impetus must come from the outside, ultimately, from the overall commitment of our entire culture toward helping our troubled young.

The pattern of care for those children who need institutionalization is taking the general form of the residential treatment center. This is true whether the agency is private or public, hospital or school. Where new centers are being planned, rather than or in addition to converting older institutions, certain general principles need to be borne in mind. By and large, the majority of youngsters in these institutions will need residential care for some period of time. Such centers need to be carefully dispersed to avoid bigness—50 to 80 youngsters are enough for any one institutional setting to handle—and the actual group living should be in units of 12 to 16. A typical structure would be a group of 5 to 8 cottages, with fewer youngsters per cottage if the overall number of units is greater. Boys and girls should be on the same campus or on adjacent campuses, and intensive treatment should be the basic approach to each resident along with active involvement of the family. This treatment begins in the milieu: every detail of the environment around the child, human and material, is planned for in therapeutic terms. A self-contained school, a group activities program, and some vocational possibilities are also necessary. Given these elements plus adequate therapists for individual and group treatment, it is reasonable to hope that a great many youngsters can be salvaged from the otherwise endless and hopeless treadmill that institutionalization for adolescents has become all over the United States.

Although this is the most glaring deficiency in the way we deal with the treatment needs of our youth, it is scarcely the only problem area. Many communities are seriously lacking in *any* of the necessary structures which therapy with adolescents requires. They might have a child guidance clinic, for example, but it takes youngsters only up to eleven or fourteen. For the older adolescent, even the relatively commonplace clinic service is lacking. And the outpatient clinic is only one of the whole sequence of necessary services. For example, the nature of adolescence is such that to meet its needs there must be a facility that will offer emergency service for the upset teen-ager at any time. This can be part of the child guidance clinic setup —but whatever its auspices, it must be known to the youth of the community as a place that you can go and get help whenever you need it. With adolescents minutes can count, as their high suicide, accident, and runaway rates show all too convincingly.

Backing this up there must be a whole array of services beginning with a group-living halfway house. This would be a sort of professionally run youth hostel, with provisions for long-time residents who would live there for an extended period in a sort of protected and supervised state of full community adjustment; at the same time the residence would include facilities for transients, for youngsters under pressure who could leave home for a night or two or a week or two if they must and find a haven under socially approved auspices, where they could also look for some contacts and help. Many an otherwise dangerous situation could be cooled down by a brief judicious intervention at the time of greatest tension. A skilled, objective person could be available to contact the family, and often enough, an adequate solution could be found. Currently, every major city has its quorum of youth-created resources of this sort, where teen-agers on the run seek whatever help they can find and where, ultimately, they take care of one another as best they can. Since the youngsters are running in any case, it would seem wiser to give them a socially created situation to run to where something could be done for them and for the constellation that caused the runaway in the first place. Left to their own devices, drugs, sexual difficulties, and social problems often follow. Every runaway youngster means a family in trouble; at the time of a first runaway it might mean a family peculiarly open to help.

We emphasize this type of adolescent-oriented facility because it is so conspicuously lacking in most communities. Needless to say, however, a great many adolescents and their families need long-term help as well as the above-described emergency services. The clinic and private practitioner type of resources continue to be necessary; they carry much of the burden of adolescent treatment today, and they will certainly have a vital role in this area in the future.

Protected work situations are necessary for many youngsters, where on-the-job training can give them a sense of career and direction and, for the sicker boys and girls, a day-care setup where work training, school, activities, therapy, group work, and in short, a total treatment program are all provided under one roof.

Community or city hospitals need to have a certain number of beds set aside for adolescents with emotional problems—the youngster with the wild hysterical outburst, the suicide attempt, the abrupt runaway, and many other kinds of emergency eruptions need sudden care, care *now*, and the facility to serve that need must be available.

To put it briefly, insofar as our mental health care is concerned, as a society we fail our teen-agers at almost every level.

PREVENTION

The best friend of the adolescent is the one who gives him a socially meaningful, idealistically connected, group-involved role to fill. The harness-ing of adolescent energy and idealism is a major task of any society—the integration of youth into ongoing creative social activity is a culture's best guarantor of growth and stability. Adolescents certainly need some distance from their homes and parents, but it is not at all the same thing as saying they need distance from their society. Where a society has no causes and no goals, or where its goals are dubious and its causes hypo-critical, then youth unrest is inevitable. The Peace Corps was one example of how young people could be brought to share in and further social goals, the "freedom riders" down south were another. The one was organized by the nation, the latter almost in spite of it. Youth is prone to "isms"—the problem becomes one of finding ongoing meaningful outlets for teen-age enthusiasm and commitment. This is not a clinical problem per se, but clinicians can usefully work with planners in considering such concerns. Given an acceptable and meaningful social role, it is likely that many of the healthier aspects of adolescent functioning will be maximized and the more morbid potentials kept at bay.

One of the more dramatic examples of such institutional help has been the Job Corps. Where such centers have functioned well, they have un-doubtedly been the salvation of many a young person who was otherwise inevitably bound for serious social difficulties. Some clinicians who have been in touch with such groups have been deeply impressed at the changes effected in otherwise "unreachable" youths. The combination of realistic tasks, meaningful opportunity, group participation, and positive *esprit de corps* seems to be universally serviceable to adolescents.

Nor must this process be confined to operations at a national level. Neighborhood youth projects and the work of roving leaders with indigenous groups have given concrete testimony to the capacity of many youngsters to share in and respond to such group-designed programs. While again not in itself a clinical issue, the involvement of clinicians in such operations has often been of major benefit to everyone. The mere act of making sense of hard-to-understand motivation, the recognition of the defensive component in many socially difficult attitudes, the understanding of how fear can conceal itself as arrogance or toughness or rage, and the ability to help a staff tolerate much behavior that would otherwise be insupportable are major factors in allowing such a program to continue.

When all is said and done, the relationships among an adolescent, his family, and his society are obviously an area requiring intensive research. The inner world of the teen-ager needs study, his use of social institutions and social roles as externalizations of or displacements from internalized familial conflicts is only vaguely understood, and the problem of determining the forces at work which lead to the different choices youngsters make is one of the major study horizons for clinicians and social scientists of all disciplines. It is clear that there must be a stepwise progression within the adolescent that brings him to grips with his society, but we don't know enough about it. What we do know is that within the process of acculturation, a great many issues arise. The major channel to social integration for the middle-class youth is college, whereas for the lower-class youth the high school diploma serves as his ticket of entrance to certain vocational training opportunities, labor union membership, civil service jobs, etc. Signs of failure and defeat in relationship to school are often the harbingers of serious troubles building up; the lower-class school dropout in high school is a person at risk and a signal for concerned intervention. By the same token many middle-class youths run into deep trouble their first year at college and need very active help indeed to cope with their difficulties. This condition is so common today that it literally assumes the proportions of an epidemic. Dr. Hyman Lippman has called these "suffering psychotic-like people who are not psychotic." High schools need close involvement with the network of community services available to teen-agers. The youngster who is doing badly, who is obviously at odds with schooling, and who is clearly on the way to dropping out as soon as it's legal should be reviewed by the teacher, counselor, and principal and have at least the opportunity for consulting with a professional in order to see what can be done to help with his dilemma. Many younger adolescents can use an older youth or young adult as a companion and model, and a prime role for paraprofessional workers thus emerges.

Keeping youngsters out of trouble involves a great deal of ingenuity and devoted activity—but it is well worth the effort.

Once they are in trouble with court involvement in the picture, another site for major preventative work opens up. The juvenile court is currently the focus of a great deal of criticism—the chances are that the combination of inadequate residential facilities for the more serious cases and insufficient day-care and outpatient services for the less disturbed youngster makes the courts' work a dubious business at best. Much can certainly be done with the limited clinical staff that might be attached to the court itself (often one lone psychologist and a couple of inadequately trained social workers who double as probation officers); the very existence of probation and the implied feeling of social control can help some youngsters and their families. But a very important opportunity for preventative work is usually lost at this point because of the sheer lack of facilities and personnel.

From society's point of view, a first court appearance should be considered quite a serious matter. In addition to being a red flag of trouble, it is also a very special opportunity—often enough it is a moment of major fluidity in the experiences of parent and child. For a brief time, they may all be very much open to influence, and intensive work done at this juncture might have more useful return than extensive work done at a later period.

TOWARD OPTIMAL GROWTH AND DEVELOPMENT

M. LaBarre (1969) observes that teen-agers constitute the largest and fastest-growing age group in our population. In 1960, there were 22 million people fourteen to nineteen years old: this figure has swelled each year; the estimate for 1970 was 40 million teen-agers! Public recognition of the creative and sublimatory efforts of this teen-age population needs enormous strengthening. A national poetry contest, a nationally sponsored magazine for publishing teen-agers' essays, stories, cartoons—with a largely teen-age editorial board evaluating the contributions—national leagues and contests for drag racers supported and sponsored by the government, national dance contests or combo band competitions, dramatic performances, a "mechanic-of-the-month" award, a chance to display crafts exhibits on tour, and other kinds of recognition for many forms of teen-age accomplishment could be built in without great difficulty. There is literally no end to the areas and kinds of recognition youngsters can be given for their positive and productive efforts. The Golden Gloves was once a major channel for young men to get somewhere, and sports are still a vitally important avenue of opportunity for many. The Westinghouse Science Search, the National Merit Scholarship Award, and many other such existing practices have shown how crucial such experiences can be for intellectually oriented youth; what we need now is to recognize and reward effort of all kinds and give our youngsters incentive to creative growth on a wide variety of fronts.

The kind and quality of youth participation in the ongoing life in the community, particularly in developing programs affecting other young people, is again a measure of the interest and motivation of the adults. There is much for young people to do—do they feel that they are asked to do anything, that their contribution is valued, that it has any impact on the real world? Our social planning needs to reorient itself to make room for an active and meaningful participation of the young in the total living of community life—to the extent that they are excluded they will develop their own eccentric community life rooted in nothing but adolescent protest and presently give everyone trouble, starting with themselves.

Appendix A

PSYCHOSOCIAL DISORDERS IN CHILDHOOD
AND ADOLESCENCE:
THEORETICAL CONSIDERATIONS AND
AN ATTEMPT AT CLASSIFICATION

by Dane G. Prugh, M.D.

"Come now and let us reason together."
—Isaiah 1:18

INTRODUCTION

During the course of the work of the Joint Commission, its Committees, and its Task Forces, various communications have energetically and incisively pointed out the limitations in our present conceptualizations regarding states of mental health and of mental and emotional disturbances in childhood and adolescence. Many have called for a bold new system of classification, comprehensible to workers with children from many disciplines and based upon concepts of psychosocial functioning and dysfunctioning. Few have chosen, however, to undertake more than a fleeting reference to observed levels of social or educational dysfunction. Most have rested, as has the Executive Committee, upon characterization of current classifications as "inadequate," while admitting that the approach to classification is "hazardous."

Among other available systems, the classification of the Group for the Advancement of Psychiatry (GAP)[1] of psychopathological disorders in childhood has rightfully been criticized for limiting itself to disturbances or deviations in personality development and psychopathology in the individual

1. Group for the Advancement of Psychiatry, *Psychopathological Disorders in Childhood: Theoretical Considerations and a Proposed Classification*, 2d printing, 1967 (New York: GAP, 1966).

334

child, while admittedly begging the more complicated questions of the child's functioning in the transactional systems of the family, the community, and a society as a whole. A courageous committee of the American Orthopsychiatric Association is indeed addressing itself currently to the complex psychosocial issues involved in classification of disorders in functioning, drawing upon a few attempts described in the literature as well as its own resourcefulness. Because of the enormity of the task, however, its report is unlikely to be formulated in time for use by the Joint Commission. The writer, having been involved in the GAP effort, recognizes, as did the others also involved, the validity and importance of a psychosocial approach to classification, and is constrained to offer the following scheme, admittedly tentative and exploratory, for consideration by members of the Clinical Issues Committee.

THEORETICAL CONSIDERATIONS

A truly sophisticated approach to this vital but elusive problem would call for an integration, at the least, of available theories of learning, personality development, family functioning, and, more broadly, the behavior of the individual in society. Such outstanding but diverse theoreticians as Piaget, N. Miller, H. Werner, Skinner, Luria, Bruner, and G. Gardner and his colleagues, to mention only a few, have addressed themselves to differing aspects of the developmental issues involved in the process of learning. Special treatment of individual questions has been offered, such as the importance of the interrelation between the self-concept and motility, as emphasized by Naville and Blom; the nature of infant perception by Fanz and others; the concept, put forth by Hendricks, of mastery of the environment as a separate instinctual drive; the inclusion of field considerations by Witkin, or the recognition of different cognitive styles of learning by a number of investigators.

Personality development and its vicissitudes have been examined by many capable persons holding quite disparate views. These include psychoanalytic workers, beginning with Sigmund and Anna Freud and followed by ego psychologists such as Hartmann, Rapaport, Erikson, L. Murphy, and Escalona; field theorists such as Lewin and Grinker; "open systems" theorists such as Allport, G. Murphy, and the "role theorists"; behavior theorists such as Skinner and Sears, and many others, among them those who emphasize the importance of inborn or temperamental qualities interacting with the environment, as do Chess, Birch, and Thomas, and those who, with Kallman, lay greatest emphasis upon hereditary factors.

Dynamic but differing concepts of family functioning have been offered by Lindemann, F. Kluckholm and Spiegel, Bell and Vogel, Jackson, and Lidz and his co-workers, among many others. Special subgroup operations within the family, including parent-child relationships, parental attitudes, and child-rearing techniques, have been scrutinized from various points of view by Levy; Havighurst; A. Johnson; W. Finzer; Sears, Maccoby, and Levin; Ausubel; Caldwell; and Douvan, to name but a few. The influences of society and culture upon child-rearing techniques, family functioning, and the mental health of the individual have been explored by anthropologists such as Mead, F. Kluck-

holm, Whiting, and Linton, and, from a different value orientation, by sociologists, including Parsons, Hollingshead, Simmons, Ross, and D. Reisman.
Special examination of the effects of poverty upon the development of children has been carried out by social scientists such as F. Reismann and O.
Lewis, as well as by workers from other fields, including Pavenstedt, M.
Deutsch and his colleagues, and Borowitz and Hirsch. The devastating impact
of racial discrimination, overlapping with poverty, upon children's development has been documented by a host of able individual investigators and, in
relation to violence, by groups such as that producing the *Report of the National Advisory Commission on Civil Disorders.*

Investigations of the behavior of small groups of persons by Bales, Hare,
and others have produced important implications for interactional or transactional theory. Theoretical and empirical contributions regarding the impact
of urbanization and industrialization upon individuals and groups are available
from the studies of social scientists, beginning with M. Weber and including
Faris and Dunham, Merton, and Opler, among others. Investigations of the
effects of a disintegrating community upon the individual's mental health, as
reported by Leighton, and studies of geographically shifting populations, of
social class transitions of families upward or downward, and of changes in
symptomatic pictures over historical epochs, offer additional theoretical views,
not to mention contributions to the understanding of the behavior of even
larger groups from the field of political science. Finally, general systems theory,
cybernetics theory, and communications theory have been applied by many
workers to many aspects of the behavior of individuals in society.

THE "MEDICAL MODEL"

The above sketchy and superficial listing of various theoretical approaches
serves only to point up the multiplicity and complexity of the issues, at a
variety of levels, which confront the individual or group who may attempt a
truly psychosocial classification. Perhaps it has been easier for some to attack,
admittedly with some justification, a narrow adherence on the part of certain
theorists to an analogy between psychological disorder and physical illness,
and for others to defend, also with a certain amount of justification, the
necessity of attention to biological factors in mental "illness," than it has been
for either group to face the bewildering complexity of what is probably nearest
the truth, or to see the partial truths in both of their approaches. Oversimpli-
fications such as "the little white clinic model" or "the little red schoolhouse
model" suggest a polarity in approaches which is probably not a real one.
They all too easily lend themselves to the development of unfortunately competitive professional hegemonies, sometimes related to available funds, which
can do little good for children.

It is true, as Blom (7) has pointed out, that the mental health professions
have generally tended to follow a clinical model, employing diagnostic and
treatment approaches to patients with problems in personality development
and addressing themselves to psychopathology and its consequences. Their
general expectation has been that, as patients improve with treatment, healthy

development and receptiveness to new experiences, such as learning, will follow "like the night the day." As now is clear, such may or may not occur. It is also true, as Blom further indicates, that the education and training professions have tended to follow a functional-competence model, based upon the approach to the development of various social, physical, academic, and cognitive skills. Thus they have felt dissatisfied with the lack of help in education or in management of the child offered by the clinician, with his generally limited knowledge of the child's environments other than the family.

The emerging psychoeducational approach in day treatment settings, the development of special educational diagnostic and remedial techniques which transcend diagnostic categories, and the recently available training of mental health professionals in offering help to teachers around problems in classroom management offer avenues for a new type of future collaboration. These can avoid an "either-or" approach, and may offer possibilities for classification of psychosocial disorders of children which can be mutually understood and employed effectively by both educators and clinicians, as well as other professions.

Other misunderstandings and miscommunications have arisen around the concept of the "medical model," even within subgroups among the individual clinical professions, where it may at times be used as a rallying point. For example, the criticisms of Szasz (50) regarding certain aspects of the management of mentally "ill" patients in mental hospitals, as carried out in the past, are cogent and relevant, if provocative and sometimes overdrawn. Such sophisticated clinicians as Turner and Cumming (52) can be driven to say, however, in a 1967 publication, that the "medical model" (largely derived from psychoanalysis, with contributions from many nonmedical analysts) accepts the notion "that personality can be understood as a relatively closed and mechanical system." It is true that some of Freud's analogies, drawn from the biomechanistic and Newtonian scientific concepts of his time, partake of this character; the fact is often overlooked, however, that they were analogies or metaphors, recognized as such by Freud, though not perhaps by some of his disciples.

Nevertheless, individuals who can quite appropriately laud Allport's (2) emphasis in 1960 upon the acceptance of "open systems" as a prerequisite for modern mental health theory, as well as White's 1959 (55) concept of "competence" and "effectance motivation," based on the importance of skills, and yet can still see the "medical model" as a wholly negative, tension-releasing, compensatory model, based on drive gratification, the frustration-conflict axis, and an exclusively defensive orientation, have not laid sufficient emphasis upon certain theoretical developments in the latter field, at least along the "cutting edge." Although many early psychoanalytic formulations did have such a character, Hartmann's discussion of the importance of positive adaptation and his concept of a "conflict-free" portion of the ego was first put forward in 1939 (though unfortunately not translated from German into English by Rapaport until 1958). Hendrick's proposal of an "instinct for mastery" was published in 1942, the same year that Schilder laid emphasis upon interest, action, and experimentation. Erikson's "search for identity" was crystallized fully in 1950, but his earlier writings reflect a trend toward something more positive and supracompensatory than "homeostasis."

In relation to the biological aspects of emotional and mental disorders, which cannot be ignored, it is important to note that the "open system" concept had been available, implicitly at least, since the psychobiologic emphasis of Adolf Meyer (35) in 1915. It was elaborated with increasing sophistication in the 1950's by such psychosomatic and psychosocial theorists as Romano (45), Mirsky (36), Engel (18), Richmond (43), Green (23), and Lindemann (34), and applied, with transactional and sociologic theory, to family behavior in 1954 by Kluckholm and Spiegel (29). Contributions to the understanding of the relationship between "human ecology" and states of health or disorder were offered in the late 1950's by Corwin (14) and Hinkle and Wolff (28), among others. In 1959, Grinker (25) essayed a "unitary theory of human behavior," drawing upon field theory and systems theory in dealing with physiological, psychological, and social levels of human behavior. Engel's (18) articulation in 1960 of a "unified concept of health and disease," based on his and Romano's earlier work, tied together many theoretical contributions from physiology, psychophysiology, dynamic psychology, ethology, the social sciences, and other fields. Such concepts were discussed in relation to children, in the context of developmental theory, by Prugh (41) in 1963, and were further elaborated in the theoretical introduction to the GAP-proposed classification of psychopathological disorders in 1966.

In this view, *there can be no strictly "medical" model*, but rather a "psycho-physio-social" one, shared by a number of disciplines. Other criticisms refer, often rightly, to problems in the pattern of delivery of services. Even so, in the recent rush toward action, it is often forgotten that the idea of "crisis intervention" was first put forth in 1944 by Erich Lindemann, a psychoanalyst who undertook in the late 1940's the first community mental health survey and program, and that Healey and Bronner, originators of the child guidance approach, stood alone in the community in 1909 in dealing with delinquent children. The writer happens to believe that many things still need changing in the medical approach to mental and emotional disorders, and feels that criticism of certain psychiatric and medical psychoanalytic professional activities, though at times painful, has been growth-promoting to the professions (with further growth still to come, as, for example, in relation to the need for some to recognize, with Freud, that psychotherapy and psychoanalysis are not the exclusive province of physicians). At the same time, it is possible that Augean stables may still need cleaning in some other professions as well.

This cursory review of conceptual developments tends only to underwrite *the increasingly constructive convergence of streams of thought from a variety of disciplines.* This convergence was emphasized, among other ways, by the use of the word "disorder" by the GAP committee. The writer believes that such developments should lead to increasing cooperation and harmony, rather than conflict, among the various disciplines who must work together positively to promote the mental health of children. At this time a classification of psychosocial disorders, based upon an explicit definition of terms (nomenclature) related to the functioning of the child in the family and transcending (while encompassing) "personality diagnosis," is vital in order to enable a wide variety of professional persons to communicate effectively, to make possible the collection of comparable "disorder-relevant" (17) data for research purposes, including epidemiological investigations, and to aid persons from various disciplines in the earlier recognition, prevention, or treatment of such disorders.

PSYCHOSOCIAL CONSIDERATIONS REGARDING PERSONALITY DEVELOPMENT AND FUNCTIONING IN THE CHILD AND ADOLESCENT

As was pointed out in the introduction to the GAP report, three propositions must be taken into account in any theory of personality development and its vicissitudes: (1) the *psychosomatic concept*, involving the unity of intrapsychic processes (mind) and bodily functions; (2) the *developmental dimension*, dealing with the interaction of maturation and experience (resulting in learning) and including the "epigenetic" concept; and (3) the *psychosocial* proposition, including parent-child and other diadic relationships within the family, other family subgroup operations, and other characteristics of the family as a small group (leadership and communication patterns, cohesiveness, value orientations, etc.), as well as other aspects of the transactions among individual, family, and external society.

In a narrower, descriptive sense, four dimensions of personality development can be identified: *physical, intellectual, emotional* (affective), and *social*. Using a general systems theory approach, these can be reduced to *three major systems*, with various subsystems: (1) *physiological*, involving molecules, cells, tissues, organs, and organ systems; (2) *psychological* (intellectual and affective), involving perceptual-motor processes, cognitive functions, self-concepts, and thoughts, fantasies, memories, or emotions registered by the perceptual systems; and (3) *social* or interpersonal, involving relationships with key persons (especially caretaking figures) and transactions with the family and community, as well as sociocultural influences from region, state, nation, and society. Interrelationships among these "open systems" (or *levels of organization* of the human organism) operate at "nodal" points, coordinated by the "central regulating system" (brain and mental apparatus) and the neuroendocrine system, with the psychophysiologic mechanisms fairly well understood at the present time.

Concepts of health and illness or of function and dysfunction in children differ somewhat from those applicable to adults, depending upon the child's capacities at a particular stage of development, the current nature of the family transactional operations, and other factors. Nevertheless, the concept of *adaptation* to the environment (or of effective coping, mastery, or psychosocial functioning) is central in relation to both children and adults. In the modern *unitary theory of health and illness* (18, 41), health and "dis-ease" are considered "phases of life." Health represents the phase of positive adaptation by the human organism and, in the child, the phase of growth and development. In this phase, the child is able to master his environment and himself, within stage-appropriate limits, to learn effectively, and is reasonably free from pain, disability, or limitations in social capacities. Illness or dysfunction represents the phase of failure in adaptation or of breakdown in the attempts of the organism to maintain an adaptive equilibrium or the "dynamic steady state" (at any one moment in the forward development of the particular child).

Stressful stimuli of physical, psychological, or social nature may impinge upon the individual, producing dysfunction, "illness," or adaptive breakdown when operating quantitatively or qualitatively in sufficient degree. *Stressful stimuli are relative—not absolute—however.* The nature and degree of any noxious stimulus at any particular time are determined by *hereditary, constitutional, developmental, and experiential* factors. Thus the child's *"adaptive capacity"* (capacity for psychosocial functioning) is influenced by his own innate characteristics, as well as by his past experience, the reactions of key persons, and within broad limits, the degree of noxious influence of the current stimulus (including its specific meaning to himself at his developmental level and to his family or the community). Significantly stressful stimuli may initially come into play at physiological, psychological, or social levels of organization, with reverberations taking place in systems other than the one originally affected. *States of "illness" or "dysfunction" may thus assume predominantly physical, psychological, or social characteristics,* depending upon the point of initial impingement of the particular stressful stimuli, the adaptive capacity of the child in his family, and the nature of the reverberations "up" or "down" the intercommunicating open system. *Multiple etiologic or "shaping" forces,* of *predisposing, precipitating, contributory,* and *perpetuating* nature, are thus involved in the production of any state of dysfunction in the child. The *balance of internal and external forces* helps to determine the adaptive outcome, as does the *degree of vulnerability* of the child's particular developmental phase ("critical periods") or situation.

The *definition of states of psychosocial dysfunction* is thus to some extent an arbitrary one, depending not only upon the *level of organization* in the child most prominently involved, the *situational factors,* and the adaptive outcome but *also upon the segment of experience with the child by the evaluating adult.* A certain *cultural and historical relativity* are also involved in the definition of states of dysfunction (or indeed in the definition of maturity, the goal of development, which may vary from culture to culture or from point to point in historical time). As implied earlier, *sociocultural forces* may play a role in the shaping of personality characteristics, and in the production of disturbances in function of individuals, as the result of poverty or discrimination, the movements of ethnic groups, the disintegration of communities, the transition of the family from lower- to middle-class socioeconomic status, or other factors. *Variations in the degree of tolerance (or even encouragement) of "sick" or deviant behavior or dysfunction,* as it is regarded by the majority group, may also occur among subcultural groups, in addition to differences in definition.

From this point of view, psychosocial dysfunction in the child can be said to include marked behavioral *regression* to more safely established levels of adaptation in the face of stressful stimuli; *fixation* at a particular level in different dimensions of development; a significant developmental *lag,* a serious *retardation,* or a blunting or *distortion* in one or another aspect of personality development; *limitation in function* at physical, psychological, or social levels, or *adaptive breakdown,* as in overwhelming physical illness, severe emotional disturbance, or mental disorder. All of these can be said to produce some degree of *social dysfunction,* although the degree may vary and may not correlate with the psychiatric diagnostic category (e.g., adolescent suicides). *Some disorders in social function, bearing on the relationship between the individual and his community, may not fall within the traditional range of mental and emotional disorders.* This is beginning to be recognized, as in the American Psychiatric Association's Diagnostic and Statistical Manual of Mental Disorders (2d edition), which includes other "social disorders" without psychiatric illness, and in the GAP classification of "sociosyntonic" disorders. However, *the perception of particular components of dysfunction may vary,* from the physician who has traditionally looked at the child's level of physical competence, the psychiatrist or psychologist who observes his psychological and psychophysiologic capacities, the educator who sees his difficulties in academic functioning, or the welfare worker or probation officer who is confronted with the child's problems in social adaptation. Thus the *"diagnosis" of psychosocial dysfunction today must include elements of educational and social evaluation, offered by appropriate professional persons, in addition to the study of physical and psychological factors provided by physicians and mental health clinicians.*

As implied by the unitary theory mentioned earlier, in considering etiologic or shaping forces which act to promote healthy development or to produce deviations, distortions, adaptive limitation, or breakdown at one or another level of organization, no one overriding position regarding any one set of factors—physical, psychological, or social (innate or experiential)—can be taken. Hereditary tendencies; individual differences at birth; temperamental or other constitutional factors; disturbed parent-child relationships; negative feedback or "fit" between child and parents; parent-child conflict; "localized neurotic interaction"; inadequate "parent development"; physical illness or handicap; unhealthy family functioning (disturbances in family interpersonal adaptive equilibrium or in "family development"), or socioeconomic or other social forces may be predominantly involved. More commonly, a number of these factors may operate in some combination to produce psychosocial dysfunction or ineffective coping or adaptation.

In addition, no one theory of personality development currently available can be employed to the exclusion of all others. As mentioned earlier, contributions to our knowledge regarding personality development have come from many sources. Three main theoretical streams include: psychoanalytic theory, learning theory, and field theory. No one of these has total explanatory power, although psychoanalytic theory tries to be as all-inclusive as possible. As modern psychoanalytic ego psychology has broadened to include cognitive functions and "autonomous" and other ego functions, it has moved closer to sophisticated learning theory with its assumption of motivation and the principles of reinforcement involved in operant conditioning, as well as field theory, with its implications for the social sciences.

PROPOSED CONCEPTUAL FRAMEWORK

It is the belief of this writer that the broadest and most helpful view of personality development available today is the psychosocial scheme of Erikson (19). His conception of psychosocial tasks in development involves the need for solution by the child of psychosocial conflicts which are characteristic of each phase. These must be resolved by the child with the help of parents and later figures within his expanding "social radius," permitting "problem resolution" and the passage through a "developmental crisis" to the next developmental stage. The crystallization of certain "value orientations" is possible at different stages, with the relative emphasis on each of these influenced in part by familial, sociocultural, and other interpersonal forces. This view allows for the existence of mutually reciprocal, "interreactional," transactional, or feedback systems between parent and child, with the characteristics of each simultaneously influencing the other, beginning with the first feeding experience. Since Erikson regards personality development as continuing throughout adult life, his approach lends support to the idea that a "fit" is needed between continued parental solutions to later psychosocial tasks and the child's developing social needs. It also is in harmony with G. Bibring's concept of pregnancy as a "maturational task" and with that of Benedek regarding parenthood as a "developmental phase."

Into Erikson's "house of many mansions" thus can fit various types of learning theory, including operant conditioning; Piaget's and other concepts regarding intellectual development; cybernetic theory; small group and family theory; sociocultural theories; field theory; systems theory; and communications theory, not to mention the more classical theory of psychosexual development derived from Sigmund Freud, and Anna Freud's recent elaboration of "developmental lines." Correlations between such psychological and social dimensions and that of physical growth and development, particularly the development of the central nervous system, are evident. The concept of heightened vulnerability of the child during a developmental "crisis"—"openness" to forward leaps or to ego damage—corresponds well with the "critical periods" of ethological theory.

In particular, Erikson's scheme embraces comfortably the concepts of self-actualization and of social competence, as put forth by White and others. The latter assumes the existence of independent ego energies, implied by Hartmann's earlier concepts, and of a "maturational thrust" (comparable to the "built-in time table" of physical growth and development) in the child toward the achievement of social competence or mastery. It also adds a "sense of efficacy" to Erikson's developmental tasks. This approach is based on an estimation of skills and strengths in the child or of potentialities for these in various dimensions of personality development. In terms of psychoanalytic theory, it assumes, among other things, that "skills are to the executive portion of the ego what defense mechanisms are to the synthetic portion" (16). This view does not do away with tension-reduction; rather it transcends it. With Allport, it tends to go "beyond steady states and to strive for an enhancement and elaboration of internal order, even at the cost of considerable disequilibrium" (2).

Finally the broad concepts and categories proposed by Erikson are comprehensible and congenial to persons from a wide variety of disciplines, from the mental health professions through education and pediatrics to welfare workers and probation officers, as the writer has occasion to know. Put into lucid prose such as that employed by Witmer and Kotinsky (56) in their beautifully cogent and condensed summary of the proceedings of the 1950 White House Conference, at which Erikson presented his paper "Growth and Crises in the Healthy Personality," his concepts, and many of those others which attach themselves so easily to them, can also come through with compelling power to nontraditional professionals, parents, and the average citizen as well.

AN ATTEMPT AT A PSYCHOSOCIAL CLASSIFICATION

In a hasty and incomplete review of the literature, a number of attempts at classification on the basis of "social functioning" have been reported in work with adults. One of the earliest was the estimation of the "degree of psychiatric impairment" included in the *Diagnostic and Statistical Manual*, published as a supplement to the *Standard Nomenclature*, by the American Psychiatric Association in 1952. This, as in the case of the form used recently by the New York State Department of Mental Hygiene and the "degree of impairment" in the capacity for development, play, learning, socialization, etc., in the GAP classification for children, represents simply a reminder that such impairment should be evaluated, and that it may not correspond with the psychopathological diagnosis (e.g., relatively limited impairment with certain mild, chronic psychotic disorders).

More formal attempts at rating the degree of disability or impairment in functioning, somewhat similar to the ratings of physical impairment by the New York Heart Association and the Commission on Chronic Illness, have been offered recently by Katz et al. (32), Spitzer et al. (49), Thorne (51), Zigler and Phillips (57), and Hetznecker et al. (27). These draw upon rating scales of recorded interviews, questionnaires, and clinical observations. Methodological problems remain (21), however, relating to problems in judgment (8, 13), and to differing perception by different disciplines (12), among other factors. A "community adaptation schedule," with systematized rating scales for evaluating the integration of individual adults into the community, has recently been put forth (44). Descriptions of a "social breakdown syndrome" and an "inadequacy syndrome" have been offered by Gruenberg (26) and Cumming (15), respectively.

In the field of childhood and adolescence, much less systematic work has been done, partly because of difficulties raised by age differences, developmental changes, etc. In addition to the rating by IQ of the American Association on Mental Deficiency (and the rough estimates of the social functioning of retarded children by workers in England), a "vulnerability index" for infants (37) and a "deviant behavior inventory" for school-age boys (6) are available, as well as the GAP symptom list for children of all ages, but these

APPENDIX A

DIMENSIONS OF PERSONALITY DEVELOPMENT
Physical, Psychological, Social
SCHEMATIC REPRESENTATION *

PERIOD	AGE	PSYCHOSOCIAL TASKS (Crises)	PSYCHOSEXUAL STAGES	RADIUS OF SIGNIFICANT RELATIONS	CENTRAL VALUE ORIENTATION	STAGES OF INTELLECTUAL DEVELOPMENT
	Birth					**Sensory-Motor**
INFANCY	3 mo.	Trust vs. Mistrust (I am what I am given)	Oral-Respiratory Sensory-Kinesthetic (Incorporative Modes)	Maternal Person	Hope	The infant moves from a neo-natal reflex level of complete self-world undifferentiation to a relatively coherent organization of sensory-motor actions. He learns that certain actions have specific effects upon the environment. Minimal symbolic activity is involved. Recognition of the constancy of external objects and primitive internal representation of the world begins.
	6 mo.					
	9 mo.					
	1 YR					
	18 mo.	Autonomy vs. Shame, Doubt (I am what I "will")	Anal-Urethral Muscular (Retentive-Eliminative Modes)	Parental Persons	Will	
	2 YR					
PRESCHOOL	3 YR	Initiative vs. Guilt (I am what I imagine I can be)	Genital Locomotor (Oedipal) (Intrusive, Inclusive Modes)	Basic Family	Purpose	**Preoperational Thought** (Prelogical)
	4 YR					The child makes his first relatively unorganized and fumbling attempts to come to grips with the new and strange world of symbols. Thinking tends to be egocentric and intuitive. Conclusions are based on what he feels or what he would like to believe.
	5 YR					
	6 YR			Neighborhood, School		

Concrete Operational Thought

Conceptual organization takes on stability and coherence. The child begins to appear rational and well organized in his adaptations. The fairly stable and orderly conceptual framework is systematically brought to bear on the world of objects around him. Physical quantities, such as weight and volume, are now viewed as constant despite changes in shape and size.

Formal Operational Thought

The individual can now deal effectively not only with the reality before him but also with the world of the abstract, propositional statements and the world of possibility ("as if"). Cognition is of the adult type. The adolescent uses deductive reasoning and has the ability to evaluate the logic and quality of his own thinking. His increased abstract powers provide him with the capacity to deal with laws and principles. Although egocentrism is still evident at times, important idealistic attitudes are developing in the late adolescent and young adult.

					Virtue
SCHOOL AGE	7 YR	Industry vs. Inferiority (I am what I learn)			
	8 YR		"Latency"		Skill
	9 YR				
	10 YR				
ADOLESCENCE	11 YR		Puberty	Peer In-Groups and Out-Groups	
	12 YR				
	13 YR	Identity vs. Identity Diffusion (I know who I am)	Early Adolescence	Adult Models of Leadership	
	14 YR				
	15 YR		Middle Adolescence		Fidelity
	16 YR				
	17 YR		Late Adolescence		
	18 YR				
EARLY ADULTHOOD		Intimacy vs. Isolation	Adulthood (Genitality)	Partners in Friendship. Sex Competition, Cooperation	Love
MIDDLE ADULTHOOD		Generativity vs. Self-Absorption or Stagnation	Maturity	Divided Labor and Shared Household	Care
LATE ADULTHOOD			Menopause Male Climacteric		
		Integrity vs. Despair, Disgust	Senescence	"Mankind" "My Kind"	Wisdom

* The writer wishes to acknowledge the help of Anthony Kisley, M.D. in the preparation of this chart.

345

PERIOD	AGE	PHYSICAL GROWTH	DEVELOPMENTAL STEPS (LINES)	DEVELOPMENTAL PROBLEMS
INFANCY	Birth	RAPID (SKELETAL)	"Normal Autism" (0-3 mo.) Anticipation of feeding	Birth defects Feeding disorders: colic, regurgitation, vomiting, rumination, failure to thrive, marasmus, pylorospasm, feeding refusal, atopic exema
	3 mo	Muscle constitutes 25% total body weight		
	6 mo.	Aeration maxillary and ethmoid sinuses	Symbiosis (4-18 mo.) Stranger anxiety (6-10 mo.)	Extreme stranger anxiety Early infantile autism
	9 mo.	Eruption of deciduous central incisors (5-10 mo.)	Separation individuation (8-24 mo.)	
	1 YR	Anterior fontanel closes (10-14 mo.)	Separation individuation (12-28 mo.) Self-feeding	Physiologic anorexia Sleep disturbances: resistance or response to over-stimulation Extreme separation anxiety Interactional psychotic disorder Bronchial asthma Pica
		Eruption of deciduous first molars (11-18 mo.)	Oppositional behavior Messiness Exploratory behavior	
	2 YR	Increase in lymphoid tissue	Parallel play Pleasure in looking at or being looked at Beginning self-concept	Teeth grinding Pseudo-retardation Temper tantrums, negativism Toilet training disturbances: constipation, diarrhea Excessive feeding Bedtime and toilet rituals Speech disorders: delayed, elective mutism, stuttering
PRESCHOOL	3 YR	SLOWER (SKELETAL) Deciduous teeth calcified	Orderliness Disgust Curiosity Masturbation Cooperative play Fantasy play Imaginary companions	Petit mal seizures Nightmares, night terrors Extreme separation anxiety Excessive thumb sucking Phobias and marked fears Developmental deviations: lags and accelerations in motor, sensory, and affective development Food rituals and fads
	4 YR	RAPID (SKELETAL)	Task completion Rivalry with parents of same sex	Sleepwalking School phobias
	5 YR		Games and rules	
	6 YR	Eruption of permanent first molars (5½-7 yrs.) Eruption of permanent central incisors (6-8 yrs.)	Problem-solving Achievement Voluntary hygiene Competes with partners	Developmental deviations: lags and accelerations in cognitive functions, psychosexual, and integrative development Tics Psychoneuroses Enuresis, soiling and excessive masturbation Schizophreniform psychotic disorder
		SLOWEST (SKELETAL)		

346

Stage	Age	Physical Development	Psychosocial Development	Disorders
SCHOOL AGE	7 YR	Frontal sinuses develop		
	8 YR	Cranial sutures ossified	Hobbies Ritualistic play	Nail-biting Learning problems Psychophysiologic disorders
	9 YR	Uterus begins to grow	Rational attitudes about foods Companionship Invests in: community leaders, teachers, impersonal ideals	Personality disorders: compulsive, hysterical, anxious, overly dependent, oppositional, overly inhibited, overly independent, isolated and mistrustful personality, tension discharge disorders, sociosyntonic personality disorders, and sexual deviations Pre-delinquent patterns
	10 YR	Budding of nipples in girls Increased vascularity of penis and scrotum		
	11 YR			
ADOLESCENCE	12 YR	Pubic hair appears in girls SPURT (SKELETAL) (Girls 1½ yrs. ahead)		Legal delinquency Anorexia nervosa Dysmenorrhea Sexual promiscuity Excessive masturbation Pseudopsychotic regressions Suicidal attempts Acute confusional state
	13 YR	Pubic hair appears in boys Rapid growth of testes and penis	"Revolt"	
	14 YR	Axillary hair starts	Loosens tie to family Cliques	
	15 YR	Down on upper lip appears Voice changes	Responsible independence Work habits solidifying	
	16 YR	Mature spermatozoa (11–17)		
	17 YR	Acne in girls may appear	Heterosexual interests	
	18 YR	Acne in boys may appear Cessation of skeletal growth Involution of lymphoid tissue Muscle constitutes 43% total body weight. Permanent teeth calcified Eruption of permanent third molars (17–30 yrs.)	Recreational activities Preparation for occupational choice Occupational commitment	Schizophrenic disorders (adult type)
EARLY ADULTHOOD			Elaboration of recreational outlets Marriage readiness Parenthood readiness	Affective disorders: manic-depressive psychoses
MIDDLE ADULTHOOD				Involutional reactions: depression, suicide
LATE ADULTHOOD				Senile disorders: chronic brain syndromes, etc.

347

PERIOD	AGE	ADAPTIVE MECHANISMS	EEG DEVELOPMENT	CNS MATURATION	DEVELOPMENTAL LANDMARKS
INFANCY	Birth		Neonate: Low amplitude and polyrhythmic 4-6 and 6-8 cycles per second appear	Brain weight: 350 grams; Level of neural function: sub-cortical; Transitory reflexes present (i.e.,moro,sucking,grasp,TNR)	Social smile (2 mo.); 180° visual pursuit (2 mo.)
	3 mo.				Reaches for objects (4 mo.); Rolls over (5 mo.)
	6 mo.	Incorporation; Imitation; Denial; Avoidance	Spontaneous K complexes appear (evidence of cortical response to stimulation)	Brain weight: 600 grams; Brain stem in advanced or complete state of myelination; Transitory reflexes disappear.	Raking grasp (7 mo.); Crude purposeful release (9 mo.); Inferior pincer grasp (10 mo.)
	9 mo. 1 YR	Regression		Brain weight: 900 grams; Cranial nerve myelination complete	Walks unassisted (10-14 mo.); Words: 3-4 (13 mo.)
PRESCHOOL	18 mo.	Withdrawal; Inhibition; Displacement; Projection	Subalpha 5-8 cycles per second become more evident; Anterior fast activity disappears; Alpha development more dominant	Progressive integration of sub-cortical and cortical areas; Babinski reflex extinguished; Bowel and bladder nerves myelinated	Builds tower of 2 cubes (15 mo.); Scribbles with crayon (18 mo.); Words: 10 (18 mo.); Builds tower of 5-6 cubes (21 mo.)
	2 YR	Undoing	Irregularities in rhythms and distortions in waves give EEG "abnormal look."	Brain weight: 1000 grams; Spinal cord and cerebellum myelination complete	Uses 3 word sentences (30 mo.); Names 6 body parts (30 mo.); Uses appropriate personal pronouns, i.e. I, you, me (30 mo.)
	3 YR	Suppression; Acting out in play and fantasy	Sleep spindles may appear "spikelike." Drowsy record may show slowing paroxysms. Distorted sleep patterns can appear.		Rides tricycle (36 mo.); Copies circle (36 mo.); Matches 4 colors (36 mo.); Talks of self and others (42 mo.); Takes turns (42 mo.); Tandem walks (42 mo.)
SCHOOL AGE	4 YR	Repression		Beginning single finger localization	Copies cross (48 mo.); Throws ball overhand (48 mo.)
	5 YR	Identification	14-6 per second positive spikes start to appear.	Beginning right-left orientation; Cerebrum myelination complete; Level of neural function:cortical	Copies square (54 mo.); Copies triangle (60 mo.); Ties knots in string
	6 YR	Isolation; Pseudo-compulsions in thought, play; Turning of emotions into the opposite; Reaction formation; Sublimation	Transient disorganization of awake and sleep tracings is common.	Body image solidifying	
	7 YR				Prints name; Ties shoelaces; Simple functional similarities; Rides two-wheel bike; Copies diamond; Simple opposite analogies; Names days of week
	8 YR			Cerebral dominance evident (laterality)	Repeats 5 digits forward; Can define brave and nonsense

Age	Defense Mechanisms	Physiological	Cognitive
9 YR			Knows seasons of the year Able to rhyme
10 YR	Rationalization	Increase in alpha voltage and regularity Brain weight: 1300-1400 grams (adult size)	Repeats 4 digits in reverse Understands: pity, grief, surprise Difficult functional similarities
11 YR			Knows where sun sets Can define nitrogen, microscope, shilling Knows why oil floats on water Can divide 72 by 4 without pencil and paper Abstract similarities Comprehends belfrey and espionage Knows meaning of C.O.D. Can repeat 6 digits forward and 5 digits in reverse
12 YR	Intellectualization	(Growth in thickness of myelin sheaths continues for life)	
13 YR	Regressions		
14 YR	Asceticism	14+6 per second positive spikes begin to disappear	
15 YR			
16 YR		Gradual evolution of stable adult patterns at all levels of consciousness	
17 YR			
18 YR			

349

are not standardized. Some systematic observations of sex and age differences in symptom patterns of preschool children have been reported (5), as have fears in children at different ages. A developmental typology of disadvantaged four-year-olds has been described (9), as have other typologies based on factor analysis of symptoms of children seen in child guidance clinics (31), children's response to drugs (30), etc. A developmental profile has been in use for some time by Anna Freud (22) and her associates, although systematically collected data have not yet appeared. Epidemiologic data are available regarding deviant behavior in school-age children in relation to sex, race, family size, and social class (33). Difficulties in ascertaining deviant behavior in children, related to differing perceptions by parents and professional persons, and inaccuracies in historical data (3, 39), have been discussed.

After the writer had developed the rough definitions and descriptions of developmentally related psychosocial functioning and dysfunctioning to be proposed in the next section, a developmental definition of degrees of psychopathology was published by Senn and Solnit (48). A four-point scale somewhat similar to that of the writer was discovered in the literature several weeks ago, offered by Ruesch (47) in relation to adults.

A variety of ways of looking at the functioning of the child at different levels of development can be discerned. One can attempt to judge the degree of "adequacy" or "inadequacy" of the child's functioning in different areas, as some have suggested. Such terms all too easily can lend themselves to pejorative implications, however, and involve a certain relativity in regard to situational factors. One can look for points where the child has gotten "off the track" (R. Lourie) in different dimensions of personality development. This is a rather general approach, however, and demands careful descriptive norms for different stages. One can also use a model based on systems analysis, looking at the overall social system in which the child develops and the various subsystems, including the parent-child relationship and family interactions. With this approach, the clinician can seek for points at which "systems overload" (Sperber) has occurred to produce interference with the child's functioning, and can offer intervention in particular systems (home, school, etc.) or work with the "overloaded" (or sometimes understimulated) child at points of crisis which may change the ongoing system. This approach, although most helpful, demands a rather sophisticated estimate of the balance between external and internal forces, related to the degree of internalization of conflict by the school-age child, in the determination as to whether consultation with the school, environmental manipulation, indirect therapy or counseling for the parents, or formal psychotherapy for the child and parents is indicated.

Although many references to "normal" or normative behavior at different levels of development can be found, standardized studies are few and sketchy. Even the available longitudinal studies, though stimulating, do not solve the issue, because of social class limitations in sampling, as well as for other methodological reasons. The GAP classification offered "healthy responses" as a classificatory category for the first time; the model offered was that of a school-age child only, however, and the criteria for healthy behavior, though defined, were unstandardized.

The approach offered by this writer for consideration (and, hopefully, modification or, less hopefully, condemnation) by the Clinical Issues Committee draws upon some features of a number of the ones already discussed. It involves an estimation of the child's skills and strengths in various dimensions of behavior characteristic of: (1) *optimal functioning*; (2) *functioning but vulnerable*; (3) *incipient dysfunction*; *moderate dysfunction*; (4) and *severe dysfunction*.

The description of "optimal functioning" is spelled out at each level rather arbitrarily in relation to *social, psychological,* and *physiological* levels of organization, using the holistic conceptual framework described earlier. This approach was not followed out consistently in the other categories, for reasons of limitations of time, and may be more confusing than helpful. Disturbances at the physiological level of functioning, where included, are regarded, unless specified as the result of physical illness or injury, as arising from the effects of stressful stimuli at the social or psychological level, through the psychophysiological interrelationships mentioned. This also may be confusing to some, and it is possible that individual "bits" of deviant behavior, where mentioned, might be better subsumed under broader headings such as "academic," "social," etc.

Children who fall into the categories of "functioning but vulnerable" and "incipient dysfunction" are regarded as being able to remain in the home, school, and community if the family is intact. Children exhibiting "moderate dysfunction" may often be able to remain in the home, frequently in the school, and ideally within the community, while receiving appropriate intervention for themselves and their families. (A variety of variables related to family functioning, community attitudes, etc., must be considered in arriving at a decision as to whether the child should remain in the home, school, or community, in addition to the availability of placement settings *appropriate* to the child's needs; whatever the situation, the feelings of the parents and the child also must be taken into account, within certain limits, in order to avoid the "human engineering" which could result from the "perfect" classification.) The same relativity applies, in lesser degree, to children showing "severe dysfunction" (sometimes total), who must be cared for more frequently outside the home, often outside the school (in special day-care programs), and at times outside the community, though ideally within the geographical region.

From these descriptions, "rough and ready" operational categorizations of psychosocial function or dysfunction can be derived fairly readily for the individual child, using terms (hopefully) comprehensible to all professional and nontraditional professional or semiprofessional groups. The final section offers such "sample" descriptive criteria, spelled out for each level of development (following Erikson's scheme and White's [54] competence model, with some criteria for differing levels of functioning drawn from the works of L. Murphy, Neubauer and his associates, and Borowitz and Hirsch, among others mentioned earlier). The categories employed are of course somewhat arbitrary, and the behavioral definitions are obviously not standardized.

Correlations with GAP nomenclature are indicated where possible for mental health professionals, following the suggestion made by Rome (46) in his position paper for the Joint Commission. Many of the descriptions of deviant behavior at various levels of dysfunctioning are drawn from the GAP symptom list and the developmental chart included herein. (It was the hope of the GAP Committee on Child Psychiatry that the symptom list would aid in the collection of data regarding clusters of deviant behaviors at different developmental levels, which could eventually result in the standardization of behavioral descriptions.) Any possible correlations between clinical diagnoses of healthy responses or of disorders in personality development and formation and various levels of psychosocial functioning or dysfunctioning can only be helpful, in the view of the writer. The use of any such functional-competence model, of the type offered here, can extend the usefulness of a clinical-mental health model; the two should not be considered from an "either-or" approach.

The tentative psychosocial classification offered is on the basis of the *individual child,* although some of the vulnerable or "high-risk" categories involve the consideration of problems in family functioning. A classification of parent-child relationships was not even attempted at this point, since vicissitudes in some of these do not correlate with the problems in functioning of the individual child. A valid classification on the basis of overall *family functioning* is still more difficult to construct, since no conceptual model of the family as yet exists which is universally acceptable to persons from differing professional backgrounds. Some dimensions of family functioning have been identified, as indicated earlier, and these have been drawn upon, with others added, in the rough definitions and descriptions offered by the writer as a point of departure (or "something to shoot at") in regard to family function or dysfunction.

As pointed out by the Orthopsychiatric Committee on Psychosocial Classification, current family classifications, or rather typologies of pathology, such as those offered by Ackerman (1), Buell (10), Voiland (53), and Fleck (20), while helpful in certain respects, have for various reasons, often good and sufficient, tended to oversimplify complex interpersonal relations, usually focusing on one or another dimension of family functioning to the exclusion of others. As a result, they offer little aid in identifying family strengths in particular or certain weaknesses as well. A truly valid family classification, however, which would be helpful to mental health clinicians, family and children's agencies, welfare agencies, courts, etc., cannot be achieved before a truly valid individual classification on the basis of social functioning gains general acceptance.

In the literature known to the writer, only Buell and his associates (10) have offered a scale of family impairment, with some attempt to predict improvement or deterioration related to type of intervention offered. In their approach to the assessment of family dysfunctioning, they have employed such categories as *level A disorders* (divorce, desertion, neglect, truancy, crime, unmarried parenthood, etc.) and *level B disorders* (behavior representing failure to meet individual, family, and child-rearing responsibilities, which most people would see as socially undesirable or open to question).

In the approach offered tentatively herein, a parallel classification to that of the individual is offered, with criteria roughly spelled out: *optimal family functioning; functioning but vulnerable; incipient dysfunction; moderate dysfunction;* and *severe dysfunction* (sometimes total). In the tentative scheme proposed, following the systems theory approach to delivery of services, the *prognosis* for individual and family functioning is sketched for each category, as far as it is known by the writer; the *type of intervention* indicated and the locale are suggested; and the necessary *clinicians* (and nontraditional professions) and *agencies* are listed for each level of functioning (with some overlap between the interventions for individual and family situations). Perhaps a better approach would be to include the *goals* of intervention, such as the maintenance of optimal functioning; primary, secondary, and tertiary prevention; removal of the child from a noxious family or environmental situation, etc. In any case, the writer was not equal to any such approach within the limits of time available.

In addition to the services suggested, which are certainly incomplete, a great deal of further knowledge is necessary in order to restructure community systems of delivery of services along the lines (program planning, organization of services) suggested by Greving and Lourie (24) and others. Careful collection of "systems-relevant" data, related to the organization and operation of clinical practice, the development of program, staff functions, community relationships, and the economics of child care, as recommended by Eiduson (17), is urgently necessary.

Such data have lagged even behind the limited "disorder-relevant data" available regarding individual clinical pictures, not to mention the even more limited epidemiologic data (both of the latter being affected by the lack of a universally acceptable classification).

Finally, methods of evaluation of "systems-relevant" and "disorder-relevant" data require considerable work. It is easy (and important) to call for evaluation, but the question of how to evaluate qualitatively as well as quantitatively still remains open in many areas. Collaborative planning among public, private, and voluntary agencies at all levels will be necessary in order to develop successful methods of evaluation. Whether intervention can be employed for disintegrating or changing communities remains an open question, but "urban diagnosis" and planning are urgently needed. In the planning for the development of mental health services in individual communities, much help can be gained from the stepwise phasic approach, in relation to community size and readiness, which was outlined by Hutcheson in the booklet "Planning Children's Psychiatric Services in the Community Mental Health Program" (42).

I. CRITERIA FOR INDIVIDUAL PSYCHOSOCIAL FUNCTIONING—BIRTH TO 1 YEAR

GAP DIAGNOSIS	LEVEL OF FUNCTIONING	PROGNOSIS
	A. Optimal Functioning (by 1 year)	
Healthy responses, other	*Social*—basically trustful; socially responsive; imitation and simple games (peek-a-boo, etc.). *Psychological*—wish to feed self; self-other differentiation begun (evidenced by stranger anxiety and separation anxiety); appropriate developmental milestones; exploration of body. *Physiological*—good appetite; reasonably regular biological rhythms (sleep, activity), etc.	Excellent
	B. Functioning but Vulnerable	
Healthy responses, (developmental crisis; situational crisis). Developmental deviation, mild.	In phase of developmental crisis (trust vs. mistrust); situational crisis (mother ill, etc.); developmental variations in sensory, motor, or other patterns, in relation to "fit" with parents, especially mother; infant with physical illness undergoing hospitalization in second half of first year; premature infant; infant with physical defect (blindness, deafness, handicap, etc.); infant in family experiencing discrimination, economic deprivation, marital conflict; infant in broken family, of unmarried mother, working mother; sibling of battered child.	Very good if preventive intervention
	C. Incipient Dysfunction	
Developmental and situation crises, mild to moderate. Reactive disorder, mild. Developmental deviation, mild to moderate. Psychophysiologic disorder, mild. Brain syndrome, mild.	Mistrustful; socially unresponsive; marked stranger or separation anxiety or absence of one or both; feeding or sleeping disturbances; mild delay in development; overresponsive, underresponsive; restlessness, paroxysmal fussiness (colic) beyond 3 months; constant crying; mild diarrhea; delayed weight gain, etc.	Good response to preventive or early therapeutic intervention

I. CRITERIA FOR INDIVIDUAL PSYCHOSOCIAL FUNCTIONING—BIRTH TO 1 YEAR (Cont'd)

TYPE OF INTERVENTION	CLINICIANS OR AGENCIES INVOLVED

A. Optimal Functioning

Health supervision; anticipatory guidance; pediatric counseling; overnight stay by mother if infant hospitalized, especially in second half of first year, etc.	Prenatal clinics; pediatricians; family physicians; health associates, nurse practitioners; well-baby clinics; neighborhood health centers; public health nurses; social workers; community health workers; mental health consultation available to all above, etc.

B. Functioning but Vulnerable

Same as A above plus parent counseling; home visits (within one week optimally, especially when infant premature or born with defect); day care if working mother; enrichment programs if in deprived or ghetto area; family financial support; adoption services; community work against discrimination, etc.	Same as A above plus welfare agencies; family and children's agencies; mother's helpers in home; mental health consultation available to all above, etc.

C. Incipient Dysfunction

Parent counseling or therapy; marital counseling; diagnostic services; mother's helpers in home; day-nursery services; etc.	Same as B above plus marital counselors or agencies; private mental health practitioners; child psychiatric facilities; community mental health centers, etc.

I. CRITERIA FOR INDIVIDUAL PSYCHOSOCIAL FUNCTIONING—BIRTH TO 1 YEAR (Cont'd)

GAP DIAGNOSIS	LEVEL OF FUNCTIONING	PROGNOSIS
	D. Moderate Dysfunction	
Developmental and situational crises, moderate to severe. Reactive disorder, moderate. Developmental deviation, moderate to severe. Psychophysiological disorder, moderate. Brain syndrome, moderate. Mental retardation, mild. Psychotic disorder, mild.	Markedly mistrustful, marked withdrawal; little discrimination between adults; extreme stranger or separation anxiety; moderate apathy, lethargy, listlessness, or depression; head banging; moderate vomiting, diarrhea; moderate delay in development; poor weight gain or growth; battered infant, etc.	Fair if specialized services available
	E. Severe Dysfunction	
Reactive disorder, severe. Psychophysiological disorder, severe. Psychotic disorder, moderate to severe (early infantile autism, etc.). Brain syndrome, severe. Mental retardation, moderate to severe.	Failure to develop relatedness to persons or extreme withdrawal; severe apathy or depression; marked feeding refusal; marked failure to thrive, marked delay in development; severe diarrhea, vomiting, eczema, etc.	Fair to guarded

I. Criteria for Individual Psychosocial Functioning—Birth to 1 Year (Cont'd)

TYPE OF INTERVENTION	CLINICIANS OR AGENCIES INVOLVED
D. Moderate Dysfunction	
Parent therapy; marital counseling; positive use of pediatric hospitalization, with mother substitutes and work with parents; mother's helpers in home; placement services, etc.	Same as C above plus public and private placement agencies; foster homes; family courts; mental health consultation to above, etc.
E. Severe Dysfunction	
Psychotherapy for parents; marital therapy; positive use of pediatric hospitalization with mother substitutes and work with parents; homemaker services; day-nursery services; placement services.	Same as D above plus foster grandmothers in home, etc.

II. Criteria for Individual Psychosocial Functioning—1 to 3 Years

GAP DIAGNOSIS	LEVEL OF FUNCTIONING	PROGNOSIS
	A. Optimal Functioning (by 3 years)	
Healthy responses, other.	*Social*—trustful; tie to mother resolving; separation anxiety largely under control; relative autonomy established; normal negativism generally resolved; social interaction; parallel play; usually bowel-trained. *Psychological*—developing sense of self (appropriate use of personal pronouns, interest in own body); working on sense of mastery over objects in environment and control over own impulses; thinking still egocentric, beginning to distinguish fantasy from reality; stage-appropriate adaptive mechanisms; curiosity and exploratory behavior; communicative speech; symbolic play. *Physiological*—regular biological rhythms; still may need nap; appetite good; physically vigorous; well-developed locomotor capacity; uses large muscles well.	Excellent
	B. Functioning but Vulnerable	
Healthy responses (developmental crisis; situational crisis). Developmental deviation, mild.	In phase of developmental crisis (autonomy vs. shame, doubt); situational crisis (mother ill, family crisis, etc.); developmental variations in motor or sensory responses (temperament), related to adequacy of "fit" with parents; child with physical defect or illness or undergoing hospitalization; child who was premature infant; child in family experiencing violence, economic deprivation, living in ghetto, or marital conflict; child in broken marriage, of unmarried mother, working mother; sibling of battered child, etc.	Very good if preventive intervention
	C. Incipient Dysfunction	
Developmental and situational crises, moderate. Reactive disorder, mild. Psychophysiologic disorder, mild. Developmental deviation, mild to moderate. Brain syndrome, mild.	Marked negativism; marked separation anxiety; hyperactivity; persistent food refusal; frequent tantrums, breath-holding spells; marked resistance to bowel training; delayed speech, mild stuttering; marked shame, doubt, or frequent fears; rigid food or toilet rituals; perfectionistic behavior; mild apathy, depression; chronic diarrhea or constipation; mild sleep disturbances; head banging or teeth grinding; marked clumsiness, etc.	Good response to preventive or early therapeutic intervention

II. Criteria for Individual Psychosocial Functioning—1 to 3 Years (Cont'd)

TYPE OF INTERVENTION	CLINICIANS OR AGENCIES INVOLVED

A. Optimal Functioning

Health supervision; anticipatory guidance; pediatric counseling; day care if working mother; overnight stay by mother if infant hospitalized, etc.

Pediatricians; family physicians; health associates; nurse practitioners; well-baby clinics; neighborhood health centers; public health nurses; social workers; community health workers; indigenous workers; day nurseries; mental health consultants available to all of above, etc.

B. Functioning but Vulnerable

Same as A above plus parent counseling; homemaker services; home visits; overnight stay by mother in hospital, mother substitute available, recreation program, mental health consultation available to hospital staff; day-care services with enrichment programs in deprived or ghetto areas; family financial support; adoption services; community work against discrimination, etc.

Same as A above plus family and children's agencies; welfare agencies; marital counselors and agencies; infant care workers; trained nursery school teachers; foster grandmothers, trained recreational therapists, teen-age and other volunteers on hospital staff; mental health consultation to all of above, etc.

C. Incipient Dysfunction

Parent counseling or therapy; marital counseling; crisis intervention; homemaker services; day-care services; nursery school and mental health consultation (pre-Head Start) for 2–3-year-olds in deprived or ghetto areas; early short-term psychotherapy for child (play therapy, behavior modification, etc.) and parents, etc.

Same as B above plus child psychiatric facilities; community mental health centers, with child mental health consultation, child guidance clinics and children's community mental health centers with trained child therapists; therapeutic nurseries attached to above independent, with child mental health consultation, etc.

II. Criteria for Individual Psychosocial Functioning—1 to 3 Years (Cont'd)

GAP DIAGNOSIS	LEVEL OF FUNCTIONING	PROGNOSIS
	D. Moderate Dysfunction	
Developmental and situational crises, moderate to severe. Reactive disorder, moderate. Developmental deviation, moderate to severe. Psychophysiologic disorder, moderate. Brain syndrome, mild to moderate. Mental retardation, mild. Psychotic disorder of early childhood, mild.	Extreme shame or doubt; markedly oppositional behavior; extreme separation anxiety or absence of separation anxiety; indiscriminate acceptance of adults; markedly fearful behavior; runaway behavior; marked tantrums; marked withdrawal; extreme overdependence; marked aggressive behavior; marked apathy, lethargy, or depression; extreme hyperactivity; persistent head rolling or head banging; severe nightmares; night terrors; marked thumbsucking, masturbation; delayed speech, marked stuttering; persistent constipation, diarrhea, vomiting, asthma; marked sleeping problems; moderate delay in development; repeated ingestion of nonnutritious objects (dirt, hair, toxic substances, etc.); moderate failure to thrive; battered or neglected child, etc.	Fair if specialized services available
	E. Severe Dysfunction	
Reactive disorder, severe. Developmental deviation (maturational patterns), severe. Psychophysiologic disorder, severe. Psychotic disorder of early childhood, interactional type, moderate to severe. Brain syndrome, severe. Mental retardation, moderate to severe.	Extreme withdrawal and lack of relatedness to persons; failure to develop relatedness; extremely bizarre or stereotyped behavior; extreme depression; marked failure to thrive; markedly disorganized, destructive, antisocial behavior; marked delay in development, etc.	Fair to guarded

II. Criteria for Individual Psychosocial Functioning—1 to 3 Years (Cont'd)

TYPE OF INTERVENTION	CLINICIANS OR AGENCIES INVOLVED

D. Moderate Dysfunction

Marital therapy; intensive psychotherapy for child and parents; individual psychotherapy for parent; therapeutic nursery programs (for 2–3-year-olds); day-care services; positive use of pediatric hospitalization, with mental health consultation, parent substitutes, therapy with parents; placement services; nursery programs for mildly mentally retarded children with associated emotional problems, etc.	Same as C above plus public and private placement agencies, foster homes, family courts, child protective agencies, with child mental health consultation available; diagnostic facilities and therapeutic nursery schools for mildly mentally retarded children, etc.

E. Severe Dysfunction

Same as D above plus drug therapy as indicated, etc.	Same as D above plus therapeutic nursery programs with mental health consultation for moderately retarded children with associated emotional problems or severely retarded children, etc.

III. Criteria for Individual Psychosocial Functioning—3 to 6 Years

GAP DIAGNOSIS	LEVEL OF FUNCTIONING	PROGNOSIS
	A. Optimal Functioning (by 6 years)	
Healthy responses, other.	*Social*—trustful; relatively autonomous; adequate initiative in peer group; warmth in social relationships; cooperative play; usually bladder-trained. *Psychological*—positive self-concept; developing sense of efficacy; control of impulses fairly well established, though still somewhat inconsistent; interested in the world about him; still some prelogical thinking, but can distinguish fantasy from reality and shows relative readiness for task-oriented and beginning learning; capacity for fantasy and creative play; stage-appropriate adaptive mechanisms; transient fears (death, injury, etc.) and phobias (irrational fears of animals, etc.); sexual curiosity; sexual differentiation established; sex-role functioning perceived; identifies with but is rivalrous with same-sexed parent; shows concern over stage-appropriate developmental issues; minimum of conflict regarding earlier stages; conscience formation in process. *Physiological*—increasing coordination; beginning capacity for fine muscle activity (hands, fingers); nap no longer necessary.	Excellent
	B. Functioning but Vulnerable	
Healthy responses (developmental and situational crises). Developmental deviation, mild.	In phase of developmental crisis (initiative vs. guilt); situational crisis (mother/father ill, family crisis, etc.); developmental variations in motor, sensory responses, etc. (temperament) related to adequacy of "fit" with parents and siblings; child with physical defect or illness or undergoing hospitalization; child who was premature infant; child with mild developmental lag in perceptual-motor functioning (inherent or related to lack of stimulation); child in family experiencing violence, discrimination, living in ghetto, economic deprivation, or marital conflict; child in broken marriage, of unmarried mother, of working mother; boy in all-female family; sibling of battered child; child in family with chronically depressed or seriously ill parent.	Very good if preventive intervention

III. Criteria for Individual Psychosocial Functioning—3 to 6 Years (Cont'd)

TYPE OF INTERVENTION	CLINICIANS OR AGENCIES INVOLVED

A. Optimal Functioning

Health supervision; anticipatory guidance; pediatric counseling; nursery school optional; kindergarten mandatory; overnight stay by mother if child hospitalized (at least up to 5 years); day-care services if mother working, etc.

Pediatricians; family physicians; health associates; nurse practitioners; well-child clinics; neighborhood health centers; public health nurses; social workers; indigenous workers; nursery school teachers; kindergarten teachers; day nursery staff; mental health consultation available to all above, etc.

B. Functioning but Vulnerable

Same as A above plus parent counseling; marital counseling; homemaker services; home visits; preparation for hospitalization or surgery, overnight stay by mother available if necessary, recreational program, parent-substitute figures available, mental health consultation available for hospital staff; day-care services if mother working, with enrichment program in deprived or ghetto areas; nursery school helpful, with available mental health consultation; consultation also for kindergarten; job opportunities for parents, etc.

Same as A above plus family and children's agencies; welfare agencies; trained recreational therapists, foster grandmothers, teen-age and other volunteers on hospital staff; nursery schools; public and private kindergartens; trained nursery school teachers; kindergarten teachers qualified in early childhood education; teacher's aides, adolescent volunteers; vocational counselors, rehabilitation workers for parents; mental health consultation available to all above, etc.

III. Criteria for Individual Psychosocial Functioning—3 to 6 Years (Cont'd)

GAP DIAGNOSIS	LEVEL OF FUNCTIONING	PROGNOSIS
	C. Incipient Dysfunction	
Developmental and situational crises, moderate. Reactive disorder, mild to moderate. Psychophysiologic disorder, mild. Developmental deviation, mild to moderate. Brain syndrome, mild.	Overly guilty, or absence of guilt; overly limited initiative and task completion; developmental arrest in significant areas though recovering; lack of motivation for learning; absent sexual curiosity; negative self-concept, uncertain sex-role identifications; absence of healthy rivalry with same-sexed parent; afraid of own fantasy; sleepwalking, frequent nightmares, night terrors; rigid sleep rituals, or food fads; persistent phobias, fearfulness; moderate developmental lags in sensory or motor patterns, coordination, perceptual-motor functions, speech, or social behavior; mild stuttering; infantile speech; continued oppositional behavior; continued struggle over toilet training; excessive thumbsucking or masturbation; persistent regressive behavior (related to illness of parent, birth of sibling, own illness and hospitalization, etc.); persistent and vivid imaginary companions; recurrent diarrhea, vomiting, headaches, abdominal pain, etc.	Good response to preventive or early therapeutic intervention
	D. Moderate Dysfunction	
Developmental and situational crises, moderate to severe. Reactive disorder, moderate to severe. Developmental deviation, moderate to severe. Psychophysiologic disorder, moderate. Brain syndrome, moderate. Mental retardation, mild. Psychotic disorder of early childhood, mild.	Marked lack of initiative; extreme fearfulness, marked phobias, or total absence of fears or phobias; destructive or antisocial behavior; cruelty to animals or siblings; extreme separation anxiety; markedly compulsive behavior; hyperactivity, short attention span; repeated accidents or ingestion of toxic substances (medicines, etc.); markedly shy, inhibited, withdrawn, or isolated behavior; markedly oppositional behavior; markedly infantile behavior; preponderance of concern and conflict over earlier stages; arrested development in significant areas without recovery; moderate to severe developmental lags in cognitive, psychosexual, or integrative dimensions; marked stuttering, elective mutism; marked feeding disturbances (food refusal; overeating); persistent soiling; recurrent diarrhea (with or without bleeding), deprivation dwarfism; pseudoretardation; battered child; mental retardation, mild.	Fair if specialized services available

III. Criteria for Individual Psychosocial Functioning—3 to 6 Years (Cont'd)

TYPE OF INTERVENTION	CLINICIANS OR AGENCIES INVOLVED

C. Incipient Dysfunction

Parent counseling or therapy; marital counseling; crisis intervention, home visits; homemaker services; nursery school with available mental health consultation, enrichment programs, developmental screening (DDST); kindergarten with mental health consultation, continued enrichment programs, special reading readiness programs; early short-term psychotherapy for child (play therapy, behavior modification, etc.) and parents, etc.

Same as B above plus Head Start program in deprived or ghetto areas, with trained nursery school teachers, teacher's aides, volunteers, and available child mental health professionals; all-purpose mental health clinics with child mental consultation; community mental health centers, with child mental health division; child guidance clinics, and children's community mental health centers with trained child therapists, and other child mental health professionals including mental health nurses; therapeutic nursery schools independent of or attached to clinics or centers; diagnostic facilities and therapeutic nursery schools for mildly mentally retarded children, etc.

D. Moderate Dysfunction

Marital therapy, intensive therapy for child and parents; psychotherapy for individual parents; special programs for disturbed children in nursery school and kindergarten; positive use of pediatric hospitalization with mental health consultation, parent substitutes, therapy for parents; placement services; courts; therapeutic nursery programs for mildly mentally retarded children with associated emotional problems, etc.

Same as C above plus disturbed Head Start programs, public and private placement agencies, foster homes with semiprofessional foster parents, family courts, with mental health consultation available; diagnostic facilities and therapeutic nursery schools for mildly mentally retarded children, etc.

III. Criteria for Individual Psychosocial Functioning—3 to 6 Years (Cont'd)

GAP DIAGNOSIS	LEVEL OF FUNCTIONING	PROGNOSIS
	E. Severe Dysfunction	
Reactive disorder, severe. Developmental deviation (maturational patterns), severe. Psychotic disorder of early childhood, moderate to severe. Psychophysiologic disorder, severe. Brain syndrome, severe. Mental retardation, moderate to severe.	Persistent failure to develop relatedness to persons or extreme withdrawal; absence of speech or inability to use speech for communication; severe depression, apathy; intense separation anxiety or complete inability to separate from mother; overwhelming fears or phobias; extremely destructive or anti-social behavior; totally disorganized or extremely bizarre behavior; severe pseudo-retardation; mental retardation, moderate to severe; severe diarrhea with bleeding, protracted vomiting, etc.	Fair to guarded

III. Criteria for Inidvidual Psychosocial Functioning—3 to 6 Years (Cont'd)

TYPE OF INTERVENTION	CLINICIANS OR AGENCIES INVOLVED

E. Severe Dysfunction

Same as D above plus drug therapy as indicated; occasional use of residential treatment for child *over 5* with severe dysfunction either from psychosocial origins or with moderate to severe mental retardation from physical origins with associated emotional problems, etc.

Same as D above plus residential treatment centers, independent or as part of community mental health center; therapeutic nursery groups with mental health consultation for moderately retarded children with associated emotional problems or for severely retarded children, etc.

IV. CRITERIA FOR INDIVIDUAL PSYCHOSOCIAL FUNCTIONING—6 TO 12 YEARS

GAP DIAGNOSIS	LEVEL OF FUNCTIONING	PROGNOSIS
Healthy responses, other.	*A. Optimal Functioning (by 12 years)* *Social*—capable of industry and achievement in school; oriented toward task completion, though still needs some support at times from parents and teachers; invests in teachers, community leaders, etc.; plays games with rules and rituals; interested in companionship with same-sexed individuals and groups but limited interest in opposite sex (boys especially). *Psychological*—capable of conceptual problem solving, though still largely concrete approach; shows curiosity, motivation toward learning; well-developed sense of efficacy; working on skills, strengths, hobbies; identifications with same-sexed parent solidified; likes being boy or girl; shows some impersonal ideals; conscience fully established, though still concrete ideas of right and wrong; impulse control generally steady; can postpone gratifications most of the time; stage-appropriate adaptive mechanisms; body image solidifying; capable of voluntary hygiene, organization of habits; concerned over stage-appropriate developmental issues. *Physiological*—growth gradual and steady; capable of highly skilled coordination and fine motor activities; cerebral dominance established.	Excellent
Healthy responses (developmental and situational crises). Developmental deviation, mild.	*B. Functioning but Vulnerable* In phase of developmental crisis (industry vs. inferiority); situational crisis (illness of parent, family crisis, etc.); developmental variations in motor or sensory responses, etc. (temperament), and learning style related to adequacy of "fit" with parents, siblings, teachers, and other adults; child with physical defect or illness or undergoing hospitalization; early school-age child who was a premature infant; early school-age child with a mild developmental lag in perceptual-motor or cognitive functions (inherent or related to lack of stimulation); child in family experiencing violence, discrimination, living in ghetto, economic deprivation, or working mother; early school-age boy in all-female family; sibling of battered child; child with chronically depressed or seriously mentally ill parents; frequent moves by family.	Very good if preventive intervention available

IV. CRITERIA FOR INDIVIDUAL PSYCHOSOCIAL FUNCTIONING—6 TO 12 YEARS (Cont'd)

TYPE OF INTERVENTION	CLINICIANS OR AGENCIES INVOLVED

A. Optimal Functioning

Health supervision; anticipatory guidance; parental cooperation with teachers, guidance counselors; Scouting and other group activities; beginning supervised activities with opposite sex; integrated schools and communities, etc.

Pediatricians; family physicians; health associates; nurse practitioners; well-child clinics; neighborhood health centers; social workers; public health nurses; indigenous workers; schoolteachers (qualified in early childhood education in first three grades), teacher's aides, counselors, smaller classes, training in child development in teachers colleges; mental health consultants available to all of above, etc.

B. Functioning but Vulnerable

Same as A above plus parent counseling; marital counseling; homemaker services; home visits; preparation for hospitalization or surgery, unrestricted visiting, education and recreational program, parent-substitute figures, mental health consultation available to hospital staff; gradual return to full school during convalescence from significant illness, continuation of enrichment programs in schools past third grade, tutoring for reading difficulties available in schools in first grade, other remedial educational measures available; also mental health consultation in schools; parent-substitute figures (Big Brother, welfare workers), etc.

Same as A above plus in-service sensitivity training for teachers; trained remedial education teachers; welfare agencies, family and children's agencies, family courts, with available mental health consultants, etc.

IV. Criteria for Individual Psychosocial Functioning—6 to 12 Years (Cont'd)

GAP DIAGNOSIS	LEVEL OF FUNCTIONING	PROGNOSIS
	C. Incipient Dysfunction	
Developmental and situational crises, moderate. Reactive disorder, mild to moderate. Psychoneurotic disorder, mild. Personality disorder, mild. Psychophysiologic disorder, mild. Developmental deviation, mild to moderate. Brain syndrome, mild.	Lack of industry (about to fail in school); daydreaming; overindustrious, overcompetitive, or overanxious behavior, overritualized behavior; limited capacity for curiosity or play; apathetic or withdrawn behavior in school or peer group; significant conflict over earlier stages; uncertain male or female identifications; beginning overeffeminate (boys) or overmasculine (girls) behavior; overly aggressive, oppositional, or overly dependent behavior; inadequate hygiene and organization of habits; mild hyperactivity and difficulty in concentration; overfatigued or overscheduled; inadequate diet; mild developmental lags in speech, coordination, perceptual-motor functions; persistent tics, thumbsucking, nailbiting, etc.; persistent enuresis; mild stuttering, recurrent diarrhea, headaches, vomiting, fainting, etc.	Good response to preventive or early therapeutic intervention
	D. Moderate Dysfunction	
Developmental and situational crises, moderate to severe. Reactive disorder, moderate. Developmental deviation, moderate to severe. Psychophysiologic disorder, moderate. Psychoneurotic disorder, mild to moderate. Personality disorder, mild to moderate. Brain syndrome, mild to moderate. Mental retardation, mild. Psychotic disorder, schizophreniform type, mild.	Markedly inhibited, withdrawn, or isolated behavior in group; marked reluctance to go to school (school phobia); overly mistrustful, provocative, or manipulative behavior; markedly dependent or pseudo-independent behavior; markedly impulsive, aggressive, or destructive social behavior; cruelty toward animals, siblings, or younger children; markedly effeminate behavior in boys or markedly masculine behavior in girls; repeated accidents; persistent learning disorders (emotional blocking, marked daydreaming, negativism, rebellion, etc.); preponderance of concern and conflict over earlier stages; marked stuttering or other speech disorders; blindness, deafness, or other handicap or chronic illness with associated emotional problems; persistent soiling; battered child; chronic diarrhea with or without abdominal pain or bleeding, recurrent headaches, vomiting, arthritis, asthma, etc.; mental retardation, mild, etc.	Fair if specialized services available

IV. CRITERIA FOR INDIVIDUAL PSYCHOSOCIAL FUNCTIONING—6 TO 12 YEARS (Cont'd)

TYPE OF INTERVENTION	CLINICIANS OR AGENCIES INVOLVED

C. Incipient Dysfunction

Parent counseling or therapy; marital counseling; crisis intervention ("first aid") for early school phobia, family crises, etc.; early short-term psychotherapy for child and parents; special ungraded classes and remedial tutoring in schools; neighborhood activity groups, etc.

Same as B above plus mental health consultants, teen-age volunteer tutors in schools, private schools; neighborhood activity centers; child guidance clinics (1 per 250,000 population); community mental health centers, with child and adolescent mental health division; all-purpose mental health clinics, with child mental consultation; children's community mental health centers, with trained child therapists, mental health nurses, and other child mental health professionals, etc.

D. Moderate Dysfunction

Marital therapy; psychotherapy for individual parent; intensive therapy for child and parents (tandem, family, group, behavior modification, drug therapy, etc.); day care (psychoeducational) programs, educational therapy; emergency services; residential treatment services of "open" and "semiopen" type; placement services; correctional and probation services with available mental health consultation; special classes in schools for disturbed, retarded, or physically handicapped children, including blind or deaf; positive use of pediatric hospitalization and mental health services, etc.

Same as C above plus child mental health consultants to juvenile courts, detention centers, and corrective services; treatment-oriented small institutions for predelinquent children; trained semiprofessional foster parents for individual and group (including "medical") foster homes; services of child mental health professionals available to schools for blind and deaf, hearing and speech clinics, etc.; residential treatment centers (public, private) in region available to family, etc.

IV. Criteria for Individual Psychosocial Functioning—6 to 12 Years (Cont'd)

GAP DIAGNOSIS	LEVEL OF FUNCTIONING	PROGNOSIS

E. Severe Dysfunction

Reactive disorder, severe. Developmental deviation (maturational patterns), severe. Psychoneurotic disorder, severe. Personality disorder, severe. Psychophysiologic disorder, severe. Psychotic disorder, chronic schizophreniform type, moderate to severe. Brain syndrome, severe. Mental retardation, moderate to severe.	Markedly bizarre, stereotyped behavior; persistent failure to develop relatedness to persons or extreme withdrawal; preoccupation with fantasy, constant obsessive rumination or incapacitating phobias; homicidal, self-mutilative, or suicidal behavior; mental retardation, moderate to severe; severe and chronic diarrhea with bleeding, severe arthritis, asthma, epilepsy, skin disorders, etc., associated with marked emotional problems, etc.	Fair to guarded

IV. Criteria for Individual Psychosocial Functioning—6 to 12 Years (Cont'd)

TYPE OF INTERVENTION	CLINICIANS OR AGENCIES INVOLVED

E. Severe Dysfunction

Same as D above plus "semiclosed" settings for the treatment of those children who run away or are dangerous to themselves and others; placement services for living-care and long-term treatment of children with chronic total dysfunction who have reached maximal benefit in residential treatment or hospital inpatient units and cannot return home, with adequate speech and hearing consultation and educational facilities for those who are blind, deaf, or otherwise handicapped; more adequate mental health services to programs for moderately mentally retarded children with associated emotional problems and for severely retarded children, etc.

Same as D above plus hospital inpatient units for diagnostic study and relatively short-term treatment of children with relatively acute severe dysfunction (1 per 500,-000 population); regional public or private residential treatment units for children with chronic dysfunction; professional group foster homes with trained foster parents for aftercare and treatment, established by residential units or public or private placement agencies, etc.

V. Criteria for Individual Psychosocial Functioning—Adolescence

GAP DIAGNOSIS	LEVEL OF FUNCTIONING	PROGNOSIS
	A. Optimal Functioning (by 18 years)	
Health responses, other	*Social*—resolving individual identity while loosening tie to family, in direction of approval by peer group, teachers, and other models; shows some criticism and rebellion against authority without revolt; capable of responsible independence most of the time; has healthy heterosexual interests with reasonable controls; develops satisfying recreational patterns, alone and with others; possesses respect for others, even if at times involved with cliques; thinking of occupational choice (has occupational commitment and ambition to achieve). *Psychological*— capable of abstract, logical (adult-type) thinking; has sensitive awareness of self; possesses standards involving at least some idealism, altruism, and moral concern, even if egocentric at times; work habits generally solidified; body image solidified; bodily concerns resolved. *Physiological*—growth spurt usually completed; normal acne disappears; sexually mature; motor coordination of adult type; capable of tremendous bursts of energy in direction of motivation.	Excellent
	B. Functioning but Vulnerable	
Healthy responses (developmental and situational crises). Developmental deviation, mild.	In phase of developmental crisis (identity vs. identity diffusion); situational crisis (illness of family member, father's loss of job, other family crises, etc.); developmental variations in motor, sensory, etc., responses (temperament) and learning style, related to adequacy of "fit" with parents, siblings, teachers, and other adults; adolescent with physical defects or illness or undergoing hospitalization; adolescent in family experiencing violence, discrimination, living in ghetto, economic deprivation, marital conflict, separation, desertion or divorce; sibling of battered child; adolescent with chronically depressed or seriously mentally ill parent; frequent moves by family, etc.	Very good if preventive intervention

V. Criteria for Individual Psychosocial Functioning—Adolescence (Cont'd)

TYPE OF INTERVENTION	CLINICIANS OR AGENCIES INVOLVED

A. Optimal Functioning

Health supervision, opportunity for comfortable relationship with physician permitting discussion of bodily concerns and misunderstandings; pediatric counseling of adolescent or parents; parental cooperation with teachers, school counselors; family life courses in school, volunteer experience with preschool children, discussion courses in current problems, some opportunity to participate in administrative and academic decisions, etc.; advanced Scouting and other group activities; limits, mutually agreed upon by teen-ager and parents, regarding amount of dating, time for return home at night, etc.; supervised group activities with opposite sex; some time to be alone; some opportunity to be involved in work experiences offering help to others; integrated schools and communities, etc.

Pediatricians, internists, and family physicians; health associates; nurse practitioners; adolescent clinics in pediatric or general hospitals; neighborhood health centers; social workers, public health nurses; indigenous workers; school teachers, teacher's aides, guidance and vocational counselors, smaller classes, training in development in teachers colleges; neighborhood youth centers and other agencies offering group experiences; mental health consultants available to all of the above, etc.

B. Functioning but Vulnerable

Same as A above plus parent counseling; marital counseling; homemaker services; home visits; preparation for hospitalization or surgery, unrestricted visiting, educational and recreational program, mental health consultation available to hospital staff; tutoring and other remedial measures, as well as school work program and mental health consultation in schools; parent substitute figures (Big Brother, welfare workers, etc.), mental health consultation available to ministers, physicians, lawyers, etc.

Same as A above plus in-service sensitivity training for teachers, trained remedial education teachers; family and children's agencies; welfare centers; lawyers; cottage-type group-living settings for dependent adolescents; mental health consultation available to all of above; college mental health programs, etc.

V. Criteria for Individual Psychosocial Functioning—Adolescence (Cont'd)

GAP DIAGNOSIS	LEVEL OF FUNCTIONING	PROGNOSIS
	C. Incipient Dysfunction	
Developmental and situational crises, moderate. Reactive disorder, mild to moderate. Developmental deviation, mild to moderate. Psychoneurotic disorder, mild. Personality disorder, mild. Psychophysiologic disorder, mild. Brain syndrome, mild.	Confusion or diffusion regarding identity; somewhat isolated socially; withdrawn or overly quiet in school; reluctance to go to school; limited capacity or motivation for work (habits or concentration) or recreation; persistent daydreaming, sudden drop in grades at school; overly preoccupied with egocentric concerns; overcompulsive, indecisive, overly preoccupied with work or ascetic needs; mildly impulsive, rebellious, boastful, defiant, clowning, exhibitionistic, antisocial, or destructive behavior in groups; able to relate to adults but not to peers; significant conflicts over earlier stages; moderate dissatisfaction with appearance, bodily or other self-attributes, or unhappy with sex role; inadequate hygiene and organization habits; absence of any interest in opposite sex; overly anxious, oversensitive behavior; overly rivalrous behavior toward siblings or overcompetitive toward peers; overly demanding or dependent on parents or friends; shifts friends more frequently than average; unhappy or overly moody; threatens to drop out of school or makes suicidal threats; actual runaway from home; overeasily fatigued or lethargic; persistent tics, nailbiting; onset of mild stuttering; overclumsy; moderate obesity; moderate dysmenorrhea; inadequate diet; recurrent headaches, fainting, abdominal pain, diarrhea, vomiting, etc.	Good response to preventive or therapeutic intervention

V. Criteria for Individual Psychosocial Functioning—Adolescence (Cont'd)

TYPE OF INTERVENTION	CLINICIANS OR AGENCIES INVOLVED

C. Incipient Dysfunction

Parent counseling or therapy; marital counseling; crisis intervention for early adolescent school phobia, family crises, etc.; early short-term psychotherapy for adolescent and parents; special ungraded classes in school; neighborhood or other activity groups, etc.

Same as B above plus neighborhood youth centers; child and adolescent guidance clinics; community mental health centers, with child and adolescent mental health division; all-purpose mental health clinics with adequate adolescent mental health consultation; children's and adolescent community mental health centers, with trained adolescent therapists, mental health nurses, and other mental health professionals, etc.

V. Criteria for Individual Psychosocial Functioning—Adolescence (Cont'd)

GAP DIAGNOSIS	LEVEL OF FUNCTIONING	PROGNOSIS
	D. Moderate Dysfunction	
Developmental and situational crises, moderate to severe. Developmental deviation, moderate to severe. Reactive disorder, moderate. Psychoneurotic disorder, moderate. Personality disorder, moderate. Psychophysiologic disorder, moderate. Brain syndrome, mild to moderate. Mental retardation, mild. Psychotic disorder, mild (confusional, regressive, etc.).	Chronic learning disorders (emotional blocking, daydreaming, negativism, rebellion, etc.); markedly withdrawn, inhibited, or isolated behavior; inability to attend school; poor self-image; negative identity (opposite of parents); preponderance of concern and conflict over earlier stages; markedly mistrustful, impulsive, manipulative, provocative, narcissistic, defiant, aggressive, runaway, destructive, or antisocial behavior; recurrent accidents; markedly dependent or passive behavior; moderate depression or suicidal attempt; persistent drug abuse; marked effeminate behavior in boys or over-masculine behavior in girls; persistent homosexual behavior; unmarried mother or father; attempted molestation of younger children; sadistic behavior toward siblings; marked stuttering or other speech disorders; pseudo-retardation, mild; delayed growth spurts, deprivation dwarfism, blindness, deafness, or other handicap or chronic illness with associated emotional problems (strong denial of illness, overdependence, etc.); persistent enuresis, soiling; inadequate diet; episodes of confusion; chronic diarrhea with bleeding, recurrent vomiting, marked loss of appetite, arthritis, asthma; mental retardation, mild, etc.	Fair if specialized services available
	E. Severe Dysfunction	
Reactive disorders, severe. Developmental deviation (maturational patterns), severe. Psychoneurotic disorder, severe. Personality disorder, severe. Psychotic disorder, moderate to severe (confusional state, regressive type, adult-type schizophrenic, etc.). Brain syndrome, severe. Mental retardation, moderate to severe.	Severely or chronically withdrawn, isolated, aloof, bizarre, or stereotyped behavior; persistent failure to develop relatedness with persons or extreme withdrawal; complete preoccupation with fantasy, constant obsessive rumination, or incapacitating phobias or anxiety; sweepingly regressed behavior; homicidal, self-mutilative, repeated suicidal behavior; mental retardation, moderate to severe; severe loss of appetite with bleeding, severe arthritis, asthma, obesity, epilepsy, diabetes, etc., associated with marked emotional problems, etc.	Fair to guarded

V. Criteria for Individual Psychosocial Functioning—Adolescence (Cont'd)

TYPE OF INTERVENTION	CLINICIANS OR AGENCIES INVOLVED

D. Moderate Dysfunction

Marital therapy; psychotherapy for individual parent; intensive therapy for adolescent and parents (individual, tandem, family, group, behavior modification, drug therapy, etc.); 24-hour emergency psychiatric services; day-care (psychoeducational) programs; placement services; adolescent inpatient or residential treatment services of "open" or "semiopen" type; correctional and probation services with available mental health consultation; special classes in schools for disturbed, retarded, or physically handicapped adolescents (including blind or deaf); adequate mental health consultation to vocational, rehabilitation programs; positive use of pediatric hospitalization, with mental health consultation and therapy with parents, for suicidal attempts, psychosomatic problems, etc.

Same as C above plus mental health professionals available to vocational habitational programs, juvenile courts, detention centers, corrective services, youth service boards; smaller treatment-oriented institutions for predelinquent adolescents; adequate mental health facilities to make institutions for delinquent treatment-oriented; temporary shelters (nonlegal) for runaway adolescents or those on drugs, with adequate mental health consultation; trained semiprofessional foster parents for group foster homes (including "medical"); services of mental health consultants available to schools for blind, deaf, hearing, and speech services; diagnostic and relatively short-term adolescent inpatient units; residential treatment centers (public, private) in region available to family; special school programs and homes for unmarried mothers; speech and hearing personnel for inpatient or residential units treating disturbed blind and deaf adolescents, etc.

E. Severe Dysfunction

Same as D above plus "closed" and "semi-closed" settings for the treatment of those adolescents who run away or are dangerous to themselves or others; placement services for living-care and long-term treatment of adolescents with chronic severe dysfunction who have reached maximal benefit in residential treatment or hospital inpatient units and cannot return home, with adequate speech and hearing consultation and educational facilities for those who are blind, deaf, or otherwise handicapped; more adequate mental health services to programs for severely mentally retarded adolescents; facilities for protection and economic self-support of moderately mentally retarded, mental health consultation for programs for severely retarded, etc.

Same as D above plus inpatient units for diagnostic study and relatively short-term treatment of adolescents with relatively acute severe dysfunction (1 per 500,000 population); regional public or private residential treatment units for long-term treatment of adolescents with chronic severe dysfunction; professional group foster homes with trained foster parents for aftercare and treatment; sheltered workshops for moderately mentally retarded adolescents; mental health consultation for smaller, cottage-type group-living situations for long-term care of severely retarded adolescents, etc.

VI. CRITERIA FOR FAMILY FUNCTIONING

LEVEL OF FUNCTIONING	PROGNOSIS

A. Optimal Functioning

Intact family; flexible *interpersonal (adaptive) equilibrium; cohesive* in response to crises; patterns of *communication, leadership,* and *role functions* clearly defined; adequate *financial functioning; marital relationship* involves mutual and reciprocal need satisfactions; *parent-child relationships* involve comfortable "fit" between parents' and children's needs, respect for each child as individual, congenial patterns of discipline; *children's development* proceeding adequately; *value orientations* reasonably clear-cut, with minimum of conflict between generations; balanced *integration into external community.*

Excellent

B. Functioning but Vulnerable

Family experiencing crisis (illness and/or hospitalization of parent or other family members; marital crisis; financial crisis; out-of-wedlock pregnancy in adolescent girl, etc.); minority-group family; family moving to new school district, neighborhood; family adopting infant or child; birth of premature infant or infant with congenital deformity, birth injury, serious illness at birth or soon after; family with child or adolescent in developmental crisis; marriage of teen-age parents; parents of infant who are overly anxious or markedly unconcerned, etc.; family in disintegrating community, etc.

Very good if preventive intervention available

C. Incipient Dysfunction

Family experiencing discrimination on racial, ethnic, or socioeconomic basis; problems in communication or value orientation (between parents, between generations, with external community, etc.); continued financial difficulties; continued mild marital discord; repeated or prolonged absence of father; death of parent with adequate parent substitute; parents experiencing conflicts or struggles over children's developmental crises or reactions to situational crisis (grieving over death of grandparent, reactions to illness and/or hospitalization, move to new school district, etc.); parents of infants or very young children who exhibit moderately overprotective, overcontrolling, overpermissive, overindulging, overstimulating, understimulating, or inconsistent attitudes and behavior; family in rapid transition upward socioeconomically; family showing mildly disorganized, noncohesive, or other types of nonadaptive response to family crisis, etc.

Good response to preventive or early therapeutic intervention

VI. CRITERIA FOR FAMILY FUNCTIONING (Cont'd)

TYPE OF INTERVENTION	CLINICIANS OR AGENCIES INVOLVED

A. Optimal Functioning

Health supervision; anticipatory guidance; parental cooperation with teachers, guidance counselors; Scouting and other group activities; family recreational, religious, and other activities; integrated schools and communities, etc.

Pediatricians; internists; family physicians; health associates; nurse practitioners; social workers; indigenous workers; neighborhood health centers; teachers, teacher's aides, guidance counselors, etc.; ministers; lawyers; mental health consultation available to all above, etc.

B. Functioning but Vulnerable

Crisis intervention (at times supporting strongest member, etc.); marital counseling; parental counseling; homemaker services; financial counseling; job opportunities; day-care services if mother working.

Same as A above plus remedial education teachers; welfare agencies; family and children's agencies with psychiatric consultation; marital counselors and agencies; mental health consultants in family courts; family life education in churches, schools, etc.

C. Incipient Dysfunction

Same as B above plus parental (or child or adolescent) counseling or supportive therapy; home visits; enrichment programs, developmental screening and other preventive programs for preschool and school-age children; mental health consultation in schools; family counseling; psychotherapy for individual family member, etc.

Same as B above, plus Head Start, job opportunity, etc.; all-purpose mental health clinics and community mental health centers with child mental health consultants; child guidance clinics, private mental health practitioners; neighborhood social centers for families, youth, and senior citizens, etc.

VI. Criteria for Family Functioning (Cont'd)

LEVEL OF FUNCTIONING	PROGNOSIS

D. Moderate Dysfunction

Severe problems in verbal communication or communication of feeling (between parents, between parents and child or adolescent, among whole family, etc.) with communication mainly through acting out of feelings; severe marital discord; markedly man-dominated or woman-dominated patterns of leadership; reversal of parental role functions or of parent-child role functions; immature, unbalanced, or unhealthily interlocking (complementary, dovetailing) marital relationships; involvement of children in marital struggle or conflict over child-rearing issues; vicarious use of child for parent's or parents' emotional needs, with individual or mutual devaluation or overevaluation of child's capacities, power alignments, triangular relationships, unconscious condonement for child's acting out of parent's wishes, etc.; scapegoating, stigmatization, or isolation of sick family member; families with parents who exhibit markedly overprotective, overcontrolling, overdemanding, overperfectionistic, overpermissive, inconsistent, seductive, neglectful, or rejecting, etc., attitudes and behavior, with children exhibiting various types of psychosocial dysfunctioning; family with repeated out-of-wedlock pregnancies in adolescent girl or girls; transmission of unhealthy attitudes or behavior over several generations; family in poverty circumstances, with inability to deal with financial matters, or drifting downward socioeconomically; broken marriage (divorce, desertion); death of parent without adequate parent substitute; recurrent involvement with law agencies, truancy, etc.; one parent seriously mentally ill, etc.

Fair if specialized services available

E. Severe Dysfunction

Guarded

Family as disintegrating collection of individuals; incestuous relationship between parent and child; desertion of children by parents; complete neglect of children by parents; multiproblem families; both parents mentally ill, etc.

VI. Criteria for Family Functioning (Cont'd)

TYPE OF INTERVENTION	CLINICIANS OR AGENCIES INVOLVED

D. Moderate Dysfunction

Same as C above plus marital therapy; family therapy if indicated; psychotherapy of parents and children; placement of children; legal protection for battered or neglected children; hospitalization or day care for seriously mentally ill parent; programs for alcoholic, addicted, etc.; financial assistance; adequate housing, etc.

Same as C above plus hospital and day-care units; walk-in clinics; 24-hour emergency psychiatric service; mental health consultation to courts (family, divorce, juvenile); block workers, probation officers, with mental health consultation; hospitalization facilities, clinics, halfway houses for alcoholics, addicted; guaranteed income; fair housing; urban renewal; model cities programs, etc.

E. Severe Dysfunction

Same as D above plus psychotherapy for adolescents alone if parents cannot participate, etc.; hospitalization or day care for seriously mentally ill individuals; "reaching out" to multiproblem families; financial support, etc.

Same as D above plus in-service training for welfare workers, probation officers, indigenous workers, etc.

REFERENCES TO APPENDIX A

1. Ackerman, N. W. *The Psychodynamics of Family Life.* New York: Basic Books, 1958.
2. Allport, G. W. "The Open System in Personality Theory," *J. Abnorm. Soc. Psychol.* 61:301 (1960).
3. Ausubel, D. *Theory and Problems of Ego Development.* New York: Grune & Stratton, 1958.
4. Bell, N. W., and Vogel, E. F. (eds.). *The Family.* Glencoe, Ill.: The Free Press, 1960.
5. Beller, K. E., and Neubauer, P. B. "Sex Differences and Symptom Patterns in Early Childhood," *J. Amer. Child Psychiat.* 2:417 (1963).
6. Block, D., Rosenfeld, E., and Novick, J. *Deviant Behavior Inventory for Latency Age Boys.* 1963. Revised, 1968, by E. Rosenfeld, N. Frankl, and A. Esman. Pub. in mimeographed form by Jewish Board of Guardians, New York, N.Y.
7. Blom, G. E. "The Psychoeducational Approach to Emotionally Disturbed Children," *Med. Rec. & Ann.* 61:348 (1968).
8. Blum, R. H. "Case Identification in Psychiatric Epidemiology: Methods and Problems," *Milbank Memorial Fund Quarterly* 40:253–288 (1962).
9. Borowitz, G. H., and Hirsch, J. G. "A Development Typology of Disadvantaged Four-Year-Olds." Paper presented at Annual Meeting of the American Orthopsychiatric Association, Chicago, 1968. Summary published in *Research: News and Notes,* Spring 1968, Vol. 4, No 1. A publication of the Institute for Juvenile Research, Department of Mental Health, Chicago, Ill.
10. Buell, B., and Associates. *A Public Accounting for Social Service Operations.* Community Research Associates, Inc., 124 E. 40th St., New York, N.Y., 1967.
11. Caldwell, B. M. "The Effects of Infant Care," in *Review of Child Development Research,* L. Hoffman and M. Hoffman, eds. Vol. I. Russell Sage Foundation, 1964.
12. Chance, E., and Arnold, J. "The Effect of Professional Training, Experience, and Preference for a Theoretical System Upon Clinical Case Description," *Human Relations* 1:195 (1965).
13. Clausen, J. A. "Some Implications of Classification in Psychiatry and Psychopathology," in *The Role and Methodology of Classification in Psychiatry and Psychopathology,* M. Katz, J. Cole, and E. Barton, eds. Washington, D.C.: U.S. Government Printing Office, 1968.
14. Corwin, E. H. L. (ed.). *Ecology of Health.* New York: Commonwealth Fund, 1949.
15. Cumming, J. "The Inadequacy Syndrome," *Psychiat. Quart.* 37:723 (1963).
16. Cumming, J., and Cumming, E. *Ego and Milieu.* New York, Atherton Press, 1962.
17. Eiduson, B. T. "The Clinic in the Year 2000," *Arch. Gen. Psychiat.* 19:385 (1968).

18. Engel, G. L. "A Unified Concept of Health and Disease," *Perspectives in Biology and Medicine* 3:459 (1960).
19. Erikson, E. H. "Identity and the Life Cycle," *Psychol. Issues* 1, No. 1 (1959).
20. Fleck, Stephen. "Family Dynamics and Anger of Schizophrenia," *Psychosomatic Medicine* 22:333–344 (1960).
21. Fleiss, J. L., Spitzer, R. L., and Burdoch, E. I. "Estimating Accuracy of Judgment Using Recorded Interviews," *Arch. Gen. Psychiat.* 12:562–567 (1965).
22. Freud, A. *Normality and Pathology.* New York: International Universities Press, 1965.
23. Green, W. A. "Process in Psychosomatic Disorders," *Psychosomat. Med.* 28:150 (1956).
24. Greving, F., and Lourie, N. "Restructuring Community Services for Orthopsychiatric Practice." Paper presented at 38th Annual Meeting of the American Orthopsychiatric Association, New York, N.Y., March, 1961.
25. Grinker, R. R. *Toward a Unitary Theory of Human Behavior.* New York: Basic Books, 1959.
26. Gruenberg, E. M. Brandon, S., and Kasius R. V. "Identifying Cases of the Social Breakdown Syndrome," *Milbank Memorial Fund Quarterly* 54:150–155 (1966).
27. Hetznecker, W., Gardner, E. A., Odoroff, C. L., and Turner, R. J. "Field Survey Methods in Psychiatry: A Symptom Check List, Mental Status, and Clinical Status Scales for Evaluation of Psychiatric Impairment," *Arch. Gen. Psychiat.* 15:427 (1968).
28. Hinkle, L. E., and Wolff, H. G. "Ecologic Investigations of the Relationship Between Illness, Life Experience, and the Social Environment," *Ann. Int. Med.* 49:1373 (1958).
29. "Integration and Conflict in Family Behavior." Formulated by the Committee on the Family, J. Spiegel and F. Kluckholm, eds. Report No. 27, Group for Advancement of Psychiatry, New York, Aug. 1954.
30. Jenkins, R. L., and Cole, J. O. (eds.). "Diagnostic Classification in Child Psychiatry." Psychiatric Research Report No. 18. Washington, D.C.: American Psychiatric Association, 1964.
31. Jenkins, R. L., and Glickman, S. "Common Syndromes in Child Psychiatry: I. Deviant Behavior Traits," *Amer. J. Orthopsychiat.* 16:244 (1946).
32. Katz, M. M., Cole, J., and Barton, W. E. (eds.). *The Role and Methodology of Classification in Psychiatry and Psychopathology.* Washington, D.C.: United States Government Printing Office, 1968.
33. LaPouse, R., and Monk, M. A. "Behavior Deviations in a Representative Sample of Children: Variation between Sex, Race, Social Class, and Family Size," *Amer. J. Orthopsychiat.* 34:436 (1964).
34. Lindemann, E. "The Psychosocial Position on Etiology," in *Integrating the Approaches to Mental Disease,* H. D. Kruse, ed. New York: Hoeber-Harper, Inc., 1957.
35. Meyer, A. "Objective Psychology or Psychobiology, with Subordination of the Medically Useless: Contrast of Mental and Physical," *J.A.N.A.* 65: 860 (1915).

36. Mirsky, I. A. "Physiologic, Psychologic, and Social Determinants of Psycho-somatic Disorders," *Dis. Nerv. Syst.* 21:50 (1960).
37. Murphy, L. B. *The Widening World of Childhood: Paths Toward Mastery.* New York: Basic Books, 1962.
38. Neubauer, P. B., Cramer, S., and Silverman, M. "The Use of the Developmental Profile for the Pre-Latency Child." Paper presented at Annual Meeting of American Association of Psychiatric Clinics for Children, New York City, Nov. 1968.
39. Novick, J., Rosenfeld, E., Bloch, D. A., and Dawson, D. "Ascertaining Deviant Behavior in Children," *J. Consult. Psychol.* 30:230 (1966).
40. Phillips, L., Broverman, J. K., and Zigler, E. "Social Competence and Psychiatric Diagnosis," *J. Abnorm. Psychol.* 71:209 (1966).
41. Prugh, D. G. "Toward an Understanding of Psychosomatic Concepts in Relation to Illness in Children," in *Modern Perspectives in Child Development,* A. Solnit and S. Provence, eds. New York: International Universities Press, 1963.
42. Prugh, D. G., and Leon, R. (eds.). "Planning Children's Psychiatric Services in the Community Mental Health Program." Washington, D.C.: American Psychiatric Association, 1964.
43. Richmond, J. B., and Lustman, S. L. "Total Health: A Conceptual Visual Aid," *J. Med. Ed.* 29:23 (1954).
44. Roen, S. R., and Burnes, A. J. "Community Adaptation Schedule" (CAS-Form 5A-1968). Behavioral Publications, Inc., 2852 Broadway, Morningside Heights, New York, N.Y. 10025.
45. Romano, J. "Basic Orientation and Education of the Medical Student," *J.A.N.A.* 143:409 (1950).
46. Rome, H. P. "The Problem of Nomenclature." Position paper with acknowledgment to the Group for Advancement of Psychiatry. Prepared for the Joint Commission on Mental Health of Children.
47. Ruesch, J., and Brodsky, C. M. "The Concept of Social Disability," *Arch. Gen. Psychiat.* 19:394 (1968).
48. Senn, M. J. E., and Solnit, A. J. *Problems in Child Behavior and Development.* Philadelphia: Lea and Febiger, 1968.
49. Spitzer, R. L., Endicott, J., and Cohen, G. M. "Psychiatric Status Schedule: Technique for Evaluating Social and Role Functioning and Mental Status." Pub. in mimeographed form by Biometrics Research Division, N.Y., State Department of Mental Hygiene and cooperating agencies, 1967.
50. Szasz, T. *The Myth of Mental Illness.* New York: Hoeber-Harper, 1961.
51. Thorne, F. C. "Diagnostic Classification and Nomenclature for Psychological Status." Clinical Psychology Monograph. Vol. 20. Supplement No. 17, 1964.
52. Turner, R. J., and Cumming, J. "Theoretical Malaise and Community Mental Health," in *Emergent Approaches to Mental Health Problems,* E. Cowen, E. Gardner, and M. Zax, eds. New York: Appleton-Century-Crofts, 1967.
53. Voiland, Alice L., and Associates. *Family Casework Diagnosis.* New York: Columbia University Press, 1962.

54. White, R. W. "Ego and Reality in Psychoanalytic Theory," *Psychol. Issues* 3, No. 3 (1963).
55. White, R. W. "Motivation Reconsidered: The Concept of Social Competence," *Psychol. Review* 66:297 (1959).
56. Witmer, H., and Kotinsky, R. *Personality in the Making.* New York: Harper and Row, 1952.
57. Zigler, E., and Phillips, L. "Social Competence and Outcome in Psychiatric Disorder," *J. Abn. & Sc. Psychol.* 63:264 (1961).

Appendix B

RECOMMENDATIONS ON RESEARCH BY THE CLINICAL COMMITTEE OF THE JOINT COMMISSION ON MENTAL HEALTH OF CHILDREN

Clinical work characteristically generates many questions and hypotheses. Because of the special aspects of the clinical perspective, these questions differ greatly from those asked by others interested in the growth and development of children as well as in services.

I. TYPES OF CLINICAL RESEARCH

1. *Applied Clinical Research*

a. Evaluative Clinical Research (the utilization of scientific method to assess the effectiveness of ongoing services in terms of stated goals; it is closely tied to administration program planning and program development). All clinical services and training programs should be evaluated so as to determine whether or not they are meeting the anticipated goals. Such evaluation should be planned in early stages of the development of the program. Exploratory and demonstration projects in clinical areas need to be encouraged with evaluation seen as an important element of these programs. The evaluation of clinical programs is relatively new; therefore, it has not as yet developed a tradition and a methodology. It is important that new ideas, new methodologies, and new measurement techniques be encouraged which can encompass the breadth and scope of clinical activities.

b. Experimental Research (the exploration in a systematic way of a clinical problem using experimental methodology; often these programs are autonomous administratively from a general operation of the agency, yet the problems explored have direct clinical applicability). Much clinical research falls into this category. However, there still remains a need for stimulating further research

388

of this type with the realization that sometimes, because of the complexity of the variables, it is impossible to get adequate control groups or to control the dimensions along which change occurs.

2. *Basic Clinical Research*

Many basic problems in clinical areas remain unanswered. We need studies of the etiological mechanisms leading to desirabilities in children, studies of predispositions of vulnerabilities to various psychological dysfunctions, studies of reversibility and change, studies of the development of affectional ties, etc. Although such research may not have immediate operational program relevance, it forms the basic scientific foundations for any clinical action or activity and is essential for intelligent future clinical decision making.

II. TRAINING

Active support should be given to those practicing clinicians who are interested in developing skills in clinical research and evaluation as well as to encourage those skilled in research to become more active in bringing their skills to bear in clinically related problems in the area of children. Where researchers do not have experience in clinical problems with children, they should be subsidized with scholarships and fellowships to obtain supervised clinical experience so they can bring their skills to bear in the clinical area.

III. RESEARCH UTILIZATION

Ways should be developed so the research in many areas of child development and clinical work can be related to and translated into both clinical activity and social policy. One example of this was the research in England on hospitalization of children which has been used now to set social policy regarding the construction and administration of children's hospitals.

IV. GENERAL ISSUES AND CLINICAL RESEARCH

The clinical situation generates many hypotheses, observations, and insights. Out of these have come many new directions for explorations in more systematic fashion. However, it is out of such clinical observations that studies of the affectional systems in man arose. It is extremely important that encouragement be given to innovative, creative, and often intuitive stages in the development of research and ideas. Often the ideas arise before adequate methodologies have been developed to systematically explore them. This flexibility is essential if one is to break into new areas. New opportunities to think, conceptualize, and systematically organize ideas in preparation for more detailed exploration later (as in Dr. Piaget's work) are necessary. This means the inclusion of the systematic and careful study of one individual as well as groups of individuals.

Appendix C

UTILIZATION OF PARAPROFESSIONALS
IN CLINICAL SETTINGS

by Rena S. Shulman, M.S.W.

The development of new types of mental health workers subsumed under the term "paraprofessional" has been spurred by a number of current trends in the mental health and social welfare field.

A discussion of manpower recruitment and training for the clinical fields must today include consideration of the development of cadres of new workers outside of our traditional clinical disciplines. Such workers are required to perform a variety of new tasks resulting from the development of a broader range of mental health care. The necessity for the improvement, intensification, and extension of services previously provided only as custodial services, such as in the correctional institutions, the psychiatric hospitals, or children's institutions, also requires new task definitions and the development of appropriate personnel for their performance. The extension of mental health services in the area of preventive programs for infants and young children, such as day care and the development of new programs for supplementary and substitute family care for young children, will require the use of additional helping personnel. Incorporation of mental health and family services in such programs as Head Start similarly set up needs for additional and new kinds of workers.

Two other factors are operative in the current burgeoning of new careers in mental health and social welfare. One is the employment aspect of anti-poverty programing which has stressed the provision of employment opportunities for the untrained and uneducated who make up our "hard-core" poor and for whom special opportunities and training must be made available in order that they may enter the employment market. The other and an interrelated factor is the developing use of the so-called indigenous populations to serve as intermediaries or bridges with the groups who have been alienated from our traditional mental health services. Because such groups are familiar with their

390

community and can often communicate with their neighbors better than the outside professional, they are able to inform the community more adequately about the mental health service and consequently bring about the utilization of professional services. In addition, they may provide many of the necessary intermediary or supplementary services.

The necessity, particularly, for providing minority-group staff who are presently in most short supply in the clinical professions to enable our services to reach minority-group members more effectively and to provide role models for minority youth is a further spur to the utilization of new personnel.

And finally, there is the major issue of manpower shortages in the mental health and social welfare field. With the vast expansion of services, it is unlikely that we will, for many years, have sufficient professionally trained personnel (requiring long years of education and postgraduate training) to adequately staff our new services. For example, in the field of social work, a 1966 report of a Health, Education, and Welfare Department Task Force on Social Work Education and Manpower indicated a vacancy rate of more than 10 percent in social work positions. There was an estimate that with the rapid expansion of programs, by 1975 there would be 178,000 vacancies in social work positions. Only 4,000 new social workers are graduated each year, and the capacity of schools of social work to train and the limitations of recruitment severely hamper the development of a sufficient force of professionally trained staff. This picture is equally true in the other clinical disciplines.

To effectively staff services and provide the new services required, more effective utilization of professional personnel is required with a definition of the tasks to be performed which may not require the highest level of professional training. This follows the medical model in which certain technical tasks have been defined which can be performed by technicians or aides, releasing the doctor or nurse for higher-level duties and thus increasing the personnel force available.

The term "paraprofessional" covers a wide range of levels of services to be performed by personnel possessing a range of education preparation and training including those without high school education or graduation, those with some technical preparation and/or college, and those with baccalaureate degrees. In general, one might define the tasks to be performed by the paraprofessional as those which are concrete and tangible, with built-in controls or where segments of service can be defined. These should be tasks which can be taught in a relatively brief period of training, which are probably repetitive in terms of the techniques to be employed, and in which the method of approach is sufficiently well defined so that independent decision making requiring diagnostic knowledge or deeper understanding of individual personality dynamics is unlikely during the actual process. Such tasks are generally performed under supervision, usually require on-the-job training rather than didactic preparation (or a limited degree of educational or didactic preparation), and would embody assistantship, aide, or apprentice-type functions as well as specific technical tasks which can be assigned for independent functioning. Or at the upper end of the spectrum may be assignments which require college education for direct work with individuals and groups of a supportive and counseling nature and requiring the acquisition of basic diagnostic understanding and knowledge of interviewing techniques and specific intervention methods. The level of intervention, the "vulnerability" of the client, and the objective of the intervention are additional factors in the nature of tasks which can be assigned to the nonprofessional.

Criteria for selection, the nature of the training and supervision, and clarity of role definition and function are necessary prerequisites in the utilization of the paraprofessional. The concept of the "career ladder," possibilities for furthering educational and professional development, and concern about the development of "non-dead-end" occupations must be borne in mind. With respect to selection criteria, basic human qualities necessary for all those in the helping professions in the capacity for relationship and concern and the aspects of teachability and flexibility of personality are essential.

With respect to training and supervision, one must caution against the transposition of the same kind of training and supervision presently utilized for the professionals in the clinical disciplines. There is a necessity for *task-oriented* training and supervision. We must be able to define the basic knowledge of personality, individual and group behavior, and child development which are required for anyone working in the field of human behavior, which must be included in the didactic content of the training. On-the-job training and supervision is essential.

The utilization of ancillary personnel in the mental health field is not a totally new development. We have been utilizing the child care counselor, the psychiatric attendant, the untrained social worker, or the volunteer for many years as part of our treatment process, and certain roles in the mental health field have been traditionally assigned to the nonprofessional. Such personnel, at times, have been totally untrained, or partially trained through in-service training programs and supervision, or more recently "professionalized," as in the child care field through the provision of educational preparation as well as in-service training and career recognition. The inclusion of the nonprofessional as an integral member of the treatment team has been an important step in improvement of services; it has moved the ancillary personnel in our institutions, where they have been most frequently utilized in the role of custodians, to active participants in milieu treatment.

In the development of categories of paraprofessional staff or categories of tasks which may be assigned to the paraprofessional, one might utilize a diagnostic and developmental model.

The following categories of staff may be proposed:

Volunteer	Case Aide
Child Care Aide	Recreational Aide
Family Assistant	Group Work Assistant
Community Assistant	Recreational Worker
Child Care Counselor	Educational Aide
Psychiatric Aide	Tutor
Mental Health Technician	"Special Teacher"
Mental Health Aide	Family Aides
Case Assistant	

Categories of paraprofessional staff have been developed by various manpower programs and other groups working on "new career" training. I have tried in the following breakdown to relate some of the titles in current use to particular tasks in mental health settings. The level of educational preparation and training is tied to the nature of the tasks to be performed. One may organize the utilization of the paraprofessional in relation to the developmental framework. Thus, for example, in preschool programs in which a large component of *care* is involved, the paraprofessional would need to be trained in child care. The personnel serving the school-age child may be engaged in more specific *educational tasks* requiring a different level of preparation and training, etc.

1. CHILD CARE AIDES

This would include *child care aides, pediatric aides, baby nurse aides, home aides,* etc. The major function of this group would be in child care. They may be used in programs for preschool children which require a large component of "care" programing, providing supplementary and complementary care for infants and young children for both preventive and corrective purposes or substitute care outside the child's home. Settings include pediatric services of hospitals, foundling homes and institutions for young children, family day-care or group programs for day care of infants and toddlers, or the more traditional day-care services for children aged two to six. Or they may be used in homemaking functions where substitute or supplementary parental care is provided in the child's own home in the absence or disability of the maternal figure in performing housekeeping and/or child-caring functions.

Such personnel would be responsible for physical care of children and appropriate nurturing and stimulation of individual children or small groups. They may also be used for baby-sitting functions in clinics so that mothers with large families, who could be present only if care is provided for the other children in the family, can participate; or they may provide escort service to bring children to a clinic or special program.

Personnel for such functions should be selected on the basis of personality characteristics and capacities for warmth and trainability in the tasks to be performed. Educational preparation is not necessary, and the training needed is less in didactic areas than in the specifics of child development and the concrete tasks to be performed. The functions themselves should be performed under the supervision of professional staff such as nurses, social workers, early childhood educators, child development specialists, or other clinicians.

Into this group, too, would fall the "foster grandmother," either volunteer or paid, who may be utilized for visits and playing with young children in hospitals or foundling homes or other settings, thus providing some of the individual care and nurturing required.

2. AIDES AND ASSISTANTS

A second category of paraprofessional personnel would include such jobs as *family assistants* or *family workers, community assistants, educational aides* or *teacher's assistants, health aide, child care worker, foster family, day-care mothers, foster mothers,* etc.

Such personnel may be assigned in special infant and young child programs, Head Start and day-care centers, child psychiatry clinics or other mental health programs, well-baby stations, or community mental health programs which involve school or community consultation. They serve as intermediaries between the professional services and the local neighborhood families. They may be involved in case finding, and in paving the way for minority or ghetto families to be able to utilize mental health services. They may serve as interpreters, may accompany families on school visits or clinic or court visits to assist in making contact with authority figures generally avoided or frightening to the poverty family. They may assist in filing applications or filling out forms. They may be able to make contact with mothers to help them make use of health services; with unmarried mothers to interpret the need for prenatal care or postnatal services or special programs for unmarried mothers. They may recruit children for Head Start or other special programs. They may assist in conducting surveys to secure demographic data or other information. They may be utilized for demonstration child care, teaching mothers appropriate modes of infant care, appropriate stimulation, etc. With mothers they may interpret nutritional needs and food preparation and homemaking suggestions.

This would also include psychiatric aides (attendants or aides in psychiatric hospitals who work under the supervision of the psychiatric nurse in child care). As teacher's assistants or educational aides they would assist teachers in educational functions with individuals or groups of children in the classroom. They may perform clerical functions in clinics or hospitals, including record keeping, filling out of forms, etc.

The tasks to be performed require an ability to communicate verbally, to be able to interpret social and mental health services to clients and the community, or the capacity to teach, as in performing demonstration child care functions or as teacher's aides. They may serve as intake receptionist or take telephone applications requiring securing identifying data and the nature of the complaint and may be trained to make appropriate referrals to other services.

Such tasks require some intellectual preparation, formal or informal, preferably a high school education or its equivalent, or may involve the high school dropout with potential for high school graduation. Training includes some knowledge of human behavior, an ability to describe behavior and problems, and knowledge of basic interviewing techniques. In the educational setting such as day-care centers, schools, or special remedial educational services in clinics, they would perform specific educational functions such as story reading, tutoring, or other educational tasks under supervision of a teacher or clinician. In the handling of individuals and groups, they must be able to learn where to gratify and where to limit, and to differentiate in handling. They may require training in making referrals and a knowledge of community resources. Training is mainly "on the job" and involves specific or concrete tasks in which choices of actions are within a limited range. They work under supervision.

Child care counselors, or psychiatric aides, fall into this group to the extent that their functions are more custodial and parenting than those in which a more active treatment role is required, which would involve more technical knowledge and training and a greater degree of differentiation in approach and techniques.

This category may also include the high school student, who may be assigned on a paid or volunteer basis to tutor younger children, who may be in the process of training for child care, or who may serve as a recreational aide, taking children on trips or playing with children.

3. TECHNICIANS

Falling into this group would be the *psychiatric* or *social work technician,* the *social work* or *case assistant,* the *mental health aide,* the *child care counselor,* or the *recreational aide.*

Such staff members perform segments of clinical functions including taking applications, which involves interviewing either in person or on the telephone, or working with individuals or groups as part of a clinical team. The psychiatric technician in the state hospital may be assigned to work with ward patients on specific preparation for leaving the hospital or for entering the world of work. As a technician on the ward, they may be assigned individual cases in which the focus is on relational work. The social work assistant or case assistant may take telephone applications requiring some evaluation of the appropriateness of the referral, with steering to other services or rejection or acceptance of applications, and sufficient data gathering to permit professional disposition of the application. They may interview "walk-ins" and determine the level of urgency of the request, or they may be assigned to individuals in a Big Brother or Big Sister type of relationship with children or adolescents. Technicians may also be assigned to specific case functions with families. They would usually deal with concrete problems such as health, housing, vocational counseling, or job placement referrals. They may be assigned to follow up on cases on medication, for checking that medication is taken, and for checking of effects. They may assist the professional by securing reports from collateral sources such as schools or probation officers, pediatricians, etc. They may lead recreational trips and serve as day camp counselors or as assistant group leaders.

As child care counselors, they are active members of the treatment team, utilizing life-space interviewing techniques with the end of on-the-spot interventions. They work with groups and utilize group process toward the objective of modification in behavior and/or personality change.

The technician requires some educational preparation including high school graduation and some college, preferably the associate degree. Educational preparation is supplemented by close professional supervision and on-the-job training. Educational preparation would include courses in child development, knowledge of community resources, group techniques, and dynamics of individual and group behavior. Supervision or on-the-job training should provide some orientation to diagnostic entities, symptom manifestations, and interviewing techniques. Some awareness of the existence of transference phenomena, resistance, ambivalence, the reasons people do not utilize services, and the obstacles to change would be required as well as some self-awareness. Tasks are performed under close clinical supervision.

This group may include the graduates of "housewives" training programs, or volunteers who undergo organized training and ongoing supervision in the performance of specific clinical tasks.

This category may provide a next career rung for the paraprofessional in category 2 who may undertake educational courses while working.

4. UNTRAINED SOCIAL WORKERS OR CASE AIDES OR GROUP LEADERS

This group includes the untrained social worker, generally called a case aide, who may work in psychiatric or social work settings; the child development specialist; the recreational worker, or group leader; the "special teacher," etc. Such staff members are assigned to work with individuals or groups under supervision but in tasks which involve concrete services as well as the objective of rehabilitation, or modification of functioning. They may work with groups as in street club work or in community centers or in special adolescent programs.

Educational preparation required is a bachelor's degree and basic courses in psychology and human behavior or specialization in early childhood education. Training is generally on the job and through supervision and some didactic content. Such workers carry responsibility for groups of cases and have some degree of choice, and judgment is required with respect to actions to be taken requiring evaluations during the process. Interviewing techniques are required as well as some training in psychosocial diagnosis. Knowledge of transference phenomena, resistance ambivalence, and self-awareness is necessary.

The "special teacher" (called that for want of another name) is usually a nursery school teacher, or occupational therapist, or other specialist, who has some special training for work with individual children in a special, educative-psychotherapeutic relationship, or to provide the special one-to-one relationship which some children may require. The emphasis here is on the relationship and the teaching function, and some knowledge must be acquired of specific techniques to be utilized. Therapeutic tutoring is another area of special functioning, with training in techniques as well as understanding of relationship aspects.

Emphasis in these assignments is both on concrete services and on relationship, support, and counseling rather than on exploration, insight, or interpretation.

The child development specialist is suggested as a new specialist. This should be someone with a baccalaureate degree in child development who may be involved particularly in preventive preschool programs currently being developed. Possibly the case aide may also be trained in some test administration. They work under close clinical supervision.

The untrained social worker has been part of our social work and mental health manpower pool for many years, working in public welfare, foster home, state hospital, and aftercare programs and probation services which have not been able to attract professionally trained staff, whether because of shortages or salary standards. However, the trend has been toward professionalization, and such staff have generally been encouraged through scholarships or other aid to undertake professional training. There has been, in recent years, increasing emphasis because of manpower shortages on utilization of on-the-job training or university courses for the untrained social workers to enhance their level of functioning. However, they have not generally been utilized in highly professionalized clinical settings such as child guidance clinics, residential treatment programs, etc.

With the increasing demand for mental health personnel required by the expansion of mental health and social services, it is apparent that many of these functions will continue to be performed by the untrained social worker or case aide. Special attention needs to be given to modes of training for this group which can emphasize development of professional skills without the necessity of undertaking graduate training. Programs for preprofessional specialization in undergraduate schools may be required as well as training through supervision and courses designed for the preprofessional group. At the same time, it will undoubtedly be necessary for psychiatric settings, such as child guidance services, and other treatment services to examine the tasks to be performed and cull out specific tasks which may be able to be assigned to the nonprofessional in the area of application and intake, data gathering, interviewing of collaterals, and possibly the assignment of individual cases in which an educational therapeutic role is required or where the focus may be on supportive relationships being maintained. The follow-up of cases on medication may be assigned to such workers, who would need to be afforded some very special and specific training in this area.

The above is by no means offered as an exhaustive list of tasks which can be performed by a range of nonprofessional personnel but as a guide to either new tasks which are developing or segments of mental health activity which can be assigned to workers without graduate professional education. The skills of the professional are required for supervision and training of such personnel.

Appendix D

PSYCHOPHARMACOLOGIC AGENTS

by D. G. Prugh, M.D., and A. Kisley, M.D.

PSYCHOPHARMACOLOGIC AGENTS[1]

Psychoactive drugs have achieved a place in the treatment of emotional disorders of childhood. They cannot replace the interpersonal relationship which is the main tool of the physician's armamentarium; however, they can be effective in reducing anxiety and overactivity. The reduction of impulsivity and irritability is usually accompanied by less anxiety and improved attention span. On occasion, they can increase spontaneous activity and responsiveness in states of apathy and depression. The effects upon complex behavior patterns, on the other hand, are much more difficult to predict during drug therapy. There is no evidence that such drugs can improve intellectual functioning directly. Although it is possible to modify a child's responses to current experiences, psychoactive drugs cannot undo previously learned behavior or alter neurotic patterns. Much information is still needed on the effects of specific drugs and their mode of action, as our knowledge remains largely empirical.

The psychological effect of administering medication can undoubtedly be a major factor in a child's improvement. The drug may influence the child either directly through his own expectations or indirectly through changed parental conduct, because they anticipate a change in the child. The physician assessing the behavior may project into the response the expected outcome in the form of confidence. One-third of the effect of *any* drug has been shown to be a "placebo" effect, which is gained if a positive doctor-parent-patient relationship is present; such may be lost (and more) if not.

1. To be published in H. Kempe and H. Silver (eds.), *Current Pediatric Therapy* (Los Altos, Calif.: Lange Medical Publications, Inc.).

PRINCIPLES OF DRUG TREATMENT

A disturbed child's condition must be accurately diagnosed if the child is to receive the most effective treatment. Choosing appropriate drugs and applying them with discrimination can help control some target symptoms in moderately severe psychoses and chronic brain syndromes. Some severely disturbed children may become amenable to psychotherapy, which may otherwise be impossible. Dosage must be carefully regulated so as not to impair a child's intellectual acuity. Although neurotic disorders rarely respond to available drugs, some children with intrapsychic conflict and suffering from persistent anxiety, inhibitions, and phobias become more spontaneous and increase their adaptive functioning. Personality disorders and mental retardation are generally not benefited by drugs, unless hyperkinesia appears as a dominant element, in which case stimulant drugs have a role. Reactive disorders rarely justify drug use unless sedation is necessary for cases with acute anxiety following physical or emotional shock.

The physician who uses drugs should have a thorough knowledge of their pharmocologic properties, especially the side effects and toxic manifestations. The severity of the child's disorder, combined with the potential for improvement, must exceed the impact of the side effects as well as the possibility of toxicity. A child's response to a psychoactive drug may be quite different from that of an adult. Special screening of drugs potentially valuable for disturbed children is essential, as a drug's action may be unpredictable because of the immature and developing qualities of the child. In addition, *dosage must be individualized* for each patient, since undertreatment as well as overtreatment may ensue because of metabolical uniqueness.

A well-tested and familiar drug should be employed before a newer or unfamiliar one. Unexpected toxicity from a less well-known agent may not become apparent until after prolonged administration. Related to this problem is the adage that drugs should not be used any longer than is necessary. Lowering the dosage periodically will help track symptom change with dynamic shifts in the child.

Since pharmacotherapy affects symptoms, not disease pictures, the physician must *continue to seek and eliminate the etiological factors* in the emotional disturbance. Failure to correct physical, psychological, or social elements contributing to the child's dilemma is not in keeping with sound medical practice.

TYPES OF DRUGS

Psychoactive agents are divided into *major and minor tranquilizers, hypnotics, stimulants, antidepressants, and psychotominetics.*

1. Major Tranquilizers

The major tranquilizers have found their greatest influence in the treatment of hospitalized, severely disturbed, or psychotic children because of their calmative effect on agitated, impulsive, or excited states without clouding of consciousness. They can facilitate social adjustment, reduce or eliminate delusions and hallucinations, and thus make these children more communicative. The dosage of a major tranquilizer is increased at intervals of several days until a satisfactory response is obtained, or until side effects limit or preclude its administration. These agents should ordinarily not be used to alleviate anxiety of the type found in the psychoneuroses.

a. *Phenothiazine Derivatives.* These drugs are the most potent of the tranquilizers and have received the most extensive clinical use since the discovery of chlorpromazine (Thorazine) in the 1940's. To all intents and purposes, the phenothiazines are equally effective, except for slight variations. Thus the physician should familiarize himself with one or two agents in this group and learn to use a particular drug well. They include chlorpromazine (Thorazine), promazine (Sparine), thioridazine (Mellaril), trifluoperazine (Stelazine), and perchlorperazine (Compazine). On the whole, most of the phenothiazines have relatively low toxicity. This provides a fairly good safety margin of therapeutic activity over toxicity, *except for Compazine, which is not safe for children.* Common nonserious side effects include autonomic or anticholinergic responses (constipation, blurred vision, dryness of the mouth, difficult micturation, gastric upset); skin changes (dermatitis, photosensitivity); extrapyramidal syndromes (Parkinsonism, dystonias, akathisia), and lethargy or drowsiness. Less commonly, endocrine abnormalities and unexplained bodily temperature changes occur. Potentially serious toxic effects include blood dyscrasias, hepatitis, marked hypotension, and seizures which may occur on high dosages. *Regular blood studies* should be a routine part of drug administration. Toxicity or troublesome side effects can be handled by decreasing the dosage or changing to another drug. Extrapyramidal signs can usually be relieved by anti-Parkinsonism drugs.

b. *Rauwolfia Alkaloids.* These drugs appear to have a less reliable effect than the phenothiazines. Reserpine probably acts by reducing brain serotonin levels. It has been used in severely psychotic and disorganized children with brain damage with variable success. With adequate doses, lethargy, nasal congestion, weight gain, and other disturbing side effects are frequently encountered.

c. *Butyrophenones.* Although this group of compounds, which has been used extensively in Europe with adults, is unrelated to the phenothiazines, the pharmacologic action is quite similar. Their usefulness for children is still not completely established. Haloperidol (haldol) seems to have a marked effect on tic syndromes, however, especially those involved in the syndrome of Gilles de la Tourette.

2. Minor Tranquilizers

These agents, because of their effects on milder psychiatric disorders and their lesser toxicity, are employed frequently in outpatient treatment of children. They may be useful in psychoneurotic and occasionally in reactive and psychophysiological disorders. Occasionally these medications are helpful with moderately disturbed children if their patterns are more malleable. In contrast to the major tranquilizers, these agents do not appear to be equally effective.

a. *Diphenylmethanes.* This group contains several agents which have anti-histaminic properties as well as tranquilizing effects. Toxicity is not commonly encountered, although the usual precautions should be taken. Hydroxyzine (Atarax, Vistaril) has been found to be useful in mild anxiety states, night terrors, reactions to somatic difficulties, and school phobias. Diphenhydramine (Benadryl) has been used extensively as an antianxiety agent as well as a sedative, but its effectiveness seems to drop off at puberty.

b. *Propanediols.* Meprobamate (Equinol, Miltown) may give rise to drowsiness, rashes, and withdrawal effects. Although habituation has been reported in adults, this does not seem to occur in children. Acute toxicity has resulted from accidental ingestion of large amounts. Because of muscle-relaxing qualities, these drugs have been useful in treating cerebral palsy and allied disorders. These agents have limited effect upon hyperactivity.

c. *Benzodiazepines.* Chlordiazepoxide (Librium) and diazepan (Valium) have apparent antianxiety effects in adults and animals, but there is as yet insufficient data available as to their effectiveness in children. Diazepan has been claimed to have potent muscle relaxant properties in addition, and may be useful in spastic conditions.

3. *Hypnotics and Sedatives*

These agents have been available to physicians for a long time. Barbiturates have been of limited value in the treatment of moderately or severely disturbed children. At times these agents can be useful for acutely agitated children, but chronic administration of barbiturates, except in convulsive disorders, is no longer wise because of the confusion, disorientation, and increased agitation frequently produced. They may paradoxically stimulate preschool children or children with hyperactivity from either anxiety or brain damage. Chloral hydrate continues to be one of the most effective sedatives and is an extremely safe drug. Although paraldehyde is equally potent and safe, its odor is a problem with children.

4. *Stimulants*

The amphetamines have been used to treat children with behavior disorders for more than twenty years. They are most effective in the treatment of children who are hyperactive and distractable as the result of anxiety or brain damage. In such children, they have a paradoxically depressant effect, seeming empirically to "dampen down" or monitor incoming stimuli, resulting in quieter, more organized behavior and a longer attention span. Prolonged therapy with these agents can be maintained without significant toxicity. Side effects are manifested primarily by anorexia and insomnia, which can be controlled by lowering the dosage. Overdoses can result in toxic psychosis, and there is a risk of habituation in adolescents. Occasionally the mirrored form of the amphetamine will succeed when its relative did not.

Treatment for school-age children is initiated with 5 milligrams daily in the morning before breakfast, and increased 5 milligrams every several days in divided doses, in the morning and early afternoon, until improvement occurs or side effects ensue. Doses up to 30 milligrams per day are not infrequently needed to effectively treat a hyperkinetic child. Beginning and maintenance doses of about half of the above are often effective in preschool children. If after two weeks no noticeable change in symptomatology has occurred, the drug (usually Dexedrine initially) should be discontinued as ineffective, and another amphetamine (Benzedrine) or Ritalin (Methylphenidate) tried. If effective, the drug can be continued until puberty, when it is usually no longer necessary.

Deanol (Deaner) has been reported to act on the reticular activating system, leading to an improved integration of stimuli impinging on the disorganized child. Investigations are still limited, and consequently its usefulness has not been proven to date.

5. Antidepressants

Whether the newer antidepressant drugs will find a place in the treatment of children has not been completely established. The types of depressions treated successfully by these chemicals in adults do not occur in childhood or adolescence. However, several of these agents have been used for disorders other than depressions with equivocal results. Nialamide (Niamid) and phenelzine (Nardil), both monoamine oxidase inhibitors, were used with autistic and seriously withdrawn adolescents, who showed an increase in awareness of their surroundings. These drugs appear to produce a protective action on serotonin and norepinephrine. Toxicity is a serious problem, however. The iminodibenzyl derivatives have been said to alleviate enuresis in children. Imipramine (Tofranil), the most commonly used of this class of drugs, has appeared as the most successful in some studies, but further tests are needed to clarify its effectiveness.

6. Psychotominetics

These agents, which include lysergic acid diethylamide (LSD-25), mescaline, and psylocybin, may have some possibilities in the treatment of disturbed children. However, the safety of these drugs is still uncertain, and their use is not recommended. Their use is at present limited to experimental application.

REFERENCES

Eisenberg, L. "The Role of Drugs in Treating Disturbed Children," *Children* 11:167 (1964).
Freedman, A. M. "Drug Therapy in Behavior Disorders," *Pediat. Clin. N. Amer.* (Aug. 1958), 573.
Lucas, A. "Psychopharmacologic Treatment," in *The Psychiatric Disorders of Childhood*, C. R. Shaw (ed.). New York: Appleton-Century-Crofts, 1966.

Appendix E

STATEMENT ON RACISM

by the Committee on Clinical Issues[1]

As clinicians we are greatly aware of the depth of the disturbances produced by prejudices of all kinds. We are also aware of how early experiences with discriminations by race, color, religion, and/or national origin significantly affect behavior in later life. We are particularly sensitive to the unconscious elements that contribute to discriminatory behavior in a variety of subtle ways, behavior which has clearly been found to be destructive not only to the adequate growth and development of those individuals discriminated against, but also to those who are doing the discriminating. Complex personal needs as well as social and economic ones are often satisfied by discrimination, prejudices, and scapegoating of all kinds. These personal needs begin in the earliest years of life, when fear and anxiety about strangers and the unknown often result in people who are different in some ways being used as objects for the expression of one's own psychological problems and difficulties. The development of a sense of self-worth, for example, has been found to be very closely related to the development of attitudes about others, especially those considered different. Tied in with this also is the self-fulfilling prophecy in which responses are often evoked from other people which tend to confirm one's initial suspicions on the grounds that such behavior is typical of a given group.

We recognize the need to be especially aware of how deeply rooted feelings influence our attitudes, the distribution of our mental health services, and other areas of work with minority groups.

Recognizing the existence of prejudice, we as clinicians dealing with children recommend: (1) Special sensitivity and awareness of clinicians to the

1. Prepared by Milton F. Shore, Zanwil Sperber, and Jerome S. Silverman, appointed members to a special subcommittee on racism.

forces of prejudice and discrimination, since these forces severely disrupt the adequate development of children with regard to their full potential and affect the distribution and quality of the mental health services given to those children and families who need assistance. (2) Clinicians should be encouraged to contribute their skills to planning how to remedy the destructive forces of racism, prejudice, and scapegoating of all kinds, since all of these are based on irrational elements deeply tied to personality functioning. (3) The roots of discrimination lie not only in psychological dimension but in many political, historical, social, and economic elements as well. Psychological explanations, although contributing to the total understanding of this phenomenon, should not be seen as the only leverage for intervention and change. Mental health professionals should not only contribute their skills but also be aware of the political implications of psychological explanations lest they be used in ways contrary to their intent. Clinicians should also be aware of how subtle forces may influence even the definition of mental health as well as the interpretations given to behavioral patterns within a given social context. (4) Training programs for clinicians (graduate programs, residencies, fellowships, etc.) should include emphasis on the understanding of and intervention with minority groups and the underprivileged. New intervention techniques should be studied and encouraged. These techniques should be of high quality and should be evaluated as to the appropriateness for the handling of particular problems, not for political or other nonprofessional reasons. This is particularly true to techniques such as brief therapy, crisis intervention, and the use of drugs which sometimes have been used in arbitrary fashion in certain groups. Generalization about various groups and the indiscriminate use of a particular technique can often foster the already existing prejudices and reactions. (5) Active efforts should be made to train and recruit competent personnel from minority groups who can participate in and accept administrative and professional responsibility for mental health services. Experts who are not members of the particular minority group should make themselves available as consultants when called in by these administrators. (6) In consultative and educative activities, efforts should be made by the clinicians to make lay and other professional groups aware of the destructive and subtle influences of discrimination, prejudice, scapegoating, etc., in the normal development of children and in the establishment of the services to children and their families. Programs should be developed from the earliest years which focus around the handling of aggression, love, feelings of self-worth, and fear in such a way as to reduce the efforts to project badness onto others. Educationally, socially, and culturally, the focus should be on developing programs that respect differences and variability, especially in times of crisis, when polarization becomes an almost natural psychological phenomenon.

Appendix F

A CLINICIAN'S OVERVIEW

by Meyer Sonis, M.D.

In approaching the rather broad topic of the clinical needs of and requirements for the emotionally disabled, mentally ill, and retarded children, and
for our current and future planning for these children, it would seem to me
that attention must be paid to a whole host of factors, including some of the
following: the number of children requiring clinical intervention as might
be given through the auspices of child psychiatric services; the spectrum of
disabilities in these children brought to the attention of such services or
potentially so; the spectrum of services required to match the disabilities in
the children; the patterns of existing services; access to, delivery of, and gaps
in these services; the manpower available, and the deployment of such manpower; and current problems and trends in child health, education, and welfare which have implications for clinical services to these children.

During the past two years, the Joint Commission on Mental Health of
Children has certainly addressed itself to the various factors relating to clinical
services for children, beginning with the recommendations of the Studies Committee, and continuing on through the work of the Task Forces, their reports,
the contracted studies, and the reports of various organizations to the Joint
Commission. From material available to those of us on the Joint Commission,
it would seem that the data and knowledge emerging will no doubt provide
significant opportunity for advances to be made in behalf of the clinical needs
and requirements of emotionally disabled, mentally ill, and retarded children.
In the remarks to follow, it will be my intent to address myself to these various
factors, but from the vantage point of a clinician who has turned teacher and
administrator and who has gained experience in the delivery of clinical services
to children.

405

I. NUMBER OF CHILDREN

Experience to date suggests that whether one likes it or not, the fact of the matter is that our estimates of the number of children requiring the clinical services are gross and may be an overestimate or underestimate of the size of the problem. Though most of the states in our nation have completed their own comprehensive mental health planning and arrived at some estimate of the size of the problem, there yet is much variance between the base rate utilized. Our lack of agreement on mental health professions and services, as well as in the child caretaking professions, on terms, definitions, and frames of reference in collecting data has not made it possible to as yet arrive at valid comparisons. Lack of interest on the part of many clinicians, at least until recently, in epidemiological data collection has also added to the problem. In the collection of data by the Biometrics Branch of the National Institute of Mental Health, further problems have emerged in that the data collected to date have not been geared specifically to children's disorders, and the age breakdown of their data does not coincide with the age breakdown of data collection in other resources.

With existing patterns of service, it is entirely possible that the same child is being counted a number of times and, at the same time, other children such as might be seen in a family agency, a pediatric hospital, a general hospital, or a practitioner's office are not being counted. The problem is further compounded by the fact that since there are many more inquiries for services than persons who are actually seen, the data of demographic and epidemiological nature available in many of our resources simply tell the picture of those children who have been seen. It is possible that if we had even some gross data on all children referred to our resources, we might be in a better position than we are currently.

Because of our lack of agreement, it is also possible that the same child is seen by the school as a learning problem, by the court as an offender, by the pediatric clinic as a child with a physical disability, by the psychiatric clinic as a youngster with an emotional disorder.

It would seem that thought must be given to establishing a uniform data basis of collection, and that the reservoirs in which emotionally disturbed children are kept also should be included. It is unfortunate that many of our mental health centers in existence or on the blueprint have as yet not taken steps to build in the necessary machinery for giving us some future data which might be more valid than that currently available.

II. SPECTRUM OF DISABILITIES

In approaching the question of the spectrum of disabilities in children which would bring them to child psychiatric attention, one source from which some data can emerge is that of the existing diagnostic classification of the American Psychiatric Association (APA). Despite the problems that this classification has posed for those of us in the children's field, it has become a frame of reference for estimating the size and nature of the population to be served. In many ways, it has also become a frame of reference for evolving the spectrum of services required. As clinicians, many of us have gained experience during the past decade in using this classification system, and I would like to call on my personal experience with this and share general impressions that have arisen.

It would seem to me that most of our outpatient child guidance clinics have been serving children predominantly in the age bracket of six to fifteen, with children under the age of six seen in greater numbers in those clinics related to pediatric hospitals, and children above age fifteen seen in greater numbers in the multipurpose clinics, general psychiatric clinics, state hospitals and clinics, and by the private practitioner in the community. It has almost become axiomatic to state that the ratio of boys to girls in outpatient child guidance clinics seems to run in the order of 2 to 1 in favor of boys, with a shift in this to a ratio closer to 1 to 1 during the adolescent period. During the past decade, as some of our communities developed other resources regarding the health, education, and welfare of children, I believe there has been a shift in the nature of referrals to the child guidance clinic with less of these referrals from social agencies than previously and more from sources such as physicians, hospitals, self-referrals, and schools. I also believe that the larger number of children referred by the school to the child guidance clinics takes place at around age seven to eight, or in the second and third grade, and that referrals generally from the schools increase toward the end of the school year and at the beginning of the school year.

If one looks at this data in terms of the spectrum of diagnoses made, it is interesting to note that in most of our outpatient child guidance clinics, 30 to 40 percent of the cases referred are terminated with no diagnosis made, since the children were never seen, and, additionally, a very small percentage terminate with a diagnosis of no psychiatric disorder. It is important, therefore, to keep in mind that when speaking of the spectrum of disabilities brought to the child guidance clinic, one is not able to say much about 30 to 40 percent of the cases accepted. It is also interesting to note that in our outpatient child guidance clinics, 40 and sometimes up to 50 percent of the children diagnosed are done so with diagnoses indicating chronicity, with the records of these cases documenting the fact that many of these children have had difficulties antedating by years the referral to the psychiatric facility.

At the outpatient child guidance clinics, an impression is also gained that the diagnosis of personality disorder is made more frequently in children over the age of ten than below, while diagnosis of chronic brain syndrome, mental deficiency, and psychosis would be made in greater numbers under the age of ten. In regard to the diagnosis of transient situational reactions, the data of the American Association of Psychiatric Clinics for Children (AAPCC)[1] suggest that, in their group of clinics, this diagnosis is made less frequently than in the general clinics reporting to the Biometrics Branch of NIMH, which suggests the possibility that the more specialized facilities exclusively serving children may be more discriminatory in their diagnoses than others.

1. AAPCC, *Children and Clinics,* a survey by the American Association of Psychiatric Clinics for Children, 1968.

From work done by myself previously in Philadelphia, and reported generally by others, it would seem that families of low socioeconomic means, and with a tendency to a high number of social agency contacts in the community, have a tendency to refer their children to the psychiatric facility when the child is older, in trouble more frequently, and when the prognosis is guarded to poor—in comparison to families other than low socioeconomic. It would also seem that the rate of referral of children diagnosed as chronic brain syndrome/mental retardation by the low economic group is similar to the rate of referral by other groups—that the behavioral symptoms manifested by this group of children are such as to bring earlier and quicker attention.

During the past ten years, there have been a number of studies done by various child guidance clinics on the demographic nature of the population served, but unfortunately not as much has been done with this data as one would hope. I believe, however, that in a certain group of our clinics, concerted and conjoint effort has been made to begin relating the data to one another in order to arrive at some common frames of reference. From such studies an impression is gained that first school difficulties come out in a rank order of presenting symptoms at a child guidance center. It is also an impression that the child guidance clinic population has many children in its midst who have learning difficulties resulting primarily from perceptual-motor developmental problems.

However, if one wanted to gain a more valid picture of the spectrum of disabilities in children requiring or potentially requiring psychiatric intervention, I believe it can best be done through combining the data of various child psychiatric services so that one has a picture of children within the pediatric hospital, the outpatient child psychiatric clinic, the inpatient service, the day-care center, and the state hospital backstop service. I believe that an even more valid picture than this would be one in which the spectrum of disabilities in children included the reservoir system in our communities. Such an approach to a more valid spectrum of disabilities which might require psychiatric intervention could be taken if we were to focus our attention on the development of the child and behavioral symptoms as a barometer to deviation in that development, regardless of whether such behavioral symptoms are etiologically produced by neuronal disorders, metabolic deficiencies, genetic or inborn errors of metabolism, social pathology, developmental phase, psychopathology, perceptual-motor developmental disorders, or any combination of these. Utilizing such a scheme, one could then more validly estimate the total range of disabilities in children and the spectrum of services of a psychiatric nature which may be required. Utilizing such a scheme, for example, one will have a net which will capture the diabetic child whose diabetes control is closely interwoven with the psychological control system; the child with congenital defects producing psychological decompensation in the family; the children in foster home institutions ostensibly on the base of dependent and neglected status; the child whose behavioral symptoms have brought him into the court as a social offender; the child whose phase of development is producing manifestations of phobic response, etc.

For myself, I believe that even more attention must be paid in the years ahead to evolving a common base of data collection, and to the utilization of the GAP diagnostic classification system. As I have gained some experience with this diagnostic classification, I believe at some future time it would be more possible to examine the spectrum of disabilities with which the child psychiatric services must be concerned.

III. SPECTRUM OF SERVICES

By this time in our growth as a subspecialty, there has been a great deal written about the total spectrum of psychiatric services required for the various disabilities which children manifest. The Conference on Planning Psychiatric Services for Children and the Comprehensive Mental Health and Retardation Law and Act certainly give some background and substance to the kinds of services which are required. For this reason, I will not detail this aspect, but would prefer to underline the fact that in our thinking about the spectrum of services required, it would seem that we seldom explore in depth the evolution of these services as a reflection of unresolved problems in our pattern of servicing the community. I am aware that this probably is a special hobby horse of mine, and for this reason I no doubt bring bias to my discussion of these issues. In other words, I have often wondered that if steps were taken to identify and resolve some of the problems now existing in our community regarding our pattern of services for emotionally disturbed children, we might find that existing child psychiatric services could do an even better job than they have been able to until the present. One might say that as long as our services for disturbed children were not developmentally focused and based, our communities had a tendency to evolve services which were symptom focused and a specific service oriented. For this reason, I believe that despite the criticism of the child guidance clinic for its one method of approach, the problem is the contrary—namely, that in some of our clinics we have developed as many as 57 different varieties of treatment without having truly understood the reasons why model number 51 or 2 did not work.

If one were to examine some of the data in the AAPCC study, attention is most beautifully called to the total gamut of services which clinicians deem necessary to match the total disabilities in children. For me, this list is far more comprehensive than that currently mandated on the Comprehensive Mental Health Law. In fact, one might wonder, in cases where the necessary community services were not available, whether this meant that the clinics, of necessity, developed comprised plans for a child, recognizing full well that this was not the most effective plan. The data of AAPCC reminds us of the fact that a child psychiatric service can function best if it is part of a total pattern of community services.

In thinking about the total spectrum of services required to match the disabilities in children and in utilizing the developmental approach referred to earlier, it would be possible to contemplate the development of a spectrum of services in which child psychiatry would be directly administratively responsible for some, collaboratively responsible for others, and consultatively related to still others. I have referred to such a scheme in the paper entitled "Implications for a Child Guidance Clinic," as well as elsewhere in this "Clinician's Overview."

IV. PATTERNS OF SERVICE

Were I an impartial observer with responsibility for developing an efficient, meaningful plan of providing community services to children with behavioral symptoms, and were I to do this by utilizing the limited manpower available in the most efficient way, I believe I would immerse myself in becoming familiar with the existing pattern of services totally within the community. I would explore the nature of child psychiatric services, protective services for children, educational and health services, social agency and welfare services, and I believe I would generally find the following observations pertinent to specific areas:

A. *Child Psychiatric Services*

In many of the outpatient child guidance clinics, I would find that contrary to criticisms made, a good proportion of cases referred do come from the low socioeconomic group. The question here is not whether they get referred, but what happens to them in the process at the clinic. Experience, I believe, would bear out the fact that many of these families do not go very far beyond that of an initial contact or two and that in comparison to other groups of children, a small proportion of these enter into the treatment contacts. It has been said that this tendency is a result of the middle-class value system of the professional staff at our child guidance clinics, and this may be so. However, I have often wondered whether this may not also be a reflection of the fact that in the clinic's approach to this group of children and their families, the clinic does not distinguish between the seeking of relief from the child on the part of the environment and the personal investment on the part of the environment required for a psychological commitment to change. I believe at times that an attitude, on the part of the clinician, has crept into clinic work which tends to devalue the person seeking relief and wanting advice. It is one thing to ask an already overburdened mother to commit herself to giving more of herself in behalf of her child at a time when she is wanting relief from the burden, and it is another thing to ask this of her by bringing in other community agents to offer support during the process.

This attrition of this group of patients is also related to what would seem to be a natural attrition process at our clinics in which about one-third of the referrals accepted do not go beyond the intake process, and one-third of the group seen through the diagnostic process does not go beyond this. As a result of this attrition process, many of the clinics utilize intake as a means of screening in or out, but I believe unfortunately do not really develop sufficient and valid data on which to base decisions. An examination of any of our clinics would reveal that many of them have undertaken studies of all kinds in search of evolving characteristics of the families who terminate as differentiated from those who remain, but in so doing have not as yet evolved meaningful criteria. In many of our clinics, the intake process is similar in philosophy and approach to that of intake into a social agency offering a concrete type of service. Because of the need to ostensibly screen in or out, many of our clinics utilize the most experienced social workers in the intake process. This may be valid, but I suspect that if one truly examines the intake interview in order to arrive at the criteria which were the basis of the decision, one would find lack of agreement among other experienced professionals.

At many of these outpatient clinics, it would seem that the case load at any one time is a reflection of a whole host of variables: children who are being offered some program at the clinic in lieu of there being the necessary services available in the community; a number of children who have been seen by a variety of nonpsychiatric facilities in the community over a number of years, but who were adjudged to require specific medical intervention; more children in treatment proportionately diagnosed as personality disorders, psychoneurosis, situational reactions, than chronic brain syndrome, mental retardation, psychosis, and psychosomatic disorders; more white children than nonwhite in treatment; the lack of a direct correlative relationship between diagnosis and treatment, the nature of treatment modalities utilized, and the rate of improvement; a whole gamut of reasons as to which profession is directly responsible for the child, the parent, and the family; and the utilization of a range of modality—individual psychotherapy, group therapy, social group work, social casework, drugs, remedial education, family therapy—without any clear criteria for deciding which modality was used to meet which disorder.

In many of our clinics, one would find a great deal of duplication of effort and spinning of the wheels, with minimum attention paid to evolving a systems approach to data collection, analysis, billing, case assignment, case flow, and evolvement of criteria on which decisions are made. In many of these clinics, a great deal of time is devoted by the organization to consultative activity with various agencies in a community, but this amount of involvement is not reflected in data that are kept by the organization. If one examined the amount of professional effort devoted by a clinic to various of its cases, one would find that a great deal of thought, energy, and concern is given by the organization to each child. Though much criticism has been leveled at the clinics for such efforts, I believe a detailed study of the nature of the population served would indicate the reasons for such a heavy concentrated effort.

In an examination of the other child psychiatric services, such as that within the pediatric center or that of the inpatient psychiatric center, one would find impressions similar to those listed for the outpatient clinic. However, in the pediatric center, it appears that more time is spent in giving diagnostic services and that the case load spectrum is somewhat different from that of the outpatient child guidance clinic. In such a pediatric center, the psychiatric service is often unable to perform its broader role in the pediatric setting because it is utilized for offering direct service. In these pediatric settings, the child psychiatric service is many times utilized by the pediatrician as a means of dichotomizing the psychological from the medical.

B. *Others—Community Services*

In a community which has evolved to a point of offering some services for children in terms of protective services, social and welfare services, health services, and educational services, and were I an impartial observer exploring these services as they may relate to children with behavioral symptoms, I

believe I would find some of the following impressions pertinent: a competitiveness among the various agencies, with each zealously guarding its
intake policy and autonomy; insufficient community funds to have truly made
possible the growth of each agency, thus fostering a competitiveness in funds;
a lack of agreement between various agencies and the child psychiatric service
on terms, definitions, and frames of reference regarding the child with behavioral symptoms; a pattern in which some children with behavioral symptoms
who should be treated are being contained, while some children who should be
contained are being treated; a pattern in the community wherein the environmental fabric for support of child development has been torn down, thus
precipitating the psychiatric emergency; a separateness in various agencies
wherein the same child is viewed and treated by the agency as an educational
problem, a physical problem, a personality problem, a family problem, a social
offender; an informal and transfer referral system which consistently aims the
disruptive child toward the long-term care of an institution such as a state
hospital, a group home for delinquents; and a rivalry between the various
mental health professions in the various child caretaking agencies.

V. MANPOWER

At the present point, a great deal of emphasis has been placed on this
question of manpower, its availability and its utilization. It is clear that the
Joint Commission has paid attention to this aspect, as have other national
studies such as the National Health Advisory Council, NIMH, etc. It has been
predictable for some period of time that in the children's mental health field,
perhaps more than in the adult services, there will be need for more concentrated development of new professions and technicians. I believe that this
question is not simply related to the fact that there are fewer child psychiatrists
than general psychiatrists, but is also related to the fact that children's services
require a greater relationship to the environment than adult services.

I will not address myself in detail to this manpower situation except to
share some general impressions and feelings that I have.

To begin with, I believe that those of us in the children's field, and especially those of us charged with medical responsibility for child care, will probably have to make peace with the need to develop a whole cadre of nonmedical
personnel to aid us in the task of intervening with children manifesting behavioral symptoms. The cadre, at the present point, may run the gamut from
the child care worker, to the mental health aide, to the indigenous worker, to
the child development specialist, to the teacher aide, to the associate social
worker and social group worker. Increasingly, I am of the mind that child
psychiatry will have to assume leadership for providing educational supervision and programs for this group of people, since I believe that medicine
will continue to separate care of children from that of diagnosis of them and
treatment, that medicine will continue to put emphasis on the scientific nature
of medical practice, relegating the development of children and the behavioral
symptoms as barometers of their deviancy to others. It would seem that similar
situations will evolve in relation to social work and clinical psychology, with

the field of social work tending to minimize the clinical, and psychology tending to increase its identity in the research area.

In reviewing the material submitted to date by the Joint Commission, and specifically relative to manpower, I believe that the American Psychiatric Association Manpower Study, contracted for by the Joint Commission,[2] holds

out the promise of giving us a much more rational approach to looking at our trends. In other words, it would seem that any study of manpower, its availability, and its future development must be tied to the nature of services offered and the trends in these services.

VI. ALTERNATIVE DIRECTIONS

Continuing on with the clinician's overview, as has been done in the previous sections, I would now like to address myself to the potential of alternatives available to meet the various problems posed.

As a start, I believe that most clinicians and clinical facilities are in agreement with many of the statements that I have made previously and many of the findings that are emerging as a result of Joint Commission study, investigation, and review. However, I believe that the continued criticism of the clinician and the outpatient child guidance clinic can only lead to destructive action and defensiveness of the clinician in regard to his training, investment, and competence. I am almost of the mind that continued blame of the clinician for all of the problems that have been identified is simply beating a dead horse and, dynamically speaking, seems to serve the purpose of utilizing the clinician and clinical facilities as a scapegoat for all of the guilt feelings that other professions and our communities have in regard to their own lack of activity in meeting the needs of children. I also believe that continued blame of the clinician may also be serving the purpose of providing a cover for the power, prestige, and status-striving issues among the various child caretaking professions.

It seems to me that this continued pastime of blaming clinicians and minimizing the needs of emotionally disturbed children is a similar phenomenon to that of the community in its previous attempts to contain and temporize with the behavioral symptoms in children, to extrude them from the system which they are clogging up, and to avoid the fact that mental illness in children will be with us for some period of time.

In fact, if we as a society are now acknowledging the existing problems that we have in education of children, the lack of adequate structure for rearing of children, the horrible gaps in community services needed for children, and if we as a society are also acknowledging that these problems and gaps have existed for some period of time, how can we then continue to place the blame for these problems on the clinical facilities and clinicians? In fact, the current acknowledgment by our society of the many gaps that exist supports the contention of clinicians that they have been placed in an untenable position during

2. J. F. Whiting, J. Carper, and R. Feldman, *Needed: A Scientific Basis for Manpower Utilization in Mental Health Services.* Prepared for Task Force IV of the Joint Commission on Mental Health of Children, Inc., Oct. 1967.

the past decade of attempting to offer their services in lieu of other needed services. I am belaboring this point in my belief that the Joint Commission itself has participated in the phenomenon, referred to previously as the community phenomenon, and that this issue of blaming clinicians is not yet settled for the Joint Commission.

As a clinician, I am of the mind that if a poll were taken, or opinion sought of the many clinicians in clinical facilities serving emotionally disturbed children, one would find the following:

a. that there is more agreement among them on: the belief that there is a multiple causality of behavioral symptoms in children and, therefore, the need for multiple solutions; the need for a systems approach to our clinical data collection and analysis, and an approach which would not only yield demographic and epidemiological data, but information to be utilized for case flow, case assignment, billing; the need for more services in our communities and the coordination and integration of these services into some unity of purpose to minimize the existing duplication, fragmentation, and mismatch; the need for a pattern of services which would meet the needs of children and their families and the total spectrum of disabilities in children; the value of a developmental approach in delivery of our services to children; the need for new manpower and systems of better deployment of existing manpower; the need for changes in our educational and welfare systems; upgrading of professions such as teaching, child care, nursing; the need for resolution of existing problems among the various mental health professions; the need for truly testing out the effectiveness of programs offered; the reorganization of existing services; a better utilization of services available, etc.

b. that there will be less agreement among the mental health professions, the clinicians, and the clinical facilities on the questions: whether there is role confusion and diffusion now existing between social work, psychology, psychiatry—child psychiatry; whether there are differences between social casework and psychotherapy; which theory should underlie our developmental approach; which frame of reference should be established as the base for our data collection and analysis; not simply whether the mental health professions should be social action oriented or not, but also the question of what and when is something social action and when is something professional action; what is a medical model as differentiated from a psychological model; the criteria by which decisions are made as to modality of treatment utilized; less agreement on the similarities and function of the various mental health professions than on their differences; and more dissension on the method for models suggested to resolve problems than on the need for such a model.

As with all clinicians who have lived through, participated in, and learned from the multiple issues of the current state of the field, I too have attempted to cope with the situation through evolvement of models of approach. The thoughts in the remaining section of this overview are simply one man's thoughts, the thoughts of a clinical facility, and a collection of clinicians in their attempts to cope. The results of this thinking and action have emerged for a group of us during the past ten years; some of this has been written and published, some organized and in action but not published.

As a result of this experience and learning, I have developed a model. However, this model is based on a whole set of assumptions which, if valid, must be taken into consideration if one is to build solutions. The following is an outline of such assumptions:

1. that every citizen, including children, has the right to the best of health, education, and welfare;

2. that the maintenance and promotion of health and the prevention of illness in children are a shared responsibility of agencies of health, education, and welfare, and that the identification of deviancy in health and the diagnosis and treatment of disease and illness are a responsibility of agencies of health;

3. that the health of children, as differentiated from that of adults, and the care of children in health and illness, as differentiated from that of adults, require a greater participation of the environment in their promotion and in the etiology of deviation, and require a greater participation of many professions and a greater financial investment in their implementation;

4. that, in light of the current structure of mental health as a health profession, and in light of the need for more valid data to emerge as the basis for change, arbitrarily, mental health should be maintained as a component of health;

5. that, within this framework of health and mental health, infant and child development thus is construed as the capacity of each child to thrive and not simply survive;

6. that behavioral symptomatology in children, with its multiple causality, provides a barometer to deviancy in development and child-rearing practices, and that the behavioral clinician can provide the expertise of judgment in this area;

7. that, with the current lack of agreement in our mental health professions and facilities on frames of reference, definition of terms, and theoretical persuasion, it is important to arbitrarily begin with an agreed-upon frame of reference for a systems approach which will allow a feedback of data and information on which corrections can be made;

8. that, within our communities, there already exists a variety of entrees to the health, education, and welfare systems, and that the problem currently facing us regarding delivery of services is not so much that we do not have services available, but that these services may not be providing what is needed;

9. that there are differences in responsibility and function for the agencies of health, education, and welfare, and that role confusion and diffusion exist because of misapplied responsibility and function;

10. that better coordination and integration of existing services will not take place unless constructive steps are taken to explore the issues inherent

in autonomy of operation of each agent from the other while attempting to achieve a common goal, and that such solutions may require centralization of intake or common intake based on an agreed-upon developmental model;

11. that mental health services must be part and parcel of a total community plan for health, education, and welfare of children, and that such a plan must be based on the developmental model as a means of organizing the community and its services for children.

In belief that the assumptions listed are valid or, on further study, will be shown to be valid, I am of the mind that a clinician is faced with the following possibilities:

1. that continuation of our clinical services for emotionally disturbed children as they are provided currently in most communities will not only impede the development of our goals but possibly aid in bringing about even more of a devaluation of their services;

2. that simply the addition of new services or a changing emphasis in service aimed at supplanting existing services or complementing them without any attention to evolving new patterns of organization for these services will also impede the goal of comprehensive health care of children;

3. that the clinician will do a disservice to his clinical heritage of experience if he continues to avoid seeking answers to the question of the efficacy of the services he offers;

4. that, unless the clinical personnel are willing to evolve an open-ended approach to testing out the various modalities of treatment utilized, the "newer" models of treatment based on current theories will emerge, unfortunately, as the panacea for all problems in children;

5. that, unless the clinicians and the existing mental health professions of social work, psychology, and psychiatry are willing to accept responsibility for development of new manpower, such new manpower will develop to the detriment of quality of service offered;

6. that the pressure for programs of prevention and early identification, without adequate attention to support the clinical facilities for disturbed children, will produce an even greater problem in providing services than currently exists;

7. that new models of approach, without an equal opportunity for evaluation of programs offered, may produce, at some later time, an even greater number of chronically disturbed children as a result of having temporized with underlying pathology;

8. that continued emphasis in our programs of child psychiatry on training the resident for his primary role as a psychotherapist, rather than as a developmental expert, will seriously impair the contribution of child psychiatry to the broader responsibilities for comprehensive health of all children;

9. that, despite the criticisms leveled at clinicians for their continued empiricism by which various clinical decisions are made, criteria can be evolved and tested in regard to clinical judgments.

During the past ten years, in anticipation of the current problems and issues posed for the clinical facility, a number of clinicians in various clinical facilities have been seeking means of resolving these problems. These solutions included, for example: new patterns of reorganization of all services for children; models for delivery of services; programs of data collection and analysis; systems approach; manpower utilization models; information availability and retrieval systems. A search of the literature would reveal a number of ideas that have emerged regarding such solutions.

I believe I have been fortunate in working with John Rose at the Philadelphia Child Guidance Clinic in the evolvement of such solutions and the testing out of their efficacy. Some of these concepts and experiences have been published in papers of Dr. Rose, Dr. Ora Smith, Dr. Isobel Rigg, Dr. Richard L. Cohen, and myself; others have not been published.

As noted, a group of clinicians under the leadership of John Rose began experimentation with such a model in 1957, at which time it had become glaringly clear that the child guidance clinic, in cooperation with other agencies of child health, education, and welfare, must evolve and test out new patterns for delivery of services if we were to collectively provide constructive avenues for growth of parents, children, and the community services. This "model" was basically aimed at the following: evolving an instrument for testing out of the effectiveness of the child psychiatric services; a common agreed-upon frame of reference for data collection and analysis among the various agencies serving children; exploring ways and means of more effectively deploying the limited professional manpower available; and developing a more systematic approach to providing child psychiatric services. Since 1967, this experiment has continued to the present, with modifications made in the model based on experience.

The remainder of this clinician's overview will be devoted to a brief exposition of this experience.

A. *Organization of Community*

In order to provide the greatest opportunity for resolving many of the current problems facing our communities in the delivery of services for children in light of our need for data which can be more meaningful in regard to our services, and in light of the belief that agencies will continue to guard their autonomy, it is important that there be a centralized administrative organization at a county or subcounty or geographic area level for the mental health and retardation services in the community. Such an organization should administratively be related to the local governmental organization, via a department of health, or mental health and retardation, and, through this means, relate itself to the state governmental machinery. This organization for mental health and retardation services should have a board of directors, consisting of knowledgeable and interested citizens to whom the staff of this organization is responsible. This organization should become the vehicle through which funds for provision of mental health and retardation services are secured.

This organization should become the responsible agent in the community for the planning, development, and implementation of mental health and retardation services for children and, through its auspices, integration with other agents of the community such as Community Chest, health and welfare associations, hospital planning associations, etc. Such an organization, through the utilization of its funds, can become the vehicle for coordination and integration of mental health and retardation services for children and the development of a common basis in the community for data collection, analysis, and comparison. Through its auspices, it can support and stimulate the development of new services in areas where there are none, while at the same time it can support and strengthen existing services. In other words, such an organization can provide for centralization of planning and purpose, while allowing for decentralization of effort and delivery of services. Through such an organization, it is possible to provide a channel for communication among the various agencies, while at the same time, it can utilize its funds to constructively bring about greater unification of purpose.

B. *Organization of Services*

Within the framework of the above community organization, the community agencies of health, education, and welfare, providing and delivering services to children, can be organized in such a way as to allow the collective efforts of the community to be focused on: development of children rather than on the service offered; minimizing duplication and fragmentation; maintenance of a child in the community; evolving data which are more meaningful and comparative; and an open-ended approach to evaluation of services offered.

As noted in our own discussion as a Clinical Committee, as noted in the various studies conducted by the Joint Commission, and as noted by the many clinicians who have been concerned about the nature of services available and offered, we must evolve a developmental frame of reference, not simply for our studies, but as the basis for delivery of our services. Whether such a developmental frame of reference uses the psychoanalytic model, the Erikson model, the learning theory model, the model of Piaget, or any other model is not the major factor to be considered. For myself, the major factor to be considered is the use of a model which, at one and the same time, can allow for agreement of all services on its use and an open-ended feedback system approach to evolving the criteria by which we can test the developmental model utilized and correct the model based on experience.

C. *Developmental Focus*

Such a developmental focus is based on the belief that normal *behavioral development* in the neonate, infant, child, and adolescent:

1. reflects the functional capacity of the central nervous system for integration and its ability to respond to environmental stimuli;
2. will progress in successive steps, unless interfered with, toward an increasing capacity of the organism for conceptualization, abstract reasoning, and warmth in social relationships;
3. can be measured in terms of age appropriateness, and thus offers a yardstick, even if gross, for prediction and outcome of child development;

4. may be interfered with as a result of the organism's equipment (disease, damage, defective) and/or the environmental influences on the organism and the interaction of each on the other, *but that* the *deviation* in behavioral development produced will be reflected in behavioral symptomatology of the organism;

5. with its relationship to behavioral symptomatology, can thus *serve* as a barometer to the quality and the function of the organism's central nervous system, the quality of the child-rearing environment, and the result of the interaction of each on the other.

D. *Entree to Service Delivery System*

With the developmental focus as one aspect of our "model," it was believed that new patterns of community services for children must be evolved to add yet another dimension to the model. If one keeps in mind that one of the goals of this model is the development of an instrument for measuring effectiveness of the programs offered, in their capacity to support normal child development, then it becomes clear that the new patterns of community services for children must be based on an extension of the developmental focus into the service system of a community.

Such a new pattern of services, therefore, was to be based on the following beliefs:

1. that a *key* to deviant development in the neonate, infant, child, and adolescent is behavioral symptomatology;

2. that the current pattern of community services for children has impeded the development of a base for more valid data collection which could serve the purpose of epidemiology, program planning, testing out of program effectiveness, program comparisons and evaluations;

3. that, however, even with the gross and uncertain knowledge now available regarding etiology of behavioral symptoms in children, the multiple causality of behavioral symptoms in children and the natural life history of these symptoms can still provide an *entree* into the system of community services which could serve the purpose of providing a base for promoting constructive child development, preventing, identifying, diagnosing, and treating the deviant development, and for testing the value of these services;

4. that such an entree to the service system, for the purposes outlined, can also provide the *most natural avenue* utilized ordinarily by parents and parent surrogates in the course of life events for themselves and their children, and in their attempts to rear their children;

5. that such *natural avenues* have already been utilized and patterned by the population of a community in the natural course of their life events, whether or not this population is defined in terms of color, class, economics, or religion, but that since the service offered to the population has not been focused on the comprehensive requirements for constructive child development and child-rearing, problems in their utilization have emerged;

6. that such natural avenues could be utilized more fully if the focus were *developmentally based, health oriented,* and aimed at assessment in the

population served of both assets and liabilities, *rather than disease and pathology focused;*

7. that such *natural avenues,* in most instances and in most communities, will probably be those agencies already in existence and available in the community for the health, education, welfare, and protection of children;

8. that such natural avenues are also *natural vehicles* for provision of comprehensive services to children and their parents through a body of available manpower, and in a form which can be utilized by the parent, parent surrogate, and child at appropriate times and in appropriate settings in the course of the natural events of living;

9. that all elements of this network of community services for children, while maintaining their individual autonomy, functions, and manpower, can collectively and individually provide the basis for a comprehensive service to children which can yield more valid data in regard to child development, deviancy in that development, programs required, program effectiveness, program comparison and evaluation.

In summary then, our network of community services for children should be such as to collectively provide for a pattern of service delivery which would, at one and the same time, allow for:

1. utilizing behavioral symptoms in the child as a key to identifying and correcting deviancy in development and promoting normal development;

2. an entree to the service system which affords a *natural avenue* of approach to identifying and correcting deviancy and promoting normal development;

3. data collection and analysis which, over a period of time and in feedback method, will aid in evolving more valid data collection on our current knowledge of behavioral development, program utilization, and efficacy.

The method by which the network of community services can provide a pattern to fulfill the above requirements can be found in the answers to this composite question: *What* behavioral symptoms or set of behavioral symptoms in the child, in which *period of time* in the life of the child, reflect deviation or potential deviancy from normal behavioral development as a result of which *possible etiology,* and *in which* particular agency or agencies of the community might these children be brought to attention most likely and naturally, and *what* might be done by *whom* to identify and correct the deviancy or promote normal development?

Such a guide to the pattern of service delivery required can be illustrated by placing the natural life history of behavioral symptoms in juxtaposition to the following qestions:

1. *Why* are these behavioral symptoms present, i.e., neuronal disorders, metabolic abnormalities, perceptual-motor deficits, social pathology, psychopathology, developmental phase of growth, or any combination?

2. *How* are these behavioral symptoms shown, i.e., irritability, sleeplessness, colic, failure to thrive, phobias, separation anxiety, poor peer relationship, etc.?

3. *When* do these behavioral symptoms show themselves, i.e., pregnancy, neonate period, infancy, preschool, school age, or adolescence?

4. *Where* are these behavioral symptoms most likely and naturally to show themselves, i.e., obstetrical office, prenatal clinic, physician's office, well-baby clinic, city health clinic, nursery school, child care center, public welfare office, school, social agency, psychiatric clinic, hospitals, etc.?

5. *What* can be done to constructively intervene in promoting normal behavioral development and in preventing, identifying, diagnosing, and treating the deviancy in that development, i.e., attention to the various complaints of the pregnant woman, which may reflect her inadequate psychological readiness for pregnancy; identification of the high-risk mothers in pregnancy and provision of the necessary support; adequate opportunity for allowing the parent of a defective neonate to cope with her feelings of guilt and shame; attention to environmental climate of the child-rearing wherein the baby is unrewarding and unrewarded, producing colic, restlessness, and a demanding crying infant; the earlier identification of the preschool-age child in the nursery where he manifests problems of coordination and integration, and the intervention of specialized methods for visual, motor training, etc.?

6. *Who* can most constructively intervene in the natural entree and avenue wherein the deviancy in behavioral development has shown itself, i.e., the obstetrician, nurse, public health nurse, social worker, associate social worker, psychologist, etc.?

E. *Principles of Operation*

In keeping with the *basic notion* expressed, the significance of the model or theory of development utilized lies in its capacity to do a better job of validating the data that we currently have been using as the basis of planning our programs, estimating our needs, determining the requirements of manpower, and deciding on program effectiveness. The seriousness of the current dilemma for the clinician and clinical services warrants as open-ended an approach as can be mounted, and a minimum of defensiveness in regard to any specific model or theory. The converse, it must be stated, is also true, namely, that the seriousness of the situation also warrants that critics of current clinical services place their specific models or theories into the same open-ended approach so that we might collectively be in a better position to evaluate effectiveness.

In order to fulfill the requirements of this basic notion, it would seem, therefore, of importance that the following principles be adhered to:

1. that all community agencies serving children, and in whose facilities and programs children with behavioral symptoms will be brought to attention, agree on a frame of reference, even though arbitrary to begin with, as a point from which to identify, categorize, and diagnose the behavioral symptoms in children;

2. that the frame of reference must be such as to allow for the mutual evolvement by all agencies of the terms and definitions which will be utilized by them in data collection, analysis, and comparison;

3. that the entree to any and all community services for children must be such as to allow each agency to elicit data (in common with and agreed upon by all other agencies) of such description and fact that a determination can be made on the level of normal behavioral development in the child and/or the deviancy in that development, as well as a determination of the assets and liabilities in the child-rearing environment for constructive child development;

4. that, based on the above determination of developmental level and needs, the decision be made by the agency as to what service or services are required to promote normal child development or correct deviancy in that development, and that involvement of other agencies or referral be instituted at this *entree* phase;

5. that the decision made by the agency regarding the nature of service to be offered should be done in such a way as to allow for their statement of the basis for this decision, prediction as to outcome, and follow-up of outcome; and that through such attention to clinical decision-making choices in each and every agency, data can eventually emerge for a better refinement of criteria of matching the need to service required.

There are other principles of operation which have been outlined in a previous paper submitted to each member of the Clinical Committee. Among these principles is that of a *common intake interview,* which could be utilized by each agency as a point of entree and as an arbitrary frame of reference for elicitation of developmental data for decision-making determination. This *common intake interview* is to be *distinguished from* a *central intake* approach, since it can allow each agency to operate within its own structure and function and setting while converging each agency to a common basis of approach to behavioral symptoms in children.

The literature of our field now abounds with various suggested alternate routes to the end point of a model for better delivery of services. As noted in this clinician's overview, a number of clinicians who have shared a common experience have chosen a route for evolvement of such a model based on a semistructured interview, utilized at the point of entree to the service, as a meaningful instrument for: elicitation of data on the behavioral development of the child and the child-rearing environment, with this data capable of rating, reliability testing, and modification based on feedback experience; a focus of agreement with other agents of child health, education, and welfare; evolving the basis of comparable data for epidemiological, demographic, and decision-making purposes; establishing an information and retrieval system— testing out of prediction and outcome. This instrument, growing out of a child psychiatric setting, has been explored in and modified by settings and personnel of social agencies, pediatric centers, practicing pediatricians, nursery schools, public school teachers, and obstetrical clinics. It is interesting to note, in terms of manpower deployment, that this instrument has been utilized by medical students, nurses, college students, residents in child psychiatry, social work students, psychology interns, pediatric residents, obstetrical residents, and residents in psychiatry.

F. *Child Psychiatric Services*

In concluding this clinician's overview, and last but not least, attention will be called to the organization of child psychiatric services.

It would seem axiomatic, and perhaps redundant, to state that the success of a developmental focus in new patterns for delivery of community services to children will be greatly dependent on the nature of specialized services available for children with behavioral symptoms. In other words, if we, as the specialized clinical experts of behavioral symptoms in children, are requiring the community at large to accept responsibility as the generalist for promoting normal behavioral development, identifying and correcting deviancy in that development, then we, as the specialists, must be prepared to provide the gamut of backstop support required—backstop support which must include: the spectrum of specialized services to match the nature of disorders in children; the educational and training programs for both the specialist and the generalist, whether this is training of child psychiatrist, education of the mental health professions, or in-service training programs for the professions of health, education, and welfare; the consultative services; development of the new manpower; research staff for operational studies, data collection and analysis, clinical problems, program evaluation, and developmental studies.

Though such backstop support may seem unobtainable, it is to be remembered that such potential is already available and on the horizon in terms of the mental health and retardation centers, the comprehensive health service plans, regional medical centers, neighborhood health centers, Medicare, the reorganization of the Public Health Service, the technology of information availability and retrieval, the plans for implementation in each state of mental health and retardation centers, management technology, Head Start, OEO programs, Model Cities, Allied Health Manpower Act, etc.

Within the framework of evolving this required backstop for our developmental approach to delivery of community services for children, and within the umbrella of the "model" for such service proposed, and in light of the potential for evolving such a backstop, consideration should be given by child psychiatry to the following:

1. the necessity of evolving the administrative organization for child psychiatry within our universities and existing mental health and retardation centers which would support the development of a child psychiatric center, capable of ultimately providing the spectrum of services required, a meaningful relationship to pediatrics, obstetrics, preventive medicine, public health, education, psychology, social work, nursing, agents of community health, education, and welfare;

2. the necessity for such a child psychiatric center to be comparatively autonomous within the university in order to assure its potential capability

of securing funds for the support of children's services unencumbered, as has been the practice, by the needs of general psychiatric programs and services;

3. the revising of training programs in child psychiatry and the mental health professions, so that increased emphasis is placed on providing education and experience for all students in growth and development of children, the deviancy in that development, and the nature of services required for promotion of normal development and identification and correction of deviancy in that development;

4. the development of a system approach for these services, including:

a. a *data bank* capable of producing patient, staff, facility, and business data;

b. a *central patient registry,* no matter at what point of entree for the patient into the system;

c. the *common intake* as the basis for elicitation of required and descriptive patient data, and the use of this for the measuring of future changes in the patient;

d. *central scheduling* of clinical appointments for all staff, utilizing an agreed-upon number of clinical appointments for all staff;

e. *centralized case assignment and flow;*

f. *quality control* through arbitrary and established points in the clinical process for evaluation of data available and decisions made, with measure of this periodic evaluation against previous criteria and decisions made;

g. procedures for testing out of *follow-up effectiveness* of services offered but procedures which flow from the total clinical process evaluations and parallel these processes through independent ratings;

h. controlled *entree into and exit from* the services of the child psychiatric center of each patient, so that at all times a constant community link is maintained for the child, so that always and in each case, opportunity is provided for assessment of the community fabric required to support constructive child development;

i. the development of *administrative procedures* which can automatically relieve professional and technical staff of details, but which support professional purpose with research intent, i.e., fee setting, billing, third-party payments, case statistics, record keeping;

j. *fiscal control methods* aimed at producing the basis for cost accounting;

k. a *common base of data collection and analysi*s with all other health, education, and welfare services for children;

l. the *periodic report* on staff and facility data to each member of the staff;

m. the *feedback system* for periodic correcting of various arbitrary criteria established through systems of recording and reporting tied to every critical point of decision making in the clinical process for each case, i.e., decision as to whether the initial intake adequately presents data on which to make a decision, decision as to case assignment and to whom, decision as to service required and offered, decision of the supervisor to assign or not assign a case, decision as to continue or not continue with service, decision to alter plans agreed upon, decision as to transfer of case, decision on diagnosis, etc.

5. the nature of services best offered by the child psychiatric center, the nature of services in the community affiliated with the child psychiatric center, the nature of services in the community independent but related to the child psychiatric center, with all of this aimed at supporting the community in a developmentally focused health-oriented model for delivery of services to children.

VII. CONCLUSION

In the space of this long, and yet brief, overview, this clinician has attempted to share his thoughts on the issues facing those clinicians offering clinical services to children with behavioral symptoms. In sharing my thoughts with the remainder of this Clinical Committee of the Joint Commission on Mental Health of Children, I have also shared the dilemmas I have experienced as a clinician and some attempts to resolve these dilemmas.

Appendix G

RECOMMENDATIONS BY THE CLINICAL COMMITTEE OF THE JOINT COMMISSION ON MENTAL HEALTH OF CHILDREN

1. Every child has a right to receive those experiences that would assist in his positive growth and development psychologically and to receive the necessary professional assistance when problems arise. Diagnosis and treatment should be available to every child, every family, and every group responsible for the care of children. Need should be the determining factor for clinical service, not social, economic, or political factors.

2. All mental health services to children should be set up along developmental lines. This means that different types of services and special services are necessary at different ages. Special services, for example, are necessary for preschool children and their families, school-age children, adolescents, young adults, etc. These services will have a different focus because of the specific needs of each of these groups. It is necessary to train specialists to deal with characteristic problems of an age period and to organize those services appropriate to a given age.

3. All mental health services to children and their families must be comprehensive and coordinated. Children need a greater diversity of services than adults, often including educational, recreational, and vocational services as well as psychotherapy. It is necessary that services be available to the significant adults in the child's life and that these services be coordinated with the help given to the child. A coordinator or ombudsman who would integrate the services needed and coordinate them for the child and his family should seriously be considered.

4. At the present time there are two major priorities in the development of mental health services. The gaps in these areas are great, and immediate attention is necessary. These are: (1) services for preschool children and their families, and (2) services for adolescents. For preschool children, services such as well-baby clinics and family and child centers, where help can

be given early, are essential. Critical needs for adolescents are in emergency services (suicide prevention), residential centers, hostels, and special outpatient services geared to their specific needs. A punitive approach to setting up services for adolescents is all too common and should be avoided in evolving adolescent services.

5. The distribution of mental health services has been markedly uneven. It is essential that adequate mental health services be established for the lower socioeconomic groups and for the many minority groups for whom services have been noticeably lacking. Extra effort is necessary to develop appropriate mental health services for these groups and to explore the mose valuable ways of developing these services rapidly. Members of the lower socioeconomic groups and minority groups need to be actively involved and recruited in the establishment of these services.

6. Clinical research of all kinds must be encouraged. Federal support should be given to those who might be interested in basic clinical research, program evaluation, and experimental research. Good epidemiological studies are of high priority (very few in the children's area). All programs that are developed for children should include evaluation so that their success can be determined. There is a need for innovation and exploration in the children's field. Much research in the children's area is not translated into social policy. It is necessary, therefore, that the research findings that are available be adequately utilized in the formulation of national programs for children and youth, and that mechanisms be developed so that scientific results form the foundation for national and state programing.

7. A major prerequisite for good mental health is adequate physical development. Poor prenatal care, for example, is highly correlated with increased problems over mental health. Therefore, optimal physical care at all ages should be seen as forming the foundation on which constructive psychological development takes place. Major efforts should be undertaken to see that physical care forms a part of all mental health programs.

8. High levels of competence in mental health work should be sought and maintained. Support should be given to all efforts to develop high standards of clinical training and professional functioning. Federal, state, and local financial support should be available to those seeking to gain training in mental health and mental health-related fields as well as to those who seek to reach high levels of competence. Rewards and encouragement, both financial and otherwise, should be given to those young adults and adults who seek to work with children of all ages in various ways relating to mental health— education, vocational work, recreation, medical fields, welfare, etc. Rewards are necessary to encourage people to undertake work with children and youth, since work with these groups is often exceedingly difficult and time consuming.

9. All clinical activities and intervention should be looked at from the point of view of their effect on individuals. It should be remembered that it takes only one person acting alone to change the course of history. Efforts toward large-scale interventions must not ignore the individual. There will always be individuals who cannot profit from large-scale interventions. These individuals need individual services—these must be available.

10. Nontraditionally trained people must be encouraged to assume certain responsibilities in the mental health area. There are many opportunities for these people to work with children and youth. Some of these are community workers; others are foster grandmothers and technicians. All of these people should be compensated adequately. There must be adequate career lines in the nontraditional area with opportunities for those who would like to become professional mental health workers. Federal funding for a massive children's program in the "nonprofessional" area should be undertaken with study and evaluation.

11. Mental health services for communities should be community based with close ties to local residents, involving these residents in mental health activities both on operational and on administrative levels. Community involvement and often community control of mental health services can be a major factor in improving the mental health of residents in a community. This is particularly important with regard to minority groups, many of whom have experienced severe discrimination which has alienated them from society. Minority groups should be involved actively in positions of responsiblity in the mental health services, and encouraged to seek high-quality service.

12. The structure of the mental health service for children should be closely tied to community needs. There are many models of services. Some examples are: community mental health centers, the child development center, the mental health unit affiliated with the university, and the total health center. The selection of one of these models should occur on the basis of its appropriateness to meet the specific needs of a local situation, as determined by the local citizenry wherever possible.

13. Early identification of mental health problems and prevention of these problems before they become severe is essential. There is an urgent need for developing a mechanism whereby children are evaluated at all ages and at regular intervals with regard to their progress and development. The mechanism may be through the child development centers or the well-baby clinic. Special staff should be trained to be sensitive to problems arising at different ages and to help families and children immediately when problems are beginning to arise. Families or children at high risk need to be given high priority.

14. Education is essential. Mechanisms should be developed for the wide sharing of information that is known in child-rearing to all groups through mass media and other mechanisms. This includes establishing courses in all schools on family planning, sex, the handling of crises, care of children, etc. Teachers should be especially aided by mental health professionals to identify and deal with problems that might arise in these courses. Parent education *for all socioeconomic levels* should be given major consideration. This includes intimate one-to-one assistance to certain groups in how to handle children as well as mass education. Such education should take place throughout the school system, at all ages, and in the community.

15. Mental health consultation should be seen as a major aspect of clinical activity with children. Mental health knowledge should be made available to welfare workers, general practitioners, nurses, teachers, pediatricians, lawyers,

etc. Incentives should be provided by national, local, and state governments to encourage professionals in various areas to involve mental health consultants in helping them with the mental health aspects of their work.

16. The birth and the development of children should be seen as social as well as personal issues. It therefore becomes mandatory to think about the care and protection of children. Advice regarding genetic problems, family planning, and abortions, as well as counseling and emotional support during pregnancy, should be available to all. Abortion laws need to be reevaluated and most likely liberalized. Family planning information should be widely disseminated. Special services should be available for nonmarried parents (mothers *and* fathers).

17. Society should take responsibility to see that basic adequate physical and psychological care of children in the early years has taken place. This means liberalization of the laws that give parents the right to their children when the child has no chance of being adequately cared for. Children should be able to be adopted or placed in foster care. But foster care needs major improvements. It needs to become a well-rewarded professional activity. The care of children should be seen as a specialized and important activity with financial as well as psychological rewards (high status). If there is reason for a child to be placed in an institution in his early years, these institutions should be staffed with a large and competent staff who can meet the individual needs and who are expert in caring for young children. Day-care centers need to be set up for all socioeconomic groups to care for children, but these day-care centers should be strictly supervised by trained staff and should have high standards. For parents who are not able to care for their children, adequate financial support should be available so that children get their psychological as well as their physical needs taken care of.

18. All institutions in society should be evaluated in terms of their ability to contribute to the positive growth of children. Schools, families, churches, employment, all should be critically reviewed with a focus on changes that are needed to contribute to a child's growth. For example, the laws regarding employment need revision so that many adolescents can become involved in work at earlier ages. Opportunity should be available for adolescents to participate in meaningful social tasks from early adolescence. Support should be given to assist children and their families in coping with natural transitional points and crises that arise in development.

19. A major reorganization and revamping of many institutions for youth is necessary (hospitals, training schools, group homes, etc.) so that they are not geared toward a punitive orientation but toward rehabilitation and growth. Major financial support is necessary on federal, state, and local levels to bring about change so that these institutions are modernized and have competent staff. For example, there is a need for smaller community-based institutions, especially in correctional settings. It is essential that children and adolescents be separated from adults in these institutions when they require institutionalization.

20. Self-scrutiny is an important part of clinical functioning. It is essential that we be constantly aware of the self-fulfilling prophecies that tend to per-

petuate certain social ways of handling situations, and sometimes prevent the change that is necessary. Constant awareness of unconscious motivational factors can aid in bringing about intelligent changes and should be used in the service of change in the development of services and in recommendations for national policy.

21. The clinician has a great deal to contribute in regard to the understanding of prejudice and racism. Personal needs on the part of both the aggressor and the victim must be considered along with the major economic, social, and political dimensions. Early training in respecting diversity is essential. Also, systematic planned programs to encourage the adequate development of a positive self-image in groups that have been discriminated against for many years is necessary. Such a positive self-image is a prerequisite to adequate personality functioning in later life.

22. The clinician is aware of the fact that there are no simple answers to complex problems and that a high degree of understanding and skill is necessary to deal with the clinical aspects of all situations—treatment, prevention, and the fostering of optimal growth and capacity for each child. All effort should be undertaken on a national level to see that clinical thinking is included in evolving and implementing a federal program for children and youth.

References

American Association of Psychiatric Clinics for Children. *Children and Clinics.* A Survey by the American Association of Psychiatric Clinics for Children, 1968.

Bettelheim, B. *The Empty Fortress.* New York: Free Press, 1967.

Bibring, G. "Some Considerations of Psychological Processes in Pregnancy," in *Psychoanalytic Study of the Child,* 14 (1959), pp. 113–121.

Caplan, G. "Emotional Implications of Pregnancy and Influences in Family Relationships," in *The Healthy Child,* H. Stuart and D. G. Prugh (eds). Cambridge: Harvard University Press, 1960, pp. 72–82.

Jones, M. C. "A Laboratory Study of Fear: The Case of Peter," *Journal of Genetic Psychology,* XXXI (1924), 308–315.

LaBarre, M. "The Special Treatment Challenge of Pregnant Teenagers." Presented at the annual meeting of the American Association of Psychiatric Clinics for Children, Boston, Mass., Nov. 2, 1969.

Lieberman, James E., M.D. "Informed Consent for Parenthood." Paper presented at the California Committee on Therapeutic Abortion, 2nd Annual Conference, San Francisco, May 9–11, 1969.

Mann, E. C. "Habitual Abortion: A Report in Two Parts, on 160 Patients," *American Journal of Obstetrics and Gynecology,* 77 (1959), 708–718.

"Newsletter Section on Clinical Child Psychology," American Psychological Association, Vol. VIII (1969), 5.

Silverman, J. S. *The Child-Adolescent and Urban Psychiatric Clinic.* Summary of a survey of Mental Health Clinic Care for Children in New York City. Jerome S. Silverman, M.D., Director, Research Project, Committee on Clinics, New York Council on Child Psychiatry, Inc., 1968.

Index

73 74 75 10 9 8 7 6 5 4 3 2 1